Leicester–Nottingham Studies in Ancient Society

Volume 5

WAR AND SOCIETY IN THE ROMAN WORLD

WAR AND SOCIETY IN THE ROMAN WORLD

Edited by

JOHN RICH and GRAHAM SHIPLEY

London and New York

First published 1993
by Routledge
11 New Fetter Lane, London EC4P 4EE

Simultaneously published in the USA and Canada
by Routledge Inc.
29 West 35th Street, New York, NY 10001

Printed in Great Britain by T.J. Press (Padstow) Ltd,
Padstow, Cornwall

British Library Cataloguing in Publication Data
A catalogue record for this book is available from the British Library.

Library of Congress Cataloging in Publication Data
War and society in the Roman world / edited by John Rich and
   Graham Shipley.
      p.   cm. — (Leicester–Nottingham studies in ancient society; v. 5)
      Selected, revised versions of papers from a series of seminars
   sponsored by the Classics Departments of Leicester and Nottingham
   Universities, 1988–1990.
      Includes bibliographical references and index.
      1. Military art and science—Rome—History.   2. Rome—History,
   Military.   3. Sociology, Military—Rome—History.   I. Rich, John.
      II. Shipley, Graham.   III. Series.
   U35.W34   1993
   355'.00937—dc20   92-36698

ISBN 0-415-06644-1

Contents

Illustrations

Figures

Table

Contributors

David Braund is Lecturer in Classics at the University of Exeter.

Brian Campbell is Lecturer in Ancient History at the Queen's University of Belfast.

Duncan Cloud is Associate Senior Lecturer in Ancient History at the University of Leicester.

Tim Cornell is Senior Lecturer in History at University College London.

Wolfgang Liebeschuetz is Emeritus Professor of Classics and Ancient History at the University of Nottingham, and a Fellow of the British Academy.

Stephen Oakley is Fellow and Director of Studies in Classics at Emmanuel College, Cambridge.

John Patterson is a Fellow of Magdalene College, Cambridge, and University Lecturer in Ancient History.

John Rich is Senior Lecturer in Classics at the University of Nottingham.

Harry Sidebottom is doing post-doctoral research at Corpus Christi College, Oxford.

Dick Whittaker is a Fellow of Churchill College, Cambridge, and University Lecturer in Ancient History.

Greg Woolf is Andrew and Randall Crawley Fellow in the History of the Ancient World at Magdalen College, Oxford.

Adam Ziolkowski is Lecturer in Ancient History at the University of Warsaw.

Preface

'There is and has been a powerful reluctance among historians to discuss ancient warfare and its consequences with a steady eye.' Thus Moses Finley, in one of his last published works (*Ancient History: Evidence and Models* (London, 1985), 71). This book and its companion volume, *War and Society in the Greek World*, constitute an attempt to respond to Finley's challenge. Like the earlier volumes in *Leicester-Nottingham Studies in Ancient Society*, they are the product of seminars jointly organized by the Classics Departments of Leicester and Nottingham Universities. 'War and Society in the Ancient World' was the theme of a series of seminars held in Leicester and Nottingham between 1988 and 1990. The two volumes contain substantially revised versions of a selection of papers from that series.

We are very grateful to all the participants in the seminar series, both our colleagues in Leicester and Nottingham and those from further afield, some of whom regularly travelled long distances to take part in the discussions. We would also like to thank the Society for the Promotion of Roman Studies for assistance with the cost of Dr Ziolkowski's travel from Poland, Susan Walker for assistance with the jacket illustration and Adrienne Edwards for invaluable administrative help.

The translations of Livy, Polybius and Tacitus in chapter 3 are reproduced by permission of the publishers and the Loeb Classical Library from *Livy: Ab Urbe Condita*, 13 vols, tr. B. O. Foster and others, 1919–51, *Polybius: The Histories*, 6 vols, tr. W. R. Paton, 1922–7, and *Tacitus: The Histories*, 1925–31, tr. C H. Moore, Cambridge, Mass.: Harvard University Press. The translation of Propertius 2. 7 on p. 120 is reproduced by permission of the publishers from *Propertius: The Poems*, tr. W. G. Shepherd, 1985, Harmondsworth: Penguin Books.

John Rich
Graham Shipley

Abbreviations

The names and works of ancient authors are generally abbreviated in the forms used in *The Oxford Classical Dictionary* (2nd edn, ed. N. G. L. Hammond and H. H. Scullard; Oxford, 1970).

AJP	*American Journal of Philology*
ANRW	*Aufstieg und Niedergang der römischen Welt*, ed. H. Temporini (Berlin and New York, 1972–)
BAR	British Archaeological Reports
CAH	*Cambridge Ancient History* (Cambridge)
CAH²	*Cambridge Ancient History*, 2nd edn (Cambridge)
CIL	*Corpus Inscriptionum Latinarum*
cos.	consul
CP	*Classical Philology*
CQ	*Classical Quarterly*
CR	*Classical Review*
CTh	*Codex Theodosianus*
DHA	*Dialogues d'histoire ancienne*
FGH	F. Jacoby, *Die Fragmente der griechischen Historiker* (Berlin, Leiden, 1923–)
FHG	C. Müller, *Fragmenta Historicorum Graecorum* (Paris, 1841–70)
IGBulg	*Inscriptiones Graecae in Bulgaria repertae*, ed. G. Mihailov (Sofia, 1958–70)
IGRR	*Inscriptiones Graecae ad res Romanas pertinentes*, ed. R. Cagnat *et al.* (Paris, 1911–27)
ILS	*Inscriptiones Latinae Selectae*, ed. H. Dessau (Berlin, 1892–1916)
IRT	*The Inscriptions of Roman Tripolitania*, ed. J. M. Reynolds and J. B. Ward-Perkins (Rome, 1952)
JHS	*Journal of Hellenic Studies*
JRS	*Journal of Roman Studies*

LCM	*Liverpool Classical Monthly*
MGH, AA	*Monumenta Germaniae Historica, Auctores Antiquissimi*
MRR	T. R. S. Broughton, *The Magistrates of the Roman Republic* (Cleveland, Ohio, 1951–86).
Not. Dig. Oc.	*Notitia Dignitatum . . . in partibus Occidentis*, in O. Seeck (ed.), *Notitia dignitatum* (Berlin, 1876)
Nov.	*Novellae*
OLD	*Oxford Latin Dictionary* (Oxford, 1968–82)
ORF	*Oratorum Romanorum Fragmenta*, ed. H. Malcovati, 3rd edn (Turin, 1967)
PBSR	*Papers of the British School at Rome*
PG	*Patrologia Graeca*, ed. J. P. Migne
PL	*Patrologia Latina*, ed. J. P. Migne
PLRE	A. H. M. Jones, J. B. Martindale, and J. Morris, *The Prosopography of the Later Roman Empire* (Cambridge, 1973–)
PRG	*Papyri russischer und georgischer Sammlungen*, ed. G. Zereteli, O. Krueger, and P. Jernstedt (Tiflis, 1925–35)
RE	*Realencyclopädie der classischen Altertumswissenschaft*
RG	*Res Gestae Divi Augusti*
TLL	*Thesaurus Linguae Latinae*
TLS	*Times Literary Supplement*

Introduction

John Rich

The Greek world, the subject of our companion volume, was a complex mosaic of communities, often at war with each other or with outside powers. Here, by contrast, the focus is on a single state. From the earliest days, war was at the heart of the life of the Roman people. They fought wars almost every year. Annual rituals marked the opening and closing of the campaigning season. All Roman citizens were liable for military service, and, apart from the poorest and freedmen (who were ineligible for the legions), most, if not all, Roman citizens under the early and middle Republic served in several years' campaigns during their youth. The censors' classification of the people into property classes and centuries served both political and military purposes and reflected the close links between military obligations and political rights (Nicolet 1980); it was no accident that, when the people met to elect their chief magistrates, who commanded the army, they assembled outside the city on the Campus Martius – the field of Mars, the war god. Valour in arms won the highest renown, and members of the élite were under heavy pressure to enhance their family's glory by distinguishing themselves in war. There were crowns and other military prizes which any soldier could win (Maxfield 1981), while a victorious commander earned the supreme honour of leading his returning troops into the city in a triumph.

In the early centuries Roman warfare was not outstandingly successful. Rome was merely one of the communities of the plain of Latium, and her citizens fought their wars against their Latin neighbours and against the peoples of the surrounding hills. From the mid-fourth century BC, however, there began a period of rapid expansion, in which the Romans won a long series of military successes (punctuated by the occasional reverse). By about 270 they controlled all Italy south of the Po. Overseas wars followed, notably against Carthage and various Hellenistic kings, and by the mid-second century all potential rivals had been defeated. Contemporaries, like the Greek historian Polybius, now recognized Rome as the ruler of the Mediterranean world. In many regions they exercised only informal empire, but a number of overseas territories were ruled directly, as provinces.

Why had the Roman military machine proved so invincible? Technically, they had shown themselves formidably adaptable. Their weaponry was improved, not by their own innovations so much as by borrowing from opponents. The looser tactical structure of the legion gave it the edge over the phalanx. Subtle generalship was not normally called for, but, when the Carthaginians produced a commander of genius in Hannibal, the Romans eventually found his match in Scipio Africanus. The most fundamental reason for their success, however, lay in the vast resources of manpower that they could dispose of as a result of the way in which they had organized their conquests in Italy. Many of the defeated communities were incorporated into the Roman citizen body, so that by the later third century about a third of the inhabitants of Italy south of the Po were Roman citizens (Brunt 1971, 44–60). The rest were made allies, and were regularly called on to serve in Rome's armies. As a result, Rome was able to field armies in several different theatres simultaneously and was able, in the early years of the Second Punic War, to withstand a series of crushing defeats which would have crippled most other states.

At first success in war seems to have benefited all levels of Roman society. The early Republic had been wracked by political conflict, which economic discontents, such as debt and land hunger, helped to fuel. Plentiful booty and the distribution of confiscated land seems to have relieved these pressures and probably contributed to the political stability of the third and early second century. By the second century, however, the benefits of war and empire came to be less equitably diffused. The élite grew steadily richer and the competition between its members constantly intensified. While poor men who were lucky enough to serve in lucrative wars like those in the East might do well, many of their fellows were less fortunate. Periods of military service now often lasted for several years at a stretch. The rich were eager to invest some of their new wealth in land, which they worked with slaves, made cheaply available by war. As a result, many peasant families were uprooted. Land distribution could have helped to resolve this, but the completion of the conquest of Italy meant that land was no longer being confiscated in the peninsula; as a result, after the 170s the Roman government ceased to make land distributions. The demand for such distributions continued, but henceforth it was met, in the teeth of senatorial opposition, by tribunes and later by generals. The Italian allies too became restive, and in 91 the rejection of their demand for the citizenship led many allied communities to rise in revolt (the Social War). This issue was resolved by the extension of the citizenship to the whole of Italy south of the Po, but the war led on to a destructive series of civil wars (88–82), which fundamentally destabilized the Republic. Civil war broke out again in 49 and continued intermittently until the eventual victory in 31–30 BC of Octavian, who went on to take the name Augustus and establish himself as the first emperor.

The central role of war in Roman society under the Republic has been discussed in a number of recent studies, notably Hopkins (1978) and Harris (1979), and is addressed by several of the contributors to this volume. Oakley provides a detailed study of the topic for the period of the conquest of Italy. My own contribution focuses on the question of the causes of Roman war-making during the middle Republic and rejects all monocausal explanations, including that of Harris (1979), who privileges the desire for the benefits of war as the principal motive force. The paper draws attention as well to changes in the pattern of Roman warfare and expansion, a point also made by Cornell. Patterson considers what lessons may be learnt for the study of the Republic by examining other societies with comparably high rates of military participation, and concentrates in particular on the topics of social mobility and veteran settlement.

What was Roman warfare like? Some aspects of this topic have been exhaustively studied, notably the organization of the army (see recently Keppie 1984). However, there is nothing for Rome comparable to Pritchett's great series of studies of *The Greek State at War* (Berkeley, Los Angeles and London, 1971–   ). In particular, not enough attention has been paid to the impact of war on the civilian population, both on the Roman side (see now Evans 1991) and on that of the victims. Ziolkowski's study of how the Romans sacked cities is a contribution towards the filling of this gap. Polybius' ideal type of such events shows the Romans behaving with terrible brutality but stern discipline; the reality, Ziolkowski argues, is likely to have been much less tidy.

Some misleading stereotypes are also exposed in Cloud's study of attitudes to war in Roman poetry. He argues against modern readings of the elegists as subversive voices, in dissent from Augustus' organization of opinion, but shows that dislike of war could find expression in, of all places, Ennius' *Annales*, the great national epic.

In the early and middle Republic extended service in Rome's wars was, as we have seen, part of the experience of most citizens. A trend away from this can already be discerned by the late Republic. The old rule that no one could stand for office unless he had served for ten campaigns was no longer enforced by the time that Cicero started his career (Harris 1979, 11–12). Distinction in war was still the most highly prized form of renown, but oratory and jurisprudence now afforded alternative ways by which an aspiring politician could make a reputation (ibid. 22–3; cf. Cic. *Mur.* 30, discussed by Cloud below, pp. 130–2). A little service in the Social War was all that Cicero saw of armies, until, late in his career and very much against his will, he was sent to govern Cilicia and was surprised to find himself subduing a mountain tribe and earning the right to a triumph (which the onset of civil war prevented him from celebrating).

The old view that Marius gave Rome a professional army can no longer be maintained (Brunt 1971, 406–11; Rich 1983). His enrolment of men without the property qualification in 107 was in all probability an isolated episode: the hostility which it aroused makes it unlikely that his successors followed suit. The traditional procedures of the levy, including the property qualification, probably ceased to operate in the chaotic conditions of the eighties. In the late Republic armies continued to be raised for the most part by conscription, but the method used now seems to have been the despatch of press-gangs to particular regions.

Overall, terms of service seem to have been no longer than in the previous century, and for the most part the men enlisted came from the same social class, namely the rural poor. (Although there is no reason to think that the property qualification was reduced during the second century, it was very low, and the censors may well have reckoned pretty well all freeborn country-dwellers as qualified.) However, the new method of enlistment may have meant that the burden of service was less evenly distributed: it will have been a matter of chance who attracted the recruiting officer's attention.

It was the army reforms of Augustus (recently analysed by Raaflaub 1980) which finally replaced the old citizen militia by a professional long-service army. The practice of raising additional troops to fight a specific war and discharging them when the war was over was ended. By the end of Augustus' reign the effective period of service for legionaries had been fixed at 25 years. In the turmoil which brought down the Republic soldiers had come to expect grants of land on discharge, but this was disruptive and from 13 BC Augustus substituted cash payments, funded initially from his own resources but from AD 6 by new taxes. It was probably Augustus who forbade soldiers to marry during their term of service, a prohibition which remained in force at least until the reign of Septimius Severus (Campbell 1978). Certain special corps served in Rome and Italy, but the bulk of the army was stationed in the frontier provinces, and from the first century AD it came to be recruited mainly from provincials.

Augustus wanted senators not to be 'ignorant of the camp' (Suet. *Aug.* 38. 2: *expers castrorum*). However, under the principate young men who aspired to the senate normally served just for a year as a military tribune, and many dispensed even with that (Talbert 1984, 14). The posts to which senators were appointed by the emperor included military commands: after the praetorship a senator might be put in command of a legion, and after the consulship he might govern one or more military provinces. Some senators earned themselves a military reputation, like Corbulo and Agricola. However, there were many senators who held no military appointments at all. The younger Pliny was an even more unmilitary figure than Cicero had been (cf. Cornell below, pp. 165–6).

The reign of Augustus also marked the end of Roman

expansion. As the Republic crumbled, grandiose conquests had helped to establish the position of powerful dynasts. Pompey had set the trend with his campaigns in the East. Caesar emulated his example in Gaul. Crassus sought to follow suit against Parthia, but lost his life in the process. Caesar as dictator planned a Parthian war, but was murdered before he could set out. Antony embarked on one, and was lucky to extricate himself with heavy losses. When Augustus established himself in power, men expected him to undertake great wars of conquests and he duly obliged, but not against the expected enemies, Britain and Parthia. He reached a diplomatic accommodation with Parthia and ignored Britain, but elsewhere he expanded the Roman empire more than ever before, subjugating northern Spain and the Alps, pushing forward Roman control to the Danube, and conquering Germany up to the Elbe. However, the disaster suffered by Varus in AD 9 led to the loss of Germany, and Augustus is said to have advised his successors not to extend the empire beyond its existing boundaries (cf. Ober 1982). His successors in the main followed this precept, with a few exceptions, of which the most notable were Claudius' conquest of Britain and Trajan's conquest of Dacia and his aggressive war against Parthia.

Thus war and the army, which under the Republic had played a central part in Roman life, were under the principate banished to the periphery. Military service had ceased to be an obligation to which all citizens were liable and which most of them underwent. Instead soldiers formed a separate section of society, viewed with a mixture of respect, incomprehension and dislike by the civilian population. The armies were stationed in the frontier provinces, and only occasionally had major wars to fight. Guaranteed by the armed forces, the rest of the empire's subjects enjoyed the *pax Romana* – the Roman peace.

This momentous development provides the focus for several of the papers in this volume. Cornell tackles the question of why expansion stopped and argues that the answer is to be found in changes which were already under way during the Republic and in the connexions between the *pax Romana* and the revolution by which the republic gave way to monarchy. Braund and Woolf both question the notion of *pax Romana*: low-level violence, such as piracy, persisted, and to some extent the concept should be seen as an ideological construct. Campbell examines Rome's relations with Parthia and shows how the diplomatic principles and techniques developed in Augustus' reign long served to maintain peace between the two powers. Sidebottom illuminates civilian perceptions of soldiers and war under the principate by examining the works of the Greek philosophers of the period.

Barbarian tribes to the north were already putting the empire under new pressure in the later second century AD. Such attacks intensified greatly in the third century, and, in combination with internal political and economic difficulties, brought the empire near to collapse. The radical reforms of Diocletian and Constantine restored stability for a time, but external pressures resumed in the later fourth century, and during the fifth the western empire disintegrated. The two final chapters in the volume examine aspects of this process.

The Roman Empire finally paid the price for Augustus' dissolution of the link between citizenship and military service. That link had assured the Republic of a vast reserve of manpower, which enabled it to surmount its deepest crises. The army of the later Roman Empire, though larger than under the principate, proved unequal to the barbarian challenge. Since Caracalla's edict of AD 212 virtually all the subjects of the empire had possessed the Roman citizenship. Yet the Roman state did not turn to them to make up the military deficit, but instead employed barbarians to fight on its behalf. The Romans had always used allied troops, but with rare exceptions (like the defeat of the Scipios in Spain in 211 BC) they had ensured that the preponderance of allies did not become so great as to threaten their security. Now this principle was forgotten. In the fifth century the Roman army disappears from view in the West, as Liebeschuetz demonstrates. The Roman state soon followed.

Whittaker shows how, as state authority collapsed, powerful landlords adopted a military role and warlords emerged, commanding personal armies. Yet Roman traditions had more staying power than the Roman state. As Whittaker brings out, landlords and warlords helped to ensure some continuity of Roman institutions and practices in the barbarian kingdoms which took its place.

8   *John Rich*

Bibliography

Brunt, P. A. (1971), *Italian Manpower 225 BC–AD 14* (Oxford).

Campbell, J. B. (1978), 'The marriage of soldiers under the empire', *JRS* 68: 153–66.

Evans, J. K. (1991), *War, Women and Children in Ancient Rome* (London).

Harris, W. V. (1979), *War and Imperialism in Republican Rome 327–70 BC* (Oxford).

Hopkins, M. K. (1978), 'Conquerors and slaves: the impact of conquering an empire on the political economy of Italy', in *Conquerors and Slaves* (Cambridge), ch. 1 (pp. 1–98).

Keppie, L. J. F. (1984), *The Making of the Roman Army: From Republic to Empire* (London).

Maxfield, V. A. (1981), *The Military Decorations of the Roman Army* (London).

Nicolet, C. (1980), *The World of the Citizen in Republican Rome* (London).

Ober, J. (1982), 'Tiberius and the political testament of Augustus', *Historia*, 31: 306–28.

Raaflaub, K. J. (1980), 'The political significance of Augustus' military reforms', in W. S. Hanson and L. J. F. Keppie (eds), *Roman Frontier Studies, 1979* (Oxford), pp. 1005–25.

Rich, J. W. (1983), 'The supposed Roman manpower shortage of the later second century BC', *Historia*, 32: 287–331.

Talbert, R. J. A. (1984), *The Senate of Imperial Rome* (Princeton).

∞ **1** ∞

The Roman conquest of Italy

Stephen Oakley

Recent studies of Roman imperialism in the later Republic are abundant,[1] and there are classic narratives of her early history.[2] Yet it is hard to find many works devoted primarily to the dynamics of the conquest of Italy before the First Punic War,[3] and the main concern of this essay will be to identify the structures which led Rome to expand in the period before 264,[4] and to discuss their origin, nature, and development; we shall also consider the rather cruder question of whether or

---

[1] I have learnt most from Hopkins 1978a and, especially, Harris 1979, whose book should be read in conjunction with the critique of North 1981.

[2] Here we need note only Beloch 1926, a work which, though over-sceptical and at times eccentric, remains the most penetrating account of early Roman history; De Sanctis 1907, probably the most balanced extended narrative of the period; and Salmon 1967, which examines in depth the wars between Rome and her most persistent opponents. Shorter pieces by Adcock and Cornell in, respectively, the old and new seventh volumes of the *Cambridge Ancient History* show how the implications of the sources have been taken increasingly seriously between 1928 and 1989.

[3] However, Humbert 1978, Starr 1980 and Rowland 1983 all deal with aspects of this theme, and the opening chapters of Tenney Frank's *Roman Imperialism* cover much of the same ground. Harris 1990 appeared when this chapter was nearly complete, and it is particularly pleasing to me that we agree on many matters.

[4] All dates are BC; the so-called 'dictator' years (333, 324, 309, 301) are ignored in all calculations.

not one should term Rome 'aggressive' or 'imperialistic' in this period.[1]

An outline of Roman expansion

Our survey begins when Rome was no more than the largest city in Latium, a position attained as a result of synoecism with other villages in the Tiber valley in the seventh and sixth centuries.[2] Indeed between the battle of Lake Regillus (499 or 496) and the Gallic sack (390) she fought all or most of her wars in alliance with the other Latin communities and, after 486, the Hernici – thereby using for the first time allied manpower to counteract the numerical superiority of her opponents. During this century all her campaigning, with only a few isolated exceptions,[3] took place in a rather circumscribed area around the city and the Latin plain against three main opponents: the southern Etruscans and in particular Veii, a city with which Rome struggled for control of the Tiber until its destruction by Camillus in 396; the Aequi, a hill tribe living in the Aniene valley above Tibur and Praeneste, whose frequent sorties out of the mountains threatened those two towns in particular and northern Latium in general; and, most menacing of all, the Volsci, a Sabellian tribe based in the mountains of the Liri valley and in the M. Lepini. In the early fifth century these Volscians had descended into the Latin plain and had overrun the land between Tarracina and Ardea; and from

[1] There is not space here for a full discussion of the reliability of our sources for early Roman history. I note merely that Livy's narrative contains both extensive invention and extensive preservation of authentic testimony; and that to circumvent the problem of the possible invention of individual items I have tried wherever possible to ground the argument on a multiplicity of passages. A fuller discussion of many difficulties will be provided in my projected commentary on Livy, Books 6–10.

[2] For the sources for the various campaigns mentioned in this brief survey, see Livy and the other evidence collected annalistically in *MRR* i. All references to unspecified ancient texts are to Livy.

[3] Amongst which note 4. 57. 7 (fighting at the Fucine Lake in 406) and 5. 31. 5–32. 5 (fighting against Volsinii and her allies in 392–1); there is no especial reason to doubt these notices, though their authenticity cannot be proven.

this powerful base they were a constant threat to the Latin states on the lower slopes of the Alban hills and to Roman territory beyond.

The triple alliance of Romans, Latins, and Hernicans had met with considerable success and Rome had become increasingly pre-eminent in it, when in 390 she was suddenly sacked by a band of marauding Gauls. This inevitably meant that her campaigning over the next few years continued to be limited to the same constricted area; and between 389 and 359 her armies operated against the Latins and Hernici (both no doubt seeing an opportunity to rid themselves of an ally growing uncomfortably powerful), against Satricum, Antium, and the other Volsci of the Pomptine plain, and in 389 and 386 against Etruscans, amongst whom Falerii was doubtless prominent. And it was only in the next fifteen years that Rome's influence began to spread further afield, culminating in the dramatic alliance with Capua (343) and subsequent First Samnite War.

From Polybius (1. 1. 5) onwards a justly recurring theme in discussions of Roman imperialism has been the short time within which Rome transformed herself from being the mistress of Italy to the dominant power in the whole Mediterranean world; but in fact the speed with which she arrived at this domination in Italy between 343 and 264 is quite as striking. This period, despite twenty-five years of uneasy and intermittent peace between the two nations, was dominated by the Samnite Wars. The First (343–341) was a small affair provoked by Rome's involvement in Campania; but the Second (327–304) developed into a grim duel for supremacy in southern central Italy; and during the Third (298–291), and what should perhaps be called the Fourth (284–272), the Samnites participated in coalitions which tried in vain to stop Rome dominating the whole peninsula. When the series began the two powers must have seemed evenly matched, and Roman territory was limited; but the Samnites at some time or other involved most of peninsular Italy in alliances against Rome, and, when Rome had finally defeated them, she had no difficulty in overrunning their erstwhile allies, whom she now had a pretext for attacking. The decisive campaign in these years was waged in 295, when the coalition of Samnites, Gauls, Etruscans, and Umbrians ranged against Rome brought the Samnite wars to their crisis; and the victory of Fabius Rullianus at Sentinum in that year was certainly more spectacular than any previously won by a

Roman general, and probably the single most important event in Rome's march to dominion in Italy.

The Romans regularly confiscated land from their defeated foes, and thus the final result of these campaigns was not just a series of treaties by which every independent state was linked to Rome, but a vast expansion of her territory. For if we adopt the approximations of Beloch, then out of a total of 130,000 sq km for peninsular Italy as a whole the *ager Romanus* (Roman territory) grew from 822 sq km in 510 to 1,902 sq km in 340, to 23,226 sq km in 264.[1] The economic consequences of this will be discussed below, but here we should note the important strategic fact that much of this territory was contiguous: the *ager Romanus* now ran unbroken from the Caudine Forks to Ostia and from Ostia to Sena Gallica. Here, then, is a classic application of the principle of 'divide and rule', and never again would it be easy for the Samnites or any other state to establish the kind of alliance ranged against Rome at Sentinum.

The nature of Rome's early warfare

These early campaigns should be placed in the context of a series of conflicts in central Italy between those dwelling in the mountains and those, like the Romans and Latins, dwelling on the plain. Overpopulation has always been a recurring problem for Italian mountain communities, and in antiquity the legends of the 'sacred springs' of Italic peoples bear testimony to how surplus warriors would depart to pastures new;[2] and the most agreeable pastures in central Italy were those plains near the coast. Hence there was constant pressure from the mountains upon coastal communities, and this explains both the downward movement of the Volsci and Aequi and the behaviour of the Samnites. A wave of Samnite invaders in the fifth century had seized Capua and Cumae from Etruscans and Greeks; but their descendants were in

---

[1]   See Beloch 1926, 620–1; Afzelius 1942, 9 and *passim*.
[2]   According to Oscan legend, all the children born in a year of particular distress were dedicated to the god Mamers and, when adult, left the community for new territory; see, conveniently, Salmon 1967, 35–6 (with references to the ancient sources).

turn to be threatened in the mid-fourth century by further excursions of mountainfolk, and this was a prime cause of Rome's First Samnite War. Samnite pressure, moreover, was not limited to the Tyrrhenian seaboard, and Livy (9. 13. 7) tells us how they also threatened Apulia, describing the conflict specifically in terms of the clash between plainsmen and mountainfolk. He used the terms of ancient ethnography, which will hardly carry conviction today; but it is a fact that throughout the history of the Mediterranean the cultures of the mountain and the plain have differed: 'The mountain dweller is apt to be the laughing stock of the superior inhabitants of the plain. He is suspected, feared and mocked.' Thus Fernand Braudel on the early modern period;[1] but the same tensions were found in antiquity and were often resolved more violently.

The loss of land consequent upon the descent of the Volsci and Aequi must have led to the impoverishment of many Romans and Latins; but above all it exposed most of Roman and Latin territory to the threat of frequent raiding. Thus the wars of the fifth century began as a struggle for survival, and, if there be any truth in the tale of Coriolanus, it lies in the fear inspired by Volscian assaults on Rome.[2] As the century progressed, the allies gradually recovered much of their land, and it is easy to see how the first expansion beyond lands held in the sixth century involved merely an extension of this defensive mentality. For it must have been believed that security would never come until the menace of the Volsci and the Aequi had been eliminated, and so a gradual advance was made into their heartland. The Samnite Wars, moreover, began before the final Roman conquest of the Volsci, and it is easy to believe that something of the mental outlook which had been formed in those years of desperate struggle in Latium was carried forward by the Romans into the wars against this new and more powerful federation of mountain dwellers (see also Sherwin-White 1980, 178).

Thus far we have scarcely implied that the campaigns of the early Republic were anything but regular warfare; but given their early date and what must have been the relatively primitive

[1] Braudel 1972, 46; but the whole chapter is a classic exposition of the relationship of mountain and plain.
[2] See e.g. 2. 34. 7–40. 13 (with Ogilvie 1965, ad loc.).

organization of both sides, many will have been no more than raids for plunder. This is not a matter on which one would expect our sources to be particularly trustworthy, but it is nevertheless interesting that enemy attacks are often viewed in this way.[1] In general Livy and Dionysius of Halicarnassus stress the regularities of Roman offensives, organized as they were by consuls and dictators; but even they sometimes state that the Romans did little more than plunder.[2] Though one should be very cautious in using details from the early books of Livy, it may be that these and other similar passages go back to authentic information. By the mid-fourth century, however, Rome must have long given up such irregularities; and certainly after the siege of Veii and the associated introduction of legionary pay in 406 (4. 59. 11) her campaigning will have become increasingly systematized and professional. Nevertheless, we shall see that Romans were obsessed with booty throughout the Republic, and this outlook may be a survival from her earliest fighting.

Thus it was in the fifth century that many of the classic structures leading to Roman expansion were born: the use of allied manpower, the need for land, the hope of profit from war, and above all the expectation that one would have to fight almost every year.

Annual warfare and the allies

For one factor will always be apparent in an account of Roman expansion in Italy: these were years in which the Romans were almost constantly at war; and no one has done more to teach us the importance of this than Harris, who demonstrated (1979, 9– 10) how rare after 327 were years without warfare. Further analysis, however, is needed (in particular for the period before

---

[1] See e.g. 4. 21. 7 (435), 30. 5 (428), 45. 6 (418), 51. 7 (413), and 5. 16. 2–6 (397). Even in Livy's account of the mid-fourth century plundering seems from time to time to be the main preoccupation of Rome's enemies; see e.g. his remarks on the behaviour of the Aurunci in 345 (7. 28. 3) and Privernum in 330 (8. 19. 5).

[2] See e.g. 4. 21. 1 (436), 55. 8 (409), 5. 12. 5 (401), 14. 7 (398), and 32. 4 (391).

327), and the evidence for the years 440–265 may be scrutinized here.[1]

This produces a striking general pattern. In the period 440–416 annual warfare is already prevalent: we have notices of fighting in fifteen of these twenty-five years, and 440, 439, 433, 432, 430, 429, 424, 420, 417, and 416 are the only years for which none is recorded. More striking still is the pattern of the next twenty-five years: between 415 and 391 Livy records no campaigning only for 412 and 411. The chronology of the next twenty-five years (that is a period covered by Livy, Book 6, and including the anarchy) is notoriously difficult and confused, but between 390 and 367 it is only for 387 and 384, the year in which Manlius Capitolinus is alleged to have been killed, that there are no notices of warfare. The next convenient segment of history, from the revival of the consular constitution in 366 to the outbreak of the First Samnite War in 343, produces five years of possible peace, in 366–364, when we know that there was a severe plague, in 347, and 344 itself; but between the outbreak of the First Samnite War in 343 and the Second in 327, Livy allows only 331 and 328 to be years of peace. Most remarkable of all are the figures for the period between 327 and 293: in this thirty-one-year period, Livy's Romans went to war every year. For the twenty-eight-year period between 292 and 265 we are handicapped severely by the loss of Livy's narrative, but our sources, defective though they are, still record no wars only for 289–285. The matter has been discussed carefully by Harris (1979, 256–7), who concluded that 288, 287, and 285 'may well have been years without warfare'; but it is worth stressing that given our poor sources we cannot rule out the possibility of fighting even in these years. After 264 the inexorable pattern of annual warfare continued, and the First Punic War dominated Rome's foreign affairs until 241.

Consequently, for the period of more or less one hundred and

---

[1] This poses the twin problems that there are years in which Livy, our main source, has recorded fighting which (rightly or wrongly) many modern scholars have rejected, and that there are likely to have been campaigns about which he was silent; but, though some details of his narrative may be unreliable, the general structural pattern produced by this analysis is unlikely to lead us far astray, and no rival reconstruction by a modern scholar could hope to gain general acceptance.

fifty years from 415 to 265, it is only for thirteen years (or less than 10 per cent) that we have no notices of fighting: 412, 411, 387, 384, 366, 365, 364, 347, 344, 328, 288, 287, and 285. Thus the pattern of annual warfare goes back far and deep into Roman history and was established long before the great period of overseas expansion. One implication of this would have been the natural assumption of Roman citizens in any winter that there would be a war in the following summer, and thus the structures of the state were geared for such fighting. A further corollary must have been that the Romans will have looked for war when none was ready at hand; for peasants do not need to work all summer, and there was time enough for fighting.[1] It would probably be absurd to describe the Rome of *c*.410 as 'imperialistic'. But any state naturally tries to win the wars in which it is engaged; and when, fifty or sixty years later, Rome's resources began to enable her increasingly to dominate her neighbours, her annual pattern of warfare must have been a great spur to conquest.

It is in this context that a remarkable passage of Livy (10. 1. 4) should be placed, relating to 303, a year for which the author has so far recounted no fighting:

> lest, however, they should pass the whole year entirely without fighting (*ne prorsus imbellem agerent annum*), the consuls made a small sortie into Umbria, because it was reported that armed men were making plundering raids on the countryside from a cave. The soldiers reached that cave . . .

and Livy goes on to describe the inevitable Roman victory. Now we should perhaps not regard the opening final clause as anything other than Livy's own deduction from his sources; but, if it were by chance to reflect the authentic Roman thought of 303, then we have a fascinating indication of the Roman expectation of, and desire for, annual warfare.

We must also consider Momigliano's well-known views on the structural significance of Rome's allies;[2] for though he was referring primarily to the fully developed system found after the

---

[1]   See e.g. Hopkins 1978a, 24.
[2]   See especially Momigliano 1975, 44–6 (p. 45 quoted); but note also Crawford 1978, 53, and North 1981, 6–7.

Second Punic War, this system had its origin and first flowering in our period:

> The *socii* (allies) . . . could not be expected to be automatically loyal. Yet they were necessary. They had to be kept busy by war, because otherwise the whole building of the Roman organization would collapse. As military obligations were the only visible tie between Rome and the allies, Rome had to make the most of these obligations lest they become meaningless or, worse, lest the allied armies turned against Rome.

Momigliano was discussing Polybius and arguing that he may have misunderstood the nature of Rome's alliances in Italy. Not all have been convinced, and Harris (1984b)[1] in particular has made some telling points against underestimating Polybius' understanding of the realities of Roman control in Italy. Yet the main thrust of the passage quoted has never been refuted. Harris argued that Roman warfare and conquest are explicable merely by reference to the structures of Roman society, and that there is no need to posit a desire to keep the allies busy. Now it is true that many of the details and the precise dates of, for example, the Punic Wars are explicable without reference to the allies; that when on occasions they were excused fighting some allies will have been relieved; that there is no evidence that Rome was worried by fears of Italian disloyalty in the period between Zama and Tiberius Gracchus; and above all that 'the habit of more or less continuous wars started before Rome established the classic system of control over the Italian allies, and therefore cannot be entirely explained by that system' (Harris 1984b, 92). But all these arguments seem to stand too close to the evidence for individual wars and too close to the conscious intentions of Roman and allied leaders. Momigliano's hypothesis certainly does not provide an entire explanation of Rome's system of alliances; but, when dealing with so complex a phenomenon, we should be searching for a multiplicity of explanations and grateful for anything which even partially illuminates. Though our evidence is – as usual – deficient, the annual warfare endemic in early Rome must also have been characteristic of many, perhaps most, other Italian states or tribes (see also Badian 1982, 166). Certainly this must

---

[1] For an earlier version of these views, see Harris 1980.

have been true of the Latins and Hernici, who time and again fought at Rome's side in the fifth and fourth centuries. It must also have been true of the Volsci and Aequi: we read in Livy and Dionysius of Halicarnassus of countless wars against Rome and the Latins, who were doubtless not their only opponents. For the Samnites our testimony for the period before 343 is less good, but between that year and 272 at least some Samnites were fighting against Rome in more or less two years out of every three. The Roman conquest of Italy deprived all these states and tribes of the possibility of regular warfare in the peninsula, but this conquest can hardly have removed from their societies all the internal structures which rested upon the expectation of war; and the great merit of Momigliano's formulation is that it points to the Roman need, consciously or unconsciously, to channel this aggression to her own purposes. Previously at war with each other and with Rome, the allies' military power was now harnessed to effect numerical superiority, victory, and conquest for Rome. But this warfare under Rome's leadership was itself productive and lucrative and would have further encouraged some facets of the bellicosity innate in the Italic peoples; hence the continuing need to keep them usefully employed. Thus Rome's Latin and Italian alliances, started in a bid to withstand Volscian, Aequian, and Etruscan pressure on Latin and Hernican territory, eventually became a powerful spur to expansion in themselves.[1]

Debt, land, and colonization

The Romans believed that they had already been planting colonies in the regal period (see e.g. 1. 27. 3, 56. 3; 2. 16. 8). That is in principle likely enough (although no individual item of evidence should be accepted uncritically), but of more moment in the shaping of their later attitudes is the series of colonies established

[1]   It has been argued that the military demands which Rome made upon Capua, her most important single ally, were in fact slight (see e.g. Bernardi 1943, 29 and Frederiksen 1984, 224–5); this may have been the case (though the evidence seems far from decisive), but the unwarlike Campani will not have been typical of Roman allies as a whole. See also Toynbee 1965, i. 201–3.

during their period of alliance with the Latin league between the battle of Lake Regillus and the war of 340–338. Now, though much is controversial about the colonization in this period,[1] it is clear that when the allies settled in strategic positions they must both have strengthened their position against their enemies and also provided themselves with a future source of reliable and guaranteed manpower. Typical of the foundations in this period are Norba (492) and Setia (around 382), both situated on the edge of the M. Lepini, and bastions against the Volsci at Antium and on the Pomptine plain.

There was no colonization in the period 380–340, and this must in part reflect less amicable relations between Rome and the Latin league. Yet after her final settlement of Latium in 338 Rome revived the concept of the Latin colony, a masterstroke which was to be of vital importance during the Samnite Wars, and was ultimately to save her in both the Hannibalic and Social Wars. The strength of this new series of colonies (sixteen founded between 334 and 263) lay above all in their strategic positions; and, since we shall be examining this colonization from a very different perspective, it is important to remember that strategic considerations dictated precisely when and where a colony was to be founded.[2]

A substantial programme of colonization meant the exporting of large numbers of settlers, and this must have had consequences for the Roman economy. Our sources provide no sophisticated analysis of fourth-century economics, but they do suggest both that debt was rife and that there was a great hunger for land; and these factors must have provided pro-plebeian politicians with their supporters. Indeed, the theme of debt recurs time and again. In the period after the Gallic sack we meet it first in the story of

[1] We do not know, for instance, whether the initiative for colonization tended to come from Rome or the Latins; whether colonies which Livy calls 'Roman' were established primarily by Rome or jointly by Rome and her Latin allies; and whether many of the notices in Livy which refer to the foundation of short-lived colonies are reliable. Contrast the views of e.g. Gelzer, *RE* 12. 958–9; Salmon 1953; Cornell 1989, 277–81.

[2] The six or seven 'citizen' colonies, founded on coastal sites with only 300 settlers should also be noted, but are less important for our purposes. For a fuller treatment of the military aspects of colonization, see Salmon 1969, 55–81.

the attempted *coup d'état* of Manlius Capitolinus in 385–4, where the support for Manlius comes from the help he gave the impoverished.[1] Under 380 we are told that the plebs complained that the election of censors had not been allowed lest the true extent of debt should be known (6. 27. 3–9). Then for 378 Livy (6. 31. 2–3) states that censors were indeed elected, but that enemy action prevented them from examining the problem of debt, and that the building of the city wall plunged the plebeians still further into debt (6. 32. 1–2). Then, in his account of the following year, 377, generalized comment on the impoverished state of the plebeians forms the background to the long narrative of the struggle for the Licinio-Sextian rogations (6. 34. 1–4). These were finally passed in 367, and, according to Livy (6. 35. 5), included a measure for the alleviation of debts by allowing previous payments of interest to help towards the repayment of the principal, for which three further years were given.

Measures to curb indebtedness and usury then become prominent in Livy, Book 7. In 357 a law was passed on *unciarium faenus*, which is best interpreted as limiting interest rates to 100 per cent per annum;[2] in 354 there is yet another notice referring to the miseries of the *plebs* (7. 19. 5); in 352 we are told that a commission of five was appointed to settle debts with money loaned by the state (7. 21. 5–8); in 347 Livy (7. 27. 3) again comments on the financial difficulties of the plebeians, and tells us that the maximum rate of interest was halved to 50 per cent; in 344 we are told that usurers were prosecuted (7. 28. 9); and in 342 the *leges Genuciae* are said to have put a complete ban on usury (7. 42. 1; see also Tac. *Ann.* 6. 16. 2 and App. *BCiv.* 1. 232–4). This last measure is preceded in Livy (7. 38. 5–42. 7) by a long account of the mutiny in the army, in which the troops complained of their impoverishment and poor land. He reveals, however, that some of his sources recorded only sedition at Rome; but that there was extensive plebeian unrest in 342 seems certain.

Several of the notices which refer to the impoverishment of the plebeians are rather impressionistic and may be little more than Livian or annalistic colouring (this applies especially to those in Book 6). Many, however, refer to concrete measures; and, even if

[1] See e.g. 6. 11. 8–9, 14. 1–10, and 20. 15–21. 1 (a pestilence).
[2] 7. 16. 1. See further Zehnacker 1980; Hölkeskamp 1987, 99–100.

Livy or his sources have misunderstood the import of some, it is hard to deny that there must have been a flurry of legislation on debt in these years. The details, however, and disputes as to their authenticity, matter rather less for our purposes: we need merely note that, however vague they may be, the notices in Book 6 cumulatively provide good evidence for the prevalence of debt amongst the poorer plebeians in the years 389 to 367, and that strong confirmation of this comes from the more concrete notices for the period 366 to 342. It would be a bold scholar who tried to sweep all the Livian evidence aside and deny that there was a problem of debt and impoverishment in these years.

The problem of debt, however, must be linked closely with the issue of the distribution of conquered land to Roman citizens. For, if through colonization or viritane distribution a poor man acquired a new or more extensive plot of land or more extensive rights to *ager publicus*, then he stood a better chance of improving his agrarian fortunes and of avoiding falling into debt. Now between the third consulship of Spurius Cassius in 486 and the distribution of land seized from Capua and the Latins in 339, a constant theme of our sources is plebeian demands for better access to land and in particular for a more equable distribution of *ager publicus*; and the passing of the *lex Licinia Sextia* (which limited holdings in *ager publicus*) is just the most famous moment in a struggle which lasted for a century and a half. Many modern scholars have regarded this agitation as no more than a retrojection of events in the late Republic, when hunger for land again became a dominant theme.[1] But this position should be rejected for many reasons, not least because any plausible model for the economy and society of early Rome needs to postulate extensive patrician landholdings, a need met by our sources' insistence upon patrician domination of *ager publicus*.

Apart, however, from the establishment of the tribes Pomptina and Publilia in 358 (7. 15. 11) and the colonization of Sutrium, Nepet, and Setia close to the Gallic War of 390, we have no record of the distribution of any land to Romans in the period 389–342 (see also Crawford 1971, 253). These are precisely the years for which Livy time and again returns to the theme of debt. In the following years, however, any remaining patrician monopoly of

[1] Gutberlet 1985, 47–72, is a recent exponent of this line of argument.

ager publicus was removed once and for all, and the great programme of colonization began, with Romans being settled all over central Italy. It is, moreover, remarkable that after 342 our sources hardly refer to what had once been the favoured theme of debt: apart from the rather mysterious Third Secession of the *plebs* in 289, which may in part have been provoked by the economic hardships of the poor, we hear only of the abolition of *nexum* (a form of debt-bondage) by a *lex Poetelia* to be dated to either 326 or 313, and this points as much to a diminution as an increase in indebtedness.[1] It might be argued that the reason for this lies in the fascination which the Samnite Wars held over the imagination of Livy, who is our dominant source, and that consequently he ignored social issues in favour of fighting. This position cannot be refuted; but Livy found the space to give great prominence to Ap. Claudius and would surely have mentioned economic matters more often if his sources had given him cause. We should rather argue that the problem of debt at Rome gradually diminished, and that the settlement of numerous plebeians on conquered territory goes some way towards explaining this.[2] Thus at a deeper level than strategic considerations there was a structural impulse in Roman society towards warfare, the subsequent acquisition of land, and colonization. Hence colonization is central to Roman imperialism before 264.

The economic rewards of warfare

We have seen already that many of the Romans' earliest wars must have been little more than plundering expeditions, but unfortunately for the main period of the conquest of Italy it is hard to document their interest in plunder and the wealth to be derived from it. This is not because of any reticence on the part of Livy, who constantly refers to Roman plundering; but the nature of the annalistic tradition is such that we can rarely, if ever, be

[1]   Perhaps as evidence for unrest in the lowest stratum of society one should point also to the fragmentary notice at Dion. Hal. *Ant. Rom.* 16. 6. 1, and to the turbulent career of Ap. Claudius Caecus.
[2]   For this argument see Brunt 1971, 26–33; Harris 1979, 60–1; Torelli 1979; Hölkeskamp 1987, 157–9; Harris 1990, 502–3.

confident that small details of this kind are authentic testimony and not plausible invention.[1] Nevertheless, Harris (1979, index s.v. booty) has amply documented the fascination of third- and second-century Romans with looting and portable booty, and it is quite inconceivable that this was not something which they inherited from their forebears. This is partly confirmed by the events of 264, where the reliable evidence of Polybius (1. 11. 2) points to Roman hopes of booty as being a prime immediate cause of the First Punic War (see e.g. Harris 1979, 182–90). If, however, this matter is not susceptible to detailed analysis,[2] others are more rewarding.

Scholars are increasingly prepared to allow that the Roman 'slave-economy' originated in the fourth and early third centuries.[3] The proposition may be supported in two ways: first by citation of evidence of varying cogency from our sources, and second by more general considerations, which ancient authors did not address.

The most substantial testimony to the importance of slavery in the mid-fourth century comes from Livy's statement that the long lasting 5 per cent tax on the manumission of slaves originated in a law passed in 357.[4] Now it is almost always possible to doubt information of this kind when it is provided by Livy's early books; but here inspection of the context of his account reveals no motive for annalistic invention or falsification. It therefore follows that if this notice is sound there must have been many slaves manumitted in the period before 355, since otherwise there would have been no motive for the passing of the law; and, if there were many

---

[1] A few passages, however, from Livy, Book 10, may be cited here: 12. 6, 17. 10, 19. 22, 30. 10, 31. 4, 39. 4, 44. 8, and 46. 6–7.

[2] Note, however, the interesting speculations of Harris 1990, 500, on Roman naval plundering.

[3] See Harris 1979, 59–60; 1984a, 23–4; 1990, 498–9; Gruen 1984, 296–7; Crawford 1985, 24 n. 34; and especially Finley 1980, 82–5; but Finley seems to underestimate the contribution of successful warfare to the provision of slaves in the fourth century (*contra*, rightly, Bradley 1984, 179). The arguments of Clemente 1982, 187–8, do not controvert this thesis.

[4] 7. 16. 7. The bizarre circumstances in which this law was passed should not affect our view of the authenticity of Livy's testimony. On the general history of this tax, see e.g. Brunt 1971, 549–50; Bradley 1984.

manumissions, then there must have been many more slaves. Some of these slaves will have come through trade, but many through warfare, and one passage often stressed in this context is Livy's account of the enslavement of the people of Veii in 396.[1] The next important testimony relates to the censorship of Ap. Claudius Caecus, which began in 312, and the most likely interpretation of his changes to the tribal structure suggests that he wanted to enrol freedmen in all the tribes and not just the urban tribes.[2] For our purposes the details hardly matter: we should note simply that if there had not been substantial numbers of freedmen at Rome the controversy would hardly have arisen. Freedmen next become significant in 296 when Livy records, presumably correctly, that they were enlisted in the army (10. 21. 3–4): again, if there were hardly any freedmen, the point would not have been worth making.

Important testimony of a rather different kind comes from the tenth book of Livy, where, in the account of fighting in central Italy between 297 and 293, there is a striking series of notices which gives figures for those captured and enslaved, set out in Table 1.1.[3] These give a total of about 69,000 enslavements in the period. As so often with Livy, this information is not unproblematic: figures of enemy captured are always liable to inflation, manuscript traditions are especially prone to corrupting numerals, and even in Book 10 his sources were not always reliable; on the other hand there is no reason to think that Livy records all enslavements which took place in this period. Here, then, it is particularly important to concentrate not on individual details of Livy's account (such as whether the enslavement of 8,000 after Sentinum is really credible), but on the general picture which he presents; and it is surely improbable that this is entirely the fantastic creation of the annalists. For even if he records twice as many enslavements as really occurred, the total figure would

[1]   5. 22. 1. Other passages from Livy's account of the warfare of the early fourth century could also be cited, but the notices are always vague and there must be much doubt about their authenticity; see e.g. 6. 4. 2 (387), 13. 7 (385), and 25. 1–2 (381).

[2]   See e.g. 9. 46. 10–15.

[3]   The information has been set out before, notably by Volkmann 1961, 153–4; Harris 1979, 59 n. 4; and Cornell 1989, 389. However, no one has yet presented all that Livy offers.

Table 1.1 Captives enslaved by Rome, 297–293 BC

Date	Livy ref.	City or people	Enslaved
297	10. 14. 21	Samnites	830
297	10. 15. 16	Cimetra	2,900
296	10. 17. 4	Murgantia	2,100
296	10. 17. 8	Romulea	6,000
296	10. 18. 8	Samnites	c.1,500
296	10. 19. 22	Etruscans	2,120
296	10. 20. 15	Samnites	2,500
295	10. 29. 17	Samnites and Gauls	8,000
295	10. 31. 3	Perusia	1,740
295	10. 31. 7	Samnites	2,700
294	10. 34. 3	Milionia	4,700
294	10. 37. 3	Rusellae	>2,000
293	10. 39. 3	Amiternum	4,270
293	10. 39. 4	Duronia	<4,270
293	10. 42. 5	Aquilonia	3,870
293	10. 43. 8	Cominium	11,400
293	10. 45. 11	Samnites	c.5,000
293	10. 45. 14	Samnites	<3,000
293	10. 46. 12	Etruscans	<2,000

still be striking. A further reason for belief in the basic credibility of this picture is that it is paralleled in the next Roman war for which we have adequate sources. That is the First Punic War, during which Polybius and others record numerous enslavements, which begin with the 25,0000 at the notorious capture of Agrigentum in 262.[1] The Third Samnite War and First Punic War are barely thirty years apart, and it is entirely credible that Roman practices should be similar in both.

Now this is the first time in Livy's narrative that we are presented with such a sequence of figures for enemy captured; and whilst this increases the probability that these figures in some way reflect the reality of the 290s, it also raises the question of whether this is a new phenomenon in Roman history. Caution is required here: the evidence for manumission which we have been

[1] Diod. 23. 9. 1. Even for this period individual figures may be suspect, but no one doubts that such mass enslavements did occur. Enslavements during and between the Punic Wars are helpfully listed at Toynbee 1965, ii. 171–3.

examining suggests that the Romans must have been enslaving people on the battlefield for many a year; and there is the possibility that the extra detail comes simply because Book 10 covers a period of history closer to the lifetimes of Livy's sources. The break, however, in the character of the evidence around 300 (before which date such figures occur only rarely),[1] is such that it is very tempting to believe that in this period the Romans began to capture far more slaves on the field of battle. This can be explained both by the Samnite Wars being larger in scale than previous wars and by a greater need for slaves. At any rate our sources provide much evidence for the importance of slavery in the period before 293.

We must turn now to general considerations.[2] The political conflicts of the fifth and fourth centuries are explicable only if we posit a vast disparity in size between the landholdings (and hence the wealth) of the rich and of ordinary peasants. Labour was needed on the large estates, and this need goes far towards explaining the existence of the various institutions of debt-bondage at Rome. Yet with the progressive amelioration of the lot of the poor in the fourth century as a result of social reforms and colonization, and with the decline in the institution of *nexum*, this traditional source of labour will have become more scarce. The slaves provided by the increasingly successful warfare of the period will have filled the gap, and it is easy to conceive of a model in which the agricultural labour of poor freeborn Romans was progressively replaced by that of slaves.[3] Increasing conquest, however, brought increasing quantities of *ager publicus* to be exploited by the rich, and this will have led to an increased demand for slaves; and even poorer farmers will have been able to find a use for one or a few slaves, as the copious evidence from Athens makes clear. Thus already in the Samnite Wars the possibility of finding more slaves as a by-product of successful warfare must have been an important factor in the way such warfare was viewed.

[1]   But note e.g. Diod. 20. 26. 3. (311), 80. 1–2 (306), and Livy, 9. 42. 8 (307).
[2]   The argument adopted here may be found already at Finley 1980, 84.
[3]   Booty, however, will have enriched even the humble and allowed them to purchase slaves; see below, p. 27 n. 4, for hand-outs to troops.

The economic rewards of warfare also manifested themselves in other ways. It is well known that the visual appearance both of Rome and of many other Italian towns was transformed in the second and first centuries by building and adornment financed by conquest overseas.[1] What is less well known is that there is sufficient evidence in our literary sources alone to suggest that this process began in the period around 300.[2] The appendix below (pp. 33–5) lists all datable building activity known at Rome for the period 400–291. It is quite remarkable how much of this evidence comes from the period 312–291. Apart from some religious activity associated with the Veientine and Gallic Wars, there is nothing comparable to this spate of building in earlier Roman history;[3] indeed, though only eighteen temples are known from the period 753–303, nine dedications of temples are found between 302 and 291. Again, a possible weakness of this argument is that it may simply reflect the increasing quantities of authentic material available for the period covered by Books 9 and 10 of Livy; but, as the rest of the list shows, records of building had long been part of the fabric of Livy's narrative, and it is thus legitimate to argue for a change in Roman policy towards building, and hence in the economy as a whole. The large number of dedications has already been pointed out, but temples form only part of a sequence of building which also included the construction of aqueducts and roads; and the new colonies would also have required much building. All this had to be paid for, and whereas slaves will have provided much of the labour, the finance must have come largely from spoil taken from the Samnites and other enemies.[4] In this context we should note the conjecture of Crawford that the Romans first struck coinage because of the need to finance the building of the Appian Way (Crawford 1982,

---

[1] For Rome see e.g. Coarelli 1977, for Italy e.g. Zanker 1976.

[2] For the difficult archaeological evidence see e.g. Wallace 1990, 281–4.

[3] The loss of Livy, Books 11–20, makes it impossible to say what happened later.

[4] General considerations would force us to posit this, but Livy also refers often to booty taken from the Samnites and Etruscans: see e.g. 9. 40. 16, 10. 30. 10, 31. 3, 37. 5, 46. 5, 14. Individual details may be suspect, but this whole series of notices shows impressively how the *aerarium*, individual generals, and even common soldiers were enriched by the spoils of war. See also Salmon 1967, 277.

99; 1985, 29). Thus the increasing dominance of Rome in central Italy was symbolized by her changing appearance.

'Continuous wars of imperial conquest', 'the plundering of conquered territories', 'the financing of further wars', 'the import . . . of booty, taxes and slaves', 'agricultural slaves', 'urban slaves', 'ostentatious expenditure in towns', 'the growth of towns and luxury in Italy', 'the purchase of land . . . the formation of large estates worked primarily by slaves'. With some slight adaptations to fit the earlier age we have here some nine of the fourteen elements in the well-known flow diagram of Hopkins (1978a, 12; 1978b, 62), which so usefully delineates an appropriate model for the economy of the late Republic. We have found evidence for all in our period, and may thus argue that, in a society shaped by continuous warfare, that model was already emerging around 300.

Roman attitudes to warfare

There are useful studies of the late republican Roman military ethos (Hopkins 1978a, 25–37; Harris 1979, 19–53), but comparable analysis for our period is much harder, since there is only limited evidence as to how fourth-century Romans thought and represented themselves. Yet, as we saw with regard to the Roman interest in booty, many of the practices and attitudes of later times must have had their origin in the wars of conquest in Italy: for if the Romans went to war every year, then fighting was one of the unavoidable hazards of life.

Nothing reveals so well the extent to which military service impinged upon Roman citizens in the middle and late Republic as the approximate calculations of Hopkins for the number of Romans under arms (Hopkins 1978a, 31–5). He estimates (ibid. 35) that in 225 legionaries comprised 17 per cent of all adult male citizens, and in 213, at the height of the Hannibalic War, 29 per cent:

> An army which accounted for thirteen per cent of all citizens (the median of the last two centuries [of the Republic]) could be raised by enlisting eighty-four per cent of seventeen-year-olds for five years, or *c.* sixty per cent for seven years, or forty-four per cent for ten years, or twenty-eight per cent for sixteen years.

But the corporate solidarity of the relatively small city-state of
c.300 is hardly likely to have been less than that c.225, and the
proportion of men enrolled will, if anything, have been higher.
Some confirmation of this may perhaps be found in Livy's
evidence for 295, when we are told that Rome put six legions in
the field (10. 27. 10–11). If these were initially at their full strength
of 6,000 men, then unless the population of Rome numbered at
least 144,000 (a high estimate), more than 25 per cent of her adult
males were serving in that year. Now Livy's evidence may not be
reliable, the legions were certainly not always at full strength in
later periods and may not have been in 295, and above all the
climactic year of the battle of Sentinum probably drew forth from
Rome an unprecedented war effort;[1] but here is an indication of
the great extent to which fighting must have affected the average
male citizen in these years.

No institution was so characteristic of the military ethos of
Rome as the triumph, and statistics provide some compensation
for our lack of a sound description of a fourth- or fifth-century
triumph. For the years of the Second and Third Samnite Wars,
and of the Pyrrhic War and its aftermath saw a greater frequency
of triumphs than any other period of the Republic: for the
eighteen years between 312 and 293 the triumphal Fasti[2] record
eighteen triumphs, and for the nineteen years between 282 and 264
no fewer than twenty-two triumphs. With this we may contrast
twenty-seven between 367 and 313, eight between 329 and 313,
thirty between 264 and 222, sixteen between 178 and 155,
seventeen between 126 and 104; only after 45 are the figures for
our period surpassed, with seventeen triumphs listed between that
year and 34; but by then the institution had been somewhat
trivialized. Thus in no period did Roman generals celebrate their
success as warriors so often as in ours.[3]

Indeed, it was in this period that at Rome the cult of Victoria,

[1] A complement of 20–30,000 men under arms may have been more
normal. Cf. Cornell 1989, 383.
[2] For the triumphal Fasti see Degrassi 1947, 64–87, 534–71. We must use
their evidence in determining structures in the same way as that outlined
above (p. 10 n. 1) for Livy. Since they are lacunose, figures are presented
only for the periods for which notices survive. I have included in the
figures ovations and triumphs on the Alban Mount listed by the Fasti.
[3] See also ch. 2 below, pp. 49–50.

later a very familiar emblem of her aspirations, first becomes prominent.[1] We may note the statue erected in 305 to Hercules, a god often associated with victory (9. 44. 16), the reference to the statue of Victoria in the prodigies for 296 (Dio, fr. 36. 28; Zonar. 8. 1), the vow of Fabius Rullianus at Sentinum of a temple to Jupiter Victor (10. 29. 14), the dedication of the temple of Victoria in 294 (10. 33. 9), the adoption in 293 of the Greek practice of wearing laurels at the games (10. 47. 3), and the likelihood that silver *quadrigati* portrayed the statue of the Ogulnii with Jupiter followed by Victoria.[2] Weinstock (1957, 212–15; 221–46) argued that both the fame of Alexander and the interest in Nike (Victory) displayed by him and his successors quickly left its mark at Rome, but did not concede (p. 247) that in the period of the Samnite Wars Victoria had yet become a potent symbol of conquest. Yet, if we add this evidence to that noted above and remember the large number of Italian states and tribes which were then succumbing to Rome, the temptation to conclude that already in the 290s Victoria had become a symbol of Roman imperialism becomes irresistible: Fabius Rullianus knew the significance of the campaign of Sentinum, and his vow there is no coincidence.

Some further pointers to Roman attitudes to warfare in our period should also be noted. The abortive attempt of P. Decius Mus to devote himself at Ausculum (Dio, fr. 40. 43; Zonar. 8. 5) shows that, whether or not they really devoted themselves, the deaths of his father at Sentinum and grandfather at the Veseris were already part of Roman military legend, and that celebration of these heroes was not just a late Republican phenomenon. The willingness of Romans to fight as champions in single combat is another indication of their bellicosity,[3] and we should perhaps accept that one such champion, M. Valerius Corvus, won an early consulship as a result of prowess thus displayed (7. 26. 12). Also revealing is the third-century inscription (*ILLRP* 309) commemorating L. Cornelius Scipio Barbatus, consul in 298, where we already see burgeoning the desire for military *laus* and *gloria*, such important factors in any explanation of later Roman imper-

---

[1]   The evidence was first noted and collected by Weinstock 1957. See also e.g. Harris 1979, 123–5; Wiseman 1981, 46 (= 1987, 198).
[2]   See Mattingly 1945, 73–4 (and cf. Crawford 1974, 715).
[3]   See Harris 1979, 38–9; Oakley 1985.

ialism. The way in which L. Postumius Megellus enhanced his own personal prestige by triumphing in 294, despite the opposition of the senate, also points to this (10. 37. 6–12); and it is easy to believe that already around 300 the desire for a military reputation made consuls fight further from Rome than might otherwise have been the case.[1]

Roman aggression?

Hungry for booty and slaves, in great need of fresh land, and impelled forward by an ideology of victory and an annual rhythm of warfare, the Romans around 300 can scarcely be regarded as fighting only to protect the fatherland. For already in this period we find them using the notoriously aggressive device of taking states into their *fides* in order to provoke others – notably the Samnites – to war;[2] and though it would be absurd to hold that the Romans started all the wars in which they were engaged,[3] Polybius' belief (1. 6. 4–6) that at the time of the Pyrrhic War they conceived a plan for dominion in Italy is perhaps credible, even though allowance has to be made for the author's schematism on such matters.[4] Livy was blind to much of Rome's aggressiveness, but even in his pages the ruthless treatment of the Aequi in

[1] A *caveat*. Hopkins 1978a, 35, claimed that 'continuous wars were largely a consequence of the competitive ambitions of a militaristic élite', and certainly in the period after 264 much of Roman expansion and the ultimate collapse of the Republic were inspired by this competition. In the earlier period, however, despite an influx of 'new' plebeian families, competition for the consulship was not so severe, and until the 290s many leading men held three, four, or even five consulships. There was thus less pressure to make the most of one's period of office, and consequently the importance of competition for office should not be overestimated in our period. *Contra*, Harris 1990, 505.
[2] e.g. the alliance with Capua in 343 in contravention of the treaty of 354 with the Samnites (7. 29. 1–32. 4) and the alliance with Fabrateria in 330 (8. 19. 1); and see further Badian 1958, 35.
[3] For example, it is not very likely that they started the Etruscan War of 311–308 or the Hernican War of 307–6, when they were still busy fighting the Samnites.
[4] For contrasting interpretations of those Polybian passages in which the Romans are ascribed a desire for world dominion, see e.g. Walbank 1963; Derow 1979; Harris 1979, 107–17.

304–303 shows how she could extirpate her neighbours (9. 45. 5–18; 10. 1. 1; 10. 1. 7–9).

The skilful settlement with the Latins and Campanians in 338 provided the backbone of Rome's power in the late fourth century and is sometimes seen as notably just and humane. This point of view is adumbrated by Livy, but no one has expressed it with more eloquence than Frank (1914, 33–4):

> But the details of this contest are of little importance compared with its results: the political reorganization of the defeated allies by some far-sighted statesmen, who, for the first time in history, showed how a republican city-state might build a world empire, and who thus shaped a policy that endured for centuries. The central idea of this statesmanship was that a prudent liberality should bind the conquered and the conqueror for the sake of their mutual interests. Its method was to remove as quickly as possible all the disabilities usually entailed by subjection and by carefully graduated stages to elevate the subject to full citizenship and thereby arouse patriotic interest in a common national welfare. The idea dominating Greek states that conquerors had a perpetual right to a parasitical life at the expense of the conquered, an idea which precluded a healthy and permanent growth of the state, was rejected entirely at Rome. A more revolutionary policy history can hardly display.[1]

Since Rome had not granted the full citizenship to Capua, her most powerful ally, by the time of her revolt in 216, the only reason for believing in a generous settlement in 338 is that she did not exact tribute from the defeated. That is quite true. But the settlement of 338 and all subsequent Roman treaties were dictated by Roman military might; however much one may admire Rome's use of her citizenship as a diplomatic weapon, the context of *civitas sine suffragio* was invariably military defeat by Rome.[2] Most of Rome's new allies lost their right to a foreign policy of their own, and those incorporated into the Roman state lost their

---

[1]   Others who take a fundamentally pro-Roman view of this settlement include Toynbee 1965, i. 272; Crawford 1978, 42; Frederiksen 1984, 207–37.

[2]   The nature of *civitas sine suffragio* has been long disputed. I have found the exposition of it by Humbert 1978, 162–284 (and *passim*) as an instrument of Roman aggression far more compelling than Frederiksen's attempt (loc. cit.) to claim that Capua was little more than a Roman ally and that the institution was akin to Greek isopolity.

very sovereignty. Rome may not have exacted tribute, but she did make extensive demands upon allied manpower and often imposed her dominion in that most galling of ways: the seizing of territory.[1] Few Campani, for instance, would have rejoiced at the far-seeing wisdom of *civitas sine suffragio*, when they had only to look at the *ager Falernus* to see what they had lost; and the Latin colonies must have stood as a symbol of all that recalcitrant allies hated.

Our sources rarely reveal the outlook of Rome's allies, and it is easy to regard them as being basically satisfied once they were safely established in the *formula togatorum*; and doubtless in such years as 225 when the Gallic threat led to the campaign of Telamon they were grateful for Roman leadership and protection. But if Capua was content with *civitas sine suffragio* why did she revolt in 216? Why did the Hernici, after more than fifty years of peaceful alliance, so foolishly decide in 307/6 to try and shake off the Roman yoke before their liberty was gone for ever? And, most bizarre of all, why did Falerii, small and isolated as she was, try to rebel in 241 at a time when Rome was not only mistress of Italy but had also beaten Carthage? Revolts against Rome were indeed few, and that is an indication of her prudent statesmanship; but it should not blind us to the real nature of her control of Italy. When the legions crossed the straits of Messina in 264 they were continuing a policy of aggression started many years before.[2]

Appendix: building at Rome, 400–291 BC

The following list (an expansion of that of Wissowa 1912, 594–5) includes all datable construction, monumentalization and decoration known at Rome for the period 400–291.

---

[1] All the colonies listed above were built on land taken from erstwhile or current foes; for specific references to this mulcting of territory, see e.g. 8. 1. 3, 14. 1–12, 10. 1. 3, 3. 5; Zonar. 8. 18 (Falerii in 241). 1. 15. 5 and 2. 41. 1 are annalistic inventions which are paradigmatic for the process.

[2] An earlier version of this chapter was read to a session of the Leicester–Nottingham seminar on 21 Oct. 1989; I am grateful to the participants for their comments and encouragement, and to Dr K.-J. Hölkeskamp, Dr P. C. Millett, and Mr J. W. Rich for improving later drafts.

396: vow and dedication of temple to Mater Matuta (5. 19. 6–23. 7).

392: dedication of temple of Juno Regina (5. 31. 3); the vow and *locatio* were made in 396 (5. 21. 3–23. 7).

388: fortifications in *opus quadratum* constructed around Capitolium (6. 4. 12).

387: dedication of temple of Mars vowed in Gallic War (6. 5. 8).

378: building of 'Servian' wall in *opus quadratum* (6. 32. 1–2).

375: building of temple of Juno Lucina (dated at Pliny, *NH* 16. 235, specifically to the anarchy).

367: possible vow by Camillus of temple of Concordia (Ovid, *Fasti*, 1. 641–4; Plut. *Cam.* 42. 3). The reliability of this notice is doubtful.

353: dedication of temple of Apollo (7. 20. 9).

345/4: vowing and dedication of temple of Juno Moneta (7. 28. 4–6).

338: Maenius places the *rostra* captured at Antium in the *comitium* (8. 14. 12).[1]

311: Appian Way and aqueduct started (9. 29. 6).

310/9: Samnite spoils used to decorate the forum (9. 40. 16).

306: Via Valeria begun (9. 43. 25).

305: dedication of *simulacrum* to Hercules (9. 44. 16).

304: Cn. Flavius dedicates temple of Concordia in *area Volcani* (9. 46. 6; Pliny, *NH* 33. 19).

302: dedication by Junius Bubulcus of temple of Salus (10. 1. 9); it was probably vowed in 311 and the *locatio* effected in 306 (9. 43. 25). The paintings inside, by the first Fabius Pictor, were famous (Val. Max. 8. 14. 6; Pliny, *NH* 35. 19).

296: Appius Claudius vows temple to Bellona; he innovates by decorating it with shields and portraits of his ancestors (10. 19. 17; Ovid, *Fasti*, 6. 201–8; Pliny, *NH* 35. 12). The statue of Victoria is first mentioned in the prodigies of this year (Dio, fr. 36. 28; Zonar. 8. 1); it is not known when it was erected, but presumably only a few years earlier (see Weinstock 1957, 215).

295: the Ogulnii pave the Via Appia from the Porta Capena to the temple of Mars; put bronze thresholds on the Capitol; place silver vessels in the temple of Jupiter and a statue of the god in a four-horse chariot on its roof; and erect a representation of

---

[1] On Maenius and the *rostra* see now Millar 1989, 141.

Romulus and Remus being suckled by the wolf at the *ficus Ruminalis*. The plebeian aediles place gold bowls in the temple of Ceres (10. 23. 11–13). Fabius Gurges sees to construction of temple to Venus (10. 31. 9); at Sentinum, Fabius Rullianus vows temple to Jupiter Victor (10. 29. 14).

294: Postumius Megellus dedicates temple of Victoria (10. 33. 9); Atilius vows temple to Jupiter Stator (10. 36. 11, 37. 15–16).

293: L. Papirius dedicates temple to Quirinus and equips it with a *horologium* (10. 46. 7; Pliny, *NH* 7. 213); Forum decked out with spoil from the Samnites (10. 46. 8); Sp. Carvilius sees to *locatio* of temple to Fors Fortuna (10. 46. 14); road to Bovillae constructed (10. 47. 4).

291: temple to Aesculapius dedicated (Ovid, *Fasti*, 1. 289–94).

Bibliography

Afzelius, A. (1942), *Die römische Eroberung Italiens (340–264 v. Chr.)* (Copenhagen).

Badian, E. (1958), *Foreign Clientelae (264–70 BC)* (Oxford).

—— (1982), review of Hopkins 1978a, *JRS* 72: 164–9.

Beloch, K. J. (1926), *Römische Geschichte bis zum Beginn der punischen Kriege* (Berlin).

Bernardi, A. (1943), 'Roma e Capua nella seconda metà del quarto sec. av. C.: II', *Athenaeum*, 21: 21–31.

Bradley, K. R. (1984), 'The *vicesima libertatis*: its history and significance', *Klio*, 66: 175–82.

—— (1985), 'The early development of slavery at Rome', *Historical Reflections (Réflexions Historiques)*, 12: 1–8.

—— (1987), 'On the Roman slave supply and slavebreeding', in M. I. Finley (ed.), *Classical Slavery* (London), pp. 42–64.

Braudel, F. (1972), *The Mediterranean and the Mediterranean World in the Age of Philip II*, trans. S. Reynolds, (London).

Brunt, P. A. (1971), *Italian Manpower 225 BC–AD 14* (Oxford).

Clemente, G. (1982), 'Qualche osservazione sulla schiavitù romana', *Opus*, 1: 187–9.

Coarelli, F. (1977), 'Public building at Rome from 201 to Sulla', *PBSR* 45: 1–23.

Cornell, T. J. (1989), 'Rome and Latium to 390 BC', 'The recovery of Rome', and 'The conquest of Italy', in *CAH²* vii. 2, chs 6–8 (pp. 243–419).

Crawford, M. H. (1971), review of Salmon 1969, *CR* 21: 250–3.

—— (1974), *Roman Republican Coinage* (Cambridge).

—— (1978), *The Roman Republic* (London).

—— (1982), *La moneta in Grecia e a Roma* (Rome and Bari).

—— (1985), *Coinage and Money under the Roman Republic* (London).

Derow, P. S. (1979), 'Polybius, Rome and the East', *JRS* 69: 1–15.

De Sanctis, G. (1907), *Storia dei Romani*, ii (Turin).

Eder, W. (ed.) (1990), *Staat und Staatlichkeit in der frühen römischen Republik* (Stuttgart).

Finley, M. I. (1980), *Ancient Slavery and Modern Ideology* (London).

Frank, T. (1914), *Roman Imperialism* (New York).

Frederiksen, M. W. (1984), *Campania*, ed. N. Purcell (London).

Gruen, E. S. (1984), *The Hellenistic World and the Coming of Rome* (Berkeley, Los Angeles, and London).

Gutberlet, D. (1985), *Die erste Dekade des Livius als Quelle zur gracchischen und sullanischen Zeit* (Hildesheim).

Harris, W. V. (1979), *War and Imperialism in Republican Rome 327–70 BC* (Oxford).

—— (1980), review of Crawford (1978), *JRS* 70: 193–4.

—— (1984a), 'Current directions in the study of Roman imperialism', in W. V. Harris (ed.), pp. 13–34.

—— (1984b), 'The Italians and the empire', in W. V. Harris (ed.), pp. 89–113.

—— (ed. 1984), *The Imperialism of Mid-Republican Rome* (Rome).

—— (1990), 'Roman warfare in the economic and social context of the fourth century BC', in W. Eder (ed.), pp. 494–510.

Hölkeskamp, K.-J. (1987), *Die Entstehung der Nobilität* (Stuttgart).

Hopkins, M. K. (1978a), *Conquerors and Slaves* (Cambridge).

—— (1978b), 'Economic growth and towns in classical antiquity', in P. Abrams and E. A. Wrigley (eds), *Towns in Societies* (Cambridge), pp. 35–77.

Humbert, M. (1978), *Municipium et civitas sine suffragio* (Rome).

Mattingly, H. (1945), 'The first age of Roman coinage', *JRS* 35: 65–77.

Millar, F. G. B. (1989), 'Political power in mid-Republican Rome: Curia or Comitium?', *JRS* 79: 138–50.

Momigliano, A. D. (1975), *Alien Wisdom* (Cambridge).

North, J. A. (1981), 'The development of Roman imperialism', *JRS* 71: 1–9.

Oakley, S. P. (1985), 'Single combat in the Roman Republic', *CQ* 35: 392–410.

Ogilvie, R. M. (1965), *A Commentary on Livy, Books 1–5* (Oxford).

Rowland, R. J. (1983), 'Rome's earliest imperialism', *Latomus*, 42: 749–62.

Salmon, E. T. (1953), 'Rome and the Latins I', *Phoenix*, 7: 93–104.

—— (1967), *Samnium and the Samnites* (Cambridge).

—— (1969), *Roman Colonization under the Republic* (London).

Sherwin-White, A. N. (1980), 'Rome the aggressor?', review of Harris 1979, *JRS* 70: 177–81.

Starr, C. G. (1980), *The Beginnings of Imperial Rome* (Ann Arbor).

Torelli, M. R. (1978), *Rerum Romanarum fontes ab anno CCXCII ad*

annum CCLXV a.Ch. (Pisa).
Toynbee, A. J. (1965), *Hannibal's Legacy* (London).
Volkmann, H. (1961), *Die Massenversklavungen der Einwohner eroberte Städte in der hellenistisch-römischen Zeit* (Mainz).
Walbank, F. W. (1963), 'Polybius and Rome's eastern policy', *JRS* 53: 1–13; = *Selected Papers* (Cambridge, 1985), ch. 10 (pp. 138–56).
Wallace, R. W. (1990), 'Hellenization and Roman society in the late fourth century BC', in W. Eder (ed.), pp. 278–92.
Weinstock, S. (1957), '*Victor* and *Invictus*', *Harvard Theological Review*, 50: 211–47.
Westerman, W. L. (1955), *The Slave Systems of Greek and Roman Antiquity* (Philadelphia).
Wiseman, T. P. (1981), 'The Temple of Victory on the Palatine', *Antiquaries Journal* 61: 35–52; = *Roman Studies* (Liverpool, 1987), pp. 187–204.
Wissowa, G. (1912), *Religion und Kultus der Römer*[2] (Munich).
Zanker, P. (ed. 1976), *Hellenismus in Mittelitalien* (Göttingen).
Zehnacker, H. (1980), '*Unciarium fenus* (Tacite, *Annales*, 6, 16)', in *Mélanges de littérature et d'épigraphie latines, d'histoire ancienne et d'archéologie: hommage à la mémoire de Pierre Wuilleumier* (Paris), pp. 353–62.

∞ 2 ∞

Fear, greed and glory: the causes of Roman war-making in the middle Republic

John Rich

The modern debate

Down to the middle of the fourth century Rome was a power of merely local significance. The Romans had fought a great many wars against their neighbours, but for most of their history they had been merely one of the more prominent of the cities in the plain of Latium. Quite suddenly, from about 343,[1] all this changed, and in a period of just over seventy years the Romans fought their way to a position of mastery over the whole of Italy south of the Po valley. This success was followed by great wars, first against Carthage, and then against various Hellenistic kings. From all of these the Romans emerged victorious, and by the middle of the second century, contemporaries like Polybius recognized them as the undisputed masters of the Mediterranean world. They now ruled a number of overseas territories directly, as provinces, and elsewhere they exercised an informal hegemony. Over the next two centuries, down to the reign of Augustus, the first emperor, the Romans continued on the same path of warfare and expansion. In the late Republic, the drive to expansion was largely fuelled by the ambitions of powerful individuals, like Pompey and Caesar. But down to the outbreak of the Social War,

---

[1] All dates are BC.

in 91, the political system remained relatively stable. Why did the Romans fight so many wars, and expand their power so widely?

Until recently, the dominant view among scholars was that Roman imperialism was essentially defensive. The principal factor which led the Romans to undertake their wars was, it was held, the fear of powerful neighbours, a fear which was in some cases well-founded, in others mistaken. Some writers also stressed the importance of accident and misunderstanding. However, it was thought that the prospect of economic gain did not play an important part in bringing about the wars, and that the Romans' territorial expansion was largely unsought. This doctrine originated with Mommsen (1877–80), and early in this century found notable exponents in Frank (1914) and Holleaux (1921). More recent statements of the case include those of Badian (1958, 1968), Walbank (1963) and Errington (1971).

From time to time various writers expressed dissent from this view, in this country notably Finley (1978) and Hopkins (1978, 25–37). However, the first full-scale attack was mounted in 1979 by William Harris in his important book *War and Imperialism in Republican Rome 327–70 BC*. Harris laid stress on the fact that the Romans had become habituated to continuous warfare, and argued that the most important of the factors which brought about the wars was the Romans' desire for the glory and economic benefits which successful warfare conferred.[1] He conceded that defensive considerations played a part in some wars, but in general sought to minimize this element. The core of his case is made in the first two chapters, where he gives a structural account of the role of war in Roman life, the attitudes both of the Roman

---

[1] In insisting on the importance of these factors Harris stands in an old and distinguished tradition. See, for example, Montesquieu 1734, ch. 1 (pp. 7 and 9 of Jullian's edition):

La république ayant des chefs qui changeaient tous les ans, et qui cherchaient à signaler leur magistrature pour en obtenir de nouvelles, il n'y avait pas un moment de perdu pour l'ambition; ils engageaient le sénat à proposer au peuple la guerre, et lui montraient tous les jours de nouveaux ennemis. . . . Or la guerre était presque toujours agréable au peuple, parce que, par la sage distribution du butin, on avait trouvé le moyen de la lui rendre utile. . . . Les consuls, ne pouvant obtenir l'honneur du triomphe que par une conquête ou une victoire, faisaient la guerre avec une impétuosité extrême: on allait droit à l'ennemi, et la force décidait d'abord. Rome était donc dans une guerre éternelle et toujours violente.

élite and of ordinary citizens to war, and the economic benefits
which Romans derived from war. He follows this up in the fifth
and final chapter with a survey of the origins of individual wars,
designed to show that they conform to his theory. Chapters 3 and
4 are devoted to Roman expansion: here he argues that expansion
was a Roman aim, and that the Romans generally welcomed
opportunities to annex territory except when special circumstances decided them against doing so.

Harris's book has aroused much interest. It was, for example,
accorded the unique distinction of receiving, in effect, two reviews
in successive numbers of the *Journal of Roman Studies*, by
Sherwin-White (1980) and North (1981). Harris himself has
returned to the fray several times (Harris ed. 1984, with responses
to his critics at pp. 13–34, 89–113; Harris 1989, 1990). Since his
book appeared, there has been a wealth of publications on various
aspects of Roman Republican imperialism: notable instances are
the books by Gruen (1984), Sherwin-White (1984), Dyson (1985),
Richardson (1986), Eckstein (1987), Ferrary (1988) and Rosenstein (1990).[1] All these works address in various ways the
questions posed by Harris. The continuing vitality of the debate is
shown by the diversity of views expressed in the present volume
(see chs 1 and 6).

A number of these recent writers have persisted in maintaining
some form of the 'defensive imperialism' view, notably Gruen,
Sherwin-White, Dyson and Eckstein.[2] These and other critics of
Harris who share their position have made some telling points.
However, none of them has fully taken the measure of Harris's
objections to the 'defensive imperialism' view. In my judgement,
no one has succeeded in producing a coherent and convincing
restatement of that doctrine, and I do not believe that such a
restatement could be produced.

Richardson, in his excellent study of the development of
Roman rule in Spain, is in general in sympathy with Harris, but
provides an important corrective to Harris's views on the annexation and exploitation of territory. He makes a good case for

---

[1]   I have discussed a number of these works in reviews: Rich 1985a,
1985b, 1988a, 1988b, 1991.
[2]   For criticisms of Harris in these works see especially Gruen 1984, chs
8–9; Sherwin-White 1984, 11–17; Eckstein 1987, xiv–xvi.

supposing that the Romans were rather slower to exploit their conquests by taxation, mining, and so on than Harris claimed. He rightly insists that to declare a region as a *provincia* originally meant just that it was marked out as an area of military responsibility, and that the development from this practice to the fully-fledged system of provincial administration was a long drawn out process. As to the question of whether it was better to assign conquered territory to Roman commanders as their province or to leave it to the inhabitants to administer it for themselves, the Roman government seems to have had no general preference but to have considered each case on its merits. In any case, as Harris himself recognized (Harris 1979, 133–6), the choice was not between maintaining or abandoning control, but between different forms of control.[1]

For many readers Harris's view of the causes of Roman warfare and imperialism has powerful appeal. There are, I think, two reasons for this. One is that it seems to accord with common sense. The 'defensive imperialism' view propounded a paradox. The Romans valued military achievements above all others and their strongly militaristic culture was displayed in such institutions as the triumph. They fought wars almost continuously and on the whole successfully, and as a result acquired both empire and great economic gains. Yet the 'defensive imperialism' doctrine requires us to believe that this warfare and expansion was not of the Romans' seeking, and was the product largely of fear. After reading Harris's trenchant attack on this position, most people tend to feel, rightly in my view, that the paradox can no longer be sustained.

The second reason why the view that the Romans were the aggressive power is so compelling is that it fits our contemporary attitudes and preconceptions. The intellectual background to the 'defensive imperialism' hypothesis has recently been explored by Linderski.[2] He shows that Mommsen's interpretation of Roman expansion derived from his German nationalist beliefs (for him the Romans' true destiny was to unite the Italian *Volk* and their overseas conquests were a historical error forced on them by circumstances). As for Holleaux and Frank, their willingness to

---

[1] Richardson 1986, especially chs 1 and 8. See also Lintott 1981.
[2] Linderski 1984. See also Frézouls 1983; Hermon 1989.

acquit Rome of seeking expansion was not unconnected, Linderski argues, with the claims made for France and the USA in their own day. It is obvious that Harris's book, too, is a product of its time. Although the great European empires came to an end only a generation ago, most people now regard imperialism as something to be deplored and find it hard to comprehend the attitude of mind, not so long ago commonplace, which regarded empire as something noble and glorious. Harris, an Englishman living in the USA, wrote his book as the Vietnam conflict was being played out.

However, the very seductiveness of Harris's interpretation should put us on our guard. The old 'defensive imperialism' thesis was too crude, too monocausal. May not Harris's alternative suffer from the same fault? John North's criticisms of Harris are pertinent here. North holds that Harris's refutation of the 'defensive imperialism' theory is conclusive: Harris has, he says, settled 'once for all the question of whether Rome's wars were aggressive or defensive' (North 1981, 9). However, he complains that Harris focuses too much on specifics at the expense of general issues, that he concentrates too much on the Romans' conscious decision-making and not enough on the structures in Roman society which made for war and expansion. At times, North over-simplifies Harris's views, but he has put his finger on a major weakness of the book. Harris is at his most compelling in his first two chapters when he discusses the structural role of Roman warfare. He is least convincing in his last chapter when he yields to the polemicist's temptation to overstate his case and seeks to show that the principal factors behind all of Rome's individual war decisions were the need to keep fighting wars and the desire for glory and economic gain. Here North's comments are just. 'Wars begin from complex situations, in which aggression, mutual fear, confusion, accident, bad communications, personal and political ambitions and many other factors play a part' (ibid. 2). 'The argument from structure cannot explain the specific, only the long-term trend' (ibid. 7).

Harris's account of the structural role of Roman warfare is partial. He devotes much space to some aspects like the part played by military success in the aristocratic ethos. Yet, to take the two examples adduced by North, he is brief and equivocal on slavery and omits altogether the Italian alliance, whose importance in this regard was first stressed by Momigliano.[1] War generated a supply of slaves, whose availability transformed Italian agriculture and so created a continuing demand for cheap slaves which only war could adequately supply. The Romans exploited their Italian allies not by taxing them, but by demanding troops, and so, if they were to continue to profit from the alliance, they had to keep finding ways of employing Italian soldiers. Moreover, the opportunity to serve in and share some of the profits of Rome's wars may actually have helped to secure Italian loyalty, for, until their conquest by Rome, continuous warfare had been as much a part of the experience of some of the other peoples of Italy as it was for the Romans. It is Harris's preoccupation with motivation and decision-making which accounts for his partial treatment. He is rightly reluctant to assert that the need to maintain the slave supply or to keep the Italians occupied directly influenced the Roman government's war decisions. However, factors of this kind could, without the Romans' being aware of it, play their part in circumscribing their range of choices, and help to explain their continuing willingness to fight wars.

North concludes (ibid. 7–8) that

> Harris is working with an unrealistic model of the senate's freedom of action. . . . The senate, in the end, had little freedom except to organize the details of the year's campaigning. . . . There were of course moments when more weighty issues arose; these were the beginnings of the major wars. . . . Even at those moments, the debates were about where to invest this year's resources or whether to defer action against a major enemy for a year or even two. . . . The senate's freedom of action lay in matters of detail, of timing, of organization.

In his view, since Harris has demonstrated that Rome's wars were aggressive, 'the focus of debate can now be shifted towards the far deeper problems of the origins, significance and eventual disappearance of the expansion-bearing structures in Roman society and organization' (ibid. 9).

Thus, while North regards Harris's interpretation of the origins of individual wars as too simplistic, he himself holds that the

---

[1] Momigliano 1975, 45–6. Harris's discussion of the topic at Harris (ed.) 1984, 89–113, is unsatisfactory. See further Cornell 1989, 385–9, and Oakley's remarks in this volume (above, pp. 16–18).

underlying structures were all working in the same direction, towards continuing war and expansion. In my view, this is mistaken. Whatever the differences between them, Harris and North are essentially in agreement on a one-sided view of Roman warfare and imperialism, which seems to me in its way almost as misleading as the old 'defensive imperialism' view.[1] Roman expansion was not a continuous process, maintained at a constant rate. Whether at the level of conscious decision-making or of underlying structures, the determining factors were many and complex and did not all pull in the same direction.

Trends and fluctuations in Roman war and expansion

The habit of constant war was as old as the Republic. There were very few years in the Republic's history when its forces saw no fighting (Harris 1979, 9–10; Oakley above, pp. 14–16). Yet the character of that warfare and the military commitment that it required underwent great changes during the Republic's history.

In the period down to 264, when the Romans' military activity was confined to Italy, their warfare had an annual rhythm. For the most part it was restricted to the summer campaigning season. An army was levied, marched out to fight for a few months, and then returned to be discharged. The command was normally held by the chief magistrates of the state – usually the consuls, but sometimes instead consular tribunes or a dictator. Sometimes they campaigned separately, but often they combined their forces.

The First Punic War (264–241) brought some important changes. During the war the Romans had to maintain a permanent military presence in Sicily all the year round, and for the first time they mobilized large war fleets. After their victory, the Carthaginians ceded Sicily (241) and Sardinia (238). What initial arrangements the Romans made for the control of these territories

[1] Cf. Doyle 1986, especially chs 1 and 6, on the inadequacy of what he classifies as 'dispositional, metrocentric theories' of imperialism, which seek to explain it simply in terms of internal drives to expansion within the dominant 'metropoles'. His principal instances of such theories are Hobson, Lenin and Schumpeter, but he cites Harris as a more recent example (p. 24).

is uncertain, but from 227 two additional praetors were elected annually for this purpose.

The Second Punic War (218–201) made unprecedented demands. Casualties were very heavy, particularly in the opening years: on a conservative estimate, some 50,000 citizens may have been lost in 218–215 – one-sixth of all adult males and over 5 per cent of the citizen population.[1] The war was conducted in several theatres – Italy, Spain, Sicily, Illyria and Greece, and eventually Africa – and in some of these the Romans had to deploy a number of armies. Thus in total the Romans mobilized far greater forces than they had ever done before, as the detailed information given by Livy shows. From 214 to 206, twenty or more legions were in service. Many of the legions were kept in being for long periods.[2] Numerous additional commanders were required besides the two annually elected consuls. This need was met by using praetors, by proroguing magistrates after the end of their term of office (a device which had been employed occasionally since 326, and from now on was to be commonplace), and by electing private citizens to special commands (*privati cum imperio* – a new expedient, which after 199 was hardly used again until the late Republic).

In the first third of the second century, the Romans' military commitments, although less than they had been during the Second Punic War, were still much greater than before that war. The period saw three great wars against eastern kings: Philip V of Macedon (200–196), Antiochus III (191–188) and Philip's son Perseus (171–168). There was also much warfare in northern Italy: it was in this period that Rome completed the conquest of the peninsula up to the foot of the Alps. The victory over Carthage had left Rome with another permanent commitment overseas, in Spain, where Rome controlled the Baetis valley and the Mediterranean coastal strip. Maintaining and extending their control in Spain involved much fighting during these years, but by 178 the Romans had succeeded in extending their authority over

[1]   Cf. Brunt 1971, 54, 419–20. Compare the First World War: for the seven original belligerent nations, soldiers killed and dying of wounds during the war amounted to 2 per cent of the total population (Wright 1965, 664).
[2]   For numbers of legions and length of service see Toynbee 1965, ii. 79–80, 647–51; Brunt 1971, 400, 417–22.

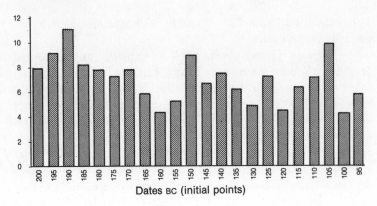

Figure 2.1 Legions in service by five-year periods, 200–91 BC (source: Brunt 1971, 422–34)

the central plains. Once again Livy supplies us with detailed information on legionary deployment. The average number of legions in service in 200–168 was 8.75; in twelve of these years ten or more legions were deployed (Afzelius 1944, 34–61; Brunt 1971, 422–6; fig. 2.1). Those who fought in northern Italy might serve for just one or two campaigns, but for the eastern wars service was for the duration, and in Spain legions were kept in post for long periods, with individual soldiers being gradually replaced. Some evidence suggests that six years' service in Spain became accepted as entitling a man to discharge (Brunt 1971, 400–1). As always down to the Social War, contingents of Italian allies served alongside the legions; in this period the ratio of allied to Roman troops varied from 2:1 to parity (Afzelius 1944, 62–79; Brunt 1971, 681–4). The main commands in the East and in northern Italy went to the consuls. From 197 the two Spanish commands were normally assigned to praetors (increased then to six per year).

After 167 we lack Livy's full narrative, but it is clear that the years from 167 to 154 were comparatively peaceful. Spain still had permanent legionary garrisons and in most (if not all) years legions were deployed in northern Italy, but both regions saw little fighting. Elsewhere there were minor wars, in Corsica and Sardinia (163–2), Dalmatia (156–5) and Transalpine Gaul (154). According to Polybius (32. 13. 6–7), one factor which led to the Dalmatian war was the Romans' concern lest 'the Italians should be made effeminate by the long peace, it being now the twelfth year since the war with Perseus'.

Serious warfare broke out again in Spain from 153, and in 149–146 the Romans found themselves fighting major wars on a number of other fronts as well – against Carthage (ending with the destruction of the city in 146) and in Macedonia and Greece. These wars led to the creation of two new provinces, Africa and Macedonia. From now on a legionary garrison was maintained in Macedonia to defend the province against the neighbouring tribes, but it saw little action until the late second century. Heavy fighting (much of it unsuccessful for the Romans) continued in Spain until 133, but thereafter the Spanish garrisons were comparatively inactive. The later years of the second century saw a number of wars in various regions, two of which led to the creation of new provinces (Asia after the war against Aristonicus in 133–129, and Transalpine Gaul after the wars of the late 120s). However, it was not until the closing years of the century that Rome was again involved in major wars on a number of fronts, most notably against the Cimbri and their allies.

Without Livy, we lack detailed information on legions from 166, but Brunt has made a plausible reconstruction of the annual deployment of legions (Brunt 1971, 426–34; see fig. 2.1).[1] It is clear that by and large the Romans' military commitment in this period was rather lower than in the early years of the second century. The overall annual average for 167–91 is 6.48. Only in seven or eight of these years were there ten or more legions in service.

Harris and North present us with a model of the Roman social system as geared to continuous war and requiring for its smooth working that a regular flow of the opportunities and profits of war should be maintained. The reality, as briefly sketched above, is rather more complex. It is true that there were few years when Rome was nowhere at war. However, the levels of Roman belligerence fluctuated very greatly. Periods of intense warfare, often on several fronts, alternated with comparatively peaceful periods with only a few minor campaigns, and sometimes, as in

---

[1] Brunt arbitrarily assumes that two legions were deployed in Northern Italy every year down to 135, but thereafter only when a military presence is explicitly attested there. This may mean that some of his estimates are too high for years before 135 and too low thereafter.

167–154, these peaceful interludes were quite extended. Warfare had once been the consuls' summer activity, but by the second century most commands lasted longer, and every year the Romans deployed forces in a number of regions, some of which they were committed to garrisoning permanently. In some periods these garrison forces were involved in heavy fighting, but in others they remained comparatively inactive (as in Spain from 178 to 154 and after 133). Overall, the years 167–91 saw a rather lower level of military activity and required somewhat lower force levels than the preceding period.

The momentum of Roman expansion was by no means constant. In the Greek East, the Romans preferred to maintain indirect hegemony and avoided permanent military commitments as long as possible. They were constantly embroiled in the affairs of the cities and kingdoms, but it was only very rarely that a problem became so critical that they deemed it necessary to despatch an armed force. Normally they limited themselves to what they could achieve by diplomatic means and by the weight of their authority. In the resultant game of brinkmanship, some eastern powers succeeded in defying Roman orders without adverse consequences. Thus Ptolemy VI Philometor ignored Roman instructions that he should hand over Cyprus to his brother, and Antiochus V Epiphanes flagrantly disregarded his treaty obligations not to maintain a fleet or keep elephants. After Antiochus' death, when the kingdom was weak, a Roman embassy had the ships burnt and the elephants hamstrung, but, when the head of the embassy was murdered, no punishment was exacted, although in the Romans' eyes there was no more fitting ground for war than offences against embassies.[1]

Even in the West, the Roman advance was in some respects surprisingly patchy. The subjugation of northern Italy was largely completed by about 170, but the Alps and their foothills remained outside Roman control. Although troops were frequently stationed in northern Italy thereafter, they seem to have engaged in little fighting and for the most part Rome left the Alpine tribes alone until Augustus undertook and rapidly completed their conquest. The provincial boundaries established for Transalpine Gaul after

---

[1]   For the events see Gruen 1984, 655–65 and 699–702, with my comments at Rich 1985a, 96.

the wars of the late 120s remained unaltered until Caesar's ambition to rival Pompey led him to undertake the conquest of the rest of Gaul. Although at least two legions were always maintained in Spain, expansion there virtually ceased after 133, and the conquest of the north of the Iberian peninsula was left to Augustus.

It is not the case that the benefits of successful war were maintained in constant supply. The most conspicuous disruption was the ending of land settlement. The two chief benefits which ordinary Roman citizens got from warfare were booty and land. From the fifth century the Roman government had confiscated land from defeated states in Italy, and much of that land had been distributed in land allotments. This practice played an important part in ending the social conflicts which troubled the early Republic and maintaining political stability thereafter. However, once the conquest of Italy was complete, the confiscation of land ceased, and as a result land allotment also ceased, about 170. The result was that an unsatisfied demand for land built up which in due course was met by tribunes and generals in spite of senatorial opposition. All this could have been avoided if the Roman government had been willing to make land allotments overseas, but they would not contemplate this solution, and stoutly opposed the few proposals of this kind which were made, notably Gaius Gracchus' attempt to refound Carthage. It was not until the dictatorship of Caesar that a large-scale programme of overseas settlement was undertaken.

Although none of the élite's benefits ceased altogether, a level flow was not maintained, as the record of triumphs shows. Information on triumphs is provided both by ancient historical writers and by the *Fasti Triumphales*, an inscribed list of triumphs set up at Rome under Augustus (Degrassi 1947, 64–87, 534–71). The data for the early centuries is of doubtful authenticity, and a lacuna in the *Fasti* for 155–129 means that some uncertainty subsists about those years.[1] However, it is clear that there were two peaks, in the late fourth and early third century, and in the

[1] The lacuna, which is about 33 lines long, probably listed fourteen or fifteen triumphs, of which seven are known from other sources (Degrassi 1947, 557–9). Over the period 160–131 triumphs probably averaged six per decade.

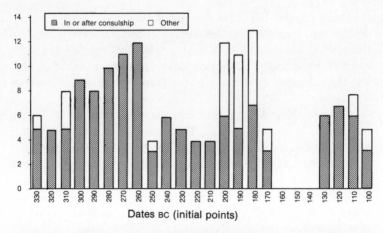

Figure 2.2 Triumphs and ovations per decade, 330–91 BC

first thirty or so years of the second century (fig. 2.2). The first peak starts with the period of the conquest of Italy and extends into the first part of the First Punic War. The second peak corresponds to the years of heavy and largely successful warfare in northern Italy, Spain and the Greek East. The decline in the level of military activity in the rest of the second century, which we have already noticed, is matched by a sharp drop in the number of triumphs: 39 triumphs were celebrated in the years 200–167, an average of 1.15 per year, whereas in 166–91 only 46 triumphs were celebrated, an annual average of 0.6.

Closer inspection reveals significant differences between the two peak periods. In the first period, most triumphs were held in or following consulships, and the rest were celebrated by dictators. In the second, the number of consular triumphs was not much higher than later in the century. The high total in the period 200–167 was the result of an exceptionally large number of non-consular celebrations – eighteen in, or following, praetorships, and two by men who had commanded in Spain as *privati cum imperio*. Before 200 only one praetor had earned a triumph (in 241). The new, wider range of Rome's commitments brought unprecedented opportunities to win glory at this earlier stage of the political career, particularly in Spain, where twelve of the praetorian triumphs were earned. It is true that the two *privati* and seven of the Spanish praetors were awarded not a full curule

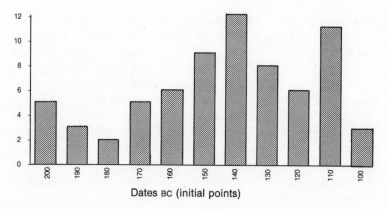

Figure 2.3 Consuls assigned overseas provinces per decade, 200–91 BC

triumph but the lesser honour of an *ovatio* (in which the victor entered the city on foot or on horseback, rather than in a chariot), and a joke in Plautus suggests that there may have been some contemporary cynicism about the frequency of triumphs.[1] Nonetheless, the value placed on these honours is confirmed by the success of those who won them in subsequent elections to the consulship (Harris 1979, 32, 262–3; Richardson 1986, 105–6).

After 167, praetors' opportunities for triumphs were sharply reduced. In the period 166–91 only six men are known to have triumphed after their praetorship.[2] This change is related to the overall downturn in military activity in this period, and in particular to a shift in the way in which the consuls themselves were deployed (fig. 2.3).[3] In the period 200–168 the consuls normally campaigned in northern Italy. The great eastern wars were conducted by consuls, but otherwise only two consuls were sent overseas in those years (Cato to Spain in 195 and Tiberius Gracchus to Sardinia in 177). The completion of the conquest of northern Italy led to a change in practice. The loss of Livy means

---

[1] Plautus, *Bacchides*, 1067–75. The slave Chrysalus represents himself metaphorically as bringing an army home loaded with booty, and then adds: 'But, audience, don't be surprised if I don't hold a triumph: it's so common, it's not worth it'.
[2] The names of a few more are probably lost in the lacuna for 155–129.
[3] The data are collected in *MRR*.

that our information on consular provinces is defective, but it is clear that it became much commoner for consuls to be sent overseas: 57 consuls are attested as holding overseas provinces in the period 167–91. Consuls sent overseas normally engaged in warfare.[1] The senate's usual practice seems to have been to send one of the consuls to wherever the main overseas trouble spot happened to be. Thus in fourteen of the years between 153 and 133, when Spain saw continued heavy fighting, one of the Spanish provinces was assigned to a consul. So in most years the best opportunities for winning glory went to consuls, and it was only exceptionally fortunate praetors who had the chance of a triumph.[2]

The consuls who were sent overseas went out to perform the traditional task of a consul, command in war. But the majority of consuls in this period still stayed behind in Italy. Although presence in Italy is positively attested for only about thirty, we can assume that most of those whose province is unrecorded also stayed in Italy, since some record is likely to survive of overseas activity. Yet only eleven triumphs were won in northern Italy in that period,[3] and only two other consuls are attested as having campaigned there.[4] Some consuls are known to have engaged in road-building (Wiseman 1970), and some appear to have spent all their year of office in Rome (for example, Scaevola in 133, Fannius in 122 and Marius and Valerius Flaccus in 100). How the

---

[1] A possible exception is M. Porcius Cato in 118: he may have been assigned Africa to carry out a diplomatic mission, the settlement of Numidia after Micipsa's death.

[2] Richardson 1975 clearly sets out the changing patterns in triumph-holding, but unnecessarily posits a stricter policy in the senate on granting triumphs to explain the drop in praetorian celebrations. The law passed between 180 and 143 requiring 5,000 enemy killed may have been the initiative of the tribune who proposed it rather than senatorial policy (as Richardson supposes), and, since most commanders would probably have had no scruples about claiming so many dead, it need not have had any significant effect on the frequency of triumphs.

[3] In Liguria: 166 (two), 158, 155. Against the Salassi: 143 (unauthorized: see below p. 57 n. 1). In and beyond the Julian Alps: 129, 117 (two), 115. Against the invading Cimbri: 101 (two).

[4] C. Papirius Carbo was defeated by the Cimbri in 113 (*MRR* i. 535). L. Licinius Crassus defeated raiders in 95 and claimed a triumph, but his colleague vetoed it on the grounds that his achievements were too insignificant (*MRR* ii. 11).

rest spent their time is a matter of conjecture, but it seems likely that most spent some time in northern Italy in effect on garrison duty, commanding an army but not fighting. This inactivity of the consuls in Italy is all the more remarkable in view of the fact that opportunities for war lay ready to hand in the as yet unconquered Alps.[1]

Thus the picture presented by Harris and North of irresistible pressures impelling the Romans to constant warfare and expansion is too simple. The levels of Roman belligerence fluctuated; fundamental changes took place in the nature of their military commitments; and in the later second century at least, opportunities for war and expansion were often missed and many consuls did not engage in warfare at all. Roman expansion was a patchy, untidy business, and we must take full account of this when seeking to explain the processes which were at work. The benefits of successful war were real enough and undoubtedly do help to explain the Romans' readiness to resort to war so often. However, there were also countervailing factors, which may in part account for the patchiness which we have observed. Two such factors were pointed out by Sherwin-White in his critiques of Harris: manpower limitations and aristocratic rivalry (Sherwin-White 1980, 178–9; 1984, 13).

The Romans' ability to call on vast reserves of citizen and allied manpower was a factor of fundamental importance in their success. It was this that enabled them to survive the crisis of the Hannibalic War. Their manpower commitments in the second century were less than those that had been required in that war, but still very heavy.[2] It would have been only prudent for the senate to seek to conserve manpower and to hesitate before undertaking new long-term manpower commitments. As Harris himself noted (1979, 144–5), this may help to explain why Macedonia was not made a province in 167, immediately after the overthrowing of the monarchy. It is commonly supposed that the maintenance of a property qualification for legionary service led

---

[1]   Consular inactivity in Italy is stressed as an objection to Harris by Sherwin-White 1980, 178; 1984, 12.
[2]   For estimates of numbers of citizens serving and of the proportion of the citizen body in arms in 218–91, see Brunt 1971, 416–34; Hopkins 1978, 33.

to a manpower crisis in the later second century as more and more citizens fell below the qualifying level. If this were true, it could have played an important part in bringing about the lower level of belligerence which we have observed in this period.[1] However, I have argued elsewhere that there is no reason to suppose that the numbers of qualified men declined steeply enough to lead to a shortage (Rich 1983).[2] There is, though, evidence of contemporary concern, not about the property qualification, but about whether the peasantry were bearing and rearing enough children.[3] Such fears were exaggerated, but they may have had some effect on decisions about wars and expansion.

As Harris has admirably shown, the traditions of their class drove Roman aristocrats to seek success and glory, and military achievements were the most highly prized. However, those same traditions would ensure that aristocrats would do all they could to prevent their rivals stealing a march on them. In the second century on average about ten senators may have become eligible every year for the six praetorships, and probably only about one in five of those senators who survived to the requisite age attained the consulship (cf. Hopkins and Burton 1983, 47–8). In that century only about one in four consuls celebrated a triumph during or after their year of office, and, as we have seen, after the early years of the century those who drew Italy in the ballot for provinces stood a much lower chance. Only a minority of praetorian provinces involved the command of an army,[4] and, as we have seen, except in the period 200–170 praetorian triumphs were a rarity. Common sense suggests that the majority who stood

---

[1]   Cf. Harris 1979, 49–50. Here and at pp. 36–8 he does show some recognition of the decline in belligerence in the course of the second century, but he fails to recognize the importance of the phenomenon or offer an adequate explanation.

[2]   There is no foundation for the widely accepted view that the qualification was progressively reduced in response to the supposed shortage: Rich 1983, 305–16.

[3]   Rich 1983, 299–305. The decline in the numbers registered at the census between 164/3 and 136/5 may have lent colour to such fears.

[4]   Every year one or two praetors were retained at Rome. After the Hannibalic War Sicily and Sardinia were normally garrisoned only with allied troops, if at all, and the same was true of the new provinces of Africa from 146 and Asia from 129.

to be disappointed of the highest prizes would not make it easy for the minority to win them, and this presumption is confirmed by the sources. Livy and other writers are full of stories of controversies in the senate over, for example, whether a commander should have his term extended or be granted a triumph. It is reasonable to suppose that this factor also operated as a brake on the initiation of war.[1]

The decision-making process

In theory Roman wars could not be begun unless authorized by the assembly of the people. In practice, however, only a minority of wars were submitted to the assembly for approval. Only about eight war votes by the assembly are known in the period from the First Punic War to the end of the Republic. There may have been some others of which no record has survived, but probably not many. Rome fought many wars in the period 218–167, but Livy records only four popular war votes in those years; since he takes scrupulous note of these, it is unlikely that he passed over others. A glance at the list of those wars for which popular votes are attested suggests that it was normally only before wars against major powers, such as Carthage and the Hellenistic kings, that the assembly was consulted (Rich 1976, 13–17; cf. Harris 1979, 41–2, 263).

Proposals for war were generally only put to the assembly after they had been approved in the senate.[2] Only once do we hear of

---

[1] North replies to this objection as follows (North 1981, 6):

> In the middle republic, if one faction failed to gain a particular command or opportunity, there was always next year to hope for better things. It must have been far more important to all factions to keep a regular flow of opportunities and profits, than to attempt to exclude rivals from command.

This seems to me to disregard the strongly individualistic nature of Roman political culture, and recalls the misguided view of Roman politics as dominated by factions which North himself has recently dubbed the 'frozen waste' theory (North 1990).

[2] Apart from the First Punic War (see below), when the issue was strictly not whether war should be declared but whether help should be sent to Messana, the only recorded exception is a not very serious proposal for war against Rhodes in 167 (Livy, 45. 21).

objections being raised in the assembly, namely against the Second Macedonian War in 200. On that occasion the tribune Q. Baebius induced the people, weary after the Second Punic War, to vote against the proposal, but a stern speech from the consul soon persuaded them to reverse their decision (Livy, 31. 6. 1–8. 1; Rich 1976, 79–80).

The readiness of the Roman people to give their consent to wars when it was sought and to acquiesce in wars being begun without their being consulted is not a mark of their political impotence, but shows rather that they were generally not averse to war.[1] On one occasion, if Polybius is to be believed, they proved more bellicose than the senate. In an account probably deriving from the Roman annalist Fabius Pictor, he tells us that in 264 the senate could not make up its mind whether to send help to Messana, but that the people decided to do so, thus initiating the train of events which led directly to the First Punic War.[2]

If Polybius is right, the First Punic War is a unique instance of the crucial decision leading to war being taken in the assembly. For other wars the real decision was taken elsewhere, either in the senate or by the commanders in the field.

War decisions which were reached when a Roman army was already in the field were generally taken by the army commander. This sometimes happened even in areas not permanently garrisoned by Rome. Thus Flamininus, after defeating Philip, went on to fight a war against Nabis of Sparta in 195, and, when Manlius Vulso arrived in 189 to take over the command against Antiochus only to find that the king had already made peace, he proceeded to campaign against the Galatians. Both decisions were essentially taken by the commanders, although the senate seems to have given some sort of authorization to Flamininus (Livy, 33. 45. 3; 34. 22. 5) and perhaps also to Manlius (see below). In areas where armies were permanently stationed, like Spain from the late third century and Macedonia from 148, war decisions were commonly taken by the commander alone, although occasionally the senate

[1] On popular attitudes to war see Harris 1979, 41–53. Millar 1984 rightly insists on the political importance of the assemblies in the middle Republic.
[2] Polyb. 1. 10. 3–11. 3. Hoyos 1984 shows that Polybius must mean that the decision was taken in the assembly, not the senate.

too might be involved, as with the negotiations with the Spanish city Segeda in 154 (App. *Hisp.* 44; Diod. 31. 39).

It might be expected that the desire to win glory and booty would have played a particularly important part in bringing about those wars which commanders began at their own discretion. Some commanders were criticized at the time for beginning war without due cause, and the fiction that wars required the consent of the people was sometimes exploited to add to their discomfiture. Enemies of Manlius Vulso unsuccessfully opposed his triumph, and one of the arguments they used was that his Galatian campaign was unauthorized (Livy, 38. 45-6). In 178, two tribunes attacked A. Manlius for launching a campaign in Histria from his province in Cisalpine Gaul without authorization (Livy, 41. 7. 7-8). M. Popillius in 173 is said to have launched an unprovoked attack on the Ligurian Statellates and then to have enslaved them after accepting their surrender; the senate ordered their restitution to freedom, and after his return Popillius was put on trial, although his family's influence ensured that the proceedings were not brought to a conclusion (Livy, 42. 7-10, 21-2). M. Aemilius Lepidus Porcina, proconsul in Hither Spain in 136, began war on the Vaccaei and persisted despite express instructions from the senate to stop; his campaign was unsuccessful, and he was stripped of his command and fined on his return (App. *Hisp.* 80-3; Oros. 5. 5. 13). M. Iunius Silanus was prosecuted unsuccessfully in connection with the defeat which he had suffered at the hands of the Cimbri in 109; the case against him included the charge that he had made war on the Cimbri without the approval of the people (Asc. 80C). A number of other second-century commanders, against whom no action was taken at Rome, are alleged by our sources to have started wars without provocation out of desire for booty and/or a triumph, namely L. Licinius Lucullus against the Vaccaei in 151 (App. *Hisp.* 51-5), Ap. Claudius Pulcher against the Salassi in 143 (Dio fr. 74),[1] and L. Caecilius Metellus against the Dalmatians (App. *Ill.* 11). Not all these allegations may have been fully justified. Thus Manlius Vulso

---

[1] Claudius was denied a triumph and celebrated one on his own authority, but the refusal seems to have been based on the inadequacy of his military achievements rather than doubts about the justice of the war (Oros. 5. 4. 7).

could point out that the Galatians had not only been a long-standing menace to peace in Asia, but had fought on Antiochus' side (Livy, 38. 47–8), and a notice in Livy (37. 51. 10) suggests that the senate envisaged the possibility of a Galatian campaign before Manlius left Rome. Both Lucullus and Lepidus made allegations against the Vaccaei in justification of their attacks, and there may have been some substance in their claims (Richardson 1986, 149–50). However, we need not doubt that at least some of these commanders began their wars chiefly or wholly in order to win glory and booty, and that the same took place on other occasions which have attracted no comment in our sources.

Harris regards the personal advantages which commanders derived from success in war as one of the main causes of Roman war-making, and Richardson has put this factor at the centre of his interpretation of Roman expansion in Spain, which he regards as a process of 'peripheral imperialism' (Richardson 1986, 177), with the men on the spot making the running and the government in Rome generally showing little interest. For Richardson, Roman warfare in the region conveys the appearance of 'an unsystematic hunt for peoples to defeat and booty to carry home' (ibid. 98).[1] Such views seem to me to take insufficient account of the patchiness of Roman warfare which we noted in the previous section. As we have seen, there was relatively little warfare in Spain in the years from 178 to 154 and again after 133. In the periods when there was heavy fighting in Spain, most of it took place in areas which the Romans already claimed to control, and those campaigns which did extend Roman authority further afield were probably at least partly motivated by the wish to ensure the security of the territory already held. While some of those consuls who held command in northern Italy in the later second century did undertake campaigns with questionable justification, like Claudius in 143 and Metellus in 119, the majority, as we have seen, seem to have done no fighting at all.

It seems then that simple triumph-hunting was the exception, not the rule. Why was this? At least part of the answer must, I think, be that unscrupulous triumph-hunting was politically risky. Richardson holds that at least in the early second century the senate regarded the commander's job as being to win victories and

---

[1] For criticism of Richardson's views see Cornell 1987; Rich 1988a.

did not care how they were come by (ibid. 108–9, 125). This seems to me mistaken. It was public policy that wars should not be begun without due cause. As the cases cited above show, commanders who flouted this might provoke an outcry at Rome. Senatorial vigilance in such matters was no doubt partly inspired by principle, but an important part was, of course, also played by personal rivalries, as in the case of Manlius Vulso. Another significant factor may have been ties of patronage between senators and subject communities. It is true that generally the penalties were not heavy. Only Lepidus was convicted, and his case was very exceptional: he had defied an express order by the senate, which was itself an extraordinary measure, prompted by a string of recent disasters in Spain. Although the senatorial consensus was firmly against Popillius, he was able to avoid conviction, and went on to hold the censorship in 159.[1] Others, like Lucullus, were never called to account. Nonetheless, any proconsul who was tempted to attack a tribe in the hope of winning booty and a triumph had to reckon with the possibility that, even if his campaign went well, he might face a scandal, or worse, when he returned to Rome. It may be for this reason that so many proconsuls played safe and took no military action during their term of office.

When starting a war involved despatching an army to a region where the Romans did not maintain a permanent presence, the decision to initiate the war was normally taken in the senate. Because of the relative ease of communications, the senate also played a much greater part in such decisions in northern Italy than it did in the overseas provinces. North, as we have seen (above, p. 43), holds that the senate's freedom of action was in reality always very restricted. In my view, the senate had a good deal more freedom of choice than he allows. The way in which senatorial war decisions were taken varied widely. At the beginning of every year the senate assigned provinces and armies. These arrangements often implied that a war would be begun in a particular region, and for many minor wars the senate took the decision to begin the war simply by decreeing the region as a

---

[1] Compare Ser. Sulpicius Galba, who massacred surrendered Lusitanians in 150, was acquitted in a celebrated trial, and went on to hold the consulship in 144 (*MRR* i. 456–7, 470).

province. However, that does not justify us in saying, with North, that all that the senate did was to 'organize the details of the year's campaigning'. The senate never began a war without reasons, just because it had to have a war somewhere.

For major wars, like those against Carthage and Hellenistic kings, the decision-making process was more complex. Such wars, as we know from Livy, were begun with due formality; in the year when war was to be begun, the consuls, on entering office, were instructed to sacrifice for the successful outcome of the war and to seek the approval of the popular assembly (Rich 1976, 13). In most cases the senate's real decision for war had already been taken months earlier (ibid. 18–55). Sometimes we can pinpoint precisely the moment when the decision was taken, as, for example, with the Second Macedonian War: the senate committed itself to this war when, in the autumn of 201, it agreed to the appeals of Attalus and the Rhodians for help. In other cases the matter is more complex: the senate took steps which were not at the time clear decisions for war, but which committed them to a course of action which turned out to lead unavoidably to war. The Second Punic War is an example. In 220 the senate warned Hannibal not to attack Saguntum. Hannibal responded by doing just that. In my view, when it learnt of his attack, the senate was unanimous that Hannibal's disregard of the Roman warning must be treated as grounds for war (ibid. 28–44). Another instance is afforded by the war with Antiochus. In 196 the senate presented Antiochus with various demands which were unacceptable to him. Both sides were prepared to make some compromises, but neither was willing to concede enough to bridge the gap. As a result war was inevitable, although it did not actually begin until 191.[1] The complexity of the decision-making process should not obscure the fact that the senate did have a real choice, which was not just confined, as North claims, to matters of timing and organization. It could have decided not to warn Hannibal off Saguntum, not to agree to the appeal of Attalus and the Rhodians, not to present its demands to Antiochus.

The senate's decisions were reached after debate. We are very

[1]   Cf. Briscoe 1981, 30–3, rightly rejecting the view of Badian 1959 that the war came about through a series of accidents and even in 192 could still have been avoided.

poorly informed about what was said in the debates relating to wars (Harris 1979, 6–7, 255). Only on a few occasions are we told anything about them, and the value of this information is often doubtful. We have substantial fragments of just one speech, that made by Cato in 167 against the proposal (which in the event was rejected) for war against Rhodes (Gell. *NA* 6. 3 = *ORF*, frs. 163–71). However, although we know so little about individual debates, it is not difficult to get an idea from the voluminous tradition about Rome's wars of the kinds of arguments which were deployed in debates on issues of war. Moral arguments will, of course, have bulked large: the enemy's unjust acts, the Romans' obligation to help their allies and humble the arrogant, and so on. Almost all belligerents, ancient and modern, have convinced themselves that they were in the right, and the Romans' concern with such questions was fortified by the tradition of the *ius fetiale*. Nor was their conscience indefinitely elastic: at least one war, the Third Punic War, may have been delayed by scruples about the justice of the Roman cause.[1] Alongside such moral consider-ations, prudential arguments will have been deployed, arguments about what was in the interest of the Roman people. Often moral and prudential arguments will have been intertwined, as they are in Cato's Rhodian speech (Astin 1978, 276–81). Prominent among such prudential arguments will have been defensive consider- ations, such as claims that, unless Rome went to war against some power, it would menace the Roman people and its interests. Our sources frequently report the use of such arguments, and, although in many individual cases their historicity is doubtful, we cannot doubt that they were a prominent part of the repertory of debate.

A much less prominent part was probably played, at least in senatorial debates, by arguments from the personal advantage, material and otherwise, which participants stood to derive from prospective wars. If speakers in the senate used this argument to advance the case for a war, they probably chose their words with care. For, in the Roman view, while it was not dishonourable to profit from war, wars should not be begun for this reason alone.

---

[1] Polyb. 36. 2; Livy, *Per.* 48–9. On Nasica's opposition to this war see especially Astin 1967, 276–80; Bellen 1985, 4–8.

Part of Cato's case against the proposed Rhodian war was that its proponents wanted to grab the wealth of Rhodes for themselves (Gell. *NA* 6. 3. 7, 52). I referred above (p. 56) to Polybius' account, probably drawn from Fabius Pictor, of how the Romans decided to help the Mamertines of Messana in 264. Whatever its historicity, it is good evidence for the value which a third-century senator put on the various possible arguments. The senate could not make up its mind, because morality told against sending help in view of the Mamertines' shameful past but prudence told in favour in view of the threat to Rome's interests if Carthage got possession of Messana. The deadlock was resolved in the assembly, in part because the consuls pointed out to the people the profits to be derived from the war. Fabius, it would seem, regarded this as an argument more appropriate for the assembly than the senate and as disreputable.

Of course, the arguments which senators deployed in debate would be a very imperfect guide to their motives for voting for a war. Defensive arguments might often be employed disingenuously, as they were by the Roman government in 238 when it claimed that the preparations being made by the Carthaginians to resume their legitimate control of Sardinia were directed against Rome (Polyb. 1. 88. 10), by Caesar to justify his campaigns against the Helvetii and the Belgae (Caes. *BGall.* 1. 10. 2; 2. 1) and by Augustus to justify his advance against Maroboduus (Vell. Pat. 2. 109). Many senators' votes in favour of war were undoubtedly coloured by their expectation of profit for themselves or their friends. However, at each such meeting there will have been more senators who did not stand to profit personally from the decision, and some for whom it would mean the advancement of their personal enemies. It therefore seems to me likely that in most decisions which led directly or indirectly to war most senators' votes were determined less by the hope of personal advantage than by their judgement of what was right and/or in the public interest.

Why did senators so frequently judge that justice and the public interest required Rome to embark on yet another war? Much of the answer to this question is, of course, supplied by the structural elements stressed by Harris and North. The Romans' possession of a magnificent fighting machine, their habituation to war and their extraordinary record of success in it, the benefits that that success brought them and the continuing demand for more of the same that it generated – it is these factors, above all, which made the Romans so ready to discern and take up occasions for war. However, other factors too played their part, and there is one in particular which must not be neglected. The Romans were not always successful in their wars and some enemies – the Gauls, Pyrrhus, Hannibal – threatened the very survival of the Republic. Memories of those dangers were real enough, and in my judgement the fear of powerful neighbours, although not, as used to be supposed, the key to Roman imperialism, must remain an important factor in accounting for it.[1] Striking testimony to the potency of such fears is afforded by the human sacrifices performed at Rome in 228, 216 and 114/13, whose purpose, as recent studies have shown, was to ward off external threats (Eckstein 1982; Bellen 1985, 12–15, 21, 36–8). Brunt once remarked that 'Roman reactions to the possibility of a threat resembled those of a nervous tiger, disturbed when feeding' (1978, 177 = 1990, 307). The image seems to me apt enough, not least because it does not dispute that the tiger was frightened.

Polybius quite often explains Roman actions in terms of fear. Thus, as we have seen, he claims that one factor in the Roman decision to help Messana was the fear that, if they stood aside, the Carthaginians would get control of Sicily and would be 'excessively vexatious and dangerous neighbours' (1. 10. 6). Fear of growing Carthaginian power reappears as the reason for the conclusion of the Ebro treaty (2. 13. 3). Polybius' account of the Gallic invasion of 225 is dominated by references to the Gallic threat and the fear it evoked at Rome (e.g. 2. 23. 7; 31. 7). The decision to retain both consuls in Italy in 197 is attributed to 'the threat from the Gauls' (18. 11. 2). In the famous passage in which, without indicating his own view, he reports Greek opinions about the destruction of Carthage, Polybius represents Greeks favourable to Rome as approving of the destruction because Carthage was a threat (36. 9. 4).[2] Polybius could, of course, err in his

[1]   Bellen 1985 is an interesting recent study of the topic.

[2]   Polybius goes on to say that those who took the opposite view saw it as part of a policy of ruthless extermination. Scholars differ about which view Polybius himself favoured: see e.g. Harris 1979, 271–2; Walbank 1985, 168–72, 286–9; Ferrary 1988, 327–43. Possibly Polybius presented

explanation of individual Roman actions. However, these passages do have a cumulative force.[1] We should not lightly disregard the belief of such a well-placed and perceptive contemporary observer that fear of other nations was at times a significant factor in Roman policy-making.

The Third Punic War is in fact a crucial case. Our sources – including the Polybian passage just cited – show that the Roman government gave as the reason for its actions that it had come to believe that Roman security required the destruction of the city of Carthage. If this is what the Romans really believed, they were in the grips of an irrational fear. Attempts to represent it as rational founder on the fact that such resurgent power as Carthage had shown had already been destroyed by Masinissa in the war which provided the pretext for the Romans' own war declaration.[2] Not surprisingly, many modern writers have tried to provide alternative explanations. Harris himself is the most recent contender. For him, Carthage, having once again attracted Roman attention, fell victim to the Romans' constant need for new wars, glory and booty (Harris 1979, 234-40; 1989, 153-6). This is a banal and implausible explanation of the Romans' terrible and extraordinary decision, and is made all the more unlikely by the fact that they had heavy military commitments elsewhere at the time. The Romans, who at the Second Punic War had accepted the survival of Carthage, now declared that the city must be destroyed. In my view, we must accept that, strange as it may seem, they did so because they had become convinced that the city was a threat which must be extirpated.

the question in this way because his sympathies were torn and he felt unable to make up his mind.

[1] This is ignored by Harris 1979, who treats these passages dismissively and in isolation (e.g. pp. 186, 198, 205). By contrast, he sets great store by Polybius' judgement when it supports his case. He is far too impressed (ibid. 107-17) by Polybius' notion that from some point the Romans consciously set out to conquer the world. That doctrine is Polybius at his worst: schematic theorizing, contradicted by his own detailed statements (Walbank 1963, not refuted by Derow 1979).

[2] *Contra* Astin 1967, 274-5; 1978, 285-6. However, Astin 1967, 48-54, 270-81, remains the best account of the preliminaries of the war.

Conclusion

Harris and his followers have exploded the old doctrine of 'defensive imperialism', but what they have offered in its place is also too one-sided. It is true that the Romans fought a war somewhere in almost every year, but at least by the second century there was no need for them to seek wars out: their far-flung imperial commitments ensured that there was generally no shortage of wars for them to fight.[1] Moreover, as we have seen, the pattern of Roman warfare and expansion was a good deal patchier than Harris' simple model implies: the nature of the Romans' military activity and commitments changed greatly over time, and in many regions there were long periods which saw few wars and little or no expansion. The wealth and prestige which success in war conferred certainly help to explain the Romans' readiness to fight, but there were countervailing factors. In particular, the ethos of aristocratic competition had more complex consequences than Harris allows. The likely participants and their friends might be impelled towards war by the prospect of the booty and glory to be won, but this same prospect might impel their rivals to thwart them. Due attention must be paid also to the workings of the decision-making process. Until the age of Caesar, the most important wars, which marked the crucial stages in Rome's advance, were the product of decisions taken in the senate, a body which on such matters is likely to have been swayed more by considerations of morality and the public interest than by personal advantage.

Roman warfare and imperialism were complex phenomena, for which no monocausal explanation will be adequate. Any attempt to provide a more satisfactory account must take the measure of

---

[1] The frequency with which the Romans fought wars is in itself not so very remarkable. As Finley remarks (1985, 67), 'Athens . . . was at war on average more than two years out of every three between the Persian wars and the defeat . . . at Chaeronea in 338 BC, and . . . it never enjoyed ten consecutive years of peace in all that period.' The history of several major powers in modern times shows a high frequency of wars, and there is a clear correlation between states' political importance and their proneness to war (Wright 1965, 220–2, 650–5; Singer and Small 1972, 258–87).

this complexity. In such an account fear, greed and glory will all play their part.[1]

Bibliography

Afzelius, A. (1944), *Die römische Kriegsmacht während der Auseinandersetzung mit den hellenistischen Grossmächten* (Copenhagen).

Astin, A. E. (1967), *Scipio Aemilianus* (Oxford).

—— (1978), *Cato the Censor* (Oxford).

Badian, E. (1958), *Foreign Clientelae (264-70 BC)* (Oxford).

—— (1959), 'Rome and Antiochus the Great: a study in cold war', *CP* 54: 81-99; = *Studies in Greek and Roman History* (Oxford, 1964), 112-39.

—— (1968), *Roman Imperialism in the Late Republic* (2nd edn; Oxford).

Bellen, H. (1985), *Metus Gallicus - Metus Punicus* (Stuttgart).

Briscoe, J. (1981), *A Commentary on Livy Books XXXIV-XXXVII* (Oxford).

Brunt, P. A. (1971), *Italian Manpower 225 BC-AD 14* (Oxford).

—— (1978), 'Laus imperii', in P. D. A. Garnsey and C. R. Whittaker (eds), *Imperialism in the Ancient World* (Cambridge), ch. 8 (pp. 159-91); = *Roman Imperial Themes* (Oxford, 1990), ch. 14 (pp. 288-323).

Cornell, T. J. (1987), review of Richardson 1986, *TLS* 21 August, p. 906.

—— (1989), 'The conquest of Italy', in *CAH*[2] vii. 2, ch. 8 (pp. 351-419).

Degrassi, A. (ed. 1947), *Inscriptiones Italiae*, xiii. 1 (Rome).

Derow, P. S. (1979), 'Polybius, Rome and the East', *JRS* 69: 1-15.

Doyle, M. W. (1986), *Empires* (Ithaca).

Dyson, S. L. (1985), *The Creation of the Roman Frontier* (Princeton).

Eckstein, A. M. (1982), 'Human sacrifice and fear of military disaster in Republican Rome', *American Journal of Ancient History*, 7 (1): 69-95.

—— (1987), *Senate and General: Individual Decision-making and Roman Foreign Relations, 264-194 BC* (Berkeley, Los Angeles and London).

Errington, R. M. (1971), *The Dawn of Empire: Rome's Rise to World Power* (London).

Ferrary, J.-L. (1988), *Philhellénisme et impérialisme: aspects idéologiques de la conquête romaine du monde hellénistique, de la seconde guerre de Macédoine à la guerre contre Mithridate* (Rome).

Finley, M. I. (1978), 'Empire in the Graeco-Roman world', *Greece and Rome*, 25: 1-15.

—— (1985), *Ancient History: Evidence and Models* (London).

Frank, T. (1914), *Roman Imperialism* (New York).

---

[1] This chapter has profited greatly from the observations of those who attended the original seminar and from Tim Cornell's comments on a later draft.

Frézouls, E. (1983), 'Sur l'historiographie de l'impérialisme romain', *Ktema*, 8: 141–62.

Gruen, E. S. (1984), *The Hellenistic World and the Coming of Rome* (Berkeley, Los Angeles and London).

Harris, W. V. (1979), *War and Imperialism in Republican Rome 327–70 BC* (Oxford).

—— (ed. 1984), *The Imperialism of Mid-Republican Rome* (Rome).

—— (1989), 'Roman expansion in the west', in *CAH²* viii, ch. 5 (pp. 107–62).

—— (1990), 'Roman warfare in the economic and social context of the fourth century BC', in W. Eder (ed.), *Staat und Staatlichkeit in der frühen römischen Republik* (Stuttgart), pp. 494–510.

Hermon, E. (1989), 'L'impérialisme romain républicain: approches historiographiques et approches d'analyse', *Athenaeum*, 67: 407–16.

Holleaux, M. (1921), *Rome, la Grèce et les monarchies hellénistiques au III⁴ siècle avant J.-C. (273–205)* (Paris).

Hopkins, M. K. (1978), *Conquerors and Slaves* (Cambridge).

—— and Burton, G. P. (1983), 'Political succession in the late Republic (249–50 BC)', in M. K. Hopkins, *Death and Renewal* (Cambridge), ch. 2 (pp. 31–119).

Hoyos, B. D. (1984), 'Polybius' Roman *hoi polloi* in 264', *LCM* 9: 88–93.

Linderski, J. (1984), '*Si vis pacem, para bellum*: concepts of defensive imperialism', in W. V. Harris (ed.), pp. 133–64.

Lintott, A. W. (1981), 'What was the "Imperium Romanum"?', *Greece and Rome*, 28: 53–67.

Millar, F. G. B. (1984), 'The political character of the classical Roman Republic, 200–151 BC', *JRS* 74: 1–19.

Momigliano, A. D. (1975), *Alien Wisdom* (Cambridge).

Mommsen, T. (1877–80), *The History of Rome*, trans. W. P. Dickson, (London).

Montesquieu, L. (1734), *Considérations sur les causes de la grandeur des romains et de leur decadence*, ed. C. Jullian (Paris, 1900).

North, J. A. (1981), 'The development of Roman imperialism', *JRS* 71: 1–9.

—— (1990), 'Democratic politics in Republican Rome', *Past and Present*, 126: 3–21.

Rich, J. W. (1976), *Declaring War in the Roman Republic in the Period of Transmarine Expansion* (Collection Latomus, 149; Brussels).

—— (1983), 'The supposed Roman manpower shortage of the later second century BC', *Historia*, 32: 287–331.

—— (1985a), review of Gruen 1984, *LCM* 10: 90–6.

—— (1985b), review of Dyson 1985, *LCM* 11: 29–31.

—— (1988a), review of Richardson 1986, *JRS* 78: 212–14.

—— (1988b), review of Eckstein 1987, *CR* 38: 315–17.

—— (1991), review of Rosenstein 1990, *CR* 41: 401–4.

Richardson, J. S. (1975), 'The triumph, the praetors and the senate in the early second century', *JRS* 65: 50–63.

—— (1986), *Hispaniae: Spain and the Development of Roman Imperialism, 219–82 BC* (Cambridge).

Rosenstein, N. S. (1990), *Imperatores Victi: Military Defeat and Aristocratic Competition in the Middle and Late Republic* (Berkeley, Los Angeles and Oxford).

Sherwin-White, A. N. (1980), 'Rome the aggressor?', review of Harris 1979, *JRS* 70: 177–81.

—— (1984), *Roman Foreign Policy in the East 168 BC to AD 1* (London).

Singer, J. D., and Small, M. (1972), *The Wages of War 1816–1965: A Statistical Handbook* (New York).

Toynbee, A. J. (1965), *Hannibal's Legacy* (London).

Walbank, F. W. (1963), 'Polybius and Rome's eastern policy', *JRS* 53: 1–13; = Walbank 1985, 138–56.

—— (1985), *Selected Papers* (Cambridge).

Wiseman, T. P. (1970), 'Roman Republican road-building', *PBSR* 38: 122–52; = *Roman Studies* (Liverpool, 1987), 126–56.

Wright, Q. (1965), *A Study of War* (2nd edn; Chicago and London).

∞ 3 ∞

Urbs direpta, or how the Romans sacked cities

Adam Ziolkowski

Ancient sources do not have much to say on the manner in which the Romans sacked cities. The thing must have been too well known to warrant lengthy comment so that when our sources do come out with a more detailed account of a sack, it invariably refers to an event which was for some reason considered exceptional. Such is one of the two exhaustive accounts of a city's sack by the Romans that have come down to us: Tacitus' description of the fratricidal capture of Cremona in AD 69. In Livy, too, more detailed dwelling upon the Romans' conduct in conquered towns refers to events which he, at least, considered anomalous. The lot of the overwhelming majority of towns that met this fate is disposed of in a bare statement of the sack's occurrence, often reduced to one of the forms of the verb *diripio.* The generally accepted modern view of the Roman way of sacking cities is based on the second of our two detailed narratives, which by its very nature and the prestige of its author seems almost tailor-made to solve at one stroke all the questions relating to the subject indicated by this chapter's title: the quasi-Weberian ideal type of a city's sack *à la romaine* afforded by Polybius' account of the capture of New Carthage in 209.[1] The aim of this chapter is to reassess the Polybian model by examining the semantic field of *diripio* in the context of the sacking of cities, and by confronting it with the information afforded by the numerous, albeit brief and

[1] All dates are BC unless otherwise stated.

fragmentary, descriptions of Roman sackings of cities in our other sources. Before proceeding with my argument I want to state in advance what is not included here, for reasons of space: the relationship between the sack's occurrence and the circumstances of the city's seizure by the Romans, and the ultimate fate of survivors of the sack.

The meaning of *direptio*

Latin authors describe the act of sacking cities with the verb *diripio* and its verbal noun *direptio*. *Diripio* is a compound made by the prefix *dis-* and the stem *rapio*. Its original meaning was: to tear apart, to mangle, to tear to pieces, which later evolved into: to deprive, to take away, to divest, with a very strong emphasis on the unruly and violent character of the act; hence its most common meaning: to sack, to plunder, to loot (*TLL* v. 1230-1, s.v. *direptio*, 1260-1, s.v. *diripio*).

As was said at the outset, passages providing a whole range of connotations of *diripio* and its derivatives are few and refer to unusual cases. Two passages in Livy are essential. One is the account of the sack of Victumulae by Hannibal's army in 218 (Livy, 21. 57. 13-14):

> The next day they surrendered and received a garrison within their walls. Being commanded to give up their arms they complied: whereupon a signal was suddenly given to the victors to sack the town, as if they had taken it by storm (*ut tamquam vi captam urbem diriperent*). Nor was any cruelty omitted which historians generally deem worth noting on such an occasion; but every species of lust and outrage and inhuman insolence was visited upon the wretched inhabitants.

The other, under 204, is a complaint to the senate by ambassadors from Locri against the Roman garrison stationed in their city (Livy, 29. 17. 15-16):

> They all rob, plunder, beat, wound, slay; they defile matrons, maidens and freeborn boys, dragged from the embrace of parents. Every day our city is captured, every day it is being plundered (*cotidie capitur urbs nostra, cotidie diripitur*).

The impression given by these passages is that *direptio* consisted in letting the soldiers loose, in giving them unrestricted freedom to loot, rape and slaughter. An *urbs direpta* would thus have been a city which had fallen prey to troops who were at liberty to do anything and everything they wanted, exactly as in the most detailed extant account of a Roman *direptio*, the sack of Cremona:

> Forty thousand armed men burst into the town; the number of camp-followers and servants was even greater, and they were more ready to indulge in lust and cruelty. Neither rank nor years protected anyone; their assailants debauched and killed without distinction. Aged men and women near the end of life, despised as booty, were dragged off to be the soldiers' sport. Whenever a young woman or a handsome youth fell into their hands, they were torn to pieces by the violent struggles of those who tried to secure them, and this in the end drove the despoilers (*direptores*) to kill one another. Individuals tried to carry off for themselves money or the masses of gold dedicated in the temples, but they were assailed by others stronger than themselves. Some, scorning the booty before their eyes, flogged and tortured the owners to discover hidden wealth and dug up buried treasure. They carried firebrands in their hands, and when they had secured their loot, in utter wantonness they threw these into the vacant houses and empty temples.
>
> (Tacitus, *Histories*, 3. 33. 1–3)

The question is, however, how typical was the image of *direptio* conveyed in these texts. The account of the fate of Victumulae – the first Roman town taken by Hannibal – could well be an illustration of the Carthaginian's alleged 'inhuman cruelty, perfidy worse than Punic' (Livy, 21. 4. 9). The Locri episode is not an account of an actual event, but an accusation put into the mouth of the most interested party, the victims of the soldiers' licence; what is more, these particular charges were grossly exaggerated (Ziolkowski 1982). In the account of the fall of Cremona we have a clear-cut case of the soldiers' disobedience. What worth should we attach, then, to these passages?

The reason why Livy focused his attention on these specific events was not any particular aspect of the troops' behaviour but the very occurrence of *direptio*, whether real or alleged. At Victumulae Hannibal's misdeed lay not in the excessive cruelty of the sack, but in his having treated people who had surrendered as if they had been conquered by storm. Locri did not in fact suffer a *direptio* in the sense outlined above, and the offences actually committed by the accused, Q. Pleminius and his men, were minor compared with the crimes with which they are charged in Livy's account. But the point is that these alleged crimes can be contained in one word: *direptio*. The Locrian envoys take the same line as Livy's in the latter's account of the sack of Victumulae: they accuse the Roman garrison of behaving every day as if the city was being taken by storm. For Livy's war-hardened audience, the list of Roman misdeeds at Locri must have read like a list of commonplaces. We thus have no reason to be sceptical about the image of *direptio* in these passages. The fact that they contain a good number of literary *topoi*, as explicitly stated by Livy in the case of Victumulae, does not diminish their value. On the contrary, with the help of such *loci communes* we can establish the kind of connotations *diripio* and the like brought to the minds of the last generation of Romans that knew war from direct, and dire, experience.

The case of Cremona is different. In Tacitus' account nothing is a matter of common knowledge, to be disposed of with a couple of catchwords; we have instead a minute description of outrages inflicted on fellow citizens, with no detail omitted. One reason of it was, no doubt, his writing in the heyday of the *pax Romana* for an audience ignorant of military matters; another, apparent throughout his account of the civil war of AD 68–9, was his abhorrence of the fratricidal character of the strife. Yet there is a possibility that the sack of Cremona was unusual also in being singularly savage and bloody. It thus remains to be seen which of the features of Tacitus' account find their counterparts in the semantic field of *direptio*.

One element of the sack – arson – was certainly not included in the normal range of connotations of *direptio*. If a city's sack was followed by its destruction, which happened quite often but was by no means the rule, our sources usually make mention of both.[1] On the other hand it can easily be shown that sexual violence was intrinsic to the notion of *direptio* on a par with looting itself. It is highly significant that the only derivative of

---

[1]   See e.g. Livy, 6. 4. 9, 10. 44. 2, 22. 20. 9, 23. 15. 6, 23. 17. 7, 24. 35. 2, 31. 45. 12, 31. 48. 7, 32. 15. 4, 32. 33. 11, 38. 43. 4, 45. 34. 6.

diripio employed in Tacitus' account of the sack of Cremona, *direptores*, is used in the sense of 'ravishers', 'violators'. The same close association between *diripio* and raping can be found in other writers. See, for example, a passage in Justin (26. 1. 7) on the sufferings of the women of Elis at the hands of the tyrant Aristotimus: 'They were robbed of everything and cast into prison, with their little boys murdered in their lap and girls ravished' (*virginibus ad stuprum direptis*), and a fragment of Cato's speech *de sumptu suo* (*ORF* fr. 203): 'Never have I imposed prefects on the towns of your allies, to plunder their property and children', where with one word – *diriperent* – he expressed two activities: plundering of property and raping (or abduction for the purpose of raping) of children.

The fact that sexual violence was inherently contained in the semantic field of *diripio* is of utmost importance for discerning the decisive connotation of the term in the context of sacking of cities, i.e. the ravagers' freedom of action. Fruits of plundering can be shared, but the pleasures of raping are ravishers' alone. Slaughter, arson and looting could all be ordered for various reasons by the commander, but it is hard to envisage a general giving his troops the order to rape. The thoroughly individualistic character of as essential an element as sexual violence implies that the character of the whole *direptio* was individualistic, in particular that other activity most gratifying to the *direptores*, looting. The second 'semantic' argument for the troops' freedom of action during *direptio* is the following. Most of the passages in which *diripio* and its derivatives are used in the context of sacking of cities are useless for determining whether the *direptio* was free-for-all or controlled. When our sources say that it was executed by the commander (e.g. Livy, 24. 35. 2, 43. 4. 9, 44. 46. 3), this is a metaphor, since those who did the sacking were the troops; when the soldiers are mentioned, the question remains of the amount of freedom they enjoyed while so engaged. But there is a third category of passages, in which generals let soldiers plunder cities or, literally, give cities to soldiers for plundering (Livy, 10. 44. 2, 25. 31. 8, 44. 45. 8). Giving implies the receiver's freedom to do what he will with the gift and this again indicates the soldiers' unrestricted freedom of action during the *direptio*.

There remains the question of killing. In this matter direct literary evidence is ambiguous: passages like those quoted above, which imply its inclusion in the range of connotations of *direptio*, can be countered with others (to be noticed below) which mention slaughter as a separate activity alongside sacking. In Latin sources we do not find instances of *diripio* being used in the sense of killing alone, as could be done with regard to raping; on the other hand, licence to kill seems an obvious corollary of that freedom of action that appears central to the notion of *direptio*. This being the case, I shall return to the matter of killing during sacking in the third section of this chapter; here the question must be left undecided.

Thus, whereas it would be rash to maintain that all the details of Tacitus' account of the fall of Cremona are also valid for the eighty or so cases where Livy uses *diripio* and its derivatives in the context of sacking cities (Packard 1968, i. 1275–7), we may take it as established that the term's range of connotations implies the plunderers' unlimited freedom to loot and rape. Whether they were equally free to satisfy their lust for blood remains for the time an open question.

The Polybian model

Polybius' account of the capture of New Carthage in 209 by the army led by P. Cornelius Scipio has a dual structure. The main thread is the description of the consecutive stages of the storming and plundering of the city. This is presented as a typical example of the Romans' conduct in a captured city, and the account thus becomes, as Walbank remarks (Walbank 1967, 216), a virtual supplement to Polybius' earlier account of Roman military organization (6. 19–42). Interwoven into this narrative is a series of comments in which Polybius explains the Romans' behaviour to his Greek audience, in particular those aspects of their conduct that were most unlike Hellenic customs and usages. For our purposes the following are the most important sections of the passage:

> When Scipio thought that a sufficient number of troops had entered he sent most of them, as is the Roman custom, against the inhabitants of the city with orders to kill all they encountered, sparing none, and not to start pillaging until the signal was given. They do this, I think,

to inspire terror, so that when towns are taken by the Romans one may often see not only the corpses of human beings, but dogs cut in half and the dismembered limbs of other animals, and on this occasion such scenes were very many owing to the number of those in the place. . . . After this [the surrender of the citadel], upon the signal being given, the massacre ceased and they began pillaging. At nightfall such of the Romans as had received orders to that effect, remained in the camp, while Scipio with his thousand men bivouacked in the citadel, and recalling the rest from the houses ordered them, through the tribunes, to collect the booty in the market, each maniple separately, and sleep there, keeping guard over it. . . . Next day the booty, both the baggage of the troops in the Carthaginian service and the household stuff of the townsmen and workers, having been collected in the market, was divided by the tribunes among the legions on the usual system. The Romans after the capture of a city manage matters more or less as follows: according to the size of the town sometimes a certain number of men from each maniple, at other times certain whole maniples are told off to collect booty, but they never thus employ more than half their total force, the rest remaining in their ranks at times outside and at times inside the city, ready for the occasion. . . . All those who are told off to spoil bring the booty back, each man to his own legion, and, after this has been done, the tribunes distribute the profits equally among all, including not only those who were left behind in the protecting force, but the men who are guarding the tents, the sick, and those absent on any special service. I have already stated at some length in my chapters on the Roman state how it is that no one appropriates any part of the loot, but that all keep the oath they make when first assembled in camp on setting out for a campaign. So that when half of the army disperse to pillage and the other half keep their ranks and afford protection, there is never any chance of the Romans suffering disaster owing to individual covetousness. For as all, both the spoilers and those who remain to safeguard them, have equal confidence that they will get their share of the booty, no one leaves the ranks, a thing that usually does injury to other armies.

(Polybius, 10. 15. 4–16. 9)[1]

Polybius' account is at the same time more and less comprehensive than the texts examined in the previous section. More, since it depicts, and comments on, the capture as well as the looting of a city. He starts with the Roman practice that must

[1]   The translation is that of W. R. Paton in the Loeb Classical Library edition, with some modifications.

have shocked the Greeks in particular, namely the pitiless massacre of all who had the misfortune to find themselves in the legionaries' path, including animals. Technically speaking, this massacre was the last phase of the assault and aimed at destroying whatever potential to resist the enemy still had after the capture of the walls. As such, it was not the same thing as the killings discussed in the first section of this paper, which took place during the *direptio*, i.e. the actual looting, distinguished by Polybius as the second phase of a city's capture. The exact equivalence of Polybius' second phase and Livy's *direptio* is assured by the fact that both start at the general's signal. Polybius' final stage, again absent in Livy, is the disposal of the booty taken in the conquered city.

On the other hand, the Greek historian, while discussing the second stage, fixes his attention on looting only; the other aspects of *direptio*, so vividly painted by Livy and Tacitus, are missing in his account. This omission might result from concentrating on what he considered essential, but the import of the whole account and especially the phrase 'upon the signal being given the massacre ceased and they began pillaging' implies that, in his view, at every stage of the sack the Romans engaged in a single activity: first they slaughtered, then they looted, and finally they disposed of their spoils. Raping, of all the aspects of *direptio* the one most strongly emphasized in the Latin sources, does not figure at all in his account; as we shall see below, this omission is rich in implications.

At the heart of Polybius' account are closely connected acts of looting and booty disposal, with regard to which he specifies several rules which he claims that the Romans rigorously observed. First, sacking was carried out by a part of the troops, never greater than half, to ensure protection for the plunderers. Second, the soldiers sent to pillage brought all their loot to the tribunes who divided it equally between all, including those who were sick and on detachment. Third, so strong was the *esprit de corps* and fidelity to the oath that nobody ever embezzled anything in secret, so that all the troops were always sure of an equal share in the profits. Finally, and inevitably, in Polybius everything – massacre, pillage and booty disposal – takes place by order.

The Roman way of sacking cities: a reappraisal

First, a point ought to be made with regard to the Polybian model: it applied to one context only, the capture of a city by assault. But *direptio* could just as well take place in a city that had opened its gates to the besiegers; all the examples quoted in the first section belong to this category. The circumstances of the sack are particularly important for the question of killing, since the purpose and significance of a massacre would obviously be quite different in a city taken by storm and in one which had surrendered.

As for the former category, cities taken by storm, the first stage of the Polybian model is corroborated by several passages in Livy and other historians, in which indiscriminate slaughter follows in the wake of a successful assault, with looting taking place after the cessation of the massacre. Clear-cut instances are Veii in 396 (Livy, 5. 21. 13 – for what it is worth), Tarentum in 209 (Livy, 27. 16. 6), Chalcis in 200 (Livy, 31. 23. 7–8) and New Carthage, though here one might suspect the influence of Polybius' account (Livy, 26. 46. 10; see Walbank 1967, 193–4, on Livy's relationship to Polybius here).

Livy differs from Polybius on one point: whereas the latter claims that the massacre was directed against all the inhabitants of a city, regardless of sex and age, the former, whenever he gets more specific, speaks of the victims of the soldiers' swords as being the men of military age, as at Chalcis, or the *puberes* (adult males), as at Antipatreia (Livy, 31. 27. 4) and at New Carthage. I think that on the whole Livy's evidence is preferable on this matter. The psychological significance ascribed to killing by Polybius cannot be overestimated, but it is hard to believe that in normal circumstances Roman soldiers took no heed of whom they were cutting down. Of course, this does not mean that no women or children ever lost their lives in the massacre phase; when, for example, Livy says that at Chalcis there remained 'no longer anyone of military age who had not perished or fled' (Livy, 31. 23. 8), he does not say that all the women and children were spared, but simply that at that stage the Romans went mainly after actual or potential adversaries. It is a fact that our sources mention several cases, discussed below, when the Romans killed all the inhabitants of a city; these, however, were unusual, if not all that rare, instances of the soldiers' rage getting the better of their lust and greed. In normal circumstances, when the object of the massacre was, as stated by Polybius, terrorizing the survivors into submission, butchery of *puberes* was in fact the most efficient way of securing it, whereas killing of women and of the young of both sexes would have been a senseless waste in view of the next phase of the sack, in which rape played so prominent a part. All other considerations apart, sexual attractiveness was surely the victims' best chance of survival.

The foregoing inference is supported by the fact that the extreme treatment Roman generals had in store for cities that surrendered was precisely killing of all the adult males, as at Leontini in 213 (reported as an enemy allegation at Livy, 24. 30. 4), Cauca in 151 (App. *Hisp.* 52), Corinth in 146 (Paus. 7. 16. 8; Zonar. 9. 31. 5–7), and Capsa in 107 (Sall. *Iug.* 91. 6–7). It is simplest to assume that in those cases the Romans simply followed the pattern practised in cities taken by storm, as is hinted by Sallust, when he excuses the commander, C. Marius, of treating Capsa 'against the law of war' (*contra ius belli*); had the city been taken by storm, the Romans' conduct would have needed no comment. One could add that in the case of the conditional surrender of a large city inhabited by a warlike population, like Cauca, the massacre proceeded to all intents and purposes as in a city taken by storm, with the bonus of surprise and unhindered seizure of the walls. The fact that in all those episodes our sources report the massacre of adult males implies that the *puberes* were chief victims of initial killings in cities taken by storm.

Before passing to the second phase we should discuss the general's signal which, according to Polybius, marked the end of the massacre and the beginning of the pillage. Livy mentions it several times, in the context both of cities taken by storm, (e.g. Veii and New Carthage), and of cities which had surrendered. One example of the latter has already been mentioned, that of Victumulae. A second is the critical phase of the siege of Syracuse in 212, the irruption of Marcellus' forces into Epipolai, which put the unfortified districts of Tycha and Neapolis at the Romans' mercy. The inhabitants duly offered their submission 'praying that they be spared bloodshed and fires', whereupon Marcellus resolved to limit the sack to plundering. Strong guards were

mounted in the camp between the two districts, 'then at a given
signal the soldiers scattered [for plundering]' (Livy, 25. 25. 5-9).
The next case, that of Phocaea in 190, is somewhat unusual. The
inhabitants of that city, having successfully repulsed a Roman
attack, eventually came to terms with the praetor L. Aemilius
Regillus on condition that their persons and property should be
unharmed. However, the agreement was thwarted by Roman
soldiers who, 'as if they had received a signal from the praetor . . .
rushed off in every direction to plunder the city' (Livy, 37. 32. 1-
12). The signal to loot, though actually not given, is in this
account mentioned in identical circumstances as at Victumulae
and Syracuse – upon the enemies' surrender and the Romans'
entrance into the city.

As can be seen, both sets of circumstances have one thing in
common: the general gives the signal, or is expected to do so, once
he has ascertained that the enemy is not capable of putting up
further resistance, the obligatory premise being that this was not
self-evident. In spite of the seizure of the city walls Scipio could
not be certain of the final capture of New Carthage as long as the
citadel held on. Marcellus, threatened from the side of the old city
and the fortress of Euryalos, could not pillage the otherwise
defenceless districts of Tycha and Neapolis straightaway, without
precautions. The pillage of Victumulae and, even more so,
Phocaea, was contingent on being admitted within the walls by
the defenders, a delicate and dangerous operation until a sufficient
number of soldiers had got inside. When plundering became not
only feasible but safe as well, some sort of sign was needed to give
the troops the go-ahead. Hence the signal mentioned by our
historians.

The question is whether the signal was needed when the
circumstances did not warrant it. A town had to be exceptionally
well defended to stand a chance of repulsing the attackers who
had managed to get a foothold within the walls; usually its fate
was sealed once the breach had been made. In such a situation the
safe run of the pillage was guaranteed without the signal; does it
follow, then, that the latter need not be given? Needless to say, the
answer depends on the signal's purpose: was it an order (or
consent) or just an intimation? The general's signal as a pre-
requisite of the sack, as an order to pass from one task to another,
goes together well with Polybius' picture of orderly pillage and

equal division of its fruits. But if normal sacking consisted in the soldiers' raping, ravaging and plundering at will and on their own behalf, the signal – a notice that the enemy's resistance was over – would have been just an invitation to the troops to start enjoying themselves.[1]

The Polybian model of looting and booty disposal is virtually uncorroborated by other evidence. In Livy's account of the sack of Veii it is explicitly stated that the killing ended with the commander's order and the plundering started with his permission, yet the soldiers plunder on their own behalf (Livy, 5. 20. 8–10, 22. 1, 23. 8–11). In his account of the capture of Anxur in 406 Livy says that the general, N. Fabius Ambustus, having seized the walls and imprisoned the populace, postponed plundering until the arrival of two other Roman armies so that all the troops might participate in looting (Livy, 4. 59. 8, 10). Had sacking proceeded according to the rules laid down by Polybius, Livy might have presented Fabius as plundering Anxur with his own troops and dividing the booty between the soldiers of the three armies. Yet, in his account, anachronistic but significant, Fabius had to wait for his colleagues. After the capture of the refuge of the Tolostobogii, a Galatian tribe, on Mount Olympus by the army of Cn. Manlius Vulso in 189, Vulso

> kept his soldiers from spoil and pillage; he ordered them each to follow as best as he could, press the pursuit and increase the panic of the fugitives. The second column, under L. Manlius, also came up; he did not permit his men to enter the camp, but sent them at once to pursue the enemy . . . When the consul had gone, C. Helvius arrived with the third column and was unable to prevent his men from plundering the camp, and the booty, by a most unjust decree of fate, fell into the hands of men who had had no part in the battle.
>
> (Livy, 38. 23. 2–4)

There is very little doubt that, contrary to what Livy later suggests (38. 23. 10), Vulso could not reclaim, let alone recover, the booty seized by Helvius' men; all he could do was to recompense, as well

---

[1] Vogel 1948 argues persuasively that the soldiers had a right to plunder; see Bona 1958 for an attempt, abortive in my view, to explode his argument. For other modern discussions of Roman booty disposal see Vogel 1953; Bona 1959; Watson 1968, 62–74; Shatzman 1972.

as possible, other soldiers for their loss.[1] The latter, however, took to heart the lesson they had learned on Mount Olympus, as is shown by what happened when the refuge of another Galatian tribe, the Tectosages, on Mount Magaba was taken a couple of weeks later:

> The victors, cutting them down from behind, followed as far as the camp; then they remained in the camp in their greed for plunder, nor did anyone pursue . . . The consul was unable to tear away from their plundering the troops who had entered the camp.
>
> (Livy, 38. 27. 3, 5)

Vulso's men there followed the principle of 'first come, first served', in patent contradiction to the rules handed down by Polybius. Equally significant are the preventive measures taken by Marcellus upon the final conquest of Syracuse in 212. On learning that key points in the city had been secured, he first sounded the recall to prevent the royal treasures from being plundered, next sent the quaestor with a force to guard them, and only then let the soldiers plunder, having first assigned guards to the houses of Rome's friends (Livy, 25. 30. 12, 31. 8–9).

Even in cases of flagrant insubordination, retrieval of booty seized by the soldiers was well-nigh impossible, as the Phocaea episode shows. Livy says that Regillus did his best to recall the troops and, 'after wrath and greed proved stronger than authority', to save the townspeople's lives, and adds: 'in everything which was under his control the word of the praetor held good; the city, the farmlands and their laws were restored to them' (Livy, 37. 32. 12–14). But it was not in Regillus' power to restore goods plundered by his men to their rightful owners.

Another argument against Polybius' model is an event he saw with his own eyes and for which he is our ultimate source: the capture of Cothon, the port of Carthage, in 146. Appian reports

---

[1] Vulso had hoped to hold his men back from plundering because he considered the storming of Mt. Olympus a battle, not an assault on a stronghold. In battle, the principle of keeping pillage under the general's control held good throughout the Republic. I know of only one case when it was violated – at Cabeira in 71, when Lucullus' men, running after loot, let Mithridates escape (Plut. *Luc.* 17. 2; App. *Mith.* 82; Cic. *Leg. Man.* 22).

that Scipio Aemilianus, having seized the walls adjacent to the port, placed four thousand men in the captured area.

> They entered the temple of Apollo, whose statue was there, covered with gold in a shrine of beaten gold, weighing 1,000 talents, which they plundered, chopping it with their swords and disregarding the commands of their officers until they had divided it among themselves, after which they returned to their duty.
>
> (App. *Pun.* 127)

In spite of sacrilege and insubordination bordering on desertion in the face of the enemy, the only thing Scipio could do was to exclude the offenders from the distribution of rewards after the final victory (App. *Pun.* 133). It is worth noticing, though, that after the capture of the first section of the wall the Carthaginians panicked and fled; the Romans' progress on that day was checked only by the coming of the night. Thus the soldiers sent to the port just before the dawn of the next day had good reason to believe that the fighting was over and that they were therefore entitled to start looting. But when it became clear that the fiercest fighting was still to come, nobody left his post until the final victory (App. *Pun.* 128–30).

The last days of Rome's greatest rival and deadliest adversary, when the Roman soldiers, conscious of the moment's historical importance, were seized with a sort of collective madness, hardly lend themselves to generalizing, but, when they are taken together with the other episodes quoted above, it becomes possible, I think, to determine what Roman generals could reasonably expect from their troops. When the situation warranted it, i.e. when military considerations dictated carrying on with the killing, it went on until the general gave the signal or until all the adult males within the soldiers' reach had been killed. In more relaxed circumstances many soldiers probably got sidetracked into plundering (and raping) from the start; what is more, they did so with impunity.

There is solid evidence to show that the troops were free to slaughter and rape in the pillaging phase, starting with the most exceptional instance of the commander's control of his troops, the capture of Syracuse. The pillage of Tycha and Neapolis almost followed the pattern set out by Polybius: there was no bloodshed and, apparently, no rapes; only 'to plundering there was no limit'

(Livy, 25. 25. 9–10). But this most unusual conduct – we do not find its like in the rest of Livy's work – was the outcome of a most unusual procedure. Marcellus and his staff deliberated on the case, then reached a decision announced to the troops as the commander's order (Livy, 25. 25. 5–8). The reason for this mildness, surprising for the Romans in general and Marcellus the butcher in particular, was obvious and promptly understood by its addressees: the inhabitants of the districts of Achradina and Nasos, which were still holding out, at the first opportunity negotiated a conditional surrender which Marcellus violated with cold-blooded hypocrisy. With the need for diplomacy gone, the *direptio* of the old city followed standard Roman practice. Cicero's and Plutarch's harangues in praise of Marcellus' benevolence are of no consequence since even Livy is compelled to admit, somewhat weakly, that 'many shameful examples of anger and many of greed were given' (Livy, 25. 31. 9). We are in a position to quote at least one specific manifestation of the soldiers' rage: the death of a certain old man at the hands of a plundering legionary (Livy, 25. 31. 9–10; Plut. *Marc.* 19. 5–6). We do not need the tale of Archimedes' absorption in a geometrical problem to account for his death; as a septuagenarian, he belonged to the category of aged men and women near the end of life, who were of no value as booty and so the most likely victims of the pillaging soldiers' thirst for blood. The cases noted above of killing first and plundering afterwards are no argument against freedom to kill in the pillaging phase since, when the adult males were all dead, there was obviously no need to carry on with killing while looting.

But the best evidence for the soldiers' freedom to kill regardless of the general's signal or the stage which the sacking had reached is afforded by those cases when all the inhabitants of a city, or nearly all, were put to the sword. For the Republic our sources mention eight such massacres, two preventive, aimed at forestalling a suspected treachery and so hardly relevant to our issue, at Casilinum in 216 (Livy, 23. 17. 10) and Henna in 214 (Livy, 24. 37. 1–39. 6), and six others, at Myttistratos in 258 (Zonar. 8. 11. 10; see also Polyb. 1. 24. 11; Diod. 23. 9. 4), Lipara in 252 (Zonar. 8. 14. 7; see also Polyb. 1. 39. 13), Ilurgeia in 206 (Livy, 28. 19. 9–20. 7; App. *Hisp.* 32; Zonar. 9. 10. 2), Locha in 203 (App. *Pun.* 15), Athens in 86 (App. *Mith.* 38; Plut. *Sull.* 14. 10), and Avaricum in

52 (Caes. *BGall.* 7. 28. 4).[1] In three cases the sources explicitly make the soldiers responsible for the slaughter. At Myttistratos the consul A. Atilius Caiatinus, seeing that all the populace was in danger of being exterminated, saved the remainder by proclaiming that prisoners would become property of their captors, thus letting the soldiers' greed prevail over their thirst for blood. In this case we clearly see that the massacre, no doubt begun after the city walls had been taken, continued during the phase which in the Polybian model would have been devoted to plundering. The same is attested in the case of Avaricum; Caesar says that his men, enraged by the massacre of their fellow Italians at Cenabum and their own sufferings during the siege, took no heed of booty and merely killed, sparing no one. The massacre of Locha – against Scipio's orders and in defiance of the agreement he had just concluded with the defenders – was actually a flagrant breach of discipline, savagely punished by the proconsul.

At Ilurgeia and Athens the generals are blamed; but the former case shows that matters were more complex. Six years before the inhabitants of Ilurgeia had killed Roman fugitives seeking shelter after the rout and death of the elder Scipios. Now, when the final conquest of Punic Spain was only a matter of time, the moment had arrived to exact the penalty. Scipio's speech before the assault, as given by Livy, is highly revealing: the general gives no orders but incites the troops 'to avenge the atrocious slaughter of their comrades' and 'by a severe example to ordain that no one should ever account a Roman citizen or soldier in any misfortune as fair game for ill treatment' (Livy, 28. 19. 6–8). Equally significant is Livy's account of the city's destruction:

> It was then in truth evident that the city had been attacked out of anger and hatred. No one thought of taking men alive, no one thought of booty, although every place was open for plunder. They slaughtered the unarmed and the armed alike, women as well as men; cruel anger went even so far as to slay infants. Then they threw firebrands into houses and demolished what could not be consumed by the flames. So

---

[1] I omit the wholesale massacres in 314 at Ausona, Minturnae and Vescia reported by Livy, 9. 25. 3–9 (cited by Harris 1979, 263), the details of which are strongly suspect, and that at Luceria (Livy, 9. 26. 1–2), which is patently unhistorical.

delighted were they to destroy even the traces of the city and blot out the memory of their enemies' abode.

(Livy, 28. 20. 6–7)

For what it is worth, this account shows that in the last analysis the destruction of Ilurgeia was brought about by the troops' anger and hatred. Besides, in the passage under discussion there is nothing to suggest any sense of guilt or trying to exculpate the general; on the contrary, the tone is that of grim satisfaction. It is pretty certain that without Scipio's egging on, his soldiers would have wiped Ilurgeia out just as thoroughly.

There remains the sack of Athens. Appian says that it was L. Cornelius Sulla who gave the order to kill all the townspeople (App. *Mith.* 38). However, the kind of troops at Sulla's disposal and his comparatively lenient treatment of those Athenians who survived the massacre suggest that he may not have been the driving force behind the slaughter. Besides, the sex appeal of women and youngsters who had lately lived on boiled leather and, reputedly, human flesh, must have been close to zero; hence, an extra motive for indiscriminate killing.

If wholesale massacres were the doing of soldiers, not generals, this means that in those particular instances the troops' rage and hatred prevailed over their lust and, to an extent, their greed. In all the cases noted above we can give reasons for this exceptionally murderous conduct. As we have seen, motives of revenge are stated in our sources for Ilurgeia and Avaricum. The same is true too for Athens: the Athenians had sided enthusiastically with Mithridates, who was credited with the butchery of 80,000 Italians, and they had put up a particularly stubborn resistance. In the case of Myttistratos we hear of dogged resistance to three successive consular armies and heavy casualties suffered by the Romans. The massacre of Lipara was most probably a revenge for the defeat of the besiegers just before the final assault. Locha surely met her doom for being the first African town taken by the Romans in the fifteenth year of a war that had hitherto brought on them unparalleled disasters.

Apart from Athens, where some of the inhabitants survived the massacre, and Avaricum all these cities were rather small. This is worth emphasizing since we know of at least two great cities as 'guilty' – in Roman eyes – of betrayal and stubborn resistance as those mentioned above, whose inhabitants, like the Athenians in 86, were not all put to the sword in spite of great carnage: Agrigentum in 210 (Livy, 26. 40. 8–13) and Tarentum in 209 (Livy, 27. 16. 5–6). The reason was probably the sheer size of these cities and the great number of their inhabitants; in both cases the Roman soldiers apparently sated their thirst for blood before they killed the whole populace.

In all these episodes the course which the sacking took was determined by the soldiers' mood rather than by the general's orders, and I do not see why it should have been otherwise in other, less bloody cases. Wholesale killing was a peculiar kind of *direptio*, unique in that the soldiers first exercised their freedom of conduct in one way – by killing – without giving heed to rape and plunder. By doing so, they irrevocably deprived themselves of violent sexual gratification; as for pillaging, it was simply put off for a short while.

The ultimate corroboration of the soldiers' freedom to slaughter, rape and plunder at will was, in my view, their almost total impunity in the few cases when, while doing so, they defied their commanders. We hear of only one case when a Roman general managed to recover from his men their ill-gotten plunder and punished them for their disobedience, namely Scipio Africanus at Locha. But the circumstances of that episode – the opening of the final campaign of the Second Punic War and the first the Romans fought on the enemy's soil – did not permit him to tolerate such misbehaviour. It is worth noticing that, of the three known cases when generals succeeded in keeping sacking under control, two – the outer districts of Syracuse and New Carthage – took place during that very war:[1] it could be said without undue exaggeration that in all these instances Rome's fate was at stake. This explains the generals' measures as well as the troops' docility, in both complying with orders and receiving punishment. With Rome's world mastery consolidated we find just one feeble attempt to imitate Scipio's conduct at Locha, that of L. Valerius Flaccus in 86, who paid with his life for trying to force his men to give their plunder back to its owners, the inhabitants of Byzantium, even though they were allies of Rome (Dio, 35. 104.

---

[1]   The third instance occurred at Tigranocerta in 69 (Dio, 36. 2. 3–5).

3–4; Diod. 38. 8). Other commanders knew better than to take such a risk.

Freedom to slaughter and rape are conclusive arguments against Polybius' ideal type. None of the rules of pillaging he sets out bears examination. The first – plundering by a part of the army – would imply that, while launching an assault, a Roman general either sent no more than half of his forces to attack or, once within the walls, he withdrew a half and let the rest plunder. The former possibility could be contemplated when the town was small enough to afford the luxury of keeping half of the besiegers out of action. The latter, apart from the virtual impossibility of putting it into effect, would have been tantamount, even in the case of equitable division of booty, to depriving a good part of the troops of the opportunity to rape, a gratification at least as eagerly sought as material gains. But most of all, in normal circumstances this rule would have been superfluous; it is not by chance that Livy alludes to it only once, speaking of the sack of Tycha and Neapolis. In that case exceptional circumstances warranted extraordinary measures; normally the Romans' crushing superiority would have made this sort of precaution unnecessary.

Polybius' second rule, emphasizing equal participation of all the troops in the profits of a pillage, is refuted by the quoted examples of looting on the soldiers' own behalf, apart from the technical difficulties which would be involved in putting it into effect (see Walbank 1967, 217). At the same time this rule, like the first, ignores that other aspect of sacking, freedom to kill and rape. In a *direptio* the question of 'equal' benefits for all did not and could not arise. During the sack, time was the paramount factor; one had to hurry in order not to be forestalled by others. *Direptio* gave no equal benefits but only equal opportunities; afterwards everything depended on luck and personal predilections. Those who preferred raping to looting had, needless to say, fewer opportunities to enrich themselves than their more materially motivated colleagues.

Last but not least, the assertion that in the Roman army nobody ever appropriated anything to the detriment of his colleagues obviously belonged to the realm of wishful thinking on the part of Polybius' informers, whose ideal was an army of robots devoid of human traits, docile executors of orders. It goes without saying that this was not the ideal of the ranks, but of their noble officers and generals who were in any case above equality and discipline. Polybius presented this ideal as a regular practice, so his account is a tribute to his qualities as a eulogist rather than a historian.[1]

If this be true, then it may not be a coincidence that he chose the sack of New Carthage to depict for his fellow Greeks the ideal picture of the Roman way of sacking cities. New Carthage was the supply base for Carthaginian forces in the peninsula and the place of custody of Iberian hostages, guarantors of the loyalty of the native tribes.[2] To exploit to the maximum all the advantages – military, political and logistic – that went with its capture Scipio could not let it fall a prey to his troops. The proof is the incident of a beautiful captive girl said to have been offered to Scipio as a gift by some young soldiers who knew their commander's liking for women. Scipio sent the girl back untouched and 'the self-restraint and moderation he displayed on this occasion secured him the warm approbation of his troops'. So Polybius (10. 19. 6; see Livy, 26. 50. 1–12). His account calls for comment on two grounds. First, one does not see how private soldiers could 'offer' captives to the general who decided the fate of prisoners; all they could do was to search for the most beautiful among captive women and set her before Scipio. Second, the reason of the troops' approbation as given by Polybius is suspect, since self-restraint and moderation towards the fair sex have never been virtues in soldiers' eyes. But it would have been an entirely different matter if Scipio, having explicitly forbidden rapes, extended the ban to his own person; in that case, and only in that case, his self-restraint would in fact

---

[1]   Polybius' statement (10. 16. 6, cited above) about the soldiers' fidelity to their oath making them hand over booty for distribution is a misunderstanding: the clause in the oath to which he alludes probably applied to theft in the camp (Polyb. 6. 33. 1–2; Gell. *NA* 16. 4. 2). I think it unlikely that the Polybian rules derive from a 'texte réglementaire', as suggested by Nicolet 1977, i. 327. It is worth noticing that similar objections can be raised against some parts of Polybius' account of the Roman army in Book 6, notably the *dilectus*, on which see Brunt 1971, 625–8.

[2]   See Scipio's speech at the army assembly before the assault on the city in Livy, 26. 43. 3–8.

have earned him 'the warm approbation of his troops'.[1] Polybius may have missed Scipio's real motives,[2] but the story proves that at New Carthage a true *direptio*, in which the troops were given free rein to murder, rape and loot, did not occur.[3]

Yet, to be fair to Polybius, it is worth stressing that in the matter under discussion he was almost entirely at the mercy of his informants, since the only Roman sack of a city he saw with his own eyes was that of Carthage herself, hardly the basis for sweeping statements. Thus, if the uninformed Greek really based his model on one of two or three cases when circumstances forced the Romans to conduct themselves more or less diplomatically, this is because he was misled by his noble informants.[4] After all, even in the day of Caesar and Cicero, Roman generals tried to keep up the pretence that soldiers obtained booty through grants on the part of their commanders (e.g. Cic. *Att.* 5. 20. 5; Caes. *BGall.* 7. 11. 9). The fiction of the general's control of his troops being so inveterate, we can forgive Polybius for having mistaken an exception for the rule, the more so as the main reason for his dilating on the Roman way of sacking cities at such length was to illustrate yet again their discipline and prudence in contrast with Greek practice.

Conclusion

Roman *direptio*, or the Roman way of sacking cities, is to be reconstructed on the basis of concrete events, Polybius' celebrated model being at best an unwarranted generalization from a most exceptional episode. Other sources depict a diversity of practice

[1] This story, together with the Chiomara episode (Polyb. 21. 38), is quoted by Harris 1979, 53 n. 1, as the proof that in Roman warfare raping of women was normal practice. I wholeheartedly agree with Harris's conclusion, but I am not sure it can be derived from these particular premises.
[2] See the trivial sermon he delivers on the occasion (Polyb. 10. 19. 7).
[3] This is also why I do not believe that at New Carthage the Romans slaughtered indiscriminately in the massacre phase. Every woman and child they encountered could have been an Iberian hostage.
[4] On Polybius' sources for the capture of New Carthage see Walbank 1967, 193–4, 198, 204.

within a quite consistent framework. Diversity resulted mainly from the soldiers' mood at the time of the sack and, obviously, the city's size and wealth. However, some basic rules appear evident. First and foremost, the essence of *direptio*, in keeping with the term's etymology, was the suspension of any form of control from above. An 'orderly' sacking is a misunderstanding; when plundering proceeded under the general's control, as at New Carthage, this was not a *direptio*.[1] More specifically, so long as it lasted, the soldiers held the power of life and death over the inhabitants and could do whatever they wanted to them; they looted on their own account and everything they laid their hands on became their property. I can think of only two limits to a soldier's spoils: his physical strength and endurance which restricted the size of each haul, and logistic and strategic considerations which put a check to the growth of the train and thus of the troops' personal impediments as well. One thing seems certain: once a thing got lost under the legionary's cloak, there was no power on earth which could snatch it away from there.

Bibliography

Bona, F. (1958), 'Sull' acquisto delle *res hostium* a seguito di *direptio*', *Studia et Documenta Historiae et Iuris*, 24: 237–68.

—— (1959), 'Preda di guerra e occupazione privata di *res hostium*', *Studia et Documenta Historiae et Iuris*, 25: 309–70.

Brunt, P. A. (1979), *Italian Manpower 225 BC–AD 14* (Oxford).

Harris, W. V. (1979), *War and Imperialism in Republican Rome 327–70 BC* (Oxford).

Nicolet, C. (1977), *Rome et la conquête du monde méditerranéen, 264–27 avant J.-C.* (Paris).

Packard, D. W. (1968), *A Concordance to Livy* (Cambridge, Mass.).

Shatzman, I. (1972), 'The Roman general's authority over booty', *Historia*, 21: 177–205.

Vogel, K.-H. (1948), 'Zur rechtlichen Behandlung der römischen Kriegsgewinne', *Zeitschrift der Savigny-Stiftung für Rechtsgeschichte, romanistische Abteilung*, 62: 394–422.

—— (1953), '*Praeda*', in *RE* xxii. 1200–13.

Walbank, F. W. (1967), *A Historical Commentary on Polybius*, ii (Oxford).

---

[1]   For what it is worth, in Livy's account of the capture of New Carthage no form of the word *diripio* is used.

Watson, A. (1968), *The Law of Property in the Later Roman Republic* (Oxford).

Ziolkowski, A. (1982), 'The case of Lokroi Epizephyrioi in 205–204 BC', *Eos*, 70: 319–29 (in Polish).

∞ 4 ∞

Military organization
and social change
in the later Roman Republic

John Patterson

Models for war and social change

For historians of the twentieth century, explaining the links between social change and warfare has become a major concern, and the problem appears in its most acute form in studies of the aftermath of the First and Second World Wars. Should the major social changes which followed these two conflicts in Britain – the extension of the franchise to women following the First World War, or the introduction of the National Health Service following the Second, for example – be explained primarily in terms of the wars which preceded them, or should they rather be seen as a product of wider social and economic factors operating on a longer time-scale?

A useful account of the debate is provided by a collection of essays edited by one of the protagonists, Arthur Marwick, entitled *Total War and Social Change* (1988). Marwick, who has sought to analyse the consequences of the First and Second World Wars in a series of important publications,[1] has stressed four main ways in

---

[1] Marwick 1965 examines the effect of the First World War on British society; 1968 expands the discussion to cover the Second World War and its aftermath; 1974 compares developments in Britain with the situations in France, Germany, Russia and the USA; 1990 is an Open University textbook covering all these issues.

which large scale warfare is likely to cause social change. War, he argues, inherently involves destruction – of life, property, and old patterns of behaviour; it tests a society's social, political and economic institutions; it provides a psychologically significant experience; and it may, especially in the case of the 'Total War' of the twentieth century, involve the mass participation of the population. Elsewhere in the same volume, Alastair Reid expands this suggestion to argue that the greater the proportion of a population which was involved in a war effort, the more likely social reforms were to result, citing in particular the increased influence of trade unions in collective bargaining in Britain following the First World War (Reid 1988).

If Reid and Marwick are right to stress the importance of the 'Military Participation Ratio' (Marwick, ibid. xvi, prefers the formula 'participation ratio' as this enables him to emphasize the importance of military-related industries as well as military service itself) as a significant factor in linking warfare and social change, there are potentially interesting implications for the historian of ancient Rome. Even before the First World War, historians were stressing the very high proportion of the Roman citizenry involved in military service during the second and first centuries BC (De Sanctis 1907, 202–3), and subsequent writers have shown that the degree of mobilization at Rome during the Hannibalic War and the civil wars of the first century BC was on a par with that of the countries of Europe between 1914 and 1918.[1] The parallels between the consequences of the First World War and those of the Hannibalic War are implicit throughout Toynbee's *Hannibal's Legacy*, and emphasized in the moving preface to the second volume of that work (Toynbee 1965, ii. v).

There seem to be obvious difficulties involved in applying Marwick's model to the situation at Rome in the last two centuries of the Republic: the pattern of twentieth-century warfare has (in the West at least) largely been one of a generally low level of military activity interrupted by conflict on a massive scale resulting in large-scale conscription into the armed forces and a transformation of peacetime economies in order to support the

---

[1] Brunt 1971a, 67, 512; Stockton 1979, 17. Hopkins 1978, 33, provides a useful chart based on Brunt's estimates of the number of Roman citizens and the size of the Roman army during the second and first centuries BC.

war effort. In second- and first-century Rome, by contrast, warfare was a normal part of everyday life, with campaigning expected annually; the absence of military activity in a particular year was more notable than its occurrence (Harris 1979, 9–10). Nevertheless, some of these wars were of greater significance than others in terms of their social and political consequences within Roman society. This was either because of the exceptionally high levels of participation involved, or because they were civil wars and resulted in the overthrow of the Roman state or its government, or because they involved significant levels of fighting in Italy itself – or a combination of all three elements, as in the case of the Social War and civil wars of the first century BC. This means that the explanatory framework provided by Marwick's 'Total War' model may potentially be helpful in a study of the last fifty years of the Roman Republic, and deserves further examination.

The concept of 'Military Participation Ratio', central to Marwick's thesis, is, however, only one element in an influential wider model of relationships between warfare and society presented by S. Andreski in his *Military Organization and Society* (2nd edn, 1968).[1] The central theme of Andreski's work – one which can be traced back to Aristotle (e.g. *Pol.* 4. 1289 b) – is that the social and political framework of a society is significantly linked to the military organization of that society: the size of its armed forces, how they are recruited, and how they operate. In particular, the degree of social stratification in a society is closely linked to the extent of participation in military activity within that society. If warfare in a society involves complex equipment or tactical skills, or for other reasons military service becomes professionalized, then that society tends to be more steeply stratified than societies in which participation in military activity is more widespread. This general principle, that the height of social stratification co-varies with the level of military participation (Andreski 1968, 73), is then qualified and elaborated in a series of further analyses and observations. Harris (1979, 51) has drawn attention to the relevance for Republican Rome of Andreski's view that a high level of military participation leads to brutality in war; and also of particular interest is the suggestion

---

[1]   Usefully summarized by Edmonds 1988, 71–2.

that warfare, especially when it leads to conquest, can lead to interstratic mobility within a society (Andreski 1968, 134–8).

This chapter sets out to examine the relationship between Roman military organization and social structure during the last two centuries of the Republic with two aims in view: to assess how far Andreski's ideas can be exploited within a study of the fall of the Roman Republic, and to examine whether Marwick's hypothesis of a likely link between large-scale war and military participation and significant social change is borne out by the situation in first-century BC Italy. It will concentrate on two interlinked phenomena: social mobility and its relationship to military service, and veteran settlement in Italy, and its social consequences.

Problems with Andreski's model

Although Andreski himself discusses the history of the late Roman Republic as part of a wide-ranging survey of military and political structure in societies through history, his analysis is based primarily on the work of Rostovtzeff and Homo written in the 1920s, and so incorporates views of Roman history which would now not receive general acceptance; for example, the idea of the third century BC as a period of 'rural democracy', that the senate was a 'closed and preponderant body' or that after Marius 'the army ceased altogether to be a militia of Italian peasants' (Andreski 1968, 53–6).

Difficulties immediately arise in applying Andreski's central arguments to Roman social and political structures. The dominant ideology of the army of the middle Republic was that it was a citizens' militia, and this was reflected in the parallels between the procedures for marshalling the army and those for assembling the Roman people for electoral purposes. The *comitia centuriata* was, in formal terms, the Roman people assembled for war, and as a result its meetings took place in the Campus Martius, outside the *pomerium*; it was this assembly which voted on issues of war and peace (Harris 1979, 263). The ideological link between membership of the citizen body and participation in the armed forces is thus very clear (Nicolet 1980, 93 ff., 129 ff.). High levels of military participation were the norm throughout the second century BC – ranging from the exceptionally high level of 26 per cent of the male citizens during the Hannibalic War to a low point of between 7 and 9 per cent in the 120s BC (Hopkins 1978, 33), so in numerical as well as ideological terms the army of the Republic can be seen as a people's army. The *comitia centuriata* was, however, a body which was extremely hierarchical in its operation; voters were divided up into groups overtly organized according to their wealth and status, although by the second century the finer divisions of this system were of marginal importance for actual military practice (Nicolet 1980, 219–24). Republican Rome thus appears to be a counter-example to the central tenet of Andreski's theory, since it combined a high level of social stratification with a high level of military participation.

The difficulties involved in fitting the situation in mid-Republican Rome into Andreski's scheme become most apparent in the final part of his book, where he argues that the three key variables within a state's military organization are the level of military participation, the degree of subordination within the army, and the level of cohesion within it (Andreski 1968, 139–56). Working from these variables, he presents six 'ideal types' of military organization, three of which seem to be potentially relevant for the Roman period: the 'masaic' or 'tribal' type (which combines a high level of participation and a high level of cohesion but a low level of subordination); the 'neferic' or 'widely con-scriptive' type (combining high levels of participation, cohesion and subordination); and the 'mortazic' or 'restricted professional' type (combining a low level of participation with high levels of cohesion and subordination).

Imperial Rome seems clearly to correspond to the 'mortazic' type; the discipline and hierarchical organization of the Roman imperial army are famous, and Augustus' reforms created a professional standing army; the level of military participation in the early Empire was very low, considering the overall population of the empire. Republican Rome presents more problems, how-ever. In essence the army of the Roman Republic seems to develop from a 'masaic' type (the army of archaic Rome, characterized by family-based contingents, small and relatively unstratified as characteristic of other small societies) into the 'neferic' type, characterized by high levels of participation, cohesion, and subordination, and usually appearing as a result of conquest. Some of the main characteristic features associated by Andreski with his ideal types do not in fact appear in the Roman context, though. The 'neferic' type, for example, should theoretically be characterized by a high level of social mobility, which is not the case in the second-century BC Roman Republic, as I shall argue; rather, the lack of mobility was a serious weakness in the social system at a time of imperial growth and potential instability. Similarly, the development of a neferic society should, according to Andreski, lead to a levelling of social inequalities, which again clearly did not happen in the second and first centuries BC; rather, an increased polarization of rich and poor is apparent, largely as a result of the influx of imperial wealth.

Nevertheless, Andreski's book represents a rare attempt to provide an overview of the structural links between warfare, society, and politics, and contains a wealth of useful insights which bear directly on the theme of this volume. In particular, Andreski's argument that there are links between social mobility and military activity has important implications in the Roman context.

Social mobility and the Roman army

In the imperial period, the potential importance of service in the Roman army as a means of gaining upward social mobility was clear. An able and courageous soldier could gain promotion to the rank of centurion after fifteen or twenty years' service (Dobson 1970, 101; Maxfield 1981, 243–4), and with it more than five times the pay he would have received in the ranks (Brunt 1950, 67). Between a third and a half of these centurions would go on to become *primipilares* for a year, and with this office became members of the equestrian order. On retirement they would receive a donative of 600,000 sesterces and might then rise to significant positions in the hierarchies of the towns of the empire and even to high equestrian office; their children could enter the senate in the next generation (Dobson 1970, 106–8). Even a comparatively low-ranking soldier could, by astute saving of his annual wages, put by a substantial sum which he could add to his retirement donative and then invest in land: Suetonius reports that Domitian prohibited soldiers from depositing more than 1,000 sesterces in the camp savings bank after Lucius Antonius

Saturninus used the collected savings of two legions to finance a rebellion in AD 89 (Suet. *Dom.* 7; see Watson 1969, 150). The army was thus an important and effective means by which the able might gain upward mobility within society in the imperial period – provided, of course, that soldiers survived until the retirement age, which some 40 per cent may have done.[1] Besides, the fact that in the imperial period soldiers were often of provincial origin (Forni 1953, especially pp. 63–75) meant that military service had the effect of integrating ordinary provincials with Roman citizenship into the structures of the Roman Empire, just as their élite counterparts were integrated into the senate (Hammond 1957; Hopkins and Burton 1983, 184–93); while those who served in the *auxilia* were rewarded with Roman citizenship at the end of their period of service (Saddington 1982, 189–92).

The potential benefits of military service under the Republic (to those who survived) were much less clear or predictable. There are, of course, difficulties in making a comparison, since the body of career inscriptions which forms the major basis of discussion in the imperial period simply does not exist for the Republic (Suolahti 1955, 12). Even so, it seems likely that comparatively few soldiers of the Republic benefited from their military service to the extent that their counterparts under the Empire did. Grants on discharge were the exception rather than the rule; and the position of centurions (a rank which was of major importance in contributing to the role of the imperial army as a channel for upward mobility) was rather different in the army of the Republic (Dobson 1970, 115; 1974, 393–5). When a soldier volunteered or was conscripted into the army, it was for a specific campaign rather than a specific number of years. The increasing size of Rome's empire in the second century BC meant that it became increasingly uncommon for soldiers to return home immediately after a campaign (which was more than likely to involve service overseas), but it was not likely to be for longer than six years on any particular occasion. If the demobilized soldier was called upon at a later date (returned veterans formed part of the reserve

[1] Corbier 1977, 216–20, estimates that between a third and a half of soldiers joining the imperial army would have survived to claim their discharge bonus.

for a period of sixteen years: Keppie 1984, 34), the military rank he gained on the first occasion did not necessarily continue into his next term of service. This meant that it was much more difficult to build a coherent career in the army of the Republic, which saw itself as a citizens' militia, than in the army of the Empire. Even when a soldier gained the centurionate by advancing through the ranks, the differentials in terms of pay between rankers and centurions were much less notable than they were under the Empire; centurions received only twice the pay of ordinary soldiers, probably until the time of Julius Caesar (Polyb. 6. 39. 12; see Brunt 1950, 67).

However, it was possible for those with a particular enthusiasm and aptitude for military service who volunteered regularly for service to build a quasi-professional career with the legions. Livy (42. 32–4) describes an episode which demonstrates this. When the consuls of 171 BC were enrolling soldiers, they assigned to the ranks twenty-three ex-centurions who had volunteered their services. The ex-centurions complained to the tribunes of the *plebs* about this treatment, and Livy provides us with a speech allegedly made by one of them, Spurius Ligustinus, who describes his military career under numerous different commanders, in the course of which he was promoted to the rank of *primus pilus* on no less than four occasions. The implication is that these soldiers expected their previous service to be taken into consideration when ranks were being allotted.

In his account of the recruitment in 171 BC Livy observes that many of the volunteers who came forward did so because they saw that those who had served in earlier campaigns in the East had become rich. Certainly a soldier could, if he was lucky, acquire substantial amounts of booty (Harris 1979, 102–4), but the length of time he would normally be obliged to serve away from home might well mean that he would find himself competing on the open market to buy land to replace his original property. Any social advancement would be largely accidental, or due to his expertise at farming the land acquired with his loot, rather than as a direct (or predictable) result of his military activities, unless, like Spurius Ligustinus and his twenty-two colleagues, he devoted himself to long-term military service.

Social mobility and colonial settlement in the early second century

There is one notable exception to this general pattern suggesting that service in the armies of the Republic was unlikely to lead to significant upward social mobility: the phenomenon of colonization in the third and (particularly) second centuries BC. Between 200 and 177 BC, 15 Roman colonies and 4 Latin colonies were established in Italy, with the primary function of providing a Roman presence in areas which had recently been conquered, and the secondary consequence of exporting some of the Roman population to the fringes of the territory under Roman control. The amount of land allocated to a settler in a Latin colony was considerably greater than that allocated to a settler in a citizen colony: for example, colonists sent to the Latin colony at Bononia in 189 BC were allocated 70 *iugera* (if *equites*) or 50 *iugera* (if of other ranks) (Livy, 37. 57. 8), whereas those sent to the neighbouring citizen colony at Mutina in 183 BC received only 5 *iugera* each (Livy, 39. 55. 6). The explanation seems to be that the larger allocations at Latin colonies were (in part at least) to compensate the settlers for loss of political rights at Rome, since the Latin colonies were independent communities (Tibiletti 1950, 219–32; Salmon 1969, 95–111; Gabba and Pasquinucci 1979, 19–20, 34). As a result, membership of a Latin colony could mean a considerable increase in wealth for a member of the *plebs*; and since Latin colonies were intended as self-governing bastions against Rome's enemies the Romans sought to create for them a timocratic governmental system like that of Rome itself. Consequently, even larger grants were given to settlers of equestrian rank: at Thurii in 193 BC, *equites* received 40 *iugera* and *pedites* 20 *iugera* (Livy, 35. 9. 7), and in the following year at Vibo *equites* received 30 *iugera* and *pedites* 20 (Livy, 35. 40. 5). However, even a grant of 5 *iugera*, and in addition the right to exploit collective pastures, might have been attractive to the poorest peasants. It seems likely that many of the colonists sent to these towns were ex-soldiers: this was particularly likely in the case of Latin colonies in strategic locations like Placentia or Cremona, both founded in 218 BC in land recently taken from the Boii (Polyb. 3. 40; Tac. *Hist.* 3. 34). At Aquileia, situated in an isolated position at the head of the Adriatic, the terms of settlement were particularly generous: 140 *iugera* were allotted to *equites*, 50 to *pedites*, and, unusually, a separate figure of 100 *iugera* was designated for centurions (Livy, 40. 34. 2).

To some extent, then, the colonial settlements of the early second century provided a route to upward social mobility (Garnsey 1975–6, 229); but at the cost to the beneficiaries of losing either legally (in the case of the Latin colonies), or in practice (in the case of the more distant citizen colonies) the rights and privileges of Roman citizenship.

Social mobility and colonial settlement in the civil war period

Andreski (1968, 134–8), following Sorokin (1957, 466–71), suggests that social mobility is most likely to be a consequence of warfare where it leads to dislocation of social structure in the areas affected, and in particular if it results in conquest and enslavement of the defeated populations. More specifically, military action leads to a shake-up within the leadership of an army, whereby the most able gain positions of authority, but the incompetent are removed from their commands. The latter assertion may be doubtful for the Roman period, since it has recently been argued that unsuccessful Roman generals suffered no particular disruption in their careers (Rosenstein 1990), and in any case the distinction between 'war' and 'peace' implied by Andreski's point here is irrelevant for the situation in Republican Rome, where the army was almost constantly in action. However, it seems highly likely that the influx of slaves into central Italy in the second century BC played a major part in the changing relationship between peasant agriculture and military service (Hopkins 1978, 1–64); and the civil wars seem to have caused massive dislocation within Italian society, for casualties were severe, and the victims mostly Italians (40,000 at Philippi, for example: Brunt 1971a, 487–8). The Social War and the struggle between Marius and Sulla were fought out in Italy itself, with widespread destruction in the areas affected; the losses involved, both human and financial, are graphically illustrated by the number of coin hoards found from these periods (Crawford 1969; Brunt 1971a, 285–93). But disaster for some meant advancement for others. The chief beneficiaries were the soldiers of the armies

who fought in the civil wars; the potential for advancement
offered by the civil wars (and the aspirations of the soldiers) is
demonstrated by the events in Sicily in 36 BC, after Octavian's
victory at the battle of Naulochus. Octavian's army mutinied and
demanded discharge on terms equal to those who had fought at
Philippi. In an attempt to mollify the soldiers (and, incidentally,
to drive a wedge between legionaries and more senior officers),
Octavian offered purple-bordered togas and the rank of *decuriones* in their home cities to the centurions. 'While he was distribut-
ing other awards of this kind, the tribune Ofillius exclaimed that
crowns and purple garments were playthings for boys, that the
rewards for soldiers were loot and money. The multitude cried out
"well said"' (App. *BCiv*. 5. 128; cf. Dio, 49. 34). Veterans clearly
hoped for land grants, cash donatives and could even aspire to
municipal office. How did this come about?

During the Second Punic War soldiers had occasionally been
given small plots of land on discharge following years of service
abroad (Gabba 1976, 39), and veterans are likely to have been
among the settlers in Latin and citizen colonies, but the distribution of land to veterans became more of a contentious issue at the
very beginning of the first century BC, following the victories of
Gaius Marius over Jugurtha and then the Cimbri and Teutones.

Traditionally, it has been thought that an increasingly serious
shortage of manpower led Marius in 107 BC to recruit soldiers
from the poorest section of the Roman population, the *capite
censi*; as a result, land had to be found for them on their
demobilization, because, unlike normal recruits, they had no
estates to which they could be expected to return on leaving the
army (Gabba 1976, 41; Mann 1983, 1). However, Rich (1983, 323–
6) has recently cast doubt on the veracity of this supposed
manpower crisis, instead emphasizing that Marius' recruits from
the *capite censi* were willing volunteers, whose enrolment won
Marius further popularity; while others have stressed that the bulk
of the army continued to be recruited from the rural peasantry
even after Marius' initiative (e.g. Gabba 1976, 14–15; Brunt 1988,
253–6; Keppie 1984, 61–3). As a result, the origin of designated
land grants for army veterans has to be ascribed to Marius'
political influence and authority rather than any increased need
for land allocations (Brunt 1971b, 99).

In 103 the tribune Saturninus proposed that Marius' veterans be awarded land grants, and, despite Saturninus' assassination in 100, these grants may well have taken place (Crawford 1974, 629–30; Brunt 1988, 278–80). Sulla followed this example, settling veterans on confiscated land in areas which had been loyal to his opponent Marius (Harris 1971, 251–98; Brunt 1971a, 300–12; Gabba 1976, 44). But the most substantial settlements of veterans took place at the initiative of Caesar, the triumvirs, and Augustus, before in 13 BC Augustus introduced cash donatives to replace the land distributions (Dio, 54. 25. 6; Corbier 1977; Keppie 1983, 208). In AD 6 a new treasury, the *aerarium militare*, was created to pay for these donatives, which had previously come from Augustus' own funds (Dio, 55. 25. 2). It has been estimated that between 47 and 14 BC more than 130,000 soldiers received allocations of land in Italy (Keppie 1983, ix).

The amount of land granted to individual veterans was often decided on the basis of their rank within the legion, as had occurred at Aquileia in 181 BC. The triumvirs in particular were keen to settle members of a legion together, and Tacitus (*Ann.* 14. 27) observes that this was how colonies were set up in the 'old days, when entire legions – with tribunes, centurions, legionaries in their proper centuries – were so transplanted as to create, by their unanimity and their comradeship, a little commonwealth'. Keppie (1983, 91–2) suggests that a problematic passage of the *Liber Coloniarum* (214. 14–15) about Volaterrae may indicate that Caesarian legionaries received allotments of 25 *iugera* there, and centurions 50 *iugera*; if that is correct, it is likely that in triumviral colonies, centurions would receive twice the normal allocation of 50 *iugera* (Keppie 1983, 124). An estate of 100 *iugera* was equivalent in size to those discussed by Cato in his *De Agricultura* (1. 7), which would make the owner a comparatively wealthy man in his community; Foxhall (1990, 104) has recently suggested that veterans may have acted as tenants on the estates of their former centurions. In addition to the land allotment, a centurion might well have acquired substantial quantities of booty in the course of his campaigns: it was notorious that standards of discipline were likely to slip in the course of a civil war. This liquid wealth might well be used to buy nearby plots of land either from other veterans or from members of the original population of the community where the colony had been founded. So centurions and tribunes were able in this way to acquire the wealth that would enable them to engage in the lifestyle of the municipal aristocracy; while their position within the hierarchy of the legion gave them also the moral authority to take the lead in municipal life. Keppie (1983, 104–12) refers to several examples of centurions and tribunes whose subsequent careers as municipal magistrates are attested by inscriptions in colonies such as Ateste and Beneventum. The fact that many new *municipia* developed in Italy during the years after the Social War (Gabba 1972) will also have been a significant factor in this process; not all the veterans were settled in colonies (Keppie 1983, 1; Brunt 1971, 300), and the more towns there were in Italy, the more opportunities there will have been for the ambitious to serve as *decuriones* on their local senates.

During the civil wars, as in the developed military structure of the imperial period, we find the rank of centurion playing an important role as a route to upward social mobility. This seems to be a consequence of the gradual 'professionalization' of the army, a development which can be traced back to the career of Spurius Ligustinus, but which accelerated with the opportunities for long-term service offered by the exceptional commands of Caesar (in Gaul) and Pompey (in the East), as well as the civil wars themselves. It also seems likely that the relationship between commander and centurions became closer during this period, as appointment by tribunes was replaced by direct appointment by the commander himself (Harmand 1967, 328–9). In this way, the centurions, who had a major influence on the morale of the legion as a whole, became more closely dependent on the commander as an individual, and as a result became locked into what was effectively a relationship of patronage with him, prefiguring the relationship of military officers and emperor under the Empire (Gabba 1976, 26–7). Lawrence Stone (1966, 38), writing on the early modern period, has stressed the importance of patronage as a means of gaining upward social mobility; the increasingly close relationship between the generals of the first century BC and their centurions can be seen as a good example of this. So the career prospects of centurions improved, and they benefited in financial terms too: although Caesar doubled the pay of his legionaries, the pay of the centurions increased by a far greater proportion – as we have seen, centurions' pay came to be five times that of the ordinary legionaries.

Social mobility and political structures

According to Andreski (1968, 137), high social mobility can be characteristic of a monocratic society, in which the ruler endeavours to promote those loyal to him regardless of their social status. The link between the institution of the principate and the encouragement of upward social mobility is clear: the most obvious example is that of the imperial freedmen who gained such prestige under the Julio-Claudians (Weaver 1967), and in general patronage became correspondingly more important within Roman society (Brunt 1988, 439). Hopkins has drawn attention to the struggle for power between emperor and senate as a major factor encouraging social mobility within the Roman Empire, together with the increasing structural differentiation of Roman society.[1]

By contrast, a low level of social mobility is for Andreski (loc. cit.) characteristic of an oligarchic society, which is trying to exclude the masses from its ruling élite. Is it correct to see the Republic as a society lacking in opportunities for social mobility?

Recent studies of the Roman élite by Brunt (1982) and by Hopkins and Burton (1983) have suggested that the exclusivity of the Roman aristocracy was more apparent than real. Badian (1990) has, however, drawn attention to the high proportion of consuls during the period 179–49 BC whose fathers or grandfathers had themselves been consuls, suggesting that the very highest offices were indeed under the control of the *nobiles*. What is less evident, however, is any mechanism for social advancement for the freeborn below equestrian rank, apart from the programme of colonization in the second century BC. This did allow some social mobility for those below the élite by granting quite large estates to members of the Roman peasantry; but it also – and crucially – had the effect of removing them from political life at Rome, and thus minimizing the effect on the social and political structures of Rome of these examples of advancement. Those who settled in Latin colonies lost their Roman citizenship as a matter of course; those who settled in citizen colonies were often too distant from Rome to be able to engage in political activity in any meaningful

---

[1] Hopkins 1965, 16–22; 1978, 74–96. For a general study of social mobility in the imperial period, see Pleket 1971.

way. The exception here was the granting, probably in 124 BC in the aftermath of the revolt of Fregellae, of the Roman citizenship to those who were magistrates in the Latin colonies (Tibiletti 1953, 54–8). It was characteristic of the Romans to give special encouragement to the élites of the towns of Italy, and it is not surprising that men from Latin colonies such as Brundisium and Aquileia are among the first Italians in the Senate (Wiseman 1971, 29). Local aristocrats could be encouraged without subverting the hierarchies at Rome to any significant degree. However, the last Latin colony was founded in 181, and between 177 and 128 it seems likely that no colonies were founded at all,[1] thus eliminating even this limited avenue of mobility for the peasantry.

Social theorists at various points on the political spectrum have stressed the importance of social mobility in maintaining continuity in a society and discouraging revolution; Marx (quoted by Heath 1981, 13) stated that 'the more a ruling class is able to assimilate the foremost minds of a ruled class, the more stable and dangerous becomes its rule', and he was followed by Sorokin (1957, 533). It could be argued that the failure of the traditional Republican system to provide any such means of advancement below the level of the landed élite was one cause of its downfall. Colonial settlements combined military practicality with a means of allowing social mobility within the traditional hierarchies of the Roman state by banishing its beneficiaries to distant regions of Italy; but the cessation of colonial activity removed this safety-valve from the Roman system at a crucial time when the tensions resulting from imperial expansion were already building up. Stone (1972, 9) has argued that what he terms 'revolutionary situations', which destabilize the established order in societies and can (but need not necessarily) lead to revolution, may be caused by rapid economic growth and imperial conquest. This picture fits well with the situation at Rome in the mid-second century BC; the expansion of empire led to an influx of wealth into Italy, much of it into the hands of the Roman élite, and the investment of this wealth in land and the exploitation of slaves captured during years of continual warfare gradually transformed the economy of much of central Italy. For those peasants who were displaced as a

---

[1] Vell. 1. 15. 3 dates the colony at Auximum to 157 BC, but Salmon 1963, 4–13 (whom I follow here), argues for an alternative date of 128 BC.

result of these developments, there were few potential alternatives available. From the 170s onwards the numbers of soldiers in the field decreased, so the scope for long-term military service was reduced (Hopkins 1978, 33); and the long-drawn-out campaigns against the Spaniards in the latter part of the century were not as lucrative as those in the East had been (Harris 1979, 49–50; Rich 1983, 318). Hence the land issue came to be a major focus of political debate at Rome, and the initiatives of first Tiberius and then Gaius Gracchus had a lasting effect both on agrarian policy in particular and politics in general. When colonization was revived in the 120s, it was in the context of Gracchan proposals to provide land for the poor of Rome, rather than having an overtly military rationale (Stockton 1979, 132–7).

Meanwhile tensions were beginning to grow in a political system which had once been closely integrated with the military structure on which it relied for its security but from which it was now becoming increasingly detached. The growth of Rome's power in Italy meant that by the second century the soldiers who formed Rome's armies tended to come not from the city itself but from more distant areas of the *ager Romanus*, from where it was difficult to attend political assemblies; or indeed from the allied communities who provided military contingents but were not involved in political activity at Rome at all (Ilari 1974, 147–73; Brunt 1988, 253–5). The problem was aggravated with the enfranchisement of the Italians by the *lex Iulia* in 90 BC; as a result of this law the Italians were theoretically equal citizens, but the further away they lived from Rome, the less likely they were to be able to participate in politics. Under the Empire, the link between military service and political activity was broken altogether.

To summarize, the expansion of the Roman state was not accompanied by the increased social flexibility which would have allowed it to survive the impact of its transformation into an imperial state; rather, one of the few means of access to social mobility was removed at a time of potential instability. The latter years of the Republic saw the relationship between military organization and political and social structure become increasingly strained; eventually effective routes to social mobility reappeared, in the form of land distributions to veterans, but these were now linked directly to long-term military service in the armies of the dynasts, and the ambitions of these generals were to bring down the Republic in the process.

Veteran settlement and social change

In *Total War and Social Change* and his other work, Marwick adopts a broad definition of 'social change', which, he argues, can involve changes in social geography, social structure, customs and behaviour, art and culture, and a variety of other developments within a society (e.g. Marwick 1988, xiv). On this analysis, the consequences of the civil wars and the veteran settlements of the first century BC undoubtedly show social change on a large scale taking place within Italy.

Perhaps most dramatic in its impact was the programme of colonial settlements. We know of about fifty settlements with colonial status founded in the period between 47 and 14 BC in Italy alone, to which must be added viritane settlements in Italy, and many more colonies overseas (Keppie 1983, 4; Mann 1983, 1–11). Land distribution schemes transformed the landscape of much of Italy, making vast tracts of the countryside into regular squares and rectangles as a permanent reminder of the civil wars and the initiative of commanders on behalf of the soldiers of the Roman army.[1] These soldiers had been recruited from all over Italy, and their transferral, often after many years of service, to a completely different part of the peninsula, had a significant cultural impact, for example transforming local practices of burial and commemoration (Beard and Crawford 1985, 83–4; expanded in Crawford, forthcoming), and encouraging the proliferation of more standardized tomb-monuments such as those with Doric friezes documented by Torelli (1968) in many areas of central and southern Italy. Their arrival also transformed local agricultural structures, as large estates were divided up into small farms for veterans or peasants were evicted from their smallholdings (as field survey has revealed in the territory of Lucus Feroniae, for example: Jones 1973, 283; Potter 1979, 132; Crawford 1980, 497–8). Meanwhile, the towns of Italy benefited from the competitive

[1]   Chouquer *et al.* 1987, especially pp. 251–5. See Purcell 1990 for the symbolic impact of centuriation.

urges of the veterans and the generosity of the *princeps* and acquired civic amenities and monumental public buildings (Keppie 1983, 114–22). Centurions and *primipilares* exploited their new-found wealth to gain access to local and central aristocracies. As Syme put it (1939, 453), 'the Principate itself may, in a certain sense, be regarded as a triumph of Italy over Rome'.

The impact of all these developments on the Italian peninsula can hardly be overestimated, and I would argue that the developments apparent in late first-century BC Italy confirm strikingly Marwick's thesis that major conflict (involving high levels of military participation and widespread suffering on the part of the population as a whole) is likely to lead to major social change. Finley (1986) has argued convincingly that 'revolution' is an unsatisfactory conceptual tool for use in analysing the fall of the Roman Republic. Exploring the concept of military participation and the links between war and social change, is by contrast, as Brunt, Gabba, and others have shown, essential to understanding the fall of the Roman Republic. 'As states change their nature, so will their policy change, and so will their wars' (Howard 1976, 76) is a maxim as true of ancient Rome as of the medieval or modern periods.[1]

Bibliography

Andreski, S. (1968), *Military Organization and Society*, 2nd edn (London).
Badian, E. (1990), 'The consuls, 179–49 BC', *Chiron*, 20: 371–413.
Beard, M., and Crawford, M. H. (1985), *Rome in the Late Republic* (London).
Brunt, P. A. (1950), 'Pay and superannuation in the Roman army', *PBSR* 18: 50–71.
—— (1971a), *Italian Manpower 225 BC–AD 14* (Oxford).
—— (1971b), *Social Conflicts in the Roman Republic* (London).
—— (1982), '*Nobilitas* and *novitas*', *JRS* 72: 1–17.
——(1988), *The Fall of the Roman Republic and Related Essays* (Oxford).

[1] I am very grateful to Michael Crawford, Lawrence Keppie and John Rich for their comments on an earlier draft of this chapter. Errors which remain are, of course, my own responsibility.

Chouquer G., *et al.* (1987), *Structures agraires en Italie centro-méridionale: cadastres et paysages ruraux* (Rome).

Corbier, M. (1977), 'L'aerarium militare', in *Armées et fiscalité dans le monde antique* (Paris), ch. 10 (pp. 197–234).

Crawford, M. H. (1969), 'Coin-hoards and the pattern of violence in the Late Republic', *PBSR* 37: 76–81.

—— (1974), *Roman Republican Coinage* (Cambridge).

——(1980), review of Potter (1979), *Athenaeum*, 68: 497–8.

—— (forthcoming), 'Italy and Rome from Sulla to Augustus', in *CAH*² ix.

De Sanctis, G. (1907), *Storia dei Romani*, ii (Turin).

Dobson, B. (1970), 'The centurionate and social mobility during the principate', in C. Nicolet (ed.), *Recherches sur les structures sociales dans l'antiquité classique* (Paris), ch. 7 (pp. 99–116).

—— (1974), 'The significance of the centurion and *primipilaris* in the Roman army and administration', *ANRW* ii. 1. 392–434.

Edmonds, M. (1988), *Armed Services and Society* (Leicester).

Finley, M. I. (1986), 'Revolution in antiquity', in R. Porter and M. Teich (eds), *Revolution in History*, ch. 2 (pp. 47–60).

Forni, G. (1953), *Il reclutamento delle legioni da Augusto a Diocleziano* (Milan).

Foxhall, L. (1990), 'The dependent tenant: landleasing and labour in Italy and Greece', *JRS* 80: 97–114.

Gabba, E. (1972), 'Urbanizzazione e rinnovamenti urbanistici nell' Italia centro-meridionale del I sec. a.C.', *Studi classici e orientali*, 21: 73–112.

—— (1976), *Republican Rome, the Army and the Allies*, trans. P. J. Cuff (Oxford).

—— and Pasquinucci, M. (1979), *Strutture agrarie e allevamento transumante nell' Italia romana* (Pisa).

Garnsey, P. (1975–6), 'Peasants in ancient Roman society', *Journal of Peasant Studies*, 3: 221–35.

Hammond, M. (1957), 'Composition of the senate AD 68–235', *JRS* 47: 74–81.

Harmand, J. (1967), *L'Armée et le soldat à Rome de 107 à 50 avant notre ère* (Paris).

Harris, W. V. (1971), *Rome in Etruria and Umbria* (Oxford).

—— (1979), *War and Imperialism in Republican Rome 327–70 BC* (Oxford).

Heath, A. (1981), *Social Mobility* (London).

Hopkins, M. K. (1965), 'Elite mobility in the Roman empire', *Past and Present*, 32: 12–26.

—— (1978), *Conquerors and Slaves* (Cambridge).

—— and Burton, G. D. (1983), 'Political succession in the Late Republic (249–50 BC)' and 'Ambition and withdrawal; the senatorial aristocracy under the emperors', in M. K. Hopkins, *Death and Renewal* (Cambridge), chs 2–3 (pp. 31–200).

Howard, M. (1976), *War in European History* (London).

Ilari, V. (1974), *Gli Italici nelle strutture militari romane* (Milan).

Jones, G. D. B. (1973), 'Civil war and society in southern Etruria', in M. R. D. Foot (ed.), *War and Society: Historical Essays in Memory of J. R. Western* (London), ch. 17 (pp. 277–87).

Keppie, L. (1983), *Colonization and Veteran Settlement in Italy, 47–14 BC* (London).

—— (1984), *The Making of the Roman Army: From Republic to Empire* (London).

Mann, J. C. (1983), *Legionary Recruitment and Veteran Settlement* (Institute of Archaeology Occasional Publications, 7; London).

Marwick, A. (1965), *The Deluge* (London).

—— (1968), *Britain in the Century of Total War* (London).

—— (1974), *War and Social Change in the Twentieth Century* (London).

—— (ed. 1988), *Total War and Social Change* (London).

—— (1990), *War, Peace and Social Change in Europe 1900–55* (Buckingham).

Maxfield, V. A. (1981), *The Military Decorations of the Roman Army* (London).

Nicolet, C. (1980), *The World of the Citizen in Republican Rome* (London).

Pleket, H. W. (1971), 'Sociale stratificatie en sociale mobiliteit in de Romeinse keizertijd', *Tijdschrift voor geschiedenis*, 84: 215–51.

Potter, T. W. (1979), *The Changing Landscape of South Etruria* (London).

Purcell, N. (1990), 'The creation of provincial landscape: the Roman impact on Cisalpine Gaul', in T. Blagg and M. Millett (eds), *The Early Roman Empire in the West* (Oxford), ch. 1 (pp. 7–29).

Reid, A. (1988), 'World War I and the working class in Britain', in A. Marwick (ed.), *Total War and Social Change* (London), ch. 2 (pp. 16–24).

Rich, J. W. (1983), 'The supposed Roman manpower shortage of the later second century BC', *Historia*, 32: 287–331.

Rosenstein, N. S. (1990), *Imperatores Victi: Military Defeat and Aristocratic Competition in the Middle and Late Republic* (Berkeley, Los Angeles and Oxford).

Saddington, D. B. (1982), *The Development of the Roman Auxiliary Forces from Caesar to Vespasian* (Harare).

Salmon, E. T. (1963), 'The *coloniae maritimae*', *Athenaeum*, 41: 3–38.

—— (1969), *Roman Colonization under the Republic* (London).

Sorokin, P. (1957), *Social and Cultural Mobility* (New York).

Stockton, D. (1979), *The Gracchi* (Oxford).

Stone, L. (1966) 'Social mobility in England 1500–1700', *Past and Present*, 33: 16–55.

—— (1972), *The Causes of the English Revolution 1529–1642* (London).

Suolahti, J. (1955), *The Junior Officers of the Roman Army in the Republican Period* (Annales Academiae Scientiarum Fennicae, 97; Helsinki).

Syme, R. (1939), *The Roman Revolution* (Oxford).

Tibiletti, G. (1950), 'Ricerche di storia agraria romana', *Athenaeum*, 28: 183–266.

—— (1953), 'La politica delle colonie e città latine nella guerra sociale', *Rendiconti dell'Istituto Lombardo di Scienze e Lettere*, 86: 45–63.

Torelli, M. (1968), 'Monumenti funerari romani con fregio dorico', *Dialoghi di archeologia*, 2: 32–54.

Toynbee, A. (1966), *Hannibal's Legacy* (Oxford).

Watson, G. (1969), *The Roman Soldier* (London).

Weaver, P. R. C. (1967), 'Social mobility in the early Roman Empire; the evidence of the imperial freedmen and slaves', *Past and Present*, 37: 3–20; = M. I. Finley (ed.), *Studies in Ancient Society* (London, 1974), ch. 6 (pp. 121–40).

Wiseman, T. P. (1971), *New Men in the Roman Senate 139 BC–AD 14* (Oxford).

∞ 5 ∞

Roman poetry
and anti-militarism

Duncan Cloud

This chapter has two parts, the first sceptical and the second more positive. In view of persisting attempts to treat Augustan personal poetry as in some sense autobiographical and to elicit from it evidence for an anti-militarist counter-culture opposed in this respect as well as others to Augustan ideology, it seems timely to rehearse in language rather less flamboyant than that of Veyne (1988) the compelling reasons for treating such attempts with great reserve.[1] In the second part I shall take a neglected text in Ennius with *prima facie* anti-militarist content, and plot its subsequent fortunes in ancient literature.

Make love, not war

The naive view that the speaker in Roman elegy is simply pouring out streams of autobiographical material, mainly about his sex life, has, I hope, no longer any proponents, although the cele-brated paper of Allen (1962) reminds us that quite recently the game of plotting the development of Propertius' affair with Cynthia was still being zestfully played. However, a version of the autobiographical game is still alive and kicking, as Stahl (1985)

---

[1] Similar arguments might be used against Hallett 1973, who sees counter-cultural feminism in the elegists. See Wyke 1989a.

demonstrates.[1] Ranged against it is the picture of the elegist as deft manipulator and romanizer of Hellenistic *topoi* and rhetorical techniques, presented by, for example, Cairns (1979a). I do not contend that the Roman elegists are solely engaged in playing Roman games with themes derived from Hellenistic poetry or their Roman predecessors and contemporaries; there is, I would argue, a constant interplay between their games with genre-themes and the Roman situation, which will at times involve some autobiographical elements. But such controls as we possess suggest that we should not equate the fictional history of the speaker in a book of elegiac poetry with the history of its creator; so, if it can be shown that anti-militarism as a theme of personal poetry has Greek antecedents and if there is no evidence for an anti-militarist counter-culture outside the Augustan elegists themselves, then we lack sufficient ground for postulating that such a counter-culture really existed. The poets provide the only evidence, nor would anyone deny the Greek roots of the anti-war stance; for Callimachus it is part, even emblematic, of his rejection of epic in favour of the smaller more intimate genres (*Aetia*, fr. 1 Pfeiffer). The fact that throughout his long literary career Callimachus enjoyed royal patronage is enough to show that the Alexandrian reader was perfectly capable of drawing a distinction between literary and court politics. There is reason to think that things were no different in Augustan Rome and that Ovid's exile was, as he himself states, a striking exception to Augustus' usual treatment of poets.[2]

What controls are there which suggest that statements made by the speaker in the course of a Roman personal poem are pseudo-autobiographical? First, we can isolate specific pseudo-autobiographical *topoi*. Although Seneca makes outrageously false statements about the climate of Corsica in *Helv.* 6 and 7 (Pierini 1980, 127), we cannot conclude that he had never been there, for other evidence confirms that he *was* exiled to that island (Dio, 60. 8; Tac. *Ann.* 12. 8); it merely confirms our suspicion that complaints about the badness of the weather are a *topos* of exilic writing.

---

[1] For a surprisingly sympathetic review see Wyke 1989b, 170–3.
[2] *Tr.* 2. 447–70 (cited in part below). Raaflaub and Samons 1990 argue cogently that there is no compelling evidence for systematic opposition to Augustus of any kind.

Consequently, when Ovid traduces the Black Sea summer weather, this is not evidence that he never went to Tomis; it merely shows that he knew what was expected of a literary exile.[1]

Second, we can bring to bear any independent evidence we may possess about the lives and attitudes of a poet and contrast it with what the poet-speaker says of himself in the poems. However, the use of ancient biographical material needs to be undertaken with great caution; what Lefkowitz (1980) has demonstrated in the case of Greek literary lives often applies to the late biographies of Roman poets. These can be constructions based solely on what one might charitably term an ingenious reading of the poems; failure to recognize this has led, for example, to Highet's grotesque ascription, given wide currency by Peter Green's Penguin Classics introduction, of a Dostoyevskian or Dickensian career to Juvenal (Highet 1954, 4–41; Green 1967, 10–22). However, such criticisms do not apply to all the Roman lives; for instance, the ancient life of the satirist Persius contains a very large number of specific facts that are not derived from the poems (like the day of the poet's birth and death) and material which shows such a detailed knowledge of the mid-first century AD that it cannot possibly be a late fiction. The same is true of surviving biographies from Suetonius' *De Poetis*. Occasionally, too, there is reliable material in other sources.

Our first task, then, must be to look at external attestation for the lives of the elegiac poets and, though this is scanty and must be approached with circumspection, it does suggest that for Tibullus and possibly for Propertius too the poets' lives and behaviour were different from those of 'Tibullus' and 'Propertius' in their poems.[2] A life of Tibullus attached to the most reliable of the manuscripts is held by a few scholars to have no independent value (e.g. Postgate 1903, 179–84; Goold 1988, 187). However, the sceptics are probably wrong; two of its statements are not only not

---

[1] *Tr.* 3. 10; *Pont.* 1. 3. 50. On the relationship between Seneca's and Ovid's climatic observations, see Pierini 1980, 126–8; Gahan 1984–5, 146. For the poetic functions of Ovid's distortions of reality, see Besslich 1979 and Helzle 1988.

[2] By 'Tibullus', 'Propertius', 'Ovid', etc., I mean the poet-speaker in the poems whose views, behaviour, and history may or may not be identical with those of their author, but should not be assumed to be so.

derived from anything in the poems but are out of keeping with
the characterization of 'Tibullus', namely that Messalla Corvinus
awarded Tibullus a prize for valour, *militaria dona*, in the
Aquitanian war, and that the poet was a member of the equestrian
order.

A further detail from Horace may be thought not only to
confirm the latter assertion indirectly but to provide the strongest
evidence that there are differences between Tibullus and
'Tibullus'. Horace addresses an ode (1. 33) and an epistle (1. 4) to
an Albius (according to the manuscripts and the life, the gentile
name of Tibullus) who writes elegies (*Odes*, 1. 33. 2–3) and is rich
(*Epist*. 1. 4. 7). By contrast, 'Tibullus' is constantly harping on his
humble circumstances. To this apparent discrepancy scholars[1]
have reacted by supposing either that Horace is addressing
another elegist with the same gentile name, a suggestion that
gratuitously flouts Occam's law, or that riches (*divitiae*) and
humble circumstances (*paupertas*) are not incompatible, a judgement contradicted by 'Tibullus' at the beginning of the first, quasi-
programmatic poem (1. 1–6). These desperate strategies arise from
an inability to accept that 'Tibullus' could be poor and Tibullus
rich, just as translators of Statius go to extraordinary lengths to
avoid making Statius describe Tibullus as rich (*Silv*. 1. 2. 255).

There is, therefore, evidence to suggest that Tibullus the author
was both rich and brave, unlike the poor and passive poet of his
elegies; consequently we should not accept anything that 'Tibullus'
says about himself as being *ipso facto* true of the poet who
invented him. Putnam (1973, 9) senses in Tibullus 'an unwilling
warrior with an intense dislike of war' and Lyne (1980, 75),
apropos of the *militia amoris* motif (military service as a metaphor
for love), asserts that the elegists used it 'to declare their dissocia-
tion from war. The conventional world made wars and war was
frightful; "war" existed in the life of love and was something other,
and more or less delightful.' In fact, however, Tibullus as anti-
militarist is one of the most suspect items in the dossier, because
(1) the Life makes Tibullus courageous enough to win the Roman
equivalent of the DSO; (2) there are enough precedents in Greek
poetry to make the poet's rejection of wealth and war a generic

---

[1]   Murgatroyd 1980, 2, gives references.

ploy;[1] (3) the speaker of the poems draws a distinction between himself and his patron Messalla: war is a suitable occupation for Messalla, but not for himself (1. 1. 53–6); the fictional 'Tibullus' is certainly an unwilling warrior, but his intense dislike of war is a personal option, not a prescription for all his fellow Romans.

Having shown that there is no real evidence to be derived from the poetry of Tibullus for the existence of an anti-militarist counter-culture in Augustan Rome, we turn next to Propertius. Of the three elegiac poets it is Propertius who is most frequently made out to be a genuine critic of Augustan militarism and indeed of Augustan ideology generally (e.g. Lyne 1980, 77; Stahl 1985). Admittedly, attempts to distinguish Propertius' views from those of the speaker in the elegies run into two difficulties that do not arise in the same acute form in the case of Tibullus. First, there is very little by way of materials in other genres, let alone a life, that would enable us to construct a different Propertius from the one the poet presents in his poetry. In fact, the only material of even the slightest substance consists of references by the younger Pliny in two of his letters (6. 15; 9. 22) to a descendant of Propertius, Passennus Paulus by name, who also wrote elegies. Pliny's statements that Paulus 'counts Propertius amongst his ancestors' (*Ep.* 6. 15. 1) and 'derives his ancestry from him' (*Ep.* 9. 22. 1) show that the poet married and either fathered or adopted a child (if Paulus had been descended from a bastard of Propertius, Pliny would not have been so fulsome about the connexion). This hint of Propertius living in bourgeois respectability at Assisi hardly accords with the protestations of 'Propertius' that he would rather be decapitated than give up Cynthia for respectable marriage and fatherhood (2. 7. 7–10). A second point may be instructive: for Pliny, Propertius is paramount (*praecipuus*) in elegy and is to elegy what Horace is to lyric (*Ep.* 9. 22. 1–2). Pliny may or may not be expressing his own opinion; what he wants is that future readers will applaud the excellence of his taste, as we can see from *Ep.* 3. 21, where Martial is a source of critical embarrassment (Pliny cannot make up his mind whether or not Martial's reputation will survive and thus enhance the value of the latter's

---

[1]   See Murgatroyd 1980, 48–9, on 1. 1. The attack on the inventor of the sword at the beginning of 1. 10 has similarities with Parthenius, fr. 5 Meineke.

connexion with himself). No such doubts assail Pliny in respect of Propertius. We may therefore assume that cultivated persons at the court of Trajan found nothing bizarre in awarding the palm in elegy to Propertius – such an assessment is not a nineteenth- or twentieth-century aberration. More to our point, Pliny's enthusiasm may also signify that Propertius was regarded as 'safe' and not as a subversive; it is perhaps significant that the names of Ovid and Lucan, unlike those of Horace and Virgil, never occur in Pliny's letters. Ovid, in a poem addressed to the emperor, provides corroboration for the respectability of Propertius as well as Tibullus:

> This (i.e. writing about how to conduct love affairs) did Tibullus no harm, but he is still read and approved; he was famous when you were already *princeps*. You will find the same precepts in charming Propertius and yet he was not grazed by the slightest slur.
>
> (Ovid, *Tr.* 2. 463–6)

Thus the Plinian and Ovidian material does suggest that Propertius himself was regarded as thoroughly respectable and that Augustus found nothing subversive in his verse.

There, however, is a second difficulty in approaching Propertius with an Augustan sensibility. Most modern readers share Pliny's high opinion of the poet. With the achievements of modernist poetry in the first half of this century, his stock, as a supposed modernist before modernism, rose even higher;[1] indeed, it is hardly an exaggeration to say that Ezra Pound with his tendentious adaptations in *Homage to Sextus Propertius* actually created the model of Propertius-as-subversive (cf. Sullivan 1965; 1976, especially pp. 13–14, 24–5). Pound's motive is clear enough; as he wrote in 1931 (Paige 1951, 310),

> [my *Homage*] presents certain emotions as vital to me[2] in 1917, faced with the infinite and ineffable imbecility of the British Empire, as they

---

[1]   Benediktson 1989 carries this trend further than any other scholar. But Hubbard 1974, 1–7, points out that antiquity regarded Propertius as 'a poet of finish, grace, and charm': his reputation as an excitingly difficult writer thus owes more to the appalling state of the manuscript tradition of his elegies than to the poet himself.

[2]   Frequently misquoted as 'men', e.g. by Sullivan 1964, 26.

were to Propertius some centuries earlier, when faced with the infinite
and ineffable imbecility of the Roman Empire.

Moreover, it is tempting for the academic critic/reader to find in a
beloved ancient author a stance congenial to the critic or the
Zeitgeist. Propertius is a natural victim for this approach; not only
do his poems show the generic preference for love over war that
we meet in Tibullus, but elegies 1. 21 and 22 suggest that he was
opposed to Octavian in the Perusine war. Elegy 2. 7 is invoked to
show that Propertius was hostile to Augustus' marriage legislation
and the poet's hostility to war is subsumed under his overall anti-
Augustan attitude. What is more, his poems often sound as if the
poet were reporting a personal experience, not exploiting a *topos*,
and so when, after a sexually explicit account of a night spent with
his girlfriend, Cynthia, he remarks that if every male were as
exhausted by sexual and alcoholic self-indulgence as himself, no
one would have drowned at the battle of Actium (2. 15. 41–6),
some are then tempted to take his comment on Actium as
seriously as they do his exploits in bed (Sullivan 1976, 58; Stahl
1985, 227–8). Now we are not concerned with ways of reading
ancient texts *per se* but only whether the texts provide evidence of
an anti-militarist counter-culture, or even of poets preaching anti-
militarist views. It is not enough to cull anti-militarist statements
from Propertius' poems, if these sentiments are 'sanitized' by
being part of the genre or counterbalanced by poems in praise of
war or set in a poetic context in which there are other signals
dissociating the poem from 'real' life.

Let us begin with elegy 2. 7:

Gavisa est certe sublatam Cynthia legem,
   qua quondam edicta flemus uterque diu,
ni nos divideret: quamvis diducere amantis
   non queat invitos Iuppiter ipse duos.
'At magnus Caesar.' sed magnus Caesar in armis: 5
   devictae gentes nil in amore valent.
nam citius paterer caput hoc discedere collo
   quam possem nuptae perdere more faces,
aut ego transirem tua limina clausa maritus,
   respiciens udis prodita luminibus.   10
a mea tum qualis caneret tibi tibia somnos,

tibia, funesta tristior illa tuba!
unde mihi Parthis[1] natos praebere triumphis?
   nullus de nostro sanguine miles erit.
quod si vera meae comitarem castra puellae,   15
   non mihi sat magnus Castoris iret equus.
hinc etenim tantum meruit mea gloria nomen,
   gloria ad hibernos lata Borysthenidas.
tu mihi sola places: placeam tibi, Cynthia, solus:
   hic erit et patrio nomine pluris amor.   20

Cynthia rejoiced indeed when the law was lifted
At the enactment of which we'd both wept long
In case it should divide us, though Jove himself
Can't separate two lovers against their will.
'But Caesar is mighty.' Caesar is mighty in war:
Nations subdued count for nothing in love.
For sooner could I suffer this head and neck
Dissevered than quench our flame in wedding's rite,
Or pass by as a husband your shut doors,
Looking back wet-eyed at the threshold betrayed.
Oh, then what sleeps the flute would sing to you,
That flute more dismal than the funeral trumpet!
How could I offer sons for Parthian triumphs?
There will be no soldier from my blood.
But if I soldiered in my proper kind
(Beneath my mistress' command), then Castor's horse
Would not be mighty enough for me:
For hence my glory has earned so great a name,
A glory spread as far as the wintry Dnieper.
I like only you: Cynthia, like only me:
This love shall rate more than the name of father.
                           (Prop. 2. 7, trans. W. G. Shepherd)

Although it contains one vigorously anti-militarist statement (14:
'there will be no soldier from my blood'), it is quite preposterous
to take the poem as serious criticism of either Augustus' marriage
legislation or the *princeps'* militarily aggressive foreign policy. I
would not want to go as far as Cairns (1979b) in arguing that, in
terms of the points that the speaker in the poem might have been
expected to make but did not, Augustus would have regarded it as
in a paradoxical way supportive. To me Propertius seems to be

---

[1] Ruhnken's conjecture, accepted by E. A. Barber in the Oxford
Classical Text. However, the MS reading *patriis* ('my country's
triumphs') may well be correct.

doing what Tibullus and himself in their different ways were always doing, namely attaching to an identifiably Roman event or pseudo-event in their own poetic story a piece of their Hellenistic inheritance. He may here also show the influence of Tibullus, Book 1, which, as is now generally accepted, probably appeared between Propertius' first and second books (Murgatroyd 1980, 13–15). The two Hellenistic *topoi* utilized in this poem are the *militia amoris* and the lover-true-to-death themes.[1] The core of the poem, lines 15–18, expresses the first *topos* with the addition that Propertius' fame as a lover (i.e. as a poet of love) has reached the Ukraine. The Roman context is twofold: the reiteration (but in the elegists' characteristic manner) of the familiar Augustan claim to be extending the Roman empire to beyond the boundaries of the civilized world,[2] and second, some withdrawn marriage legislation which would apparently have forced the speaker to marry and to abandon Cynthia.

This legislation in described in a way that cannot possibly be accurate: the *lex Iulia de maritandis ordinibus* which was eventually promulgated in 18 BC did not legally oblige bachelors to marry – it merely placed them under certain disabilities if they did not. Ironically, that statute might have enabled Propertius to marry Cynthia, since it allowed non-senators, perhaps for the first time, to contract valid marriages with freedwomen providing they were not infamous.[3] It is incredible that legislation was ever contemplated that would enforce marriage upon *equites*, the order

---

[1]   Murgatroyd 1975, 60–7, traces the Greek origins of the *militia amoris* motif back to Sappho; he finds the motif much developed by the Hellenistic poets. For examples of unwarlike poet contrasted with man-of-war see Cairns 1972, 13, 15–16. For the fidelity-unto-death motif juxtaposed with the *militia amoris* and man-of-war motifs cf. Tibullus, 1. 1. 53–68, a passage which may have provided Propertius with his starting-point, and parallels cited in Murgatroyd 1980, 48–9, 62–7.

[2]   e.g. Hor. *Odes*, 3. 5. 2–4; Virg. *Aen.* 6. 794–5; Prop. 2. 10.

[3]   Ulpian, fr. 16. 2; *Dig.* 23. 2. 43. For the debate among scholars of the autobiographical school on Cynthia's status, see Stahl 1985, 28, 39–40, 148. Most take her to be a superior *hetaira*, probably superior enough not to qualify as a common prostitute, who would be liable to *infamia* and ineligible for marriage with a knight. Stahl holds that she was a married woman engaged in a liaison with Propertius; if so, she could presumably have divorced her husband and married Propertius anyway.

to which Propertius probably belonged. At most the historical trigger for the poem may have been some preliminary discussion of marriage legislation, which Propertius has used to give a Roman background and a Roman character to his Hellenistic material. For what it is worth, the only evidence outside this poem for dissatisfaction with Augustus' marriage legislation relates to the period after the passing of the *lex Iulia de maritandis ordinibus* in 18 BC, not to a date in the early twenties when the poem was published.[1] If Badian (1985) is right that 'Propertius' is responding as a debtor to the *aerarium* to the abolition of a triumviral tax on celibates, then the poem has even less contact with the real world, since there is nothing in it at all about relief at not having to pay up tax arrears.[2] The structural function of the legislation in the poem is to provide the same kind of antithesis to the lover-faithful-to-death motif (lines 7–8) as does the extension of the Roman empire under Augustus (lines 5–6) to 'Propertius'' claim to have literary admirers in the Ukraine (line 18). This claim, like the reference to Octavian's or Augustus' legislation, is self-evidently a piece of bombastic exaggeration bordering on nonsense and a pointer to the way in which one should take 'Propertius'' declaration that no one from his blood would be a soldier.

I have spent some time on elegy 2. 7, because it is a prime specimen in the repertory of those who wish to represent Propertius as an anti-militarist opponent of Augustus; I hope I have demonstrated that another way of reading the poem is at least as plausible for its Augustan setting. The other elements in the dossier consist either of poems in which the speaker declines on the ground of his own incapacity for epic to forsake love poetry in order to write epic poems on the campaigns of Augustus, or of poems expressing sympathy for the latter's opponents in the civil war. Elegies 3. 1, 3, 4, 5, and 9 fall into the former category; they are all expressions of a preference for a life of love-making and the making of love poetry (in effect the same thing, as the lover is a poet) as against the making of war and war epics. What robs this

[1] See especially Suet. *Aug.* 34. 1, with the discussions of Levi 1951, 48; Carter 1982, 143; Badian 1985, 83–4, 91–2.
[2] This point is missed by Goold 1990, 139 n. 2, who accepts Badian's explanation.

attitude of any political significance is the fact that Horace, a 'safe' establishment figure, adopts an analogous position (e.g. *Sat*. 2. 1. 10–20; *Epist*. 2. 1. 250–9), and then in his own way celebrates the achievements of the regime. For the poet to express a preference for the smaller, less public, forms of poetry is standard after Callimachus. The Augustan reader would expect the refusal or *recusatio*; he would be surprised, perhaps even impressed, by the artfulness with which nonetheless the poet flatters the *princeps* and his military achievements.[1]

Much is made by Stahl and like-minded predecessors of 1. 21 and 22 (e.g. Fedeli 1980, 485–8, 496–9; Stahl 1985, 99–129). 1. 22. 3–8 speaks of the slaughter in the Perusine War of 41 BC between Octavian and L. Antonius, mentioning that the dead included a kinsman of Propertius. 1. 21 is a sympathetic treatment of Gallus, a dying soldier on Antonius' side, possibly to be identified with Propertius' kinsman. However, admitting support for Octavian's opponents was not an act of bravado; Horace, whose Augustan credentials are impeccable, never apologizes for having fought on the wrong side at Philippi. He first mentions the fact, without apology, in the very poem in which he announces the invitation by Maecenas to join his literary circle (*Sat*. 1. 6. 47–8), and he continues to draw attention to it in his later poetry (*Odes*, 3. 4. 26; *Epist*. 2. 1. 47–8). All three of Maecenas' protégés claim to have been reduced to poverty by the activities of the triumvirate in the Civil War (Virg. *Ecl*. 9; Hor. *Epist*. 2. 2. 49–50; Prop. 4. 1. 128, more allusively). In Horace's case this was at least partly false; we learn from Suetonius' reliable Life that he was able to purchase the position of a senior treasury official (*scriba quaestorius*; on *scribae* see Badian 1989), and he himself tells that he was of equestrian status (*Sat*. 2. 7. 53). These references to loss of lands at

---

[1] The paradigm is Hor. *Epist*. 2. 1. 250–9, addressed directly to the emperor; one and a half lines at the beginning and three at the end proclaim Horace's incapacity for celebrating the emperor's campaigns, while the five lines in the middle show him doing it quite competently. The alternative model, more Callimachean and so more Propertian, is *Odes*, 4. 15; in the first three and a half lines Phoebus forbids the poet to tell of wars, that is write an epic about Augustus, but the remaining twenty-eight and a half lines of alcaics exalt imperial successes. I cannot see more than ingenuity in Propertius' variations on these themes in the earlier poems of his third book.

the hands of Octavian and his fellow triumvirs, or to association with the beaten side in the Civil War are so normal that we are entitled to wonder why the three poets made them. I can only suppose that Maecenas and Augustus actually encouraged such protestations as patrons claiming to be more interested in literary talent than in earlier allegiances.

In short, it is quite unnecessary to ascribe to Propertius' poetry any form of anti-militarist or anti-Augustan purpose. What is more, to read Propertius' poems in this way actually creates problems when we turn to those of his poems which do overtly proclaim Augustan themes, such as the Cleopatra and Actium elegies (3. 11, 4. 6; see Sullivan 1976, 21–4, 145–7; Stahl 1985, 234–47, 250–5). Why should an opponent of the regime indulge in such gratuitous and exuberant flattery of the *princeps*? Such evidence as there is suggests that the *princeps*, at any rate until the last decade of his principate, approved of a certain measure of independence on the part of his authors providing they also from time to time made the right noises.[1]

Ovid ought to be the prize exhibit in any gallery of poets opposed to Augustus; was he not, after all, exiled in AD 8 to Tomis in part because of his poetry? However, he fits uneasily into the anti-militarist slot. His poet-speaker is not an anti-militarist in any relevant sense, as Sullivan concedes (1972, 20; 1976, 61). It is difficult to know what to believe in Ovid's own account of his exile and its causes; prudence and the desire to structure his experience in such a way that he can exercise artistic control over it, as well as making it the object of sympathy and compassion in his Roman readers, lead to obscurity, inconsistency and downright fiction (Ehlers 1988; Claassen 1988). However, from behind the smoke-screen of disinformation and exilic commonplace two points emerge quite clearly. First, of the two offences for which he was relegated to Tomis, a poem (*carmen*), namely the *Ars Amatoria* (*Art of Love*), and a mysterious 'mistake' (*error*; *Tr.* 2. 207), it was the latter that was the more important (*Pont.* 2. 9. 72; 3. 3. 72), a

---

[1]   Cremutius Cordus in Tac. *Ann.* 4. 34 states that Livy praised Pompey so highly that Augustus called him a Pompeian, 'nor did that damage their friendship'. Clearly, Livy was at liberty to laud Augustus' adoptive father's most serious foe, providing the tone of his history was right by Augustan standards.

point confirmed by the length of time which elapsed between the publication of the *Ars* and any sign of Augustus' displeasure.[1] Second, it was his attitude to sexual conduct in the *Ars*, not his attitude to war, which angered Augustus (*Tr.* 2. 345-7, 5. 12. 67-8; *Pont.* 2. 9. 73-6; Thibault 1964, 30-6). Thus the fate of Ovid is only marginally relevant to the subject of this chapter.

Finally, it has been suggested by Stahl (1985, 127-9, 304-5) that Augustus had Gallus' elegies destroyed after his fall from grace, a warning to other personal poets as well as an indication of the subversiveness of the form. However, there is no evidence that Gallus' poems did disappear – Quintilian (*Inst.* 10. 1. 93) implies that copies were available to him and his pupils – or that Augustus ever systematically tried to destroy the writings of authors of whom he disapproved.[2] The fact that, until the recent discovery of some papyrus fragments (Anderson *et al.* 1979), only one line of Gallus' poetry survived is no indication of official suppression; hardly more of M. Furius Bibaculus has survived and it would have been tempting to guess that his epigrams abusing the Caesars were suppressed, had not a speaker in Tacitus' *Annals* (4. 34) told us that Julius and Augustus had left them alone. So, if Gallus' downfall involved *damnatio memoriae*, it certainly did not entail the obliteration of his poetry, any more than Ovid's downfall entailed the destruction of *his* poetry.[3]

So, to sum up, the alleged evidence of an anti-militarist sub-culture under Augustus for which the elegists act as spokesmen is of little value. External evidence for Tibullus and Propertius points rather to their being perfectly respectable members of

---

[1] Remarked on by Ovid himself: *Tr.* 2. 90, 541-2. Nugent 1990 argues for the *Metamorphoses* as the cause of offence to Augustus, but this implies that Ovid in *Tr.* 2 is pointlessly misleading.

[2] The burning of the works of Cassius Severus and T. Labienus by the senate under Augustus is a different matter: those of the former at least were defamatory (Tac. *Ann.* 1. 72), and it must have been a symbolic gesture, as Caligula was able to find copies and restore them to circulation (Suet. *Calig.* 16). See also Raaflaub and Samons 1990, 439-47.

[3] Ovid states that his poetry had been removed from the three public libraries in Rome (*Tr.* 3. 1. 65-76), but as in *Tr.* 3. 14 he asks a friend to prepare at Rome a complete edition of his works (minus, of course, the offending *Ars Amatoria*), it is clear that the ban extended no further.

Augustan society. Even the *persona* that each of them adopts in
his poetry is of one who rejects war/war poetry *for himself* in
favour of love/love poetry. Despite their Callimachean point of
departure both poets select some themes congenial to the
princeps: in the case of Tibullus, the praise of country life and
rural cults; more obviously, in the case of Propertius, Augustus'
campaigns and victories and, in Book 4, venerable cults and even
married love (4. 11). Ovid is a somewhat different matter, but the
role played in his downfall by his poetry was probably supplemen-
tary rather than central, and in any case involved its sexual
subversiveness, not its anti-militarism.

The tale of a text

There is, however, another way of looking at texts which can be
made to yield modest results. If a text achieves classic status, we
can trace its use and abuse in later authors and their treatment of
it may have historical implications. In what follows I offer a
specimen of this approach, relevant to this volume because it deals
with a *prima facie* criticism of war in a most surprising context,
the *Annales* of Q. Ennius. Aulus Gellius (*NA* 20. 10. 4), in a
discussion of the legal phrase *ex iure manu(m) consertum*,[1] cites
a passage of the *Annales*, which is also alluded to by several other
ancient writers. The fragment goes as follows (247–53 Skutsch =
268–73 Vahlen):

> proelia promulgantur,[2]
> pellitur e medio sapientia, vi geritur res;
> spernitur orator bonus, horridus miles amatur;
> haud doctis dictis certantes, nec maledictis
> miscent inter sese inimicitias agitantes;
> non ex iure manu consertum, sed magis ferro

---

[1] Both *manu* and *manum* are found in this phrase, but the form *manu* is
better attested for Ennius (Skutsch 1985, 436).
[2] Gellius' citation starts with *pellitur e medio* . . . , but that this was
preceded by something like *quom proelia promulgantur* may be inferred
from Cic. *Mur.* 30 (Skutsch 1985, 432–3).

rem repetunt regnumque petunt, vadunt solida vi.[1]

[When] wars are promulgated, wisdom is driven from the midst, matters waged by force; the good pleader is shunned, the rude soldier loved. Not contending with learned words, nor harassing one another with curses they carry on vendettas; not by process of law to pursue claims, but rather with the sword they seek back property and seek the mastery, they proceed by brute force.

The fragment's meaning is not at every point clear, but one thing is certain: the speaker is describing the evil effects which follow the outbreak of war. The passage consists largely of a set of antitheses of which the first attracts approving epithets, the second pejorative. *Sapientia* – wisdom – is an unqualifiedly good word and it is being expelled from their midst; in such a context the contrasting *vis* – force – with which things are being carried on can only be bad. In the second line the *orator bonus* – the good pleader or possibly envoy – is chiastically replaced by the *horridus miles*, who must be the horrid or rude soldier rather than one merely bristling either with bristles or weapons. The final two lines contrast claims pursued by due process of law with those pursued by force of arms by those who aim at tyrannical power or mastery. The middle couplet is more problematic. If the manuscript text is retained, these lines do not include an antithesis. However, it seems to me that the traditional emendation of *nec* ('nor') to *sed* ('but') with a comma after *maledictis* is probably right, as this text maintains the antithetical structure of the passage ('contending not with learned words but with curses, they harass one another, carrying on vendettas'). Either a scribe or Gellius himself could easily have written *nec* by mistake for *sed*.[2] Skutsch (1985, 434) objects that war is not carried on by curses, but this brings us to the problem of the overall purport of the passage.

Skutsch apparently supposes that the reference is to the

[1] Skutsch punctuates these lines so that *ferro* is taken with *vadunt* and *rem repetunt regnumque petunt* becomes a parenthesis. However, without punctuation marks Ennius' reader had no choice but to take *ferro* with *rem repetunt . . .* (so Cic. *Mur.* 30).

[2] Gellius claims to be quoting Ennius from memory, and it was Ennius' use of the phrase *ex iure manu consertum* which primarily concerned him. His text contains a number of errors here, which we can correct from Cicero's citations, e.g. *errore* for *ferro* and *rei* for *rem*.

behaviour of nations; after the outbreak of war, instead of using
the procedures of international law to satisfy their claims, they
resort to force. This is possible, but there is an alternative which is
in my view more likely, namely that the passage is describing the
evil effects of war on a community; war leads the citizens to resort
to naked violence instead of legal procedures in their relations
with each other. One argument in favour of this interpretation is
the use of the word *inimicitia*, normally used of hostility between
individuals; it is very seldom used of hostility between states, and
no instance is known in early Latin. A further argument is
supplied by the passage of Gellius in which he cites our fragment.
Gellius goes on to explicate the phrase *manu consertum* in terms
of a procedure between litigants disputing over property at a
distance from Rome who bring a symbolic part of it (e.g. a clod of
earth) to the praetor's court in Rome. Gellius' concluding words
are textually corrupt, but the meaning must be something like:

> Accordingly, Ennius wanted to signify that property was being sought
> back, not, as was usual before the praetor, by the civil actions laid
> down by law nor by the *manu consertum* procedure just described, but
> by war and steel and by genuine and brute force; a point which he
> seems to have expressed by contrasting the symbolic force of civil law
> which is merely formulaic, not physical, with warlike and bloody
> force.
>
> (Gell. *NA* 20. 10. 10)[1]

Thus Gellius, who knew his archaic texts, had an interest in law
and had no axe to grind, thought Ennius in the words *ex iure
manu consertum* was talking about disputes between Roman
citizens, not disputes between Rome and other states.

The context of the passage in the *Annales* is quite uncertain.
Gellius cites it as from the eighth book. If this is correct, it came in
Ennius' account of events from 217 to about 211. Skutsch (1985,
430) thinks that it may come from an exordium to the book. It
could also come from a passage describing morale in Rome after a

---

[1]   *idcirco Ennius significare volens [bellum] non, ut ad praetorem solitum
est, legitimis actionibus neque ex iure manu consertum, sed bello ferroque
et vera vi atque solida <rem repeti . . .>; quod videtur dixisse, conferens
vim illam civilem et festucariam quae verbo diceretur, non quae manu
fieret, cum vi bellica et cruenta. Volens* should perhaps be emended to
voluit.

defeat, Trasimene or Cannae, or, perhaps most plausibly, from a speech in the context of dissatisfaction with the tactics of Fabius Cunctator (cf. Livy, 22. 25–6) or the election campaign that led to C. Terentius Varro gaining the consulship (Livy, 22. 34–5). Alternatively, Gellius may have got the book number wrong, as he quite often did (Skutsch 1985, 30). If so, a plausible context would be the outbreak of the Second Punic War, which Ennius narrated in Book 7. A number of scholars suppose that the reference is not to Rome but to some other community – Carthage at the outbreak of the war (Müller 1884, 173–4; Harris 1979, 35 n. 5) or Capua before its defection to Hannibal.[1] However, Gellius, as we have seen, thought that the passage referred to Rome, and the same is also implied by Cicero's perverse use of the passage in the *Pro Murena*, to be discussed below.

This is a most surprising passage to come from the stylus of the author of the *Annales*. It is a generalization, whatever the specific context, and, though it would be less telling if it comes from a speech delivered by a discredited individual, it is noteworthy that both Gellius[2] and, as we shall see, Cicero approved of the passage. Given the conventions of patriotic epic, one would hardly have expected Ennius in his account of the Second Punic War to dwell on the possibility that war could have a disastrous effect on Roman reverence for the law. However, enough evidence has survived the disinfecting of Roman history, already beginning in Polybius and more or less complete in Livy, to suggest that defeats in the Second Punic War affected behaviour, particularly that of the *plebs*.[3] It may be relevant too that a form of possessory edict

[1] Suggested by Prof. M. H. Crawford at the seminar at which the original version of this chapter was delivered. However, the Capuans did not then enter a war, but changed sides in a war in which they were already engaged.

[2] He characterizes the lines as 'composed with exceptional distinction' (*NA* 20. 10. 4: *insigniter praeter alios factos*).

[3] Both Polybius (3. 86) and Livy (22. 7–8) attest the demoralization of the *plebs* after the news of the disaster at Lake Trasimene had reached Rome; Polybius, unlike Livy, states that it affected the senate as well. The use by later historians of the Greek theory that fear of external enemies (*metus hostilis*) disciplines a community, in order to explain the collapse of the Republic, enforces an idealization of Roman behaviour before the historian's chosen cut-off point.

aimed at securing an occupier's rights against force was in existence by 166, when it is attested by Terence (*Eun.* 319). Since the law takes cognizance of new offences only when they have become a problem, the possessory interdict can only have been issued because forcible possession and the eviction of existing occupants had become a nuisance.

One final point before moving on. In addition to the opposition between peacetime legality and the violence of wartime, Ennius makes other contrasts in this passage: between the use of intelligence (*sapientia*, *docta dicta*) and violence, and between logical argument delivered by the *orator bonus* and (if we read *sed*) verbal abuse and the prosecution of private feuds. So, while the primary function of the passage is to contrast the business of the law with the activities of war, to the detriment of the latter, during a war other values too are overthrown; we should never forget that Ennius' models are Hellenistic as well as Homeric (Jocelyn 1972, 1015 and n. 289). Lactantius (*Div. Inst.* 5. 1) takes the first line in this larger sense, for he applies it to the behaviour of the pagan persecutors of Christianity infuriated by the sweet reasonableness of Christian apologetic.[1]

Gellius is our fullest source for this passage of Ennius, but it also appears, though with an unexpected function, in Cicero's speech on behalf of Murena. This was a dexterous speech; L. Licinius Murena had been one of the successful candidates for the consulship in the elections in the summer of 63 BC, the second election in which Catiline was defeated, but another unsuccessful candidate, Servius Sulpicius Rufus, a young patrician and *nobilis* skilled in jurisprudence, brought a prosecution for *ambitus*, electoral corruption, against Murena. After making all allowances for the touching-up process, we must admit that it is a lively speech for Cicero to have delivered at the same time as he was dealing with the Catilinarian conspiracy. To have got his almost certainly guilty client off in such circumstances is an achievement, to have caused Cato to smile in the process (Plut. *Cat. Min.* 21)

---

[1] Lactantius' source is probably Gellius rather than Cicero (*contra* Skutsch 1985, 433), since he cites Ennius by name and his introductory phrase *disceptatione sublata* implies knowledge of line 250, not cited by Cicero. Lactantius knew Gellius well – he is our only source for the opening lines of Gellius' seventh book (cf. *Epit. Div. Inst.* 24. 5).

possibly a greater one! The section of the speech which caused
Cato, a *subscriptor* to the prosecution, to laugh was that which
contained Cicero's sallies at the expense of Cato's Stoic beliefs,
but he must have found some amusement too in the passage in
which Cicero uses our Ennius text to demonstrate that oratorical
ability, and *a fortiori* the petty jurisprudential skills of Sulpicius,
are inferior to military glory:

> Etenim, ut ait ingeniosus poeta et auctor valde bonus, 'proeliis
> promulgatis pellitur e medio' non solum ista vestra verbosa simulatio
> prudentiae sed etiam ipsa illa domina rerum, 'sapientia; vi geritur res.
> Spernitur orator' non solum odiosus in dicendo ac loquax verum
> etiam 'bonus; horridus miles amatur'; vestrum vero studium totum
> iacet. 'non ex iure manu consertum, sed ferro', inquit, 'rem repetunt.'
> quod si ita est, cedat, opinor, Sulpici, forum castris, otium militiae,
> stilus gladio, umbra soli; sit denique in civitate ea prima res propter
> quam ipsa est civitas omnium princeps.
>
> (*Pro Murena*, 30)

> For indeed, as says a poet of genius and excellent authority, 'at the
> promulgation of war is driven from the midst' not only your verbose
> imitation of good sense but even that mistress of everything 'wisdom'
> herself; 'matters are waged by force. The pleader is shunned', not only
> the kind that is repellent and loquacious in speaking but even the
> pleader who is 'good; the rude soldier is loved'; but your profession is
> completely neglected. 'Not by process of law to pursue claims but with
> the sword they seek back property.' But if that is the case, in my view,
> Sulpicius, the Forum should yield to the camp, peaceful pursuits to
> those of war, the pen to the sword, and the study to the open air; in a
> word, that activity should take first place in the state which has made
> it the leading state in the world.

For the future author of the immortal lines *cedant arma togae,
concedat laurea linguae* ('Let arms yield to the toga, the laurel
wreath to the tongue') to adopt this position on the primacy of
military glory over eloquence was in itself good for a laugh.

Cicero's methods for contorting this unpromising passage into
an exaltation of military life at the expense of barristers and
jurisconsults involves *suppressio veri* and *suggestio falsi*. *Nec* (or
sed) *maledictis miscent inter sese inimicitias agitantes* disappears
completely. The *suggestio falsi* involves the suggestion that Ennius
actually approves of the displacement of *sapientia* and the *bonus*

orator by the *horridus miles*, which is quite the opposite of what Ennius meant.

The Ennius text, like chunks of Homer for fourth-century Greeks, has thus acquired autonomous status; Cicero has used it to engage in a *jeu d'esprit* he intends his audience and his readers to enjoy. They knew perfectly well that Murena's military career was not really very glorious; his chief exploits consisted in failing to capture Amisus and Tigranocerta in 72 and 69 from the forces of Mithridates (his commanding officer Lucullus eventually had to take these towns himself). They also knew that Cicero rated the skills of oratory, at least when practised by himself, at least as no lower in the scales than military success as a source of *gloria*. Indeed, Cicero was so pleased with this preposterous passage that nearly twenty years later, in May 44, in a letter to Servius Sulpicius, with whom he was in fact on very friendly terms, he was still saddling him with the Ennius quotation (*Att.* 15. 7). Nor should this piece of fun be used as evidence that Cicero regarded war as a calling (as it is by Wood 1988, 97).

What further use can we trace of the 'horrid soldier' motif in Roman literature? *Horridus miles* soon had its day metrically, for from Catullus onwards to scan *horridu' miles* as dactyl + spondee would be as barbarous as the soldier. In fact, *horridus miles* seems to make only one further appearance in Latin, in Livy, 9. 40. 4–5, where the phrase is sanitized in a description of Roman military equipment, with *horridus* apparently meaning no more than 'rough' in an approving sense in contrast to the eye-catching uniforms of the Samnites:

Notus iam Romanis apparatus insignium armorum fuerat doctique a ducibus erant horridum militem esse debere, non caelatum auro et argento sed ferro et animis fretum.

The Romans had already learnt of this showy and impressive military equipment, but had been taught by their leaders that a soldier ought to be roughly accoutred, not adorned with gold and silver but reliant on cold steel and courage.

More interesting are echoes of the Ennius passage in Virgil's *Aeneid*. As we have noted, the *miles* can no longer be *horridus* except by means of metrical sleight of hand. Wars however can still be horrid; for example, in the Sibyl's prophecy, in language made notorious by a former professor of Greek at Sydney, she states that the Trojans will regret ever having come to Lavinium (*Aen.* 6. 86–7):

> sed non et venisse volent. Bella, horrida bella,
> et Thybrim multo spumantem sanguine cerno.

> But they will also wish they had not come. Wars, horrid wars,
> and Tiber foaming with much blood do I behold.

This and other uses of *horrida bella* in Virgil (e.g. at 7. 41 and at 11. 96, where Aeneas' tears over his dead comrade Pallas are the result of the horrid destinies of war, *horrida belli / Fata*) at least show that *horridus* in military contexts is not, as it is for Livy, a nice, even comfortable, word. Another line, 12. 720, very Ennian in its alliteration and its spondaic character, looks as if it was influenced by a line of the Ennius fragment, *miscent inter sese inimicitias agitantes*:

> illi inter sese multa vi vulnera miscent . . .

> They with mighty force deal one another wounds.

There is, however, one passage which does indicate an interesting variation on the Ennian theme, and where Virgil seems to me to be using the Ennius passage as a sub-text, namely the climax to Jupiter's speech in Book 1, where he prophesies the reign of Augustus:

> Cana Fides et Vesta, Remo cum fratre Quirinus
> iura dabunt; dirae ferro et compagibus artis
> claudentur belli portae; Furor impius intus
> saeva sedens super arma et centum vinctus aenis
> post tergum nodis fremet horridus ore cruento.

> Grey Faith, and Vesta, and Quirinus in concert with his brother Remus shall be lawgivers; terrible in their close-wrought frame of iron, the gates of War shall be shut; within, Frenzy the impious, shall be seated on a pile of savage arms, and tight-bound with a hundred knots behind his back he shall bellow hideously (*horridus*) from bloody jaws.
> (*Aen.* 1. 292–6)[1]

---

[1] I have taken the translation from Austin 1971, 111.

Although only one word reflects our Ennius passage directly, that word is *horridus*, set in exactly the same position of the line, even though it entails coincidence of ictus and accent for the last three feet of the hexameter, something which Virgil normally avoids, and although for metrical reasons he avoids the form *horridus* elsewhere in the Aeneid. Moreover, the contrast between the legal activity of peace, expressed by Fides and Vesta with Romulus and Remus giving laws, and Furor sitting on his pile of arms and bellowing horridly with bloody mouth, is itself a re-working of the Ennian antithesis. The fact that the prosaic Gellius uses the same poetic and grand-style adjective, *cruentus*, as Virgil, in his summary of the Ennius passage (Gell. *NA* 20. 10. 10, cited above) suggests that, at least subconsciously, he also associated the two passages.[1]

The 'gates of war' are the doors of the temple of Janus, closed in 29 BC following Augustus' victory over Antony and Cleopatra. As has long been recognized, Virgil's description of them echoes another passage from Ennius' *Annales* (225-6 Skutsch):

> postquam Discordia taetra
> Belli ferratos postes portamque refregit

> After hideous Discord had broken open the iron-clad doorposts and gate of war.

In this further Ennian sub-text the fury Discordia breaks down the doors which in Virgil are being closed. Nevertheless, the Ennian echo in Virgil reminds us of *discordia* which, unpersonified, suggests civil strife.[2] Accordingly, when we eventually meet *Furor impius* we know that, as commentators have supposed on other grounds, it is civil war that Augustus has imprisoned

---

[1]   *Cruentus* occurs elsewhere in Gellius only in the story of Androclus and the lion, where it is used literally of the latter's bleeding paw (5. 14. 19), and, significantly, in a quotation from Virgil (5. 8. 5 = *Aen.* 3. 618). With its mainly high Ciceronian and poetic associations, *cruentus* is the sort of word normally avoided by a disciple of the archaizing movement who practises the plain style.

[2]   There are many examples of *discordia* in this sense, but perhaps the most telling are Cic. *Leg.* 3. 9 (a law) and Virg. *Ecl.* 1. 72-3, about an earlier stage in the Civil War.

impotently bellowing; nevertheless, the allusion is discreet, given Augustan propaganda that the Actium campaign was primarily against a foreign power. Virgil has subtly shifted the antithesis so that it is not all war which is contrasted unfavourably with peace and the rule of law, but civil war. No longer is external war a form of *furor*. No longer, either, are Romulus and Remus emblematic in their fatal quarrel of Rome's propensity for civil war,[1] but, reconciled, they give laws together. The exercise is all the more interesting because 29 BC was the first occasion when the doors of Janus were closed after what was in fact as much a civil as a foreign war.

One last point about Virgil and Ennius. We have seen that Virgil echoes two Ennian texts, lines 225–6 and 247–53 in Skutsch's edition. Vahlen printed them as a sequence (lines 266–73), omitting *proelia promulgantur*. This cannot be correct, for, as Skutsch observed, the second fragment must have been preceded by some words from which Cicero drew his phrase *proeliis promulgatis* (above, p. 126 n. 2). However, it is still possible that the two fragments may derive from the same passage, perhaps, as Vahlen supposed, from Ennius' account of the opening of the Second Punic War. The fact that Virgil echoed both fragments in the same lines is an argument in favour of this hypothesis.[2]

What, then, of value does this tale of an Ennian text tell us? First of all, that the conventions of Roman national epic, as created by Ennius, were more fluid than one might have expected. Just as Ennius was self-confident enough to evade the patronage of a single political faction at Rome (Goldberg 1989), so he was confident – and Hellenistic – enough to be able to address the undesirable consequences of war within the framework of a national epic. Admittedly, the extent to which this is true depends on the context of the excerpt; nevertheless it remains a thoroughly Roman statement, admired by Cicero and Gellius, of the evil

---

[1] Famously in Hor. *Epod.* 7. 17–20, and naughtily resuscitated by Lucan (1. 95).
[2] Skutsch accepts the alternative view that the fragment on the 'gates of war' refers to the opening of the doors of Janus in 241 or 235 BC (Skutsch 1985, 402–3, with bibliography). He is perhaps too ready to reject Latte's theory that the second-century annalist L. Calpurnius Piso, our earliest source for the Janus ritual, may have invented it, possibly prompted by Ennius' phrase.

effects of war on the civilian community. Virgil, in making the same type of point about civil war in a less direct way, because in a mythologized context, was therefore doing nothing new.

Second, the Ennian text becomes autonomous, as chunks of Virgil were later to become, in the sense that they can be played with in ways that cut across the original meaning and enjoyed as such by those who, like Cicero and his jurors, knew the source; the jury and the audience must have realized that in asserting the superiority of military glory over eloquence Cicero was being playful – the misuse of the text improves the joke. In Lactantius the Ennian text functions as totally autonomous, for Lactantius knows it only as a quotation to be used as an *ad hoc* appeal against the pagans to a great national poet in applying it to their fury when confronted by the rational persuasiveness of Christianity.

Last, the Virgilian adaptation suggests a way in which the use of a famous sub-text can conceivably carry a political charge. Whatever the Ennian context, it has to be a comment on what happens at the outbreak of a war, whereas Jupiter in Virgil is referring to the ending of a war and the coming of peace, and the Ennian resonances help. *Furor*, imprisoned, can represent all the disagreeable effects of war listed by Ennius, including the feuds of factions (*inimicitiae*) that characterized the century before Virgil wrote. Perhaps, too, Virgil can hint at something rather stronger than Augustus would have wanted; he might have preferred the horrid soldier in his wholesome Livian form, not disliked or rejected. But that would take us into another Tale.[1]

Bibliography

Allen, A. W. (1962), 'Sunt qui Propertium malint', in J. P. Sullivan (ed.), *Elegy and Lyric* (London), pp. 107–48.

Anderson, R. D., Parsons, P. J., and Nisbet, R. G. B. (1979), 'Elegiacs by Gallus from Qasr Ibrîm', *JRS* 69: 125–55.

Austin, R. G. (1971), *P. Vergili Maronis Aeneidos liber primus* (Oxford).

Badian, E. (1985), 'A phantom marriage law', *Philologus*, 129: 82–98.

—— (1989), 'The *scribae* of the Roman Republic', *Klio*, 71: 582–603.

[1] I must express my thanks to John Rich for suggestions which have greatly improved this chapter.

Benediktson, D. T. (1989), *Propertius: Modernist Poet of Antiquity* (Carbondale and Edwardsville, Ill.).

Besslich, S. (1979), 'Ovid's winter in Tomis', *Gymnasium*, 79: 177–91.

Cairns, F. (1972), *Generic Composition in Greek and Roman Poetry* (Edinburgh).

—— (1979a), *Tibullus: A Hellenistic Poet at Rome* (Cambridge).

—— (1979b), 'Propertius on Augustus' marriage law (2. 7)', *Grazer Beiträge*, 8: 185–204.

Carter, J. M. (1982), *Suetonius: Divus Augustus* (Bristol).

Claassen, J.-M. (1988), 'Ovid's poems from exile', *Antike und Abendland*, 34: 158–69.

Ehlers, W.-W. (1988), 'Poet und Exil: zum Verstandnis der Exildichtung Ovids', *Antike und Abendland*, 34: 144–57.

Fedeli, P. (1980), *Sesto Properzio: il primo libro delle elegie* (Florence).

Gahan, J. J. (1984–5), 'Seneca, Ovid, and exile', *Classical World*, 78: 145–52.

Goldberg, S. M. (1989), 'Poetry, politics, and Ennius', *Transactions of the American Philological Association*, 119: 247–61.

Goold, G. P. (1988), *Catullus, Tibullus, Pervigilium Veneris* (Loeb Classical Library; Harvard).

—— (1990), *Propertius: Elegies* (Loeb Classical Library; Harvard).

Green, P. (1967), *Juvenal: The Sixteen Satires* (Harmondsworth).

Hallett, J. P. (1973), 'The role of women in Roman elegy: counter-cultural feminism', *Arethusa*, 6: 103–24.

Harris, W. V. (1979), *War and Imperialism in Republican Rome 327–70 BC* (Oxford).

Helzle, M. (1988), 'Ovid's poetics of exile', *Illinois Classical Studies*, 13: 73–83.

Highet, G. (1954), *Juvenal the Satirist* (Oxford).

Hubbard, M. (1974), *Propertius* (London).

Jocelyn, H. D. (1972), 'The poems of Quintus Ennius', *ANRW* i. 2. 987–1026.

Lefkowitz, M. R. (1981), *The Lives of the Greek Poets* (London).

Levi, M. A. (1951), *C. Suetoni Tranquilli Divus Augustus* (Florence).

Lyne, R. O. A. M. (1980), *The Latin Love Poets* (Oxford).

Müller, L. (1884), *Quintus Ennius: eine Einleitung in das Studium der römische Poesie* (St Petersburg).

Murgatroyd, P. (1975), 'Militia Amoris and the Roman elegists', *Latomus*, 34: 59–79.

—— (1980), *Tibullus I* (Pietermaritzburg).

Nugent, S. G. (1990), 'Tristia 2: Ovid and Augustus', in K. A. Raaflaub and M. Toher (eds), pp. 239–57.

Paige, D. D. (1951), *The Letters of Ezra Pound* (London).

Pierini, R. degl' I. (1980), 'Echi delle elegie ovidiane dall' esilio in Seneca', *Studi italiani di filologia classica*, 52: 109–43.

Postgate, J. P. (1903), *Selections from Tibullus and Others* (London).

Putnam, M. C. J. (1973), *Tibullus: A Commentary* (Norman, Okla.).

Raaflaub, K. A., and Samons, L. J., II (1990), 'Opposition to Augustus', in K. A. Raaflaub and M. Toher (eds), pp. 417–54.

—— and Toher, M. (eds, 1990), *Between Republic and Empire: Interpretations of Augustus and his Principate* (Berkeley).

Skutsch, O. (1985), *The Annals of Q. Ennius* (Oxford).

Stahl, H.-P. (1985), *Propertius: 'Love' and 'War': Individual and State under Augustus* (London).

Sullivan, J. P. (1965), *Ezra Pound and Sextus Propertius* (London).

—— (1972), 'The politics of elegy', *Arethusa*, 5: 17–34.

—— (1976), *Propertius* (Cambridge).

Thibault, J. C. (1964), *The Mystery of Ovid's Exile* (Berkeley).

Vahlen, J. (1928), *Ennianae poesis reliquiae* (3rd edn; Leipzig).

Veyne, P. (1988), *Roman Erotic Elegy: Love, Poetry, and the West* (Chicago).

Wood, N. (1988), *Cicero's Social and Political Thought* (Berkeley).

Wyke, M. (1989a), 'Mistress and metaphor in Augustan elegy', *Helios*, 16: 25–46.

—— (1989b), 'In pursuit of love, the poetic self and a process of reading Augustan elegy in the 1980s', *JRS* 79: 165–73.

∞ 6 ∞

The end of Roman imperial expansion

Tim Cornell

The problem

A major change in Roman military policy appears to have occurred at the end of the reign of Augustus. Until then the empire had grown inexorably as a result of centuries of successful war. The conquest of Italy in the fourth and third centuries BC was followed by a series of major wars during the last two centuries of the Republic in Spain, North Africa, Greece, Asia Minor, Syria and continental Gaul, which resulted in the formation of a far-flung territorial empire directly controlled from Rome. The process of expansion continued under Augustus, whose armies overran Egypt, north-west Spain, the Alps, parts of Austria and most of the Balkans. An attempt to conquer Germany and to extend the Roman frontier to the Elbe had to be abandoned in AD 9, however, and the armies were brought back to the Rhine. By the end of his reign, Augustus had evidently decided against further expansion; on his deathbed, we are told, he instructed his heir to keep the empire within its existing borders.[1]

This advice was followed, broadly speaking, by Augustus' successors during the two centuries that followed, the age of the 'Roman peace'. From this point on, apart from the isolated and marginal additions of Britain, Dacia and (briefly) Mesopotamia,

---

[1] Tac. *Ann.* 1. 11; Dio, 56. 33. On these texts note Ober 1982, and see further below p. 149.

the boundaries of the Roman empire remained much what they had been at the time of Augustus' death in AD 14.

The traditional explanation of this development is that under Augustus the Romans finally attained the secure frontiers that they had always sought, and that once the natural boundaries of the Rhine, Danube and Euphrates had been reached, there was no need for any further expansion. The German adventure of Augustus can be fitted into this traditional picture in one of two ways. One could suppose that for once Augustus overstepped the mark; thus according to Tenney Frank he gave in to the jingoistic pressures of public opinion (articulated most memorably by the poets) and briefly revived Julius Caesar's grandiose dream of world conquest; but after the German experience he learned his lesson and reverted to the prudent defensive policy which he, like the Republican senate before him, had otherwise consistently followed (Frank 1914, 348). Alternatively it could be argued that Augustus was aiming to secure a more logical strategic frontier along the Hamburg–Leipzig–Prague–Vienna line (Syme 1934, 353). On this view the German adventure was not an aberration, but part of the same wise and prudent policy of establishing a safe and lasting frontier.

As far as the Republic is concerned, this reconstruction embraces the now distinctly old-fashioned notion of 'defensive imperialism' – the notion, that is, that Roman expansion was not the product of deliberate aggression, but rather an incidental result of wars that had been undertaken in response to external threats. According to this theory the Romans were continually being forced to fight in defence of their own interests or those of their allies; the protection of an ever-widening sphere of interests entailed increasing responsibilities, and, where necessary, the direct control of a growing number of overseas territories.[1]

But the idea of the Romans as a peace-loving people, reluctantly forced into wars by aggressive and threatening neighbours, and compelled against their will to undertake the burden of ruling an empire they had not sought, was always a

[1] This traditional view goes back, in essence, to Mommsen. On Mommsen see the interesting discussion of Linderski 1983.

faintly ludicrous one,[1] although for obvious reasons it had a wide currency in the colonial era, and it is now generally discredited. Recent studies have emphasized the belligerence of the Romans during the Republic, and have noted that their society was geared to war and the pursuit of military glory (Hopkins 1978; Harris 1979). The growth of the empire brought tangible benefits which the Romans were ready and willing to accept, and it was something of which they were in no way ashamed (Brunt 1978; Harris 1979). Of course they believed that their wars were just (which is not the same thing as saying that they were defensive), and they were also confident that the empire had been ordained by the gods (Virg. *Aen.* 1. 278–9; cf. Brunt 1978, 168 = 1990, 297); but that did not inhibit their warlike tendencies – quite the contrary. The Romans were imperialists and proud of it; the only surprising thing is that this truism has had to be rediscovered by scholarship.

Needless to say, modern historians have also challenged the idea of Augustus as a prudent and cautious statesman whose sole aim was to defend the empire (Brunt 1963; 1990, 446–70; Wells 1972, 3–13).[2] Here, admittedly, there is a serious obstacle in the fact that some ancient sources describe Augustus in precisely these terms. Suetonius, for instance, tells us that 'Augustus never wantonly invaded any country, and felt no temptation to increase the boundaries of the empire or enhance his military glory' (*Aug.* 21, trans. R. Graves). Dio makes similar comments more than once (53. 10. 4; 54. 9. 1). But there are good reasons for thinking that such texts are the product of the times in which they were written, and reflect the opinions of the authors who wrote them rather than true descriptions of the policy of Augustus (Brunt 1963, 172 = 1990, 100–1; A. R. Birley 1974, 14, 20; Ober 1982, 318). They are contradicted, first, by the fact that in his actions Augustus showed no such restraint (he was the greatest conqueror in Rome's history); second, by the evidence of contemporary

---

[1] The formulation may look like a caricature, but it underlies many books on Roman history written in the early part of the present century. Notice especially Frank 1914, 356, where the Romans are described as 'unambitious, peaceful, home-staying men, characterised above all by a singular respect for orderly procedure'.

[2] For a recent restatement of the traditional view see Gabba 1990.

sources. The most important of these by far is the *Res Gestae*, which clearly indicates that Augustus took pride in his conquests and was pleased to celebrate them in public. The other major contemporary source is the work of the Augustan poets, whose imperialistic sentiments reflected the ideals of the regime they served (Brunt 1963).

The work of Brunt and others has effectively demolished the thesis that Augustus' conquests were undertaken with the sole purpose of providing secure frontiers for the empire. The evidence in fact seems to point to something much more grandiose: to a continuing programme of imperial expansion, and perhaps even a dream of world conquest, although this latter speculation may go too far (Syme 1988, 237). But if we abandon, as it now seems we must, any notion of defensive imperialism or a search for secure frontiers, then the change that occurred around AD 14 appears all the more extraordinary. The termination of the process of contin- uous war and expansion, and the inception of the *pax Romana*, evidently constitute a remarkable transformation, and surely demand some kind of explanation.

Curiously enough the question has been addressed only in passing in modern studies of the subject. A variety of tentative explanations has been offered, but some of them are manifestly wrong and none is adequate. To my knowledge there has been no fully reasoned discussion of the issue. The reason is that as long as the theory of defensive imperialism dominated the field, the ending of the wars of conquest was not a problem. Expansion ceased because the Roman empire had attained its full extent, bounded by natural frontiers, under Augustus. But modern critical studies have pointed out that there was nothing god-given about the Augustan empire; the idea of a standard-size Roman empire, achieved by Augustus as the logical culmination of centuries of struggle, is merely the product of hindsight (Mann 1979, 176). It has also been pointed out that the Rhine, Danube and Euphrates do not form natural strategic frontiers. Rivers are not effective lines of defence, nor do they function historically as boundaries between ethnic, linguistic or national groups (Mann 1974, 513; A. R. Birley 1974, 22). The Rhine–Danube line was initially chosen as a temporary border for reasons of adminis- trative convenience; but the expectation in Augustus' time proba- bly was that further conquests beyond the Rhine and Danube would soon take place. With the passage of time, however, the line became fixed, and the further expansion did not materialize.

The potential strategic weakness of the Rhine–Danube line, which was fatally exposed in the invasions of the third century, also serves to confirm that imperial policy was not principally designed to protect Roman interests from attack. A defensive policy presupposes some kind of threat; but it is doubtful if the Roman empire faced any major external threats during the Principate. This proposition may seem more credible now than it did during the Cold War, which was the main inspiration for Edward N. Luttwak's brilliant analysis of the grand strategy of the Roman empire (Luttwak 1976). Luttwak gave scientific precision to the theory of defensive imperialism, arguing that the 'escalation dominance' of the legions (that is, their perceived efficacy as a weapon of last resort) would serve to deter any large-scale attack without their actually having to be used. Meanwhile a ring of satellite states (client kingdoms) was expected to cope with 'low-intensity threats' beyond the borders of the Roman provinces; and the territory of the satellite states could be used as the battle-ground if the legions had to be deployed. Needless to say, this made extremely uncomfortable reading in Europe during the 1970s, and particularly in the 1980s under President Reagan, whose leading security adviser was none other than Edward N. Luttwak.

But even Luttwak is vague about the nature of the threats Rome supposedly faced. Although the legions were stationed in 'high threat sectors', it emerges that the threats in question were potential rather than actual; the aim of Roman policy was to provide 'security against the sudden emergence of unseen threats' (ibid. 18). He even admits (and the admission is very damaging to his general thesis) that the threats were primarily internal rather than external. In the absence of any other plausible candidates for the role of an 'evil empire' beyond the frontiers, Luttwak seizes upon Parthia, whose power he thinks represented a 'systemic' threat to Rome. He is not alone in this: many Roman historians have written about 'the Parthian threat', or Rome's 'Parthian problem'.[1] On the other hand a respectable body of scholarship

---

[1]   e.g. Wacher 1987, 18: 'the serious and continuing threat of Parthia in the east'. On Rome's relations with Parthia see Campbell below (ch. 9), taking a rather different line from the present chapter.

has long maintained that the Parthians did not represent a serious menace to Roman interests in the East (e.g. Anderson 1934, 257; Syme 1936, 142).

Brunt has made a strong case for seeing Parthia as a potential menace. The Parthian empire had grown from small beginnings in the third century BC, and by the early first century had occupied all of former Seleucid territory as far as the Euphrates. That the Parthians had ambitions for further expansion could perhaps reasonably be assumed; and we know from Tacitus that in AD 35 King Artabanus III announced a claim to all the former possessions of the Achaemenids (*Ann.* 6. 31). In the event the Parthians made no attempt to realise this claim. For most of the period of the Principate internal weaknesses prevented them from mounting any serious attack against Roman interests; but the Romans could not be expected to foresee this, and the Parthians would have retained the potential for aggrandizement under strong leadership and reformed organization (Brunt 1990, 459–60).

The problem here is that we have no means of reconstructing the fears and aspirations of either side; nor can we properly say whether their fears, if any, were justified. Nevertheless it is worth repeating the point recently made by B. Isaac in his excellent study of Roman military policy in the East (Isaac 1990, 21–2), that in diplomacy and war one should distinguish between words and deeds, and that Tacitus for one did not take Artabanus' pronouncements seriously. As for deeds, Isaac shows that the record of relations between Rome and Parthia is clear and consistent: disputes always concerned the control of territory to the east of the Euphrates, and armed conflict almost always occurred as a result of Roman initiative. The Parthians never took the initiative in launching an armed attack, except in the 150s when they started a war for the control of Armenia. They never attacked Syria except as a tactical response to Roman aggression (usually in Armenia). There is no evidence that they ever attempted or even wished permanently to occupy Syria or any other Roman possession (Isaac 1990, 31–3).

On the other hand, the Romans frequently attacked Parthia. Crassus' expedition in 54 BC was prompted by megalomania and had not the slightest justification in law, morality or strategic utility (cf. Plut. *Crass.* 16). Later, Trajan and Caracalla invaded Parthia in the hope of winning fame by emulating the deeds of

Alexander. It is true that in a military sense the Parthians could be a formidable enemy; but the record shows that their skill in war was directed against the Romans only on those occasions when the legions had invaded Armenia or Mesopotamia. In a political sense Rome did not have a Parthian problem; but it is abundantly clear that Parthia had a Roman problem.

Some solutions

If we reject the idea that Roman imperialism was driven by a need to establish secure frontiers, how are we to account for the end of the process of continuous war and expansion? In my view this question has not been properly addressed in recent studies. Various possible solutions have been hinted at, but have not been supported by detailed argument or evidence, and none of them is to my mind adequate to resolve the general problem.

(1) *Was further expansion practicable?* It is sometimes suggested that the Roman empire stopped expanding after Augustus because of the increasingly difficult conditions that obtained beyond the frontiers. The empire in AD 14 was bounded by the ocean in the west, deserts in the south and east, and impenetrable forest to the north. According to Luttwak, Roman forces could advance into these regions but could not conquer them because the enemy's 'assets and sources of strength were not fixed, or at any rate, not concentrated' (Luttwak 1976, 45). Areas of forest and swamp, inhabited by nomadic populations who would disappear into the trees and adopt guerrilla tactics, were simply too difficult for the Romans to overrun and control effectively. If they persisted, their only real option 'was to attack the population base itself, in a war of extermination. In the absence of a settled pattern of life that the army could control and reorganize under Roman rule, peace required that first a desert be made' (ibid. 46). Consciously or unconsciously, Luttwak seems to be saying that Germany was Rome's Vietnam. The same held true of 'the North African semidesert, . . . in the plains of what is now the Ukraine, in the arid plateau of Iran, and in the deserts of Arabia' (ibid.).

There may be some truth in this where deserts are concerned (although the conditions did not stop Augustus from sending an expedition to Arabia Felix in 26 BC), but it is difficult to see hostile terrain as an obstacle to further Roman advances in the north, either in reality or in the perception of the Romans. It is not self-evident that the landscape of Germany or Iran should have been more hostile than that of, say, Iberia, Gaul or Illyricum. That the Germans were 'semi-nomadic' and therefore unconquerable can be questioned (Mann 1979, 178); and if we need proof that the Romans could, if they wished, deploy their forces effectively against 'the widely dispersed rural base of warrior nations whose life and whose strength did not depend on the survival of a city-based economic and social structure' (Luttwak 1976, 46), we have only to consider their success in lowland Britain, which in AD 43 was overrun and brought under effective Roman control within a matter of months (if not weeks). True, the hill country of Wales and the North took longer to subdue, but the Romans nevertheless persisted and were eventually successful except in the north of Scotland, where their failure is unlikely to have been due to the nature of the country (Brunt 1990, 474). As for Iran, it is equally hard to understand why the Romans would necessarily have failed where the Macedonians had succeeded (Mann 1979, 177–8; Brunt, loc. cit.)

(2) *Was there any point in further expansion?* Another possibility is that the Romans refrained from further expansion during the principate, not because of the physical difficulties of the task, but because it was simply not worth the effort. This explanation does derive some support from the sources, which claim that the empire already embraced the best regions of the world and that the lands beyond the frontiers were infertile and inhabited only by a few nomads. This is the view of Strabo (6. 4. 2 (288); 17. 3. 24 (839)), writing in the time of Augustus. Similarly Appian, in the time of Antoninus Pius, declares: 'Possessing the best parts of the earth and sea the Romans have, on the whole, aimed to preserve their empire by the exercise of prudence, rather than to extend their sway over profitless tribes of barbarians' (App. *praef.* 7; cf. Florus, 2. 29).

But these complacent remarks represent a rhetorical conceit, rather than a rational statement of policy. The suggestion that the Romans already ruled over everything worth having was no more than an excuse for their failure to go further; it served to explain, or rather to explain away, the fact that the conquest of the *orbis terrarum*, so confidently predicted in the time of Caesar and the early years of Augustus, had not in fact materialized (Brunt 1990, 475–7). As far as expense is concerned, Strabo makes the point explicitly in his remarks about Britain. 'Although the Romans could have possessed Britain,' he writes (2. 5. 8 (115)),

> they scorned to do so, for they saw that there was nothing to fear from the Britons, since they are not strong enough to cross over and attack us. No corresponding advantages would arise by taking over and holding the country. For at present more seems to accrue from the customs duties on their commerce than direct taxation could supply, if we deduct the cost of maintaining an army to garrison the island and collect the tribute.

This passage contrasts sharply with statements by other Augustan writers, such as Horace, who confidently refers to the imminent conquest of Britain (*Odes*, 3. 5. 3–4) without the slightest hint that it might not be advantageous to Rome. The best interpretation of this discrepancy is that Strabo reflects a changed atmosphere, and was writing at a time when the plan to conquer Britain had been abandoned – or at least postponed (Brunt 1963, 173–4 = 1990, 103–4).

(3) *Was expansion too expensive?* Whether Strabo was right about the economic consequences of occupying Britain is difficult to say. But for the present purpose all that needs to be said is that the costs of the military operation did not, in the event, deter Claudius from mounting a successful invasion. We should also note that the conquest of Britain entailed only a relatively small increase in the overall military establishment of the Roman empire – at most two legions, if we assume that the legions XV and XXII Primigeniae, raised either by Caligula or by Claudius, were created in order to release other legions for the invasion of Britain. It follows that any calculation should only take account of the marginal costs of the occupation, which were relatively low and would certainly have been covered by only a small proportion of the tribute levied on the new province. That Britain, when it became a province, was profitable is beyond question, provided we rule out the unrealistic and counterfactual 'peace dividend' that could have been realized if Claudius had decided instead to reduce

the size of the Roman army by around 50,000 men – or the 'opportunity cost' of benefits that might have been gained by dispatching 50,000 men to conquer, say, Parthia.

The fact that the Roman emperors maintained a large standing army means that there cannot have been major increases in military expenditure in wartime. Some scholars have maintained the opposite (A. R. Birley 1981, 39; MacMullen 1976, 104–5, and 1984), but have not offered any strong supporting arguments or evidence. Transport costs, and increased expenditure on arms, matériel, road building and so on, would add marginally to the normal peacetime budget; we may also suspect that army units were kept below strength during peacetime, and would have had to be supplemented by new levies (Crawford 1975, 591–2; Corbier 1978, 283). But there can be no certainty about this, and it is equally possible that troop numbers in war zones were increased by taking detachments from elsewhere. To that extent one can see that it might have cost more to put Roman army units on a war footing, but there is no evidence that the expense would have been prohibitive.

Birley cites no evidence to support his claim that 'when major wars occurred expenditure increased sharply, as Roman writers often affirm' (A. R. Birley 1981, 39). One wonders which Roman writers he has in mind; in any case it rather depends on what is meant by 'sharply'. MacMullen (1984), who places great stress on transport costs, produces figures which suggest that moving a whole legion from one end of the empire to the other would increase the state's annual military budget by no more than around 0.5 per cent. It may be that in the late Empire it was somehow more difficult and more costly for the emperor to mobilize his forces for war; but one cannot imagine that what was possible for Rome in the age of Augustus suddenly became impossible under Tiberius; in any case we happen to know (from Suet. *Calig.* 37) that under Tiberius the empire's budget was in surplus to the tune of about 100 million sesterces a year – that is, around 20–25 per cent of the amount regularly spent on keeping the armed forces in being (Hopkins 1980, 125).

On the other hand it should be noted that successful war could be extremely profitable in terms of booty, and the exploitation of conquered territory through taxation and the extraction of mineral resources. It is absurd to suggest that peoples and places beyond the Rhine and Danube were too impoverished to yield significant amounts of booty, and were in this respect different from Spain in the second century BC or Gaul in the time of Julius Caesar. The profits from the conquest of Dacia in 106–8 are in any case sufficient to disprove this notion.

I conclude, therefore, that Roman military policy in the principate was not determined to any significant extent by financial constraints. Emperors could, and sometimes did, undertake major wars of conquest; the problem is why they did so only rarely, and why in general they did not follow the precedent of the leaders of the Republic and of Augustus.

(4) *Augustus' last wishes.* The explanation most commonly advanced for this change is that the defeat of Quinctilius Varus in AD 9 caused Augustus to change his mind about the expansionist course he had previously pursued; the attempt to conquer Germany, he now realized, had been a ghastly mistake, and he was determined to see that it should not be repeated. He therefore advised his successors to keep within the existing borders. They followed his advice, and the Roman peace ensued. But one only has to state the case in this manner to see that it is not an adequate solution to the problem. It is hard to believe that hundreds of years of continuous war and imperialism could be brought to an end by one disaster, however serious, and that the alleged last wishes of one old man should have been observed for almost two centuries (Mann 1974, 511; 1979, 177). There must be more to it than that, even if we reject the possibility that Augustus still continued to make plans for further conquests after the disaster, and that the deathbed instruction in fact emanated from Tiberius, who either invented it or, more probably, forced it upon his ailing stepfather (cf. Ober 1982).

(5) *Emperors' personal inclinations.* Tacitus complained more than once that the warlike traditions of the Republic had been abandoned by the emperors, and put forward their apathy and laziness as a reason (e.g. *Ann.* 4. 32, cited below). There is undoubtedly much truth in the view that the concentration of political power in the hands of one man contributed to the long peace that characterized the early Empire, and it is likely that strong-minded, experienced and thoughtful men such as Tiberius

and Hadrian deliberately rejected the bellicose policies of their predecessors. In such cases the individual personality must be seen as an important factor in shaping historical events. But it would be wrong to place too much emphasis on the character of particular emperors, and to ascribe the Roman peace to the accidental fact that the throne was occupied by certain individuals and not by others. There are structural factors at work too, as I hope to show; and it is important not to forget that the emperor did not have complete control of events. The work of Fergus Millar has made it clear that the imperial government did not think in terms of active 'policies', and did not possess the resources to carry them out (Millar 1977; 1982). On this view the development of a frontier system, if that is a proper way to describe the haphazard jumble of *ad hoc* arrangements on the various borders of the empire, was not the result of deliberate planning. It just happened (Millar 1982; Mann 1979). It may be that some emperors were by nature uninterested, lazy, indifferent or, for whatever reason, inactive; but there must be more to it than that.

(6) *Was there a 'pax Romana'?*   A more effective way of loosing the knot might be to cut it, by arguing that the Roman peace was not really an age of peace at all. It is undeniable that wars were fought under the principate, and there is a case for saying that the change we have been examining is more apparent than real. We have already seen that the much-vaunted *pax Augusta* was nothing of the kind. War and conquest were pursued with unparalleled ferocity outside the borders of the empire under Augustus; what was celebrated as peace was the end of civil war and the restoration of order in Italy and the inner provinces. Is it possible that the longer *pax Romana* is equally illusory? Is it really true that war and imperialism came to an end with the accession of Tiberius?

The conquest of Britain under Claudius, and that of Dacia under Trajan, have already been noted as exceptions to the general pattern, and it may have struck some readers as paradoxical (to say the least) that these instances should be cited as evidence for the Roman state's capacity to conduct successful wars during the principate, and as arguments against the idea that wars of conquest were too expensive or for other reasons impracticable. Equally we should not overlook the minor campaigns that went on fairly continuously in some frontier zones, and the numerous internal wars caused by uprisings and revolts. To say that the early Empire was an age of complete and uninterrupted peace is of course an exaggeration. No one would seriously deny this; but most historians, one suspects, would argue that it is a matter of degree – that is to say, there was a marked reduction in the amount of active campaigning by Roman armies in the first and second centuries AD by comparison with what went before.

Such a proposition is not easily tested. The problem is to quantify the relative levels of military activity that took place at different periods. But we do not possess enough data to carry out a proper statistical comparison of the level and intensity of Roman warfare under the Republic and under the Empire. Calculations of such things as annual (or even monthly) casualty and fatality rates in proportion to population size, which have been used in studies of modern nations at war (Singer and Small 1972), are out of the question in Roman history. We have to make do with crude categories and largely subjective impressions, the most important and distinctive of which come from the writings of contemporaries.

Our sources leave us in no doubt that the early Empire was less warlike than the Republic, an impression that emerges at once from a comparison of Livy and Tacitus. Tacitus himself was conscious of this. Writing of the reign of Tiberius, he says :

> I am aware that much of what I have described, and shall describe, may seem unimportant and trivial. But my chronicle is quite a different matter from histories of early Rome. Their subjects were great wars, cities stormed, kings routed and captured. Or, if home affairs were their choice, they could turn freely to conflicts of consuls with tribunes, to land- and corn-laws, feuds of conservatives and commons. Mine, on the other hand, is a circumscribed, inglorious field. Peace was scarcely broken, if at all. Rome was plunged in gloom, the ruler uninterested in expanding the empire.
>
> (Tac. *Ann.* 4. 32)

But this remark is, even by Tacitus' standards, exceptionally disingenuous. Court intrigue and the corrupting effects of despotism are the topics he likes best, and his ability to analyse them is what makes him the great historian he is. As a chronicler of military campaigns Tacitus can be exceedingly dull. Of course that is not always so; his accounts of Boudicca's revolt, of Agricola's campaigns in Scotland, and of the civil wars of 69, are masterly. But they come alive because of the author's interest in their political and moral aspects, rather than because of the military details themselves. I would venture to suggest that Tacitus was not particularly drawn to military narrative as such; and I cannot agree with Syme, who takes *Ann.* 4. 32 at face value, that Tacitus gave disproportionate space to the revolt of Tacfarinas because, in the absence of great foreign wars, and in the midst of dull and deplorable domestic affairs, it provided much needed relief and variety (Syme 1951, 120). If anything, the truth is the other way round; Tacitus tends to understate the importance of military operations in the provinces during the principate, and makes it seem a more peaceful period than it actually was.

Let us briefly summarize the facts, in so far as the evidence allows. During the empire Roman army units were frequently engaged in low-level campaigns against minor incursions and unrest. In parts of the empire such as North Africa there was fairly continuous 'police' activity of this kind. In Egypt, as we know from papyri, minor insurrections and unrest in the countryside were common. On the Rhine and Danube frontiers there were frequent campaigns against peoples on the other side of the frontier, some of which are recorded in historical sources, others only known through incidental references, inscriptions, and so on. For instance the operations against the Sarmatians and Roxolani undertaken by Ti. Plautius Silvanus in Moesia during the reign of Nero are known only from the famous epitaph inscribed on Silvanus' tomb (*ILS* 986). Sometimes these clashes developed into more serious wars, such as those against the Chatti and the Dacians under Domitian. In Britain serious fighting went on fairly continuously (apart from a period of consolidation and comparative peace in the 60s) from the time of the initial invasion in 43 to the recall of Agricola in *c*.85, and intermittently after that.

In addition to this regular military activity in frontier zones, there were provincial revolts, which in some cases became major armed clashes. The rebellions of Florus and Sacrovir, Boudicca and Civilis, and the great Jewish uprisings of 66 and 132, are the best-known instances of a phenomenon that may have been more frequent and more serious than our meagre sources suggest at first sight. We have to reckon with the possibility that the suppression of internal unrest and routine campaigning in frontier zones have been systematically under-recorded in the surviving sources (cf. Woolf below, ch. 7). There may be all kinds of particular reasons for this. Official propaganda would not have wanted to make too much of campaigns in which the emperor was not personally involved. Thus the very arduous campaigns in north-west Spain that followed Augustus' departure in 25 BC are minimized or passed over altogether in some accounts; according to Velleius (2. 90. 4), not even brigandage persisted after the emperor had withdrawn – a tall story, as Syme has pointed out (1970, 103). Tacitus had his own personal reasons for underplaying the achievements of Agricola's predecessors in Britain, particularly Cerialis and Frontinus. But the principal reason, one suspects, was that small-scale frontier wars and the suppression of internal unrest conferred little prestige on the generals who carried them out, and were of minimal interest to historians and their readers.

There can be no doubt that the principate has a military history, and that warfare did not abruptly cease at the end of the reign of Augustus. The idea of an age of war followed by an age of peace is much too crude. Moreover, it is not easy to view the change simply as a matter of degree; who can say whether the warfare of the Republic was more or less intense than that of the principate? There are no suitable criteria of measurement, and the data are inadequate. On the other hand, it is not really possible to maintain that there was no change at all. Contemporary writers thought there was, and that fact in itself requires some kind of explanation. But if it is not a question of degree, it would seem to follow that the wars of the imperial period were different in kind from those that went before. Here we approach the nub of the matter. Under the Republic war was tied to imperialism, whereas under the principate most wars were fought in order to consolidate existing possessions and to put down internal unrest. The most obvious change would therefore seem to be that major foreign wars, particularly wars of conquest, were rare events in the first and second centuries AD. There can be no question that the programme of continuous imperial expansion, pursued so relentlessly by Augustus, was not continued by his successors.

The Republican origins of the *pax Romana*

The problem cannot be resolved by arguing that it does not exist. Even so it still seems to me that the best approach is to reconsider the terms of the question. So far it has been assumed that the Roman Republic was an age of continuous war and imperial expansion. The trend continued into the reign of Augustus, and only came to an end under his successors, when war continued to take place, but major foreign wars became infrequent and expansion was rarely pursued.

The weakness of this formulation lies in its characterization of the Republic. The modern orthodoxy holds that from the late fourth century BC onwards the Romans engaged in continuous wars and relentless imperial conquest. What is wrong with this picture is that it presupposes an unchanging pattern of war and imperialism over a period of more than three centuries. While acknowledging that wars were fought in increasingly distant theatres and on an ever-growing scale, the standard view today nevertheless appears to assume that the same drives, the same dynamic, the same motivating forces lay behind the process of Roman imperialism throughout the Republican epoch. In my opinion this view is mistaken.

W. V. Harris, whose work has been so influential in the formation of the current orthodoxy, ended his account of war and imperialism in Republican Rome in 70 BC. His reason for doing this was not simply that he had to stop somewhere, nor the increasing complexity of the source material; rather it was because he rightly sensed that by the early years of the first century BC a change had occurred in the phenomenon he was analysing. Harris himself defines the change in terms of a shift in the location of power within Roman society: 'foreign wars and expansion gradually ceased to be the preoccupations of the Roman aristocracy and the citizen body, and became instead the specialized policy of certain "great men" and their followers' (Harris 1979, 5). The point is well taken, but in my view Harris does not go far enough. There are two aspects to this. First, the change is more fundamental than Harris suggests. It is not simply that individual dynasts took over the direction of affairs from the senate and people. Rather, the whole pattern of Roman war-making, its frequency, intensity and duration, and its nature and function within society, were profoundly different in the first century BC from what they had been earlier. Second, the change was a gradual one, and its symptoms were manifesting themselves long before the turn of the first century. The second century was already very different from the third. It was not simply a matter of scale and distance; the very fact of continuous war, which was the dominant feature of Roman life in the fourth and third centuries BC, was already beginning to disappear in the first half of the second century.

These points can best be illustrated by giving a brief outline of the historical development of Roman warfare during the Republic. In the early years of the Republic the Romans fought for survival against the depredations of hostile neighbours. In the later years of the fifth century BC and the early decades of the fourth they became more aggressive and began to threaten the security of neighbouring cities and peoples (for details see Cornell 1989, 281–323). After the reforms of 367 BC, which transformed the political structure of the state, the stage was set for the classic pattern of Roman war-making, which was linked to the new style of political competition and the emergence of the nobility (Hölkeskamp 1987).

For nearly 150 years from this time war for the Romans was a regular annual event. Every year the two consuls conducted a levy, led out their armies from the city (sometimes jointly, but usually in different directions), invaded the territories of other states and made war on their populations. This activity was both aggressive and, in the long term, always successful. The conquered peoples, and those who chose to surrender in advance rather than be defeated, were obliged to become allies of the Romans, and to join them in subsequent campaigns. Roman military expertise and efficiency grew together with the number and strength of their allies. By the end of the fourth century BC the Romans were the dominant power in Italy, and by 264 they had conquered the entire peninsula. In the following decades they took Sicily and Sardinia from the Carthaginians, and embarked on the conquest and colonization of the Po valley.

Victory brought tangible gains in the form of movable booty, slaves and land, as well as the intangible benefits of increased security, power and glory. These benefits were shared among the citizens, who served in the army as a function of their citizenship.

Constant warfare required the commitment of a high proportion of citizen manpower to regular active service; throughout the period of the middle Republic between 10 and 15 per cent of adult male citizens were under arms every year, and at times of crisis the figure was much higher. To achieve this level every Roman citizen would have had to serve for at least four years; but since there was a property qualification for service in the legions, the actual figure was probably more like seven years among the *adsidui* (those qualified to serve) (Harris 1979, 44–5). Such service would inevitably have entailed active participation in war.

Warfare was therefore part of the normal experience of every Roman, and was embedded in the fabric of Roman society. The Republic's institutions were military in character and function; its religion, and its cultural and moral values, were suffused with a militaristic ethos. This is the warrior society that has been so well described and analysed in recent studies (Hopkins 1978, 25–37; Harris 1979, 9–53). But what needs to be emphasized is that the pattern of regular annual campaigns is characteristic of the first phase of the middle Republic, specifically the period from 362 to 218 BC.

The later years of the third century introduced a new stage in the development of Roman imperialism. At first sight it might seem that Roman military activity in the later third and second centuries BC was more of the same but on a larger scale, and that is how it is often treated by modern writers. But the period of overseas war and expansion was accompanied by important structural changes which altered the nature of Roman war-making in significant ways. From now on Roman armies were involved in far-flung campaigns in distant overseas theatres which lasted for years on end. Roman campaigning no longer followed an annual pattern, and ceased to have the seasonal, biological rhythm that it had had previously. Formal annual levies no longer took place in the traditional way. It is generally agreed that Polybius' famous account of the levy on the Capitol (6. 19–20) did not reflect the practice of his time, or even of the time he was writing about, namely the Hannibalic War (Brunt 1971, 625–34). Major commands were increasingly held by proconsuls whose appointments could be prolonged by the senate for several years; conversely, many of the annual consuls served in settled provinces and were not involved in active warfare (Sherwin-White 1984, 11–

15). The army began to change its character; from a citizen militia drawn from small farmers it came more and more to depend on recruitment among the rural proletariat. This process, which was aggravated by social pressures and made possible by successive reductions of the minimum property qualification for service, was already well advanced by the time of the Gracchi.[1]

These developments are well known and have been extensively studied. But an important aspect that has received less attention is the fact that there was a change in the frequency and the character of the wars themselves. This change has two important features that deserve emphasis. First, warfare became intermittent, and wide fluctuations can be observed between periods of intense fighting and interludes of relative calm (cf. Rich above, ch. 2). In the second century BC Roman armies were stationed permanently in Spain and northern Italy. But they were not continuously at war. In these areas wars alternated with long periods in which Roman military activity consisted of small-scale operations and garrison duty (e.g. in Spain from 179 to 154, and after 133, and in northern Italy after around 170). In North Africa and the eastern Mediterranean the Romans had no permanent military presence, and intervened only sporadically in a series of major wars (e.g. the Second and Third Macedonian Wars, the Syrian War, and the Third Punic War). Periods of relative inactivity on all fronts can be identified, for instance between 167 and 154. Polybius tells us that in 156 the Roman senate resolved to make war on the Dalmatians because 'they did not at all wish the Italians to become effeminate owing to the long peace, it being now twelve years since the war with Perseus and their campaigns in Macedonia' (Polyb. 36. 13. 6-7).

The conclusion of the Numantine War in 133 was also followed by a period of general inactivity, interrupted only by a minor revolt in Asia (131-129) and an uprising in Sardinia (126), before the conquest of Gallia Narbonensis began in 125. Further peaceful interludes occurred in the 90s, between Marius' victory over the

---

[1] Gabba 1976, 1–19; Brunt 1962. Rich 1983 has shown that the evidence underlying the reconstruction of Gabba and Brunt is extremely fragile (and at times non-existent); but his arguments nevertheless confirm that the economic and social status of the legionaries was very low even during the second century BC, and that is what matters for the present purpose.

Germans (101) and the outbreak of the Social War (91), and from 63 to 58 after the conclusion of Pompey's eastern campaigns. These periods of peace, lasting from around five to little over ten years, are quite short and may not seem particularly significant. But they represent a striking contrast with the continuous wars of the fourth and third centuries, when even a single year without a major campaign was a rarity (Harris 1979, 256–7). The argument being put forward here is that as time passed these interludes of comparative peace became longer and more frequent, and that major imperialistic ventures became increasingly rare.

At first sight this proposition may seem surprising, but this is because of two factors which have tended to mask the development of the process. In the first place the interludes of peace were not accompanied by total demobilization; Roman armies continued to be stationed in frontier provinces, even if they were not engaged in full-scale war. Second, in the period we are considering the Republic was engulfed by the internal conflicts and civil wars that eventually brought it down. The last century of the Republic was not, by any standards, a peaceful age. This observation leads us to the second important feature of the change in the nature of Roman warfare that was referred to earlier.

In the last century of the Republic most wars were caused by internal conflict, unrest and discontent within the empire. There can be no doubt that in this sense Roman military history entered a new phase around the time of the Gracchi. The wars against Jugurtha (110–105), Sertorius (79–72) and Mithridates (88–85; 74–63) involved the revolt of provinces and subject territories in Africa, Spain and the Greek East (respectively); the Social War (91–89) was a rebellion by Rome's Italian allies, and at least six distinct periods of civil war can be identified (88–86; 83–81; 49–45; 43–41; 38–36; 31–30). Lesser armed uprisings occurred in 77 (Lepidus) and 63 (Catiline), and the period also experienced serious slave revolts (136–132; 104–101; 73–71) and campaigns against pirates (102–100; 77–75; 74–72; 69–67).

These internecine conflicts were part of the Roman revolution, and must be seen as symptoms of a painful readjustment to the new conditions produced by the growth of empire and the contradictions inherent in the process of imperialism. The Roman Republic, that is to say, was a victim of its own success. Even in the midst of these trials, however, the empire continued to expand through conquest. But the imperialist wars of the late Republic were exceptional events, first because they entailed military operations on an unprecedented scale, and second because they occurred only rarely. The spectacular campaigns of Pompey in the East in the 60s, and of Caesar in Gaul in the 50s, are without parallel, unless we count Crassus' ill-fated attack on Parthia in 54–53 and Mark Antony's abortive invasion of Armenia and western Iran in 36–34.

By the late Republic, it can be argued, the nature of war and imperialism was totally different from what it had been in the age of regular seasonal campaigns in the fourth and third centuries, and had become something much closer to that of the imperial period. The beginnings of this pattern are already visible in the events of the second century BC. At that period Rome had begun to keep a regular military presence in certain provinces. Areas such as Spain and northern Italy were effectively war zones, in which an initial period of regular warfare was followed after a generation or so by more settled conditions under permanent military supervision. This is precisely what happened in Britain after the invasion of AD 43. In terms of military policy the two cases are, in my opinion, exactly parallel. Other provinces had armies permanently stationed in them in order to contain what Luttwak calls 'low intensity threats'. The most obvious cases are Macedonia from 149 BC, Transalpine Gaul after 125, and Cilicia and Syria after 61 (evidence in Brunt 1971, 432–3, 449). The function of these military forces was not essentially different from that of the Rhine and Danube armies during the first century AD. On the other hand, major imperialistic adventures occurred only intermittently in the post-Gracchan age, and were clearly exceptional: Caesar's campaigns in Gaul, the Augustan conquests, the Claudian invasion of Britain and Trajan's advance into Dacia could be listed under this heading.

In the eastern Mediterranean major wars were fought sporadically, and alternated with long intervals of peace and diplomacy. It is possible to see continuity from the Macedonian, Syrian and Mithridatic Wars under the Republic to the Parthian wars of the principate. Sometimes these eastern wars resulted in an increase in Roman territory, and sometimes they did not. On the other hand, throughout the period from the middle of the second century BC to the end of the first century AD, many annexations took place by peaceful means, as former client states such as Asia, Bithynia, Cyrene, Cyprus, Galatia, Thrace, Judaea, Cappadocia and Commagene were incorporated as provinces.

Although it would no doubt be possible to point to important differences in the conduct of Roman foreign policy between the Republic and the principate, the continuities in the pattern of military activity are, I believe, real enough. My argument is simple. The Roman peace was not a new and radical departure from previous policy or behaviour. The change was gradual, and took place in the course of the last two centuries BC. I would argue, moreover, that it is an important element of the process of transformation that we call the Roman Revolution.

War and Augustus' new regime

At this point we need to ask some awkward questions. If the above conclusion is so simple and obvious, why has it escaped the attention of historians and commentators? If the continuities I have noted are indeed real, why do they not emerge more clearly from the ancient sources and the works of their modern successors? The answer to these questions lies in the nature of the historical process under examination. There are two aspects to this. First, the underlying continuities have been obscured by the violent convulsions on the surface. It is difficult to envisage the age of turmoil and civil war in the late Republic as one in which the peaceful conditions of the principate were being formed. Nevertheless, that is what I believe was happening. The conclusion is paradoxical, and, in so far as it offers a view of what the late Republic would have been like if there had been no civil wars, it may seem absurd. But viewed in another way it looks more reasonable. The real point is that what the principate brought about was an end to political crisis and civil war, not a radical change in foreign policy.

The second aspect is that the aggressive and belligerent policies of Augustus do not conform very well to the broad picture that is being outlined here. The explanation is that the Augustan age was an exceptional period in which special factors were at work. I would argue that the reign of Augustus represents a temporary interruption of the continuing trend and one which tends to distort the overall picture. This point requires some explanation and discussion.

It could be argued, first, that Augustan policy was reactionary and anachronistic. That is to say, Augustus deliberately sought to revive the traditional warlike spirit of an earlier age. The restored Republic was being made to revert to its traditional role of fighting external enemies. It is also likely that this was seen as a way to heal the wounds of the civil wars and to unite a formerly divided society. Some such outlook is implicit in works of Augustan literature, most notably perhaps in Livy's first decade. That the regime wished to be identified with the Republican tradition of imperialism is indicated by the inauguration of the Forum of Augustus in 2 BC, in which the emperor's own conquests were memorialized together with statues of earlier generals who had made Rome great (Suet. *Aug.* 31). Augustus therefore sought to revive the old Republican tradition of continuous war and conquest, even though, as we have seen, the tradition was by now long outdated.

A second possible motive is bound up with Augustus' decision to set up a regular standing army of standard size (initially consisting of twenty-eight legions with auxiliary support), with fixed terms of service and guaranteed retirement bonuses (Raaflaub 1980). This was a major development, which ended the chronic insecurity experienced by soldiers under the Republic. It also carried to its logical conclusion the gradual transformation of the Roman army from a citizen militia to a professional force. The problem was that the maintenance of a large standing army entailed a huge recurrent cost to the treasury, and Augustus was eventually (in AD 6) obliged to introduce new taxes to help pay for it, including a 5 per cent inheritance tax paid by Roman citizens. This was not popular, and one can well understand why the emperor felt the need to justify the expense by giving the army something to do. It is most unlikely that he would have been able to keep such a large force inactive for any length of time. The programme of military conquest and imperial expansion under-taken by Augustus was no doubt partly inspired by the need to make the idea of a professional standing army acceptable to public opinion in general, and in particular to the upper classes, first in the provinces, and later among Roman citizens in Italy, who were having to pay for it through taxation. Meanwhile, poets and propagandists were kept busy with the task of commending a belligerent policy to a war-weary population.

Third, it is likely that Augustus wished, by setting out on a path of conquest and expansion, to emphasize his position as Caesar's heir. This raises the important point that the competition for military honours among the oligarchy had been eliminated in the late Republic by the monopolistic tendencies of the dynasts. Military achievements were traditionally the means to glory and political success, and it was therefore necessary for the aspiring dynasts to concentrate them into their own hands. As a result, political office came to depend on imperial patronage rather than personal achievement, and major campaigns had to be conducted either by the emperor in person or by members of his own family. Augustus therefore conducted military campaigns himself, and later gave commands to Tiberius and Drusus, to Gaius Caesar, and finally to Germanicus. Military commands gave prestige and public recognition to members of the imperial family, helped to secure the loyalty of the armies to Caesar's heirs, and served to legitimize dynastic succession. It was consequently necessary for Augustus to provide his heirs with opportunities to exercise major commands, which in turn necessitated an active and belligerent foreign policy.

On the other hand the military ambitions of other nobles had to be curtailed. After 19 BC triumphs were restricted to members of the imperial family, and the activities of senatorial army commanders in the field were carefully controlled. During the Republic triumph-hunting by ambitious commanders was a major cause of war and imperialism. The senate might disapprove of their actions, but was powerless to prevent them. The result was that foreign policy in the Republic was largely fashioned by 'men on the spot', with little in the way of central direction or control (Richardson 1986, especially pp. 172–80). Under the principate this situation was transformed. There was now a strong centralized authority, the emperor, who could and did exercise firm control over provincial governors. Millar has argued that, because of the difficulty of long-distance communication and the natural inertia of the Roman system of government, the commanders of provincial armies must have been given a fairly free hand (Millar 1981). This may be true, but within closely defined limits. For a consular legate to make war on his own initiative would have been unthinkable, and even when he was authorized to take action his movements were carefully restricted. The best illustration of this is the story (Tac. *Ann.* 11. 19–20) of Cn. Domitius Corbulo, the legate of Lower Germany, who in 47 led his army across the Rhine in the course of a war against the Chauci; the emperor ordered him back and forbade any further use of force against the Germans. According to Tacitus, a man of distinction represented a threat to peace and an encumbrance to an indolent ruler (*formidolosum paci virum insignem et ignavo principi praegravem*). Corbulo had no choice but to obey the emperor's instruction, uttering as he did so the bitter comment *beatos quondam duces Romanos* ('how fortunate were the Roman generals of old!').

The anecdote is symbolic and revealing. Emperors had a strong interest in maintaining peace except when it suited them to make war themselves for personal or dynastic reasons. Augustus, as we have seen, needed military victories to legitimize his position and to secure the succession for his heirs. The same considerations apply to the policies of some later emperors. Claudius' invasion of Britain is normally explained as an attempt to gain military prestige and to shore up his rather shaky position; the same motive probably lies behind the German wars of Domitian and the invasion of Dacia under Trajan. As time went on emperors were increasingly involved in active campaigning (Campbell 1983, 32 ff.; 120 ff.), but this happened because of the increasing military pressures on the empire during the second and third centuries. Major wars of expansion occurred only when emperors had specific personal or dynastic reasons to undertake them. Generally speaking, however, such initiatives were unnecessary. By the end of Augustus' reign the principate was well established, and the succession firmly secured. The policy of expansion had served its purpose, and the disaster of AD 9 clearly demonstrated the need to call a halt. It may well be that Tiberius himself, a man of great practical experience and good sense, deliberately reversed a policy which he saw to be misguided and unnecessary. If so the Roman world was greatly in his debt. But in any case the negative political forces predisposing emperors to restrain their armies and their commanders had by this date become far stronger than the positive desire for further expansion, which continued to appeal to jingoistic sentiment but had little practical impact on the conduct of foreign affairs.

The *pax Romana* and the Roman Revolution

The foregoing paragraphs bear out the point made earlier, that the personal decisions of individual emperors were an important factor shaping historical events, but individual emperors exercised their choice and made personal decisions within a broad political context conditioned by factors which were outside their control and of which they were probably not aware. I therefore persist in arguing that structural changes were decisive in bringing about the developments we have been considering, and that the *pax Romana* was a product of the Roman Revolution.

This general observation needs to be examined in more detail. In particular it is worth dwelling briefly on the implications of the most important structural feature of the Roman Revolution, namely the emergence of a fully professional army. This was a complete reversal of the traditional Republican ideal of an integrated society in which every citizen was a farmer, a soldier and the father of a family. The imperial legionary, by contrast, was a regular full-time professional, who was forbidden to own or cultivate land where he was stationed and legally prevented from contracting a valid marriage and begetting children. There could hardly be a more revealing symbol of the transformation of the Roman world than this polar opposition. The transformation can be summarized in general terms as a shift from a closely integrated society to a more differentiated one in which functions such as government, war and religion became the preserve of specialized groups, instead of being embedded in the totality of the citizen body (Hopkins 1978, 74–96).

During the empire the process of structural differentiation was intensified by the rapid spread of the Roman citizenship and the integration of the provinces. As far as the army was concerned, this had the paradoxical effect of enlarging its recruitment base but at the same time widening the gap that separated it from civilian society. During the first century AD the legions were increasingly, and in the end almost exclusively, recruited in the provinces (Forni 1953). The army was also physically separated from the rest of society, being stationed on distant frontiers which became military zones with their own special characteristics. The effect of these developments was that Italy and the inner provinces of the empire were gradually demilitarized, and the warlike tradition of the Roman people faded out of existence. The warrior spirit survived only in a distorted and artificial form, as people took vicarious pleasure in reconstructions of battles in the writings of historians and poets, and in the bloody spectacles of the arena (Hopkins 1983).

The change affected all levels of society, but is particularly noticeable among the upper classes. During the middle Republic, equestrians were liable to ten years' service, completion of which was a requirement for political office (Polyb. 6. 19. 2–5). Military achievements were an indispensable qualification for political success, which depended in the last analysis on the favour of the voters in the assemblies, consisting principally of men who fought in the army and whose very lives might depend on the military competence of those whom they elected. By contrast, under the principate most senators and *equites* had little or no experience of military service, and, of those who had, few would have taken part in active combat. Political advancement depended now on the emperor's patronage, for which military achievements were not necessary and perhaps not even an advantage. Too high a reputation could be dangerous, as Tacitus pointed out.

Other routes to advancement were open, and many senators followed civilian careers. An interesting example is the career of the younger Pliny. Although he served for one year as a military tribune in Syria, and was later appointed Prefect of the Aerarium Militare, Pliny clearly knew and cared little about military affairs. It is significant that his wide-ranging correspondence, with its descriptions of the daily life and daily concerns of a Roman aristocrat, makes hardly any reference to military matters, warfare, or events on the frontiers. Even the conquest of Dacia fails to merit his attention: the only allusions to it occur in a letter offering literary advice to a man planning to write a history of the Dacian Wars (*Ep*. 8. 4), and a few perfunctory lines of congratulation to the emperor on his victory (10. 14).

In Pliny's time senators who had military experience and commanded the armies were known as *viri militares*, in contrast to

the majority who followed civilian careers (E. Birley 1953).[1]
Such a distinction would have been meaningless in the middle
Republic, and did not become an important feature of Roman
public life until the first century BC, when men like C. Flavius
Fimbria, A. Gabinius, C. Memmius and L. Volcatius Tullus
emerged as early examples of military specialists (Smith 1958, 61–
6). On the other hand there are signs that by the late second
century BC military service was no longer an essential requirement
for political office (Harris 1979, 257). According to Sallust,
Marius drew a contrast between himself and nobles whose
experience of warfare was based entirely on history books and
Greek treatises on military tactics (Sall. *Jug.* 85. 12). This may be
an anachronism for the time of Marius, but it evidently sounded
plausible enough to Sallust. In Plutarch we find Marius presented
as a gruff major-general figure with no aptitude or liking for
politics or civilian life (see especially Plut. *Mar.* 31. 2; 32. 1). This
picture is unhistorical, but for us it provides useful confirmation
that a distinction between military men and civilian politicians
was a reality when Plutarch wrote in the early second century AD.

These facts have an important bearing on the question of the
pax Romana. We have seen that under the principate the Roman
empire was by no means free from war. But this fact was largely
ignored by our sources, whose authors were pleased to think that
they were living in an age of peace. The explanation for this
strange fact is not far to seek. First, as we have seen, the educated
classes of the empire had no experience of war. They had no
conception of what the frontier provinces were like, and no
particular reason to find out. For most Roman aristocrats war
was something to be read about in books, a topic offering scope
for the exercise of rhetorical skill. Lucian's unforgettable satire on
the historians of the Parthian War of 161–5 clearly shows that the
realities of war counted for nothing with historians and their
readers (Lucian, *How to Write History*, especially 14–16). For
Pliny, as we have seen, the Dacian War was no more than a
literary problem.

[1]   Campbell 1975 proves that the phrase was not a precise technical term,
but his arguments do not convince me that the republican tradition of a
senatorial career 'persisted in the empire' and that *viri militares* did not
exist.

A huge gulf separated such people from the world of the frontier provinces and the life of the soldier. Even Tacitus' much-admired account of the mutiny of the German and Pannonian legions in AD 14 is largely a skilful congeries of rhetorical effects, as Erich Auerbach showed long ago (Auerbach 1953, 33–40). Tacitus has absolutely no understanding of the problems the soldiers faced or sympathy with their complaints. What we find instead is a contemptuous reference to 'the usual issues' (*Ann.* 1. 16. 1: *nullis novis causis*) and an account which presents the whole affair as a typical example of indiscipline and low-class impudence. Similar sentiments underlie his comments about the 'madness' of the soldiery in the civil wars of 68–9 (Powell 1972). Such passages reveal a contempt bred from unfamiliarity. The Roman upper classes were terrified of the army. To them the life of the camp was an alien and hostile world, which they looked upon with fear and loathing (cf. Isaac 1990, 24).

In these circumstances ancient writers were unlikely to attach much importance to events on the frontiers. Except on the occasion of major campaigns involving the emperors, wars were remote affairs to be either ignored altogether or treated in a trivial or offhand way. Why should historians and rhetoricians bother with events that had no effect on their leisured existence and were occurring in places about which they knew little and cared even less? Here the contrast with the Republic is very striking. Then wars were always of major political importance; the interests of tens of thousands of Italian families were at stake; and the upper classes were closely involved. Senators and *equites* had all done military service in the provinces, about which they were extremely well informed and where they had important personal interests to protect. In the Empire foreign wars continued to take place much as in the late Republic. What changed was their impact on Roman society, and particularly on the consciousness of the upper classes.

In one sense it could be argued that the Roman Peace had no objective reality: it was an illusion arising from the blinkered perceptions of the educated and well-off inhabitants of Italy and the inner provinces. But in another sense it was not an illusion: the state of affairs that we have described is precisely what is meant by the Roman peace. The radical transformation of the Roman world in the last two centuries BC had brought into being a civilian society. The empire had become a world in which most people lived in peace for most of the time. War was an unfamiliar experience for the great majority of them. Soldiers were a marginal group stationed in remote areas and involved in activities that were irrelevant to the daily lives of civilians. The *pax Romana* had little or nothing to do with what was happening on the frontiers. Wars were fought from time to time, but their effect was so slight that it was possible for historians and rhetoricians to ignore them or even to state that they had not happened. The Roman peace was a great achievement, even if it was not the product of deliberate policy; but we should not allow the complacent rhetoric of sources such as Florus, Appian or Aelius Aristides to disguise the fact that in remote and forgotten corners of the empire men and women, 'Romans' and 'barbarians' alike, were paying a heavy price for it.[1]

Bibliography

Anderson, J. G. C. (1934), 'The eastern frontier under Augustus', in *CAH* x, ch. 9 (pp. 239–83).

Auerbach, E. (1953), *Mimesis: The Representation of Reality in Western Literature* (Princeton).

Birley, A. R. (1974), 'Roman frontiers and Roman frontier policy: some reflections on Roman imperialism', *Transactions of the Architectural and Archaeological Society of Northumberland and Durham*, n.s. 3: 13–25.

—— (1981), 'The economic effects of Roman frontier policy', in A. King and M. Henig (eds), *The Roman West in the Third Century* (Oxford), pp. 39–53.

Birley, E. (1953), 'Senators in the emperor's service', *Proceedings of the British Academy*, 39: 197–214.

Brunt, P. A. (1962), 'The army and the land in the Roman Revolution', *JRS* 52: 69–86; = Brunt 1988, ch. 5 (pp. 240–80).

—— (1963), review of H. D. Meyer, *Die Aussenpolitik des Augustus und die augusteische Dichtung*, *JRS* 53: 170–6; = 'Augustan imperialism', in Brunt 1990, ch. 5 (pp. 96–109).

—— (1971), *Italian Manpower 225 BC–AD 14* (Oxford).

—— (1978), 'Laus imperii', in P. D. A. Garnsey and C. R. Whittaker (eds), *Imperialism in the Ancient World* (Cambridge), ch. 8 (pp. 159–91); = Brunt 1990, ch. 14 (pp. 288–323).

---

[1] I am very grateful to John Rich for his comments on an earlier version of this chapter.

—— (1988), *The Fall of the Roman Republic and Related Essays* (Oxford).

—— (1990), *Roman Imperial Themes* (Oxford).

Campbell, J. B. (1975), 'Who were the "viri militares"?', *JRS* 65: 11–31.

—— (1984), *The Emperor and the Roman Army, 31 BC–AD 235* (Oxford).

Corbier, M. (1978), 'Dévaluations et fiscalité', in *Les 'Dévaluations' à Rome* (Rome), pp. 273–309.

Cornell, T. J. (1989), 'Rome and Latium to 390 BC' and 'The recovery of Rome', in *CAH*², vii. 2, chs 6–7 (pp. 243–350).

Crawford, M. H. (1975), 'Finance, coinage and money from the Severans to Constantine', in *ANRW* ii. 2. 560–93.

Forni, G. (1953), *Il reclutamento delle legioni da Augusto a Diocleziano* (Milan).

Frank, T. (1914), *Roman Imperialism* (New York).

Gabba, E. (1976), *Republican Rome, the Army and the Allies*, trans. P. J. Cuff (Oxford).

—— (1990), 'Le strategie militari, le frontiere imperiali', in E. Gabba and A. Schiavone (eds), *Storia di Roma*, iv: *Caratteri e morfologie* (Turin), ch. 12 (pp. 487–513).

Harris, W. V. (1979), *War and Imperialism in Republican Rome 327–70 BC* (Oxford).

Hölkeskamp, K.-J. (1987), *Die Entstehung der Nobilität* (Stuttgart).

Hopkins, K. (1978), *Conquerors and Slaves* (Cambridge).

—— (1980), 'Taxes and trade in the Roman empire', *JRS* 70: 118–25.

—— (1983), *Death and Renewal* (Cambridge).

Isaac, B. (1990), *The Limits of Empire: The Roman Army in the East* (Oxford).

Linderski, J. (1984), '*Si vis pacem, para bellum*: concepts of defensive imperialism', in W. V. Harris (ed.), *The Imperialism of Mid-Republican Rome* (Rome), pp. 133–64.

Luttwak, E. N. (1976), *The Grand Strategy of the Roman Empire from the First Century AD to the Third* (Baltimore and London).

MacMullen, R. (1976), *The Roman Government's Response to Crisis* (New Haven, Conn.).

—— (1984), 'The Roman emperors' army costs', *Latomus*, 43: 571–80.

Mann, J. C. (1974), 'The frontiers of the principate', in *ANRW* ii. 1. 508–33.

—— (1979), 'Power, force and the frontiers of the empire' (review of Luttwak 1976), *JRS* 69: 175–83.

Millar, F. G. B. (1977), *The Emperor in the Roman World* (London).

—— (1982), 'Emperors, frontiers and foreign relations, 31 BC to AD 378', *Britannia*, 13: 1–23.

Ober, J. (1982), 'Tiberius and the political testament of Augustus', *Historia*, 31: 306–28.

Powell, C. A. (1972), 'Deum ira, hominum rabies', *Latomus*, 31: 833–48.

Raaflaub, K. J. (1980), 'The political significance of Augustus' military reforms', in W. S. Hanson and L. J. F. Keppie (eds), *Roman Frontier Studies, 1979* (Oxford), pp. 1005–25.

Rich, J. W. (1983), 'The supposed Roman manpower shortage of the later second century BC', *Historia*, 32: 287–331.

Richardson, J. S. (1986), *Hispaniae: Spain and the Development of Roman Imperialism, 218–82 BC* (Cambridge).

Sherwin-White, A. N. (1984), *Roman Foreign Policy in the East 168 BC to AD 1* (London).

Singer, J. D., and Small, M. (1972), *The Wages of War 1816–1965: A Statistical Handbook* (New York).

Smith, R. E. (1958), *Service in the Post-Marian Roman Army* (Manchester).

Syme, R. (1934), 'The northern frontiers under Augustus', *CAH* x, ch. 12 (pp. 340–81).

—— (1936), 'Flavian wars and frontiers', *CAH* xi, ch. 4 (pp. 131–87).

—— (1951), 'Tacfarinas, the Musulamii and Thubursicu', in *Studies in Roman Economic and Social History in Honour of A. C. Johnson* (Princeton), pp. 113–30; = Syme 1979, 218–30.

—— (1970), 'The conquest of north-west Spain', in *Legio VII Gemina* (León), pp. 79–107; = Syme 1979, 825–54.

—— (1979), *Roman Papers I–II*, ed. E. Badian (Oxford).

—— (1988), 'Military geography at Rome', *Classical Antiquity*, 7: 227–51.

Wacher, J. S. (1987), *The Roman Empire* (London).

Wells, C. M. (1972), *The German Policy of Augustus: An Examination of the Archaeological Evidence* (Oxford).

7

Roman peace

Greg Woolf

Isn't power simply a form of warlike domination? Shouldn't one therefore conceive all problems of power in terms of relations of war? Isn't power a sort of generalized war which assumes at particular moments the forms of peace and the State? Peace would then be a form of war, and the State a means of waging it.

(Foucault 1980, 123)

War, we are told, was ubiquitous in the ancient world (Finley 1985, 67–87). Among the rare exceptions to this rule were the interior provinces of the Roman empire in the first three centuries AD. But exceptions are important. Peace is hard enough to find in any age and the means by which even a brief respite from continual warfare was achieved are worth examining. Besides, the Roman peace raises problems for the notions that war was a structural component of ancient society, that warfare played a central role in the economies of all ancient states or that making war and guarding against it were essential in the reproduction of ancient societies. Of course, the Roman empire may simply have been exceptional; this is in practice the common view, that the empire's unprecedented size and some near-unique institutions, such as a professional army, created a haven of peace unparalleled before or since. This paper presents a different view of the *pax Romana*, by placing in the centre Roman claims to have created peace as a by-product of empire, and by assessing the ideological status of those claims. Within and without the empire, Roman peace may be seen as simply a component of wider patterns of violence, a concomitant of other structures of domination.

Roman peace is far from exceptional in this respect, and a post-Gibbonian understanding of its nature and origins may help us to appreciate more fully the conditions under which peace has existed in other times and places.

Evocations of the modern world seem inevitable in discussions of war. Despite our long European peace, we still live under the shadow of war, and the same seems true of most societies described by ethnographers and historians. If there is nothing local or temporary about the phenomenon, perhaps it is time to lay the ghost of the ubiquity of warfare as characteristic of the *ancient* world in particular. The origins of war have become the locus of a debate about the moral nature of man. Some see war originating along with the state or even some more primitive political form, so that the growth of complexity has led us away from the original affluent society. Others, with the aid of primatologists and sociobiologists, look to genetic predispositions. Yet others ascribe the persistence of war to a will to power deep in the heart of man. And there is always Cain, or even Eve. Nor can the issue be simplified by imposing narrow restrictions on the use of the term war, for example to conflicts between states recognized by both as wars. It is commonplace to say that one man's war is another man's conflict or police action, rebellion or banditry, terrorism or covert operation; or that war continues politics and politics war, or that world peace, world order and world security are simply the masks of world power. The study of ancient war must therefore become the study of ancient power, or at the very least of those aspects of power involving the actual or threatened use of violence within and between states. Peace is not the absence of such power, and ancient declarations of war and peace can be accepted at face value no more than modern ones.

Images of peace

If violence and 'organized societal violence'[1] are constants, conceptions of war vary widely between and within societies. Modern discussions focus on the role of the state and on

[1] For this definition of war cf. Shipley's introduction to the companion volume, *War and Society in the Greek World.*

battlefield encounters, disputing the extent to which the terminology of warfare may be literally applied to other kinds of conflict, but the metaphorical use of the term is much wider. We are aware, then, that the language of war and peace is contestable, and discussions of definition and usage have become subsumed into broader discourses about the legitimacy of violence and of the state. Many societies probably exist, and have existed, in which these issues were not the subject of debate; the shared assumptions of members of those societies often have to be reconstructed from what is assumed or implicit in their utterances and writings. But the early Roman Empire was not, I shall argue, a world in which nothing needed to be said about violence, but rather a society characterized by debates as fierce as ours, if very different from them.

Central to understanding early imperial uses of the notion of peace is an appreciation of the extent to which they differed from the distinctions made between war and peace in the Republic. These turned not so much on an opposition between *pax* and *bellum* as on an opposition between two moral and religious spheres, *domi* and *militiae*, which were partly constructed by a series of religious rituals.

One way in which the distinction was made concrete was around the *pomerium*, the sacred boundary of the city of Rome. Outside this boundary was the Campus Martius, named for the god of war and originally the area where the Republican citizen army trained. When the citizens assembled there, they were drawn up in battle order as the *comitia centuriata*. When a Republican magistrate went out to war or his province, he first climbed to the Capitol, to perform a series of vows and to take the auspices, and then, dressed in his military garb (*paludatus*) he processed out of the city with his attendants[1]. The complement to this ceremony was the convention that, after concluding a successful campaign, a

---

[1] See Giovannini 1983, 16–19. However, Giovannini underplays the *pomerium*. While he must be correct to reject the idea that *domi* and *militiae* were geographical distinctions and that different kinds of *imperium* were exercised in each, his view does not seem to include a satisfactory account of the spatial components of these rituals. Richardson 1991 offers an account which preserves a sense of the unity of *imperium*, but shows greater sensitivity to the religious dimension.

general might request the right to celebrate a triumph. During the ceremony he led his army, under arms, across the sacred boundary from the field of Mars, by a circuitous route, to the temple of Jupiter on the Capitol. If he crossed the *pomerium* before this procession, he forfeited the chance of a triumph. For the duration of the ceremony, the convention that the army could not enter the city was suspended, and the reversal of this taboo was accompanied by other inversions that lasted throughout the sacred period of this communal *rite de passage*. The processing troops mocked their general and he himself was clothed in robes borrowed from the cult statue of Capitoline Jupiter with his face painted red, making him into the living icon of the terracotta cult statue. At the conclusion of the procession the *triumphator* returned the god's paraphernalia to the temple on the Capitol (Versnel 1970; Scheid 1986). The *pomerium* was also the site of other rituals. Burials were forbidden within it, for example, and the *pomerium* was extended each time Rome conquered more territory. A Vestal who was found no longer to be *intacta* was executed on the *pomerium*, and in Roman myth the founder of the city killed his own brother because he stepped across the original *pomerium*, marked out with a plough.

We can never fully reconstruct the ways in which these rituals were appreciated and given meaning by those who participated in them, but a certain logic can be inferred from the oppositions these rituals construct, oppositions between Mars and Jupiter, death and life, and war and peace. Other ceremonies surrounded the transition from one condition to another. Declarations of war were preceded not only by political debate, but also by rituals conducted by priests known as *fetiales* (Rich 1976; Harris 1979, 166–75). It does not matter that the rules seem in practice often to have been ignored, while particular religious rituals were freely adapted and abandoned over time. For the sake of reconstructing Republican ways of conceptualizing the dichotomy between war and peace, the normative models are more important than actual practice. Likewise, at the end of a war the doors of the temple of Janus would be closed to signify peace. But as with the extension of the *pomerium*, the ritual was rarely celebrated even if the notion was available for use by the emperors.

During the Republic it was important to signal these transitions because they entailed moral, religious and political consequences.

For example, the power of Republican magistrates over citizens was strictly limited *domi*, and until and even during the levy, citizens might still have recourse to the right of *provocatio* (appeal) and tribunes might use their veto to frustrate the actions of magistrates. But when *cives domi* became *milites militiae*, the general had the power of life and death over them. A Roman myth celebrated Titus Manlius Torquatus, the commander who executed his own son for a heroic but disobedient act while on campaign, and a disgraced body of soldiers might be decimated, one in ten being selected to be brutally killed by his fellow soldiers.

These limits were not static but were sometimes fiercely contested. For example, *provocatio* was extended to serving soldiers by a *lex Porcia*. Another debate arose about the right of the senate to suspend some of these traditional civic rights by passing a decree known as the *senatus consultum ultimum*, but, as Cicero found out to his cost, it was never universally agreed that the most dire civic emergency justified the execution of citizens without trial. Disputes over these issues are better documented for the age of Cato and Cicero than for earlier periods, but there is no reason to believe that a tranquil consensus ever existed at Rome, whatever Cicero might have believed or asserted about the middle Republic, before the Gracchi threw daggers into the *forum*.[1] But despite

debates about how to signal the distinction, it remained common ground that both leaders and followers assumed new rights and obligations when they moved across the moral boundary between civil society and its antithesis. This transformation of identities remained important to the end of the Republic; Julius Caesar was once able to rebuke a legion simply by addressing them as *Quirites*, the term used to address citizens in assemblies at Rome.

This dichotomy was not exactly equivalent to our distinction between war and peace. But the two spheres were truly and consistently opposed, each acquiring its characteristics from the other. The alternation of wars and peaces, with the repeated transformation of citizens into soldiers and back again, marked the passage of time, like the cycle of the seasons within which these transformations were originally embedded (Harris 1979,

---

[1] On attitudes to violence in the middle and late Republic, see Lintott 1968, especially pp. 175–7.

9–10; North 1981, 6), while the succession of triumphs and civil magistracies recorded in the *Fasti*, and the steady enlargement of the *pomerium* and the *ager Romanus*, created an awareness (although not the only awareness) of history and progress.

What I have been describing are normative models, beliefs about the way society operated in normal conditions. Exceptions to such norms can be easily tolerated; indeed, the very notion of an exception functions to bolster the priority of the norm. The rituals that construct these models do so by evoking symbols and suggesting oppositions and associations that combine to build up structures of meaning. The example of the *pomerium* shows how a variety of oppositions may be built up into a structure that distinguishes *domi* and *militiae* as two spheres of existence, each with varied connotations. The spatial barrier is important not as a legal-juridical limit, but as a mechanism for mapping the opposition between two moral spheres onto space, so that rituals might use spatial relationships and movements in space to express the transition between the civil and its opposite. But the central component of the symbolic system is not the spatial limit but the conceptual dichotomy.

The relevance of this Republican symbolic system to this paper is as a contrast to that which, in some respects, replaced it under the Empire. Perhaps most importantly, the contrast illustrates the mutability of such ideas, not so much in response to political transformations but as an integral part of wider social and cultural discontinuities. Ideas of war and peace changed with changed conditions. *Pax Romana* is a specifically imperial notion, and cannot be understood except in relation to empire.

Pax originally meant an agreement, including a treaty to end or prevent a war. But it early seems to have acquired the sense of peaceful conditions as opposed to hostility between states, and is used domestically to connote a state of order and security in the writings of the Ciceronian period (Weinstock 1960, 45; *OLD* s.v. *pax*). As a political slogan, especially used as a coin legend, *pax* occurs from Sulla onwards, often linked with *concordia* and always in the context of civil war (*RE* 18. 2430–6). Some connection is probable with the ideal of the *pax deorum*, the harmonious relationship between the Roman people and the gods mediated by the Roman state, since that relationship may have seemed to be imperilled by civil strife. The cult of *pax* almost

certainly began with Caesar, but was most prominent under
Augustus and his immediate successors. *Pax* recurs as a symbol
throughout the latter part of Augustus' reign, again associated
with other evocations of civil harmony, like *concordia* and *salus
publica*, most famously in Augustan poetry and in the Altar of
Pax Augusta (Hardie 1986, 133–6, 303, 358–62; Zanker 1988). But
the cult continued to be sponsored by most first-century emperors, reaching its most massive monumental expression in the
Temple and Forum of Pax built by Vespasian in Rome after the
first imperial civil war (Weinstock 1960, 44–52). Both Augustus
and Vespasian were careful to make victories over foreign opponents the ostensible occasions for promoting the cult of *pax*, as for
closing the doors of the temple of Janus, but the evocation of civil
harmony seems an inescapable sub-text. Despite an iconography
borrowed from Greek personifications of *eirene*, the cult was
wholly Roman in tone. These monuments should be seen less as
propaganda than as tangible traces of a discourse within the
Roman state, responding to public sentiment as much as forming
it. Augustus in particular experimented with various images and
symbols before he found those which enabled him and his subjects
to establish a common ideological vocabulary through which the
new order might be described and discussed, while the virtues and
ideals which became canonical for emperors bound rulers as much
as ruled. The point is important because it implies that the new
prominence of peace derived not simply from imperial fiat and
whim, but acquired its central role because, as a symbol, it had the
potential to be developed to meet the new conditions of empire.

Weinstock identifies two strands to the new imperial ideology,
pax at home depending on *concordia*, between the orders as well
as among the élite, and *pax* abroad, in the sense of an unequal
peace between Rome and those she had pacified. The inequality is
crucial: for Weinstock '*Pax* . . . stood right from the beginning for
Roman imperialism' (ibid. 45). Along with its evocations of
solidarity and security in the context of domestic relations, peace
was in the same period acquiring other connotations connected
with Rome's new role as the harbinger of *humanitas*, those values
and customs invented in Greece but destined to flourish under
Rome's benevolent rule. Already in Strabo we find a justification
of the empire in terms of its civilizing role and a conception of
civilization that contrasts the peaceful behaviour of civilized men

to the warlike habits of barbarians (Clavel-Lévêque 1974; Thollard 1987). First-century AD Latin authors conceived of barbarians as distinguished from Romans by their *feritas* and their lack of *humanitas*. Part way between men and beasts, the barbarian was characterized *inter alia* by his warlike nature (Dauge 1981; Wiedemann 1986). The humanizing effects of incorporation in the empire included pacification, as well as bringing the barbarians down from their mountain villages to cities in the plain and teaching them to speak Latin and to dress in togas. The idea that the expansion of the empire was in part legitimated by the spread of *humanitas* and *pax* is a common one.[1] As with much imperial ideology, the roots of this notion can be found in late Republican texts,[2] but *pax*, like *imperium*, receives a new prominence and nuance in the first century AD.

Pax represented the unity of the Roman people and, at the same time, was the concomitant of the *humanitas* created by Roman power among their subjects. Uniting these two strands is the association of *pax* and *imperium* as virtual synonyms. Pliny the Elder refers to the 'awesome majesty of the Roman peace' (*NH* 27. 1. 1: *immensa Romanae pacis maiestate*) as a circumlocution for empire and Seneca writes of Nero's *pax* in a similar manner (*Clem.* 1. 1. 2). This equation of *pax* and *imperium* is not found in Republican writing, despite the existence of an empire in the Republic and of a developed theory of *imperium*. Rather, it is part of the new ideology of the imperial period. A concomitant is that peace and war have a new spatial analogue, the opposed worlds of the civilized, pacific provinces and that of the savage, warlike barbarians. Between the two worlds the Roman army stood guard, and the frontier was transformed into a moral barrier (Alföldi 1952). This is the image of the empire conjured up by Aelius Aristides' *Roman Oration* and by Appian's *Preface*, but it is not confined to the writers of the Second Sophistic. The Roman peace is presented as comprising two elements: peace in the

[1]   e.g. Caes. *BGall.* 1. 1. 3; Pliny, *NH* 3. 39; Vitr. *De Arch.* 2. praef. 5, 9. praef. 2; and, inverting the moral valency, Tac. *Agr.* 30.
[2]   Weinstock 1960, 45, quoting Cic. *QFr.* 1. 1. 34 on the *pax sempiterna* won for Rome's subjects by Roman *imperium*. Cf. Richardson 1991, 6–7, for the contemporaneous emergence of a usage of *imperium* in a territorial sense to mean 'empire' as opposed to 'power'.

provinces and security at the frontier. The image of the early empire as peaceful, prosperous and content behind secure defences erected by the emperors at the edge of the *oikumene*, is one that ancient historians from Gibbon onwards have largely accepted for the period between Augustus and the third-century crisis. Yet if *pax Romana* is an ideological construct, rooted in a particular time and place and formulated with regard to particular interests, this convergence between ancient and modern images should perhaps arouse our suspicions.

Peace with the barbarians

We live in nation states, the governments of which claim sovereignty within their borders and assert the rights of the governments of other nation states to regulate their internal affairs without interference. Of course there are exceptions, both occasional and systematic, and there are alternative ideologies, for example those based on claims to global or hemispheric leadership or on the international class struggle. But the public ideology of most states, as developed, for example, in the United Nations Charter, depends on the notion of territorial sovereignty. One implication is that armies exist primarily to defend states or to engage in war between them, and that military activity between states is warfare and qualitatively different from military activity within a state. These everyday fictions must be thought away when we deal with ancient societies.[1] Romans did not conceive of the world as a mosaic of sovereign territories, and thought in terms of peoples and places rather than states and spaces, connected not so much by frontiers and international law as by routes and a variety of relationships with Rome.[2] From an early period in Rome's expansion, these relationships were rarely expressed in terms of parity, and the ambiguities of the language of political friendship allowed even relations with the Parthians to

[1] Austin 1986 discusses the problems caused by similar anachronistic assumptions for our understanding of warfare in the Hellenistic period. Isaac 1990, 1–3, discusses the impact of modern ideologies on our understanding of Roman frontiers and Roman imperialism.

[2] Lintott 1981; Purcell 1990a, 8–9; Isaac 1990, 394–401.

be represented as relations of dependency.[1] The frontiers of the imperial period were systems of communications and deployment, not the limits of Roman power (*imperium*), and Roman writers did not maintain that armies only served a defensive purpose. Nevertheless, particular frontiers have often been tacitly assumed to have been defensive in nature, and Luttwak's recent synthesis, by making these assumptions explicit, has initiated a fierce debate on the issue.[2]

Modern assumptions about frontiers, wars and armies may well have contributed to the modern image of a defended, static empire. But it should be admitted that the emphasis on the defensive aspects of frontiers does not derive entirely from anachronistic interpretations. Expansion, at least in terms of the acquisition of new provinces, did slow down after Augustus' reign. Besides, a certain amount of ancient testimony does present the empire as stable, peaceful and defended by troops stationed in a ring around prosperous provinces. Luttwak used Aelius Aristides' *Roman Oration* to great effect to show an ancient appreciation of the grand strategy he saw as implicit in the Roman frontiers. Finally, frontiers in most regions are studied through archaeology, and the most durable traces of Roman activity are static monuments like Hadrian's Wall. Even so, archaeologists have long realized that troops, roads and signal stations were as important as walls and ditches (e.g. Breeze and Dobson 1976), and an even more dynamic picture of the activity of the Roman army of the frontier emerges from the writing tablets found at Vindolanda.[3]

But more importantly, there is a danger that, in reacting against Luttwak's view of Roman defence policy, we may simply produce an inversion of it, throwing out the baby with the bath-water in the process. So Benjamin Isaac's excellent account of the activity of Roman armies on the eastern edge of the empire (Isaac 1990), although it begins by asserting that 'they are armies of conquest

---

[1]   Badian 1958; Braund 1984; Campbell below (ch. 7).
[2]   Luttwak 1976. For the reaction Mann 1979; Millar 1982; Whittaker 1989, 23–50; Isaac 1990, 372–7.
[3]   Bowman and Thomas 1983, with the new material presented in *JRS* 76 (1986), 120–3; *Britannia*, 18 (1987), 125–42; *Britannia*, 21 (1990), 33–52; *JRS* 81 (1991), 62–73.

and occupation, *as well as defence*' (my italics), concentrates on the army's role as a security force within the provinces, and presents Roman relations with Parthia almost entirely in terms of Roman imperialism. Roman defenders are recast as occupying forces and imperialists. Tacitus plays the same trick, putting into the Caledonian Calgacus' mouth a denunciation of the Roman empire, culminating in the famous claim that 'theft, murder and rape are the true meanings of their word empire (*imperium*), and where they create a desert they call it peace (*pax*)' (Tac. *Agr.* 30). Tacitus' inversion, besides being a typical device, alerts us to the relativity of values, using a barbarian to accuse Rome of crimes normally associated by Romans with barbarism. Disputes about defence and aggression belong to a discourse about the legitimacy of violence and of the state. In recognizing and rejecting any sense of identification we may have with the Roman empire, it is not necessary to side with their opponents. Rather, we should step outside the debate and assess its structure and terms.[1]

War and expansion originated under the Republic. Roman armies dominated first Italy, then the west and by the late second century the entire Mediterranean basin. The creation of permanent commands, *provinciae*, occurred later in most areas, but in the eyes of ancient writers it was not permanent commands or the imposition of *tributum*, so much as conquest, that marked the extension of Roman *imperium*. The pace of conquest accelerated dramatically over this period. For Polybius it was the period of half a century or so after the defeat of Hannibal (*c*.220–168 BC) that saw Rome's conquest of the world (1. 1. 1–2). But the period of maximum expansion was the first century, with the conquests of Lucullus and Pompey in the east followed by those of Caesar and Augustus in the west and north. The rate of conquest was probably at its peak under Pompey and Caesar. Augustus added huge areas to the empire, but with increasing caution, following revolts in Pannonia and the destruction of Varus' legions beyond the Rhine (Brunt 1963; 1990). The rate at which new territory was provincialized under his successors continued to decrease, but major wars were still fought. The main areas of military activity were in the north-west and on the eastern frontier. Germanicus

[1] For similar observations about the debate over the defensive or aggressive nature of Republican imperialism, see North 1981.

campaigned across the Rhine under Tiberius, and Claudius presided over the invasion of Britain, where modest expansion continued throughout the first century and beyond. Claudius' reign also saw campaigns across the Rhine, and Domitian conducted campaigns and annexed territory there. Several second-century emperors fought along the Danube. Trajan's Dacian campaigns resulted in the greatest territorial gains, but major wars were fought more or less continuously from Marcus' reign onwards. Campaigns also continued in other theatres. There were wars against Parthia in AD 52–63, 112–14, 155–63, 194–8 and 215–17 (Isaac 1990, 29–30). Alongside these two major theatres, there were wars in Africa and military expeditions around the Black Sea. From the end of the second century, emperors were regularly engaged in major campaigns both in the East and along the northern frontiers. While the wars in the north are usually seen as responses to barbarian attacks, at least some of those in the East are no more or less defensive than the wars of the late Republic. Rome continued, then, to wage frequent wars against neighbouring peoples in the imperial period. When it was possible and desirable, Roman emperors were ready to annex new territories. But, just as many Republican wars were not followed by annexation, so many imperial campaigns resulted in gains of prestige and booty, rather than territory. From the second century BC to Pompey's eastern campaigns and Caesar's invasion of Britain, Romans had often preferred to control some conquered peoples through client rulers, and the practice continued throughout the empire (Whittaker 1989, 32–3).

The imperialism of the imperial period is easier to understand when Roman ideas about war are considered. On many issues there was no single Roman opinion or ideology, but rather a range of positions in a developing debate. It is possible to distinguish between ideas which are the matter of fierce contention and debate and those which are taken for granted, what Bourdieu terms *doxa*, the common ground which frames that debate (Bourdieu 1977, 159–71). So, for the Republican period, there seems to have been an unquestioned view that military glory, the rewards of warfare and the extension of Rome's power were desirable ends and praiseworthy achievements (Harris 1979, 9–53), while there was less consensus about the desirability of setting up permanent commands to replace defeated states, about the treatment of the defeated or about the advisability of undertaking particular wars at particular times.[1] Imperial discourse developed out of that of the late Republic, and in many respects was very similar to it. Military glory was still a desideratum. Emperors liked to celebrate their martial glory, monopolizing the right to hold triumphs, and only allowing generals to fight under the imperial auspices. Major campaigns were almost always commanded by emperors in person or by imperial princes. Emperors spent time with the troops and advertised their connections with the armies, and had themselves portrayed in armour on equestrian statues.[2] Imperial iconography was not exclusively military: Trajan had himself portrayed wearing a toga on the Arch of Benevento as well as in military costume on the column commemorating the Dacian wars. But military success was one component of the role of the emperor, and an important one. So too among the aristocracy, military service was a key component of the training of a young man for office, whether in the equestrian service or as a senator. But not all aristocrats saw their role in military terms: Pliny's *Epistles* express a very different set of ideals than those portrayed by Tacitus in the *Agricola*. Emperors were aristocrats writ large, and they too varied in the importance they attached to martial achievements.

A difference emerges then between Republican and imperial values. Roman emperors were no less warlike than their Republican predecessors but the importance of territorial aggrandizement shifted from *doxa* to opinion, out of the universe of the

---

[1] It is not always easy to disentangle debates about particular cases from disagreements in principle on these issues. No Republican texts argue against aggression or warfare as such, but it is arguable that in the last century of the Republic there were some groups and individuals more ready than others to solve problems by setting up new *provinciae* rather than continuing to maintain dependent monarchies. To some extent these debates reflect the application of *popularis* political principles and methods to foreign affairs, and to some extent they reflect the Romans' continuing experiments in ways of dealing with the longer-term consequences of their military successes.

[2] See Campbell 1984 on the military associations of emperors. An equestrian statue found at Misenum, originally of Domitian but remodelled with the face of Nerva, is displayed in the National Museum in Naples. Cf. Austin 1986 for Hellenistic parallels.

undiscussed (because undisputed) in the Republic, into the universe of discourse under the Empire. It was now possible to challenge Republican values, or, put another way, there was now a plurality of positions on this issue. Doubts about annexation or at least about particular annexations had existed in the Republic, but a new feature of imperial discourse are pronouncements that expansion was over, that Rome ruled all that was worth ruling and disdained to rule over the surrounding peoples. Evidence for the emergence of this view has been traced back to the reign of Augustus,[1] but then it was only one view among a series of competing ideals. Augustan poets still held out hopes of world conquest. The conflict does not represent schizophrenic leadership, so much as a growing awareness among the Roman élite that the world might be bigger and more difficult to conquer than they had thought. The issue was not resolved within the first four centuries of the empire. Expressions of opposition to expansion can be found in the works of Suetonius and Dio,[2] in Strabo's explanation (4. 5. 32) for the rationale behind the decision not to conquer Britain, in the preface to Appian's *History*, and in Aelius Aristides' *Roman Oration*. Arguments in favour of expansion are best known from Tacitus, with his complaints that Corbulo and Agricola had been frustrated by imperial jealousy and that historians had nothing glorious to report under the principate of an emperor who had no interest in expansion (Tac. *Agr.* 39–40; *Ann.* 4. 32, 11. 20). Herodian was also a supporter of expansion (Isaac 1990, 24–5), and Florus, in the preface to the first book of his Epitome of Livy, complained of the laziness of emperors apart from Trajan, in comparison to Republican conquerors. It is not always easy to distinguish criticism of a general policy from criticism of a particular action or emperor: Hadrian's withdrawal from Trajan's conquests earned criticism from Fronto, Victor, Eutropius and Festus.[3] These conflicting views cannot be resolved into the typical views of expansionist and anti-

---

[1]   Nicolet 1988, with Millar 1988 and Purcell 1990b. Brunt 1990b, 468–77, and Isaac 1990, 20–8, have clearer treatments of the issue.

[2]   Brunt 1990b, 465–8, on their views of Augustus. On Dio's opposition to Severus' campaigns in the East, Millar 1982, 1–2.

[3]   Isaac 1990, 24. For the generally favourable impression of Trajan in late antiquity see Lightfoot 1990.

expansionist periods. Had a consensus existed, the issue would have moved into *doxa* and no longer been the subject of debate. Rather, conflicting views of Roman expansion characterized the entire period, as did the related debates on the military vocation of the individual aristocrat or the military role of the ideal emperor.

Ultimately, Roman expansion slowed and stopped. Few emperors tried to emulate Trajan and Severus, and fewer succeeded. The reasons for the end of expansion are not clear, not even the fundamental question of whether it was the result of a lack of will, *inertia Caesarum*, or of inability to continue. Our ignorance probably reflects theirs. From the historian's perspective it is possible to note long-term trends, and to periodize Roman imperialism accordingly, but events were much less clear at the time. It is against the background of this uncertainty that the security promised by *pax Romana* must be assessed.

Peace in the provinces

The Roman peace did not mean that provincials had no experience of violence. If the Antonine age was 'the period in the history of the world, during which the condition of the human race was most happy and prosperous',[1] it was not because the lot of the provincials was uniformly idyllic and prosperous, but because Roman provincials were spared the additional misery of warfare on top of the ill health, squalor, insecurity, poverty and low life expectancy that were the lot of most inhabitants of the ancient world (MacMullen 1974). True, some areas of the provinces never benefited fully from the Roman peace. Rome ruled the plains, plateaux and river valleys, where most of the population lived, but the inhabitants of mountainous and desert areas were never fully incorporated and banditry flourished in the interstices of Roman power (Shaw 1984; cf. MacMullen 1966, 255-68). Besides, provincials were subject to the violence of landowners and of civic and imperial officials. Relations between local magnates and their dependants can never be fully reconstructed, but abuses of power certainly occurred (Garnsey and Woolf 1989). Provincials were also subjected to conscription, billeting and other requisitions by

---

[1] Gibbon 1776-88, i. ch. 3, p. 89 in the World's Classics edition.

the army.[1] Unsurprisingly, many provincials had their own weapons, even if they were no match for trained soldiery (Brunt 1975).

What *pax Romana* did claim to mean was an end to civil war. Threats to the credibility of this claim came not from crime and banditry, but from provincial revolts and civil wars. Both existed, of course, just as they had under the Republic. A number of provincial revolts are reported by literary texts, more from the West than the East and more from the first century than from subsequent ones (Dyson 1975). Armed rebellions led by Roman officers also occurred (MacMullen 1985). Occasionally the line between provincial revolt and civil war became blurred, as in the revolt of Vindex (Brunt 1959). Little is known about the majority of these incidents, their significance or the reasons for their outbreaks and failures. Recent accounts have attributed them to tensions generated by conquest and acculturation (Dyson 1971), and to taxation (Corbier 1988), while ancient authors add debt and the viciousness of Roman commanders. Each revolt probably had a complex origin. Military coups, led by members of the aristocracy, seem easier to explain in terms of fear and ambition, but it is still unclear what determined their timing and incidence. All emperors executed some aristocrats, most had to deal with palace conspiracies, but only a few faced a serious threat of civil war. One key variable was the extent to which emperors were successful in focusing the loyalty of the troops, and in particular the centurionate, on themselves, rather than on the aristocratic high command.[2] The nature of the threats to the *pax Romana* seems to have changed over time. Revolts directed against Rome, as opposed to against one particular emperor, seem confined to the first century, while attempted military coups became more frequent. The change presumably reflects the growing Romanization of provincial élites. At all events, once barbarian invasions from the north and defeat by the Persians to the East shattered the myth of *pax Romana* in the third century, the reaction was wholly

[1]   Brunt 1974; Mitchell 1976; Isaac 1990, 282–304. For the relationship between soldiers and civilians in general, MacMullen 1963.
[2]   Campbell 1984 provides an account of the various means used to achieve this effect. For an example of the efficacy of this strategy see Suet. *Claud.* 13.

Roman in form. The collapse of the legitimacy of the Roman emperors was marked by a series of military coups, and even the secessionist rebels, like the Gallic emperors, represented themselves in Roman terms (Drinkwater 1987).

Although a number of revolts and coup attempts are known, little is known of each, and they are accorded very little importance in general accounts of the empire. Certainly this was the way that Roman emperors preferred to have them regarded. Gaul provides a good example. In AD 21 there was a revolt based among the Aedui and the Treveri, two of the most important tribes of central and northern Gaul, and affecting a large number of other communities. It was serious enough for troops from the German garrisons to be called in to supplement the local levies that had tried to suppress it. All the same, Tiberius delayed announcing the outbreak of the rebellion to the senate until he could also announce its suppression.[1] His refusal either to visit Gaul in person or to allow his son to do so and his public refusal of an *ovatio* for the victory seem designed to play down the significance of the revolt. Claudius, speaking thirty years later in favour of allowing Gauls to stand for magistracies in the city of Rome, referred to their unshakeable loyalty and service ever since Caesar's conquest.[2] In fact there had been a string of military operations in Gaul since Caesar's conquest. In addition to the revolt of AD 21, literary accounts record warfare in Gaul in the early forties, campaigns there led by Agrippa in the early thirties, and more fighting in the early twenties BC (Wightman 1974). Nor is the historical record complete. Until recently there has been a consensus that from the beginning of the Augustan wars in Germany, Gaul was demilitarized, becoming, in Tacitus' words, 'an unarmed province'.[3] But recent archaeological research has revealed traces of substantial military activity in many parts of

[1] Tac. *Ann.* 3. 40–7. Vell. Pat. 2. 129–33 gives a similar account but with different colour.

[2] *CIL* xiii. 1668: *immobilem fidem obsequiumque.* Cf. Tac. *Ann.* 11. 23: *continua inde ac fida pax.*

[3] Tac. *Hist.* 1. 16, describing the state of affairs at the time of Vindex's revolt in an admittedly rhetorical passage; cf. Joseph. *BJ* 2. 372–3 for Herod's claim that Gaul was completely pacified at this period. For the modern consensus see Wells 1972; Wightman 1977.

Gaul long after the supposed advance to the Rhine.[1] Mirebeau,
near Dijon, is the most impressive example. It comprises a stone
built fortress, with the capacity to house a legion, with *canabae*,
temples and an amphitheatre, all set in a centuriated landscape.
The fort was built in the Flavian period, but probably continued
to be occupied into the second century AD. Other major forts have
recently been excavated at Aulnay-de-Saintonge and Arlaines.
These structures cannot all be related to known revolts. The only
conclusion is that Gaul was a good deal less pacific than either
Tiberius or Claudius pretended.

Gaul was probably not a special case. Provincial revolts are
recorded in virtually every part of the empire, in 'civilized' eastern
provinces like Egypt and Achaea as well as in barbarian ones like
Gaul and Germany. The amount of energy and resources the army
spent in ensuring public order in the interior of the empire is only
now emerging from detailed archaeological work from Judaea to
Britain.[2] It seems likely, then, that both the frequency and
seriousness of revolts is under-reported in the literary sources.
Just as some military actions today are referred to, in official
parlance, as conflicts or expeditions, it may be that even major
military operations within the empire were described as operations to suppress banditry. The label 'bandit' serves not only to
play down the seriousness of a threat but also to remove its
legitimacy. Garrisons like those stationed for long periods within
the 'unarmed province' of Gaul could not conceivably be related
to the police actions that the military did undertake in the
provinces, but the imperial government chose to minimize the
extent of military activity in order to deny the seriousness of
the threat.[3]

A very different image is vividly evoked by Tacitus at the
beginning of the *Histories* (1. 2), where he summarizes the work in

---

[1]   Tassaux and Tassaux 1983–4; Reddé 1985, 1989; cf. in general the
papers gathered in *Caesarodunum* suppl. 28, *Travaux militaires en Gaule
romaine et dans les provinces du nord-ouest* (1978).
[2]   Judaea: Isaac 1990, 54–160. Britain: Hurst 1988, showing the presence
of a garrison at Gloucester, in the so-called civilian zone, as late as the
second century AD.
[3]   On the ideological content of the label 'bandit' see Shaw 1984. For a
similar argument in the context of the *bagaudae* of the fourth century, see
Thompson 1952.

terms which make plain its subversion and inversion of the ideology of *pax et imperium*. 'The work I begin is splendid in disasters, ferocious in battles, anarchic with plots and savage with peace itself (*ipsa etiam pace saevum*).' He goes on to enumerate the emperors killed, the civil wars fought, the provinces disrupted, the wars against the barbarians and the appearance of a false Nero supported by Parthia. Even Italy was struck down by disasters as Vesuvius erupted and the Capitol was set alight in the course of fighting in the city. Just as the *Germania* and the *Agricola* achieve some of their rhetorical effect by the inversion of Roman norms about barbarism and civilization, so the *Histories* participate in the same discourse as the panegyrical writings of second-century Greeks, but turn the official view of the world on its head. The events of AD 68–70 do illustrate the violence lying beneath the surface of *pax Romana*. It was not just a matter of rival armies fighting in support of their generals. Inter-city rivalries flared up into armed conflicts and provincials allied with barbarians against other provincials. Every tenet of the *pax Romana* was challenged. It is easy to see why the ideology was reasserted so vigorously under Vespasian, with the construction of the temple and forum of *pax* and those passages of the Elder Pliny's *Natural History* that forge precarious links between the world of nature and the fragile Flavian peace.

Roman claims that the provincials enjoyed unbroken peace were an exaggeration, and at least some Romans knew it. Quite apart from the routine violence that characterized life in all ancient societies, the provinces also suffered revolts and civil conflicts of a more serious nature than emperors were prepared officially to admit. The provinces were pacified, but pacified repeatedly, rather than once for all, and they were not peaceful.

Conclusion

Pax Romana is a convenient shorthand for Roman claims to have created a world freed from war. Solidarity and security were said to have been bestowed on the *orbis terrarum*, the *oikumene*, the whole of the civilized world, and that gift was guaranteed by the armies that ringed the empire, defending the emperor's subjects from the barbarians that Rome disdained to conquer. Peace meant an end to the civil strife of the late Republic and also produced the conditions for the spread of *humanitas*, of civilized values, under Rome's benevolent rule. Peace legitimated the empire of the Romans and the rule of the emperors. *Pax* was created by and justified *imperium*.

Other views are and were tenable. The claim that Rome had conquered all the world worth conquering was not accepted by all Romans, not even by all emperors, and some may have felt that peace *domi* demanded expansion *militiae* as in the middle Republic, rather than the defended ramparts described by the imperial panegyricists. Equally there was more than one view about the peaceful condition of the provinces. *Pax Romana* was thus an ideological construct. Whose interests did it serve? In the short term, the emperors were the principal beneficiaries of this view of the world. Aristocrats also benefited, but their limited chances of winning military glory in a world without war were already forcing some, like Pliny or Fronto, to construct new ideals very different to those embodied in, for example, the *Agricola*. Romans in general had more to gain from belief in *pax Romana* than peregrines who had to suffer conflicts that had been downgraded from wars to revolts and from rebellions to banditry only in name. As we might expect, then, the new knowledge of the world formed by Roman power benefited individuals roughly in proportion to their status within the new order. Ideology also had its disadvantages: emperors and their advisors, those to whom *pax Romana* must have been most real, may well have been lulled into a false sense of security by it, and the dramatic falsification of their claims in the third century caused a crisis in legitimacy that almost proved fatal.

But if *pax Romana* can be viewed critically in this way, it does not mean that it was a wholly misleading view of the world. The Romans' power was great, even if they did not rule the world, and the provinces were freer of war because peace had been declared than if it had not been. Imperial propagation of the image of peace contributed to sustaining it. So Herod is presented by Josephus as using the peace of the rest of the empire as an argument to dissuade the Jews from revolt, so Claudius set up at Lyon a copy of his speech proclaiming the fidelity of the Gauls in order to ensure it, so the *pax Augusta* was designed to prevent another civil war.

What the continued war on the frontiers and the repeated disturbances of the Roman peace within the empire show is that the Roman empire was characterized not by the absence of violence but by a carefully balanced economy of it. If war is organized societal violence, then the Roman peace qualifies as war, as the opening quotation from Foucault suggests it might. The emperors ruled not by abolishing violence but by channelling it, using and perpetuating rivalries between cities, between soldiers and civilians, between social classes and within the élite, to ensure a dynamic equilibrium which they controlled and which necessitated their participation. This form of rule has been described as capstone government, denoting a type of imperial state with weak but extensive power, which maintains itself not by increasing its own power but by divide-and-rule, preventing the coalition of any other interests in society.[1] But it seems preferable to take another Foucaultian perspective, and to see the power of the emperors as residing not so much in their ability to prevent action, as in their capacity to harness the energies of their subjects to create an empire of violence. The Roman world had not been made pacific in the sense that its members were incapable of war. The emperors' *imperium* depended on the institutions and ideologies with which they organized the warlike potential of their subjects to wage peace.[2]

Bibliography

Alföldi, A. (1952), 'The moral barrier on the Rhine and Danube', in E. Birley (ed.), *The Congress of Roman Frontier Studies, 1949* (Durham), pp. 1–16.

Austin, M. M. (1986), 'Hellenistic kings, war and the economy', *CQ* 36: 450–66.

Badian, E. (1958), *Foreign Clientelae (264–70 BC)* (Oxford).

Bourdieu, P. (1977), *Outline of a Theory of Practice* (Cambridge).

Bowman, A. K., and Thomas, J. D. (1983), *Vindolanda: The Latin Writing-tablets* (Britannia Monographs, 4; London).

[1] Hall 1985, 52–3, with special reference to China; generalized by Crone 1989, 57.

[2] I am very grateful to Tim Cornell and John Rich, whose critical comments have much improved this chapter.

Braund, D. C. (1984), *Rome and the Friendly King: The Character of the Client Kingship* (London).

Breeze, D. J., and Dobson, B. (1976), *Hadrian's Wall* (London).

Brunt, P. A. (1959), 'The revolt of Vindex and the fall of Nero', *Latomus*, 18: 531–59; = Brunt 1990a, ch. 2 (pp. 9–32).

—— (1963), review of H. D. Meyer, *Die Aussenpolitik des Augustus und die augusteische Dichtung*, *JRS* 53: 170–6; = 'Augustan imperialism', in Brunt 1990a, ch. 5 (pp. 96–109).

—— (1974), 'Conscription and volunteering in the Roman imperial army', *Scripta classica Israelica*, 1: 90–115; = Brunt 1990a, ch. 9 (pp. 188–214).

—— (1975), 'Did imperial Rome disarm her subjects?', *Phoenix*, 29: 260–70; = Brunt 1990a, ch. 11 (pp. 255–66).

—— (1978), 'Laus imperii', in P. D. A. Garnsey and C. R. Whittaker (eds), *Imperialism in the Ancient World* (Cambridge), ch. 8 (pp. 159–191); = Brunt 1990a, ch. 14 (pp. 288–323).

—— (1990a), *Roman Imperial Themes* (Oxford).

—— (1990b), 'Roman imperial illusions', in Brunt 1990a, ch. 18 (pp. 433–80).

Campbell, J. B. (1984), *The Emperor and the Roman Army 31 BC–AD 235* (Oxford).

Clavel-Lévêque, M. (1974), 'Les gaules et les gauloises: pour une analyse du fonctionnement de la Géographie de Strabon', *DHA* 1: 75–93.

Corbier, M. (1988), 'L'impôt dans l'empire romain', in T. Yuge and M. Doi (eds), *Forms of Control and Subordination in Antiquity* (Tokyo), pp. 259–74.

Crone, P. (1989), *Pre-industrial Societies* (Oxford).

Dauge, Y. (1981), *Le Barbare: recherches sur la conception romaine de la barbarie et de la civilisation* (Collection Latomus, 176; Brussels).

Drinkwater, J. F. (1987), *The Gallic Empire: Separatism and Continuity in the North-western Provinces of the Roman Empire, AD 260–274* (Historia Einzelschriften, 52; Stuttgart).

Dyson, S. L. (1971), 'Native revolts in the Roman empire', *Historia*, 20: 239–74.

—— (1975), 'Native revolt patterns in the Roman empire', *ANRW* ii. 3. 138–75.

Finley, M. I. (1985), *Ancient History: Evidence and Models* (London).

Foucault, M. (1980), *Power/Knowledge: Selected Interviews and Other Writings 1972–1977*, ed. C. Graham (New York).

Garnsey, P. D. A., and Woolf, G. D. (1989), 'Patronage of the rural poor in the Roman world', in A. Wallace-Hadrill (ed.), *Patronage in Ancient Society* (London), ch. 7 (pp. 153–170).

Gibbon, E. (1776–88), *The History of the Decline and Fall of the Roman Empire* (London).

Giovannini, A. (1983), *Consulare imperium* (Schweizerische Beiträge zur Altertumswissenschaft, 16; Basel).

Hall, J. A. (1985), *Powers and Liberties: The Causes and the Consequences of the Rise of the West* (Oxford).

Hardie, P. (1986), *Virgil's Aeneid: Cosmos and Imperium* (Oxford).

Harris, W. V. (1979), *War and Imperialism in Republican Rome 327–70 BC* (Oxford).

Hurst, H. R. (1988), 'Gloucester', in G. Webster (ed.), *Fortress into City: The Consolidation of Roman Britain in the First Century AD* (London), ch. 3 (pp. 48–73).

Isaac, B. (1990), *The Limits of Empire: The Roman Army in the East* (Oxford).

Lightfoot, C. S. (1990), 'Trajan's Parthian war and the fourth-century perspective', *JRS* 80: 115–26.

Lintott, A. W. (1968), *Violence in Republican Rome* (Oxford).

—— (1981), 'What was the "Imperium Romanum"?', *Greece and Rome*, 28: 53–7.

Luttwak, E. N. (1976), *The Grand Strategy of the Roman Empire from the First Century AD to the Third* (Baltimore and London).

MacMullen, R. (1963), *Soldier and Civilian in the Later Roman Empire* (Cambridge, Mass.).

—— (1966), *Enemies of the Roman Order: Treason, Unrest and Alienation in the Empire* (Oxford).

—— (1974), *Roman Social Relations 50 BC–AD 284* (London).

—— (1985), 'How to revolt in the Roman empire', *Rivista storica d'antichità* 15: 67–76; = *Changes in the Roman Empire: Essays in the Ordinary* (Princeton, 1990), ch. 19 (pp. 198–203).

Mann, J. C. (1979), 'Power, force and the frontiers of the empire', *JRS* 69: 175–83.

Millar, F. G. B. (1982), 'Emperors, frontiers and foreign relations, 31 BC to AD 378', *Britannia*, 13: 1–23.

—— (1988), review of Nicolet 1988, *Journal of Roman Archaeology*, 1: 137–41.

Mitchell, S. (1976), 'Requisitioned transport in the Roman empire: a new inscription from Pisidia', *JRS* 66: 106–31.

Nicolet, C. (1988), *L'Inventaire du monde: géographie et politique aux origines de l'empire romain* (Paris).

North, J. A. (1981), 'The development of Roman imperialism', *JRS* 71: 1–9.

Purcell, N. (1990a), 'The creation of provincial landscape: the Roman impact on Cisalpine Gaul', in T. Blagg and M. Millett (eds), *The Early Roman Empire in the West* (Oxford), ch. 1 (pp. 7–29).

—— (1990b), review of Nicolet 1988, *JRS* 80: 178–82.

Reddé, M. (1985), 'Le camp militaire d'Arlaines et l'aile de Voconces', *Gallia*, 43 (1): 49–79.

—— (1989), 'Vraies et fausses enceintes militaires d'époque romaine', in O. Buchsenschutz and L. Olivier (eds), *Les Viereckschanzen et les enceintes quadrilaterales en Europe celtique (actes du IXième colloque de l'AFEAF, Châteaudun 1985)* (Paris), pp. 21–6.

Rich, J. W. (1976), *Declaring War in the Roman Republic in the Period of Transmarine Expansion* (Collection Latomus, 149; Brussels).

Richardson, J. S. (1991), 'Imperium Romanum: empire and the language of power', *JRS* 81: 1–9.

Scheid, J. (1986), 'Le flamine de Jupiter, les Vestales et le général triomphant: variations romaines sur le thème de la figuration des dieux', *Le Temps et la réflexion*, 7: 213–30.

Shaw, B. D. (1984), 'Bandits in the Roman empire', *Past and Present*, 105: 3–52.

Tassaux, D., and Tassaux, F. (1983–4), 'Aulnay-de-Saintonge: un camp augusto-tibérien', *Aquitania*, 1: 49–95; 2: 105–59.

Thollard, P. (1987), *Barbarie et civilisation chez Strabon: étude critique des livres III et IV de la Géographie* (Annales littéraires de l'Université de Besançon, 365).

Thompson, E. A. (1952), 'Peasant revolts in late Roman Gaul and Spain', *Past and Present*, 2: 11–23; = M. I. Finley (ed.), *Studies in Ancient Society* (London), ch. 14 (pp. 304–20).

Versnel, H. S. (1970), *Triumphus* (Leiden).

Weinstock, S. (1960), 'Pax and the "Ara Pacis" ', *JRS* 50: 44–58.

Wells, C. M. (1972), *The German Policy of Augustus: An Examination of the Archaeological Evidence* (Oxford).

Whittaker, C. R. (1989), *Les Frontières de l'empire romain* (Annales littéraires de l'Université de Besançon, 390).

Wiedemann, T. E. J. (1986), 'Between men and beasts: barbarians in Ammianus Marcellinus', in I. Moxon, J. D. Smart, and A. J. Woodman (eds), *Past Perspectives: Greek and Roman Historical Writing* (Cambridge), pp. 189–201.

Wightman, E. M. (1974), 'La Gaule Chevelue entre César et Auguste', in *Actes du IXième congrès international d'études sur les frontières romaines* (Cologne), pp. 472–83.

—— (1977), 'Military arrangements, native settlements and related developments in early Roman Gaul', *Helinum*, 17: 105–26.

Zanker, P. (1988), *The Power of Images in the Age of Augustus* (Ann Arbor).

8

Piracy under the principate and the ideology of imperial eradication

David Braund

In his *Res Gestae*, Augustus boasts:

> I made the sea peaceful and freed it from pirates (*mare pacavi a praedonibus*). In that war I captured about 30,000 slaves who had escaped from their masters and taken up arms against the republic, and I handed them over to their masters for punishment.
>
> (*Res Gestae*, 25. 1, trans. P. Brunt and J. M. Moore)

The war in which he brought peace to the sea was that with Sextus Pompey, who is regularly characterized under Augustus as a pirate leader. The war with Sextus is called a war (*bellum*), but it is a war with slaves, dignified only by its scale: Sextus himself goes unnamed. Later, in AD 69, Vespasian's men defeated the piratical forces of Anicetus in what Tacitus calls, probably with half an eye to Anicetus' past as a royal freedman, a 'slave war' (*bellum servile*; Tac. *Hist*. 3. 47–8, with Shaw 1984, 6). These cases, and others, raise large questions. What was the relationship between war and piracy? What role, if any, did piracy have in the Mediterranean after Augustus?

War not war

In the first book of his *Institutes*, the Severan jurist Ulpian offered a simple working typology of piracy and related forms of violent conflict:

Enemies are those upon whom the Roman people has declared war
publicly or who have themselves declared war upon it: the rest are
termed bandits or pirates. (*Hostes sunt, quibus bellum publice
populus Romanus decrevit vel ipsi populo Romano: ceteri latrunculi
vel praedones appellantur.*)

(*Dig.* 49. 15. 24, Ulpian)[1]

Two aspects of this typology deserve special attention. First, it
should be noted that piracy and banditry are treated together by
Ulpian, both in this passage and elsewhere (*Dig.* 47. 9. 3,
approving Labeo). Ulpian was responding not only to theoretical
considerations, but to the realities of banditry and piracy in his
world. Bandits took to the sea, while pirates operated on land.[2]
It is scarcely surprising, therefore, that our sources seldom offer
neat distinctions between 'bandit' and 'pirate': all-embracing terms
like *latro* and *leistes* are used to encompass bandits, pirates and
others, 'since', as Shaw rightly observes, 'all form part of a
common threat to the same provincial order'.[3] Second, Ulpian's
main point, that bandits and pirates are distinct from those who
are in a formal state of declared warfare with the Roman people.
Bandits and pirates are not considered proper enemies of Rome:
rather, they are the common enemies of mankind.[4] They are, at
once, the enemies of no one and the enemies of everyone.

Ulpian's views are not exceptional: his typology is derived from a
long tradition of such thinking. Some eight centuries earlier,
Thucydides (1. 5) offered a similar analysis. Like Ulpian,
Thucydides treats bandits and pirates in the same breath. Likewise, Thucydides also considers both bandits and pirates to be alien
to and at odds with contemporary civilization, as represented
especially by the developed city-state: for him, piracy, which had
been more widely accepted in earlier times and had even had a place
in the evolution of civilization,[5] remained acceptable only in less
developed regions of his world. Nor can piratical conflicts

---

[1]   A similar formulation is given by Pomponius, *Dig.* 50. 16. 118.
[2]   e.g. Plut. *Pomp.* 24. 6; Paus. 4. 4; *Dig.* 47. 9. 3, Ulpian.
[3]   Shaw 1984, 14, with Garlan 1978, 2; cf. Garlan 1989.
[4]   Explicitly, for example, Cic. *Off.* 3. 107; Pliny, *NH* 2. 117; cf. Clavel-
Lévêque 1978, 18–19; Maroti 1962, 124–7. Scale was important: according to Herodian, 1. 10. 1, Maternus was so successful that he ceased to be
a bandit and became an enemy.
[5]   As Garlan 1978, 10, stresses. Cf. Shaw 1984, 23; Garlan 1989.

be compared with developed warfare such as that between Athens and Sparta, as his whole discussion is designed to indicate, though that war encompassed piratical actions.[1] Piracy could be a form of war and some communities might regularly connive at it or practise it openly.[2] However, it was more usually regarded as improper war – for Ulpian, undeclared war.[3] Piracy did not conform to accepted rules: it was inimical to civilization in all its aspects, including even civilized warfare.

At its worst, piracy might be so threatening as even to offer an alternative to civilization, as it did before Pompey, according to Plutarch:

> Even the wealthy, the aristocratic and would-be intellectuals took to piracy in order to gain a reputation. Pirates had bases and strongholds everywhere. The fleets which called there were remarkable for more than the strength of their crews, the skill of their helmsmen, the speed and dexterity of their ships, suited to their purpose. More appalling than their terror was their disgusting extravagance, with gilded sails and purple awnings and silver-coated oars, as if they revelled and plumed themselves upon their evil-doing. The Roman empire was disgraced by their flutes, strings and drinking along all the coast, by their seizures of imperial personages and by their ransomings of cities. . . . They plundered refuges and shrines previously inviolate. . . . They offered strange sacrifices at Olympus and performed secret rites. . . . But the Romans took the brunt of their insolence. . . . The pinnacle of that insolence was this: whenever one of their victims protested that he was a Roman and gave his name, they pretended to be awe-struck. They struck their thighs and threw themselves at his feet, begging for forgiveness. The victim would be taken in by their abject cowering. Then some pirates would put Roman shoes on his feet, while others clad him in a toga, so that there would be no further mistake. After having had their fill of mockery and pleasure, they would lower a ladder in the open sea and invite their victim to disembark and go his way in safety. When the man refused they would throw him overboard and drown him.
>
> (Plut. *Pomp.* 24)[4]

---

[1] MacDonald 1984 collects the passages. He acutely observes the distinction between proper warfare and raiding at Thuc. 5. 115. 2; cf. 4. 41. 3, 66. 1. Note also Jackson 1973; McKechnie 1989, 103–4.

[2] McKechnie 1989, 120; note Arist. *Pol.* 1256 a 37.

[3] Cf. Polyb. 18. 5. 1–3 on Aetolian raiding and laxity in declaration of war, with Berthold 1984, 98 n. 52.

[4] Possibly from Posidonius: Strasburger 1965, 43, especially n. 36.

According to Plutarch, piracy had reached such a point that it attracted even the élite. Pirates not only violated traditional religion, but had their own religion. Their principal target was the main force for order in the late Republic – Rome, its citizens and its symbols. And that target was not respected as an enemy, but ridiculed. Nor do Plutarch's pirates behave with any shame or covertness: their crime is magnified by their brazen attitude, for they 'combine shameless effrontery with defiance of the law'.[1]

Of course, the degree of piracy which Plutarch describes is exceptional and extreme. However, the extreme case serves to illuminate the threat to civilization latent in successful piracy. Pirates constituted a danger that was not only physical, but also moral and social. Particularly so, since the élite defined the rules of civilization and these certainly did not include the exercise of power by the lower orders, as pirates or in any other guise.

The complete unacceptability of piracy in the traditional thinking of the Roman élite is indicated by the severity of the punishment meted out to its practitioners. Crucifixion was routine: when Julius Caesar captured the pirates who had ransomed him, Suetonius regards it as a mark of his clemency that he cut their throats prior to crucifixion.[2] There was a special morality for the pirate: agreements with pirates, even if sworn under oath, could be broken in good conscience, 'for', as Cicero confirms (*Off.* 3. 107), 'the pirate is not a proper enemy, but the common enemy of all: with the pirate there can be no good faith or oath.'

---

[1]   Philo, *De spec. leg.* 4. 2; Mommsen 1899, 601. The effrontery of bandits and pirates is a favourite theme: the pirate who compared himself with Alexander (Cic. *Rep.* 3. 24; cf. Augustine, *De civ. D.* 4. 4), the bandit who kissed an emperor and escaped detection (Dio, 75. 2. 4), the many exploits of the bandit Bulla, whose conversation with a prefect recalls Alexander and the pirate (Dio, 77. 10), and the bandit who planned to kill Commodus, disguised as a praetorian (Herodian, 1. 10. 6–7). As with Plut. *Pomp.* 24, a substantial part of that effrontery was behaviour which mimicked the imperial establishment and highlighted common ground between the outlaw and the enforcers of law.
[2]   Suet. *Iul.* 74. 1, with Shaw 1984, 20–1; Hopwood 1989, 175. Hardly surprising then that Pompey's resettlement of pirates was criticized: Plut. *Pomp.* 29.

The eradication of piracy?

It is held that piracy simply did not exist in the Mediterranean world from the reign of Augustus until the reign of Commodus.[1] The main stimulus to that view is the claim, which recurs in contemporary sources, that the emperors eradicated piracy. However, examination of these claims shows them to be less than compelling.

The majority of such claims are made in the context of exaggerated laudation of the emperor. Thus Alexandrian Jews, in Philo's account of their embassy to Gaius:

> This was the Caesar (i.e. Augustus) who calmed the storms that raged everywhere, who healed the common plagues of Greeks and non-Greeks, which originated in the south and east and spread to the north and west, scattering the seeds of chaos over all lands and seas between. This was the man who not only loosed but broke the chains which burdened and shackled the world. This was the man who removed open warfare and the unseen warfare of bandit attacks. This was the man who emptied the sea of pirate boats and filled it with merchantmen.
>
> (Philo, *Embassy to Gaius*, 145–6)[2]

Similarly, Epictetus (3. 13. 9):

> For behold we can see that Caesar has provided us with a great peace, that there are no longer any wars or battles or great brigandage or piracy; at any time we can travel and journey from sunrise to sunset.

Epictetus does not make a habit of praising emperors (Millar 1965): he proceeds to contrast the things that Caesar cannot do. The contrast is important to his point and helps to account for his positive remarks on the imperial peace. Further, it should be noted that, even in positive mood, Epictetus is careful to state that there is no longer *great* brigandage or piracy: whether the adjective is to be applied to piracy as well as brigandage is less clear, but, as we shall see, not unlikely.

---

[1] The case is presented most fully by Starr 1941, 172–3, and 1989, 73–4, but the view is widespread: for example, Rostovtzeff 1957, 146; Garzetti 1974, 362.

[2] And more in similar vein: see Gabba 1984, 63–4.

Plutarch's comments seem to include piracy:

> On his death-bed, Antipater of Tarsus counted his blessings and reckoned even his good voyage from Cilicia to Athens. We too should not overlook the commonplace but take some account of it and rejoice that we live, are healthy, look upon the sun; that there is no war or civil strife. Rather, the land allows us to farm and the sea allows us to sail, as we wish, without fear; that we may speak, act, be silent or at leisure, as we wish.
>
> (Plutarch, *On the Tranquillity of the Mind*, 469 e)

Piracy may also have been included in the praise given to Augustus by those on board an Alexandrian ship in the Bay of Naples, who,

> . . . clad in white, garlanded and burning incense, heaped upon him best wishes and outstanding praise. They cried that it was through him that they lived, through him that they sailed and through him that they enjoyed liberty and good fortune.
>
> (Suetonius, *Augustus*, 98.2)[1]

In these passages the eradication of piracy is presented as but one aspect of something much larger, namely the establishment and maintenance of peace and prosperity through the suppression of all that might threaten it. And this is said to have been achieved not only in the Mediterranean, but more generally on land and on the seas.

More important than the exaggeration of such claims (on which, more below) is the fact that they place the eradication of piracy firmly among more familiar imperial achievements. Much-quoted verses of Horace confirm the point: under the *princeps*,

> the ox roams the fields in safety,
> Ceres and kind Prosperity nourish the fields,
> across a pacified sea fly the sailors.
>
> (Horace, *Odes*, 4. 5. 17–19)

With the bandit removed, livestock and crops flourish; with the pirate eradicated, honest sailors go their way. As Horace's poem

---

[1] For similar protestations, without mention of piracy, see Epictetus, 4. 1. 4 with Millar 1965, 146. Shaw 1984, 33–4 points out Suetonius' exaggeration of Augustus' success against bandits.

goes on to expound, the conditions of civilized life (especially morality and security) are assured by the *princeps*.

Before we can proceed further to examine this aspect of imperial ideology, it remains briefly to consider two further passages of a rather different sort, from Strabo and the elder Pliny respectively. They are usually cited out of context and therefore seem momentous; seen in context they are much less significant. Strabo (3. 2. 5 (144)) states:

> In addition, there is the present peace, the pirate-gangs having been broken up, so that sailors have no anxiety.

However, he is concerned in this section not with the Mediterranean sea as a whole, but only with the stretch of sea between Spain and Italy. His remarks relate only to that area, particularly inspired perhaps by Augustus' suppression of piratical activity on Sardinia, which had reached major proportions by AD 6 (Dio, 55. 28. 1). Later, the elder Pliny complains (*NH* 2. 118),

> A vast multitude sails a sea that is open and offers hospitable ports on all its shores, but in pursuit of profit, not knowledge.

However, his complaint is part of a larger denunciation of the lack of scholarly exploration of his world.[1] It is important to Pliny's point that he assert the ease of such exploration by comparison with that of earlier centuries; he stops a long way short of claiming the complete absence of piracy from the Mediterranean.

The ideology of eradication

The emperor is credited with the eradication of piracy as champion of civilization, peace, prosperity and proper order. The claim to the eradication of piracy was both an expression of imperial control and its legitimation: the passages quoted above particularly stress the latter, of course. Before the principate other such champions had been similarly credited.

A number of Greek myths concern the heroic suppression of

---

[1] On Pliny's morality see now Wallace-Hadrill 1990.

bandits and other threats to civilization: a notable example is Theseus, who disposed of bandits, while Dionysus made short work of the pirates who seized him from the shore.[1] But the first imperial ruler credited with the eradication of piracy is King Minos of Crete. We are told that Minos energetically suppressed pirates and thereby promoted sea travel, the acquisition of wealth and settlement in walled cities. In consequence, Minos' imperial rule was all the more acceptable (Thuc. 1. 8; cf. Lucian, *Dial. Mort.* 24. 1).

Turning from myth to history, a mark of the pre-eminence of archaic Corinth was said to be its eradication of piracy (Thuc. 1. 13. 5). Similarly, the Athenian empire was concerned to control piracy. Themistocles is credited with clearing the sea of pirates in the 480s (Nepos, *Them.* 2. 5), while Cimon cleared Scyros of pirates.[2] The so-called Congress Decree is usually taken to entail Athenian organization of measures against piracy.[3] For Isocrates (*Paneg.* 115), a symptom of the demise of Athenian hegemony was the consequent resurgence of piracy in the Aegean.

Later in the fourth century, the role of pirate-suppressor became a bone of contention between Athens and Philip II of Macedon (Hammond and Griffith 1979, 511; Cawkwell 1981, 48). The struggle for this role indicates the larger imperial role which it implied:

> With regard to the pirates, he (i.e. Philip) states that it is just that you and he together suppress those who commit evil acts by sea against

[1] Ormerod 1924, 31–2 suggests that Sciron might have a piratical connection. *Homeric Hymn to Dionysus*: the behaviour of the pirates (with a single exception) is typically disrespectful and irreligious. P. de Souza draws my attention to Ampelius, 2. 3 on Castor and Pollux, amongst others, credited with the elimination of pirates from the sea.
[2] Plut. *Cim.* 8. 3–7, according to whom Cimon also brought back the bones of Theseus from Scyros – is it simply coincidence that both dealt with brigands? Note also that Pericles worked to control the Black Sea (Plut. *Per.* 20).
[3] Plut. *Per.* 17: though its authenticity has been doubted, the decree was evidently part of the tradition by Plutarch's day. MacDonald 1982 argues that the decree is not concerned with piracy, but the clause 'that all should sail in security' (his translation) makes this difficult to argue. As MacDonald 1982, 121 sees, 'by summoning the congress Athens was making a claim for leadership of all the Greeks'. As such a leader she would have been expected to deal with pirates. On the control of pirates in Athenian treaties, see MacDonald 1984; McKechnie 1989, 122–6.

you and him alike. That amounts to a bid that you set him in control of the sea. That is to admit that without Philip you are incapable of exercising the safe guardianship of the sea . . .

(Ps.-Demosthenes, *On Halonnesus*, 14)

Alexander took over that role from Philip.[1] Hellenistici rulers, likewise: Eumelus is said to have won widespread praise for suppressing piracy in the Black Sea, while Dionysius I of Syracuse claimed to be a suppressor of pirates.[2] Despite such postures, pirates might also prove useful in actual war and at least some Hellenistic rulers were not above using those who might be regarded as pirates.[3] Nevertheless, piracy remained essentially unacceptable. Rhodes built an imperial identity upon the suppression of piracy.[4] Caere is even said to have won general praise among the Greeks simply for abstaining from piracy (Strabo, 5. 2. 3 (220)).

Influenced perhaps by Greek opinion, the expanding Roman empire set itself to deal with pirates.[5] Caesar's action against his captors was applauded (Ormerod 1924, 232). To suggest that a Roman provincial governor consorted with pirates was to make a very serious allegation (Cic. *Verr.* 2. 5. 11). It is as part of this tradition that we should understand Cicero's remarks on Pompey's much-vaunted eradication of piracy from the Mediterranean (Cic. *Leg. Man.* 31–5; cf. Plut. *Pomp.* 28. 2). The suppression of piracy was part of the Roman empire's beneficent patronage over the world (Cic. *Off.* 2. 26). It was also a cause and legitimation of Roman imperialism and territorial expansion.[6]

[1] Ps.-Demosth. 17. 19, with Hammond and Griffith 1979, 634; McKechnie 1989, 139 n. 196; Curtius, 4. 8. 15.
[2] Diod. 20. 25 (Eumelus); 15. 14. 3 (Dionysius I), considering the claim a pretext; cf. 16. 5. 3 (Dionysius II). On Carthaginian hostility to piracy, see Whittaker 1978, 82–5.
[3] e.g. Diod. 20. 83; Polyaenus, *Strat.* 4. 6. 18; Polyb. 18. 54. 7; note however McKechnie 1989, 108 and 113–14, on the unpopularity to be gained by association with pirates.
[4] Diod. 20. 81. 3; Berthold 1984, 99; Strasburger 1965, 50. McKechnie 1989, 125 is right to perceive a 'keenly felt moral obligation for leading states, or states which claimed to be such, to clear the sea of pirates'.
[5] Strabo, 5. 3. 5 (232), with an indication of Greek influence, discussed by Crawford 1978, 197; Livy, 8. 14; App. *Ill.* 3; Polyb. 2. 8. 8, cf. 3. 24.
[6] e.g. in the Balearics at the end of the second century BC (M. G. Morgan 1969), in Cyrene (Braund, 1985), Syria (Sherwin-White 1984, 213) and in Cyprus (Oost 1955, 98). It is in this context that we must understand the so-called Piracy Law of 101/100 BC.

Despite the praise heaped upon Pompey, piracy remained a problem in the Mediterranean even after his exploits. Indeed, the exaggerated eulogy of Pompey's achievement is not unlike the praise of Augustus and his successors in this regard: Florus (1. 41. 15), depriving the emperors of credit, goes so far as to suggest that no pirate was ever again seen in the Mediterranean after Pompey. But, under the Republic, there was scope for criticism, and there were contemporaries who exposed the eulogy so publicly that Cicero had explicitly to face the issue, and was forced to admit that piracy was still a problem for the governor of Asia in 62 BC.[1] Under the principate, there was no direct criticism of emperors for laxness towards pirates, but Roman governors did not escape entirely: Strabo considered kings to be more efficient in suppressing pirates.[2]

Were there pirates under the principate?

We have seen that claims that the emperors eradicated piracy are ideologically charged. That is enough to warn us against taking them at face value, particularly in view of the eulogistic manner in which they are made. However, it remains to consider the actual level of piracy in the Mediterranean under the principate. In the absence of any detailed statistics such consideration can only be broad and rather impressionistic.

It has been argued with some effect that the silence of Roman legal writers from Augustus to the Severans, particularly on the *lex Rhodia*, is a firm indication that piracy was not a problem in the first and second centuries AD (Starr 1941, 173; 1989, 74). However, although legal writers of this period are relatively under-represented in the *Digest*, some of their observations on piracy are preserved, nevertheless.[3] If the *lex Rhodia* be thought

---

[1] Cic. *Flac.* 28, 31 ff., with Reddé 1986, 326. The proposition that Pompey 'must virtually have ended' the procurement of slaves through piracy (de Ste Croix 1981, 230) is probably an overstatement; cf. Harris 1980, 124.

[2] Strabo, 11. 2. 12 (496); 14. 5. 6 (671), imputing this view to the Roman government; cf. Braund 1988, 90–1.

[3] *Dig.* 13. 6. 18 (Gaius), mentioning *piratae* as a natural hazard; cf. Gaius' similar remarks at 44. 7. 1 and Sen. *Ben.* 1. 5. 4. Piracy also seems

particularly important, we have a monograph on that law ascribed (albeit uncertainly) to L. Volusius Maecianus from the second century AD.[1] Therefore, the legal evidence tends rather to suggest the persistence of piracy. Moreover, with regard to wrecking and scavenging from wrecks, there is enough legal evidence to suggest that this may even have become a particular problem by the second century.[2]

In addition, occasional outbreaks of piracy happen to be mentioned by our sources, when they were sufficiently large and troublesome to attract attention. We hear something of the pirates (*leistai*, at least) who flourished on Sardinia in AD 6, the refractory Moors, Troxoborus in Cilicia in AD 52 and the pirate base established at Joppa as a result of the upheaval of the Jewish revolt.[3] Of course, we are not here concerned with piratical activities outside the Mediterranean: it is agreed that these persisted through the principate, though that is further to undermine ancient claims that the emperors eradicated piracy.[4]

Scattered evidence exists, therefore. However, the persistence of piracy in the Mediterranean cannot be assessed through reference to occasional major outbreaks. Epigraphy can reveal lesser instances, but it too is unlikely to record really small-scale occurrences.[5] It is chronic, everyday piracy that is at issue: for this, our meagre sources must be supplemented with broader considerations.

As we have seen, piracy and banditry were thoroughly

to be in question at *Dig.* 47. 9. 5 (Gaius); cf. 4. 6. 9, 47. 9. 6 (both Callistratus).
[1] *Dig.* 14. 2. 9, excerpted from a monograph on the Rhodian law ascribed to Maecianus, wherein is quoted Antoninus Pius' approval of Augustus' attitude towards that law, namely that it should be followed in so far as it did not conflict with imperial legislation. The ascription to Maecianus has been doubted: see *Der kleine Pauly*, s.v. 'Volusius'.
[2] Note fierce provisions against wreckers by Hadrian (*Dig.* 47. 9. 7: culprits are treated as *latrones*) and Antoninus Pius (*Dig.* 47. 9. 4). Cf. Petron. *Sat.* 114; Dio Chrys. 7. 32, 51 with Jones 1978, 59–60.
[3] Dio, 55. 28. 1; Calp. Sic. 4. 40, with Wiseman 1982; Tac. *Ann.* 12. 55, with Hopwood 1989; Joseph. *BJ* 3. 414 ff.; cf. Brunt 1975, 266; Reddé 1986, 327–8. Note also 2 Corinthians 11: 26.
[4] Reddé 1986, 329–30, gathers evidence (which, as one would expect, is not abundant: see below).
[5] *IGRR* iv. 219, more than an everyday case; cf. MacMullen 1966, 262; Levick 1976, 130.

interwoven, both in terminology and in practice. Piracy was far from being a purely seaborne phenomenon: pirates operated on land and against cities, while defence against them was also to a great extent on land (McKechnie 1989, 101–4; Reddé 1986, 452). Often, pirates and bandits were one and the same, like Troxoborus. Since banditry certainly persisted as an everyday fact of life under the principate, despite laudations of the imperial peace-bringers (Millar 1981; Shaw 1984), there is a *prima facie* case that piracy also persisted.

We should further consider the causes of piracy. Violent disturbance and poverty, whether acute or chronic, are regularly cited. The general absence of warfare in the Mediterranean under the principate can only have reduced piracy there. However, as far as we can judge, the ordinary man was hardly less vulnerable to poverty: that stimulus remained.[1] Pirates are often said to include fugitive slaves: in so far as this is true, slaves continued to flee to become potential pirates under the principate, as before. In addition, discharged soldiers and sailors might prefer brigandage to a settled civilian existence.[2] Moreover, among some communities, piracy seems to have been a social institution: though the Roman government sometimes relocated such communities,[3] there was no wholesale programme of resettlement. Most important, perhaps, is the fact that much piracy was opportunistic, conducted by part-time pirates. Fishermen took opportunities to pillage at sea,[4] as did bandit-shepherds in the mountains. Likewise, throughout antiquity, traders could consort with pirates, behave as pirates and be confused with pirates.[5]

Furthermore, if piracy ceased to be a problem after Augustus, it is difficult to explain the maintenance of large (and therefore expensive) Mediterranean fleets. The very existence of such fleets

---

[1]   Cf. the judicious remarks of Brunt 1975, 269.

[2]   e.g. Gannascus; Tac. *Ann.* 11. 8. 1, with Hobsbawm 1969.

[3]   e.g. Strabo, 4. 1. 5 (180); Livy, *Per.* 6; App. *Ill.* 10; Florus, 1. 41. 14. See in general Hanson 1988.

[4]   Petron. *Sat.* 114; Dio Chrys. 7. 32. Plato, *Laws*, 823 e, links fishermen and pirates; cf. Arist. *Pol.* 1256 a 37.

[5]   McKechnie 1989, 117–19, collects evidence. For example, both pirates and traders had an interest in slave-trading: Harris 1980, 124; cf. Brulé 1978, especially pp. 117–38.

would seem to suggest the persistence of piracy.[1] In view of the proximity of pirate and bandit, it is no surprise to find sailors of the fleet acting against brigandage on land too (e.g. Tac. *Ann.* 4. 27; Reddé 1986, 452). Meanwhile, on the land itself, *praefecti* were appointed to certain coasts to perform a function that was at least partly military: it seems probable that coasts of particular pirate activity were chosen for the attention of these officials.[2]

Augustus and his successors did not begin to eradicate piracy. But they did control it. Central government was no more interested in petty piracy than it was in the petty banditry that was rife in the empire. The priority was to forestall major outbreaks and, where necessary, to restore general order. Everyday piracy might attract the attention of a provincial governor or the like, but it is probable that, as with bandits, local communities were usually left to deal with pirates as best they could.

'Romances'

The second century AD is generally considered to have been the heyday of what is conveniently termed 'the novel', or 'the romance' or 'romances'. The numerous questions of chronology and genre raised by such a generalization cannot concern us here. We begin, rather, with the simple observation that Mediterranean pirates (and bandits) proliferate in such literature, including for example the works of Longus, Xenophon of Ephesus and Achilles Tatius (not to mention Apuleius), usually dated to the second century AD. How is the historian to deal with 'romances'? The question finds a ready answer from those who argue that piracy had been eradicated by the second century. Since these works depicted pirates at a time when pirates allegedly did not exist, they may be ignored (Starr 1941, 172–3). Ormerod (1924, 264) further suggests that the absence of 'real' piracy actually softened the 'fictional' pirate of second-century literature. Others prefer to

---

[1] Starr 1989, 72–7, does all that one could in an attempt to explain their existence in a world without piracy, but does not convince. Of course, the fleets were not only called upon to deal with pirates: see Reddé 1986, 323–662 for a comprehensive study of their activities.

[2] Reddé 1986, 417–23: the evidence is largely epigraphic and patchy.

assert that novels are evidence of historical reality (e.g. Scarcella 1977).

Although they are different, histories and romances are not neatly distinguishable, for each entails the other, particularly in antiquity (J. R. Morgan 1982; Woodman 1988). Therefore, history is 'hard to avoid in the texture of ancient fiction' (Anderson 1984, 89). As Morgan observes, 'a novelist who wishes to be plausible cannot afford to move very far away from the real world and the way things happen there'. Such a novelist seeks 'to control his unlimited imagination in the way that an historian does and so invite his audience to respond to his novel as if to actuality' (J. R. Morgan 1982, 222; cf. Reardon 1974; Wiersma 1990). To this extent, at least, romances may not be history but they are profoundly historical. As Millar (1981, 75) observes, 'the invented world of fiction may yet represent – perhaps cannot help representing – important features of the real world'. Despite occasional forays into the supernatural and excessive coincidence, romances tend to work with the credible.[1] In particular, their authors can exhibit a notable concern for accuracy of detail on seafaring (Bowie 1977).

Of course, by the second century, pirates had become a commonplace, not only of romances, but also of rhetoric. However, a commonplace cannot be assumed to be unreal.[2] Artistically, pirates offered speed, mobility and change in a world that was largely static and unchanging. In particular, they were convenient agents of a key theme of imperial literature, namely *fortuna*, the sudden rise and fall of personal fortunes: in an instant, pirates could render a wealthy princess a hapless slave and whisk her to a far land (Anderson 1984, 77; Hägg 1983, 114). Moreover, the pirate offered a splendid villain, the common enemy of mankind and civilization, with his unacceptable and sometimes horrific ways. At the same time, the extreme blackness of the pirate's villainy lends itself to parody, particularly if we

---

[1] Hägg 1983, 111–14; even the supernatural could fall within contemporary credibility, even transformation into a donkey: Augustine, *De civ. D.* 18. 18.

[2] As J. R. Morgan 1982, 263, points out with reference to piracy and shipwreck. Kennedy 1972, 334 n. 48, observes that piracy was a flourishing reality when it became a favourite theme of declamation.

suppose a literate audience ready to enjoy the bungling
incompetence and ignorance of the lower orders. And the ignorant villain gains an element of horror that may be lacking in the
reasoning evil-doer. Ormerod's soft pirates are rather lost among
the murderers, rapists and practitioners of human sacrifice who
menace the heroes and heroines of the romances and represent
gross violence to counterpoint their love stories.

Romance dealt with pirates in a way that history did not. The
historian concerned himself with greater themes, with proper war.
Bandits and pirates had to become a major nuisance to merit his
scornful or intrigued attention. At the same time, historians were
concerned essentially with the élite. Ordinary men who practised
everyday, low-intensity piracy were beneath the dignity of such an
approach to history. Cassius Dio refuses to be drawn into the
piracy of AD 6, though it had reached a level that could not be
ignored completely:

> I shall not go into all these matters in detail for much happened that is
> not worth recording and would be useless to relate.
>
> (Dio, 55. 28. 2)

Historians who included such details were open to censure.[1]
Biographers, too. Lucian illustrates the point by mocking Arrian
for writing the life of a bandit chieftain named Tillorobus.[2]

It is not surprising that we hear relatively little of Mediterranean piracy in the histories of the first and second centuries AD.
Imperial controls (the fleets, the coastal troops, local powers)
combined with the effects of relative stability to create a
Mediterranean world which suffered piracy mostly at an everyday, low-intensity level. Historians were not concerned with such
matters and tell us only of occasional major outbreaks which
attracted the attention even of central government.

Although beneath the dignity of history, everyday piracy,
wrecking and looting were not beneath the jurists and left some
epigraphic record, while the entire plot of a romance could turn

---

[1] Lucian, *How to Write History*, 28. Note, however, that Dio and others
were not above recording the more sensational actions and utterances of
bandits and pirates (above, p. 198 n. 1); such passages resemble romance:
cf. Shaw 1984, 44–9.
[2] Lucian, *Alex.* 2, with Stadter 1980, 239 n. 81, on the name.

on a single pirate ship. The emperor might even disclaim personal responsibility for everyday events at sea, as did Antoninus Pius,[1] after an incident in the Aegean, when he observed enigmatically: 'I am the master of the world, but the law is master of the sea' (*Dig.* 14. 2. 9). Despite the apparatus of imperial control, the sea – even the Mediterranean – remained a place of special difficulty. The relationship between sea and land has been seen as a relationship between nature and culture (e.g. Konstan 1983, 73–81); justly so, if we overlook the wilderness of desert, forest and intractable mountains. On the sea and in wild regions on land especially, piracy and banditry continued. It continued because it was unstoppable; for the same reason, perhaps, it was regarded as natural, like fire and storms.[2]

Bibliography

Anderson, G. (1984), *Ancient Fiction: The Novel in the Graeco-Roman World* (London).

Berthold, R. M. (1984), *Rhodes in the Hellenistic Age* (Ithaca).

Bowie, E. L. (1977), 'The novels and the real world', in B. P. Reardon (ed.), *Erotica Antiqua: Acta of the International Conference on the Ancient Novel, 1976* (Bangor), pp. 91–6.

Braund, D. C. (1985), 'The social and economic context of the Roman annexation of Cyrenaica', in G. Barker, J. Lloyd, and J. Reynolds (eds), *Cyrenaica in Antiquity* (Oxford), pp. 319–25.

—— (1988), 'Client kings', in D. C. Braund (ed.), pp. 69–96.

—— (ed., 1988), *The Administration of the Roman Empire, 241 BC–AD 193* (Exeter).

Brulé, P. (1978), *La Piraterie crétoise hellénistique* (Paris).

Brunt, P. A. (1975), 'Did imperial Rome disarm her subjects?', *Phoenix*, 29: 260–70.

Cawkwell, G. L. (1981), 'Notes on the failure of the second Athenian confederacy', *JHS* 101: 40–55.

[1] If it was indeed Pius; see Schulz 1946, 255.

[2] Sen. *Ben.* 1. 5. 4; *Dig.* 4. 9. 3 (Ulpian, quoting Labeo); 13. 6. 18, 44. 7. 1 (both Gaius). On banditry as a natural disaster, see Shaw 1984, 8–9.

A version of this chapter was read at the American Philological Association in San Francisco (Dec. 1990): I am grateful for the contributions of colleagues there, particularly to Profs Bruce Frier and John Nicols. I am also conscious of the improvements generously offered by Philip de Souza and John Rich. Of course, my gratitude to those named does not imply their agreement with my views.

Clavel-Lévêque, M. (1978), 'Brigandage et piraterie: représentations idéologiques et pratiques impérialistes au dernier siècle de la république', *DHA* 4: 17–32.

Crawford, M. H. (1978), 'Greek intellectuals and the Roman aristocracy in the first century BC', in P. D. A. Garnsey and C. R. Whittaker (eds), pp. 193–207.

de Ste Croix, G. E. M. (1981), *The Class Struggle in the Ancient Greek World* (London).

Gabba, E. (1984), 'The historians and Augustus', in F. Millar and E. Segal (eds), *Caesar Augustus: Seven Aspects* (Oxford), pp. 61–88.

Garlan, Y. (1978), 'Signification historique de la piraterie grecque', *DHA* 4: 1–16.

—— (1989), *Guerre et économie en Grèce ancienne* (Paris).

Garnsey, P. D. A., and Whittaker, C. R. (eds, 1978), *Imperialism in the Ancient World* (Cambridge).

Garzetti, A. (1974), *From Tiberius to the Antonines* (London).

Hägg, T. (1983), *The Novel in Antiquity* (Oxford).

Hammond, N. G. L., and Griffith, G. T. (1979), *A History of Macedonia*, ii (Oxford).

Hanson, W. S. (1988), 'Administration, urbanization and acculturation in the Roman west', in D. C. Braund (ed.), pp. 53–68.

Harris, W. V. (1980), 'Towards a study of the Roman slave trade', in J. H. D'Arms and E. C. Kopff (eds), *The Seaborne Commerce of Ancient Rome* (Memoirs of the American Academy in Rome, 36), pp. 117–40.

Hobsbawm, E. J. (1969), *Bandits* (London).

Hopwood, K. R. (1989), 'Bandits, élites and rural order', in A. Wallace-Hadrill (ed.), *Patronage in Ancient Society* (London), pp. 171–87.

Jackson, A. H. (1973), 'Privateers in the ancient Greek world', in M. R. D. Foot (ed.), *War and Society: Historical Essays in Honour of J. R. Western* (London), pp. 241–53.

Jones, C. P. (1978), *The Roman World of Dio Chrysostom* (Cambridge, Mass., and London).

Kennedy, G. (1972), *The Art of Rhetoric in the Roman World* (Berkeley).

Konstan, D. (1983), *Roman Comedy* (Ithaca).

Levick, B. M. (1976), *Tiberius the Politician* (London).

MacDonald, B. R. (1982), 'The authenticity of the Congress Decree', *Historia*, 31: 120–3.

—— (1984), '*Lesteia* and *leizomai* in Thucydides', *AJP* 105: 77–84.

McKechnie, P. (1989), *Outsiders in the Greek Cities in the Fourth Century BC* (London).

MacMullen, R. (1966), *Enemies of the Roman Order: Treason, Unrest and Alienation in the Empire* (Cambridge, Mass.).

—— (1974), *Roman Social Relations 50 BC–AD 284* (New Haven).

Maroti, E. (1962), 'Ho koinos polemos', *Klio*, 40: 124–7.

Millar, F. (1965), 'Epictetus and the imperial court', *JRS* 55: 141–8.

—— (1981), 'The world of the *Golden Ass*', *JRS* 71: 63–75.

Mommsen, T. (1899), *Römisches Strafrecht* (Leipzig).

Morgan, J. R. (1982), 'History, romance and realism in the *Aethiopika* of Heliodorus', *Classical Antiquity*, 1: 221–65.

Morgan, M. G. (1969), 'The Roman conquest of the Balearic Isles', *California Studies in Classical Antiquity*, 2: 217–31.

Oost, S. I. (1955), 'Cato Uticensis and the annexation of Cyprus', *CP* 50: 98–112.

Ormerod, H. A. (1924), *Piracy in the Ancient World* (Liverpool, repr. 1978).

Purcell, N. (1990), 'Mobility and the polis', in O. Murray and S. Price (eds), *The Greek City: From Homer to Alexander* (Oxford), pp. 29–58.

Reardon, B. P. (1974), 'The Second Sophistic and the novel', in G. W. Bowersock (ed.), *Approaches to the Second Sophistic* (Pennsylvania), pp. 23–9.

Reddé, M. (1986), *Mare nostrum: les infrastructures, le dispositif et l'histoire de la marine militaire sous l'Empire romain* (Rome).

Rostovtzeff, M. I. (1957), *The Social and Economic History of the Roman Empire*, 2nd edn, rev. P. M. Fraser (Oxford).

Scarcella, A. M. (1977), 'Les structures socio-économiques du roman de Xénophon d'Éphèse', *Revue des études grecques*, 90: 249–62.

Schulz, F. (1946), *History of Roman Legal Science* (Oxford).

Shaw, B. D. (1984), 'Bandits in the Roman empire', *Past and Present*, 105: 3–52.

Sherwin-White, A. N. (1984), *Roman Foreign Policy in the East 168 BC to AD 1* (London).

Stadter, P. A. (1980), *Arrian of Nicomedia* (Chapel Hill).

Starr, C. G. (1941), *The Roman Imperial Navy 31 BC–AD 324* (Ithaca, repr. 1975).

—— (1989), *The Influence of Sea Power on Ancient History* (Oxford).

Strasburger, H. (1965), 'Poseidonios on problems of the Roman empire', *JRS* 55: 40–53.

Wallace-Hadrill, A. (1990), 'Pliny the Elder and man's unnatural history', *Greece and Rome*, 37: 80–96.

Whittaker, C. R. (1978), 'Carthaginian imperialism in the fifth and fourth centuries', in P. D. A. Garnsey and C. R. Whittaker (eds), pp. 59–90.

Wiersma, S. (1990), 'The ancient Greek novel and its heroines: a female paradox', *Mnemosyne*, 43: 109–23.

Winkler, J. J. (1980), 'Lollianus and the desperadoes', *JHS* 100: 155–81.

Wiseman, T. P. (1982), 'Calpurnius Siculus and the Claudian civil war', *JRS* 72: 57–67.

Woodman, A. J. (1988), *Rhetoric in Classical Historiography* (London).

9

War and diplomacy: Rome and Parthia, 31 BC-AD 235

Brian Campbell

Parthia was unique among the lands bordering the Roman empire in that it was a large kingdom with a long and distinctive tradition of civilization, coherent government, and domination over subject peoples. Parthian armies not only inflicted unavenged defeats on Rome but even invaded Roman territory. This unprecedented situation presented the Romans with unique problems, since there was little in their historical experience to prepare them for dealing with an adversary of significant strength on a permanent basis, but also with unique opportunities for diplomatic contact. The process by which Romans and Parthians achieved an orderly coexistence, the factors in society that influenced this, and also the methods by which diplomacy was successfully accomplished, help to illustrate the interrelation of society, government, and war in the imperial period. Even within the confines of ancient warfare Rome and Parthia had a significant capacity for acting outside their borders and initiating destruction. In that sense they were superpowers, and Henry Kissinger has aptly summed up the consequences of mutual ignorance and lack of communication between great powers:

> The superpowers behave like two heavily armed blind men feeling their way round a room, each believing himself in mortal peril from the other whom he assumes to have perfect vision. . . . Of course, over a time even two armed blind men can do enormous damage to each other, not to speak of the room.
>
> (Kissinger 1979, 522)

Relations between Rome and Parthia from 92 to 31 BC did not encourage hopes of diplomatic rapport. Sulla's unfortunate decision to sit between the king of Cappadocia and a Parthian envoy at a meeting in 92, though perhaps due to ignorance, was construed as an insult by the Parthian king (Plut. *Sull.* 5). Pompey was rude and uncompromising in 65 in refusing to address Phraates III as 'king of kings' and in announcing that justice was to be the boundary between Rome and Parthia (Plut. *Pomp.* 33; *Apophtheg. Regum*, 8). From 53 BC onwards the Romans had tended to settle problems in the East by invasion and warfare: Crassus invaded Parthia largely for personal aggrandizement; Julius Caesar could not ignore the opportunities for military glory offered by a war in the East, and only his murder prevented the campaign he was carefully preparing. The Parthians responded to these acts or threats of aggression by exploiting Roman disarray in the civil wars and invading Roman Syria in 40 under the joint command of the Parthian king's son and the Roman defector Quintus Labienus, 'The Parthian'.[1] They killed Decidius Saxa, the governor of Syria, and overran the province before being repulsed in three battles in 39–38 by Antony's lieutenant P. Ventidius. Antony then tried to chastise the Parthians and add glory to his own name by another invasion of their territory, but his campaign ended in ignominious retreat with no positive achievement.

Augustus, by contrast, reached a diplomatic accommodation with the Parthian king expressed in a formal treaty, probably in AD 1, and accepted that Rome, while aiming to nominate or approve kings of Armenia, a supposedly independent kingdom much under Parthian influence, need not have a military presence there. This arrangement worked until in Nero's reign King Vologaeses ambitiously installed his brother as king of Armenia and tested how far the Romans were prepared to allow the Parthians to go in asserting their influence there. Negotiation and compromise backed up by the threat of military action and the concentration of strong forces directed by Domitius Corbulo, the distinguished governor of Syria, eventually brought a solution.

---

[1] Dio, 48. 26. For the coins issued by Labienus, see Crawford 1974, no. 524.

The Romans accepted the Parthian king's nominee as king of Armenia provided that he was crowned by Nero in Rome.

Trajan put an end to this era of diplomatic rapport; brushing aside Parthian attempts at negotiation he set out to make Armenia a Roman province and apparently to annex further territory between the Euphrates and Tigris. His efforts ended in fiasco. Hadrian repaired the damage and wisely restored the status quo. But an uneasy peace ended when the governor of Cappadocia, M. Sedatius Severianus, blundered into Armenia to expel Parthian troops and was massacred along with a legion. A war ensued (AD 163–6), requiring the personal presence of the emperor Lucius Verus who for a time, like Trajan, occupied Ctesiphon, the Parthian capital. Syria was seemingly extended to include Dura-Europus, and a few garrisons were left in strongpoints. Nevertheless, this success did not substantially alter the strategic balance in the area or intimidate the Parthians. Septimius Severus resumed the Roman offensive, and after capturing Ctesiphon created a new province in northern Mesopotamia. His son Caracalla launched another invasion, though with no tangible result. But already the balance was shifting as the Parthian regime was overthrown by the Sassanid dynasty of Persis probably in 224, and the last emperor of the Severan dynasty, Severus Alexander, found himself on the defensive against this new threat.[1]

During this period of over three hundred years the structure of government in Rome underwent significant changes. In the late Republic the senate's control of foreign policy was increasingly usurped by military dynasts who seemed to act independently. In a letter to Crassus in 53 the Parthian king shrewdly asked if the army had been sent by the Roman people or if it was a personal venture (Plut. *Crass*. 18). Autocratic rule meant that the emperors were in complete control of foreign policy with the help of their

---

[1] On Roman relations with Parthia in the Republic and imperial period and the importance of the province of Syria, see especially Debevoise 1938; Ziegler 1964; Timpe 1975; Rey-Coquais 1978; Keaveney 1981 and 1982; Sherwin-White 1984; Brunt 1963, 174–5 (= 1990, 104–6) and 1990, 456–64; Gruen 1990, 396–9; Isaac 1990, 19–53; Kennedy and Riley 1990, especially pp. 28–46. On Parthia itself see Frye 1962 and 1984.

friends and advisers. But an emperor did not have to take an interest in foreign affairs or make decisions or follow the advice of his friends; there was no organized government structure to provide experience, continuity, and consistency in dealing with foreign affairs; the senate was consulted, but largely as a mark of respect.[1] There were no permanent diplomatic representatives, and the remoteness of Parthia meant that personal contact between Roman emperor and Parthian king was rarely possible. Furthermore, Parthian internal and dynastic politics were often turbulent, especially since any member of the ruling Arsacid house could be made a legitimate king. Instability reduces confidence in diplomacy. This, however, should not be exaggerated. The long reigns of several Parthian kings[2] suggest consistent government through which diplomacy could be conducted. Indeed, the large number of potential royal claimants offered Rome some diplomatic opportunities.[3]

Roman perceptions of the Parthians

An important factor in the contacts between Rome and Parthia was the perception of the Parthians held by important people in Rome who made decisions or contributed to them. In the early first century BC the Romans were not well informed about the Parthians; at Carrhae in 53 the troops were ignorant of their strengths and fighting techniques, believing them to be like the Cappadocians and Armenians who rarely came to close quarters and who had been easily beaten by Lucullus (Plut. *Crass.* 18. 3–5). However, as Strabo pointed out, 'the supremacy of the Romans

[1]   The rivalries of the emperor's governors and army commanders must sometimes have perplexed the Parthians, e.g. the dispute between Ummidius Quadratus and Domitius Corbulo over responsibility for the reception of Parthian hostages (Tac. *Ann.* 13. 9).

[2]   Note Phraates IV, *c.*38–2 BC, Vologaeses I, *c.* AD 51–80, Vologaeses III (IV), *c.*148–92, Vologaeses IV (V), *c.*191–207. See Colledge 1967, 178–9; Bickerman 1980, 130–1; Frye 1984, 360. Between *c.*31 BC and AD 224 there were about 21 established kings of Parthia and 26 Roman emperors, though of course there were more pretenders to the Parthian throne.

[3]   For the problems of diplomacy and Roman imperial government, and in particular the role of the emperor, see Millar 1982 and 1988.

and that of the Parthians have revealed much more knowledge than had previously been handed down by tradition'.[1] By the first century AD the Parthians were well enough known to appear with the Greeks and Romans as examples of the sub-division of mankind into nations (Seneca, *Ep*. 58. 12). Later, Ulpian could casually use the phrase 'if the king of the Parthians should be alive', to illustrate legal terminology (*Dig*. 28. 7. 10. 1).

Since relations were generally hostile and suspicious, especially after the disastrous invasion of Crassus, the Parthians came to be seen as natural enemies of Rome, an idea which persisted through to the third century AD. Ulpian gives the Germans and the Parthians as stock examples of Rome's enemies (*Dig*. 49. 15. 24). There was a fear of Parthian military prowess with startling reports about their armour-piercing arrows and invincible heavy cavalry. Although in the aftermath of Carrhae the Senate was slow to take effective action to safeguard Roman interests in the East, Cicero as governor of Cilicia was worried about possible Parthian incursions into Cappadocia and Cilicia and advised the senate to send more troops 'since there is an extreme danger that all those provinces which pay taxes to the Roman people may have to be lost'.[2] According to Caelius there was talk in Rome of sending Pompey or Caesar to deal with the Parthian menace, though it is interesting that it was still seen as an adjunct of Roman politics.[3] The detailed planning of Caesar's projected campaign against the Parthians in 44 shows the respect in which they were held by this accomplished commander,[4] and their reputation was confirmed by the substantial setbacks inflicted on Antony (Sherwin-White 1984, 319–20). Their mounted archers, who could shoot while retreating, and their strong cavalry are singled out by Augustan writers, while in the fourth century, Festus (*Breviarium*, 15) could still describe war in terms of Roman

---

[1] Strabo, 11. 6. 4 (508); cf. 11. 1. 6 (491–2) – criticism of previous geographical knowledge. For the difficulty of getting detailed intelligence reports, see Millar 1982, 18–19.
[2] *Fam*. 15. 1. 3–5, cf. 2. 1–2. See also Sherwin-White 1984, 290–7.
[3] *Fam*. 8. 10. 2; *Att*. 6. 1. 3. Cf. *Att*. 5. 21. 2–3, 6. 2. 6; *Fam*. 8. 7. 1.
[4] App. *BCiv*. 2. 110; Nicolaus of Damascus, *FGH* 90 F 130. 41; Plut. *Brut*. 25, *Caes*. 58; Suet. *Iul*. 44.

javelins against Parthian arrows.[1] Indeed, the efforts made by
the Romans especially in the second century AD to develop
suitable military tactics to cope with Parthian archers and cavalry
show how seriously they took the difficulties of fighting this kind
of opponent (Campbell 1987, 13–29).

What kind of people did the Romans think the Parthians were?
There was certainly a notion of their distinct racial characteristics,
and perhaps inferiority. Septimius Severus in a letter to Aphrodisias in 198 describes the Parthians as 'barbarians' (Reynolds 1982,
no. 17. 10; cf. no. 18. 2; *IGBulg* 659. 29). Lucan could traduce all
eastern peoples as being softer than those from the North (*Phars.*
8. 365–94, with some intemperate criticism of Parthian social
customs). Polyaenus, the Greek writer who dedicated his
Strategemata to Marcus Aurelius and Lucius Verus, justifies his
effectiveness in this field by referring to his Macedonian background and the distinguished past of the Greeks, who had
mastered oriental peoples (*Strat.* 4, *prooem.*). Moreover, a belief
that the Parthians were devious or treacherous persisted after the
death of Crassus. In the *Annals* Tacitus singles out several
characteristics which sound rather like traditional clichés: a lack
of mercy and justice (12. 11); excessive luxury (2. 57); love of
hunting, horses, and endless banquets; contempt for Greek
customs; so Parthians who had been brought up as hostages in
Rome rarely found favour when they returned (2. 56; 6. 32).

By the end of the Republic the Romans had begun to recognize
Parthia as a power which was comparable with Rome. Of course
the Parthians were no match for Rome in resources, manpower,
or military might, and there is no sign, at least in the first two
centuries AD, that the Romans regarded them as a direct threat to
their control of the East, still less to the empire as a whole.
However, the Parthians' status as a permanent power in the East,
with important vassals, was such that they could not easily be
dislodged. Dio's analysis, referring to the situation after Carrhae,
probably conveys received wisdom of Roman experiences in the
East: the Parthians were very effective in war, but their reputation
was greater than their actual achievements; they were unable to
occupy Roman territory and sometimes lost some of their own,

[1]   Note also Statius' comments on the Parthians at *Silv.* 1. 4. 77–81, 2. 6.
18–19, 4. 4. 30–1.

but they could never really be defeated. Their skill in archery and horsemanship was formidable, as was their ability to use the hot climate and the terrain. But they were at their best on their side of the Euphrates. Beyond that they were better suited for sudden raids and limited battles than for full-scale war over a long period, because of supply difficulties, paying and keeping the army together, and winter weather which was not good for their bow strings (40. 14). Dio's view is supported by Tacitus, in whose account of Romano-Parthian relations Parthian respect for Rome in diplomatic terms is always tempered by the memory of Parthia's distinguished history and the king's pre-eminent position among eastern potentates.[1] Indeed in Paetus' camp at Rhandeia the nervous officers are made to reflect that Parthia rivalled the imperial might of Rome (15. 13). Yet Tacitus also identifies some characteristics that limited the Parthian military threat: dislike of distant campaigns (11. 10); their inability at sieges (11. 9); incompetent commissariat (12. 50); internal dissension (2. 2).[2]

By the late second and early third century AD, when Parthian

---

[1] Tacitus' use of *reverentia* (*Ann.* 6. 37, 12. 10–11, 13. 9, 15. 1) is an expression of a diplomatic generality, 'respect' or 'good will' towards Rome, and cannot be pressed to mean Parthian obeisance or Roman dominance. At *Germ.* 37. 3–5, Tacitus expresses the view that the freedom-loving German tribes posed a greater threat to Rome than the despotism of the Arsacids; but this is in a context where he wished to emphasize German strength, and he chooses to omit any mention of the setbacks inflicted on Antony by the Parthians. For the potential strength of Parthia, see Brunt 1990, 457–60.

[2] We find the same general ideas in Lucan, in a speech given to Lentulus Spinther urging Pompey not to seek refuge with the Parthians (*Phars.* 8. 331–439). Pliny the Elder (*NH* 5. 88) and Strabo (11. 6. 4 (508), 9. 2 (515), 16. 1. 28 (748–9)) speak of Parthia in terms that compare her to Rome. It is true that at 6. 4. 2 (288) Strabo says that the Parthians have yielded supremacy to Rome. But (i) the context of this passage is initially the settlement of 20 BC and the presentation of this in Rome (ii) there were different interpretations of the Parthian motives for sending hostages; Augustus himself wrote that Phraates sent hostages 'not because he had been overcome in war' (*RG* 32) (iii) some Parthians did occasionally seek a king nominated by Rome, but nothing much ever came of this and Strabo wildly exaggerates in his claim that the Parthians were about to hand over their entire authority to the Romans; this undermines confidence in the whole passage, which was probably written to give the most favourable picture of Augustus' achievements.

power was on the wane, Septimius Severus contemptuously proclaimed a simple imperialist motive for the annexation of Mesopotamia, though he also argued that it provided a defence for Syria. Dio was uninterested in the former and sceptical of the latter, since Mesopotamia cost more than it brought in and involved the Romans in constant wars because they were now so closely involved with peoples who were more in the Parthian than the Roman orbit (75. 3). According to Dio, the facts supported his view, and later he adverted to the increasing possibility of an attack by the now dominant Persians (80. 3). This passage is the first sign of real disquiet in Rome about a military threat in the East since Cicero wrote to the senate in 51 BC, and shows how perceptions of the balance of power were changing. Romans could fear that the Persians were preparing an invasion, and the story was that they intended to march to the shores of the old Persian empire on the Mediterranean. However there was still little clear intelligence about Ardashir's movements or capabilities, and Dio's main concern was that the appalling state of the army was undermining the Romans' capacity to resist this new threat.[1]

Augustus and the development of diplomacy

Augustus held the key to the development of Roman policy in the East. He could not ignore Parthia, whose prestige was high because of the recent successes against Rome and the capture of military standards. Rome also had a permanent presence in Asia and Syria, two wealthy and important provinces, and therefore political and economic interests to protect. In addition, independent vassal states looked to her for guidance and support.[2] So, a military presence was required. Moreover, there was Armenia, in which the Romans maintained a persistent if erratic interest. It is inaccurate to describe Armenia as a buffer state between Rome and Parthia. Tacitus says merely that Armenia lay between the two empires (*Ann.* 2. 3), and in Pompey's day the Parthians had wanted the entire Euphrates to be recognized as the frontier (Dio,

---

[1]   Isaac 1990, 31–3 seems to me to underestimate the importance of the change in circumstances brought about by the arrival of the Sassanids.
[2]   For the role of friendly kings see Braund 1984, 91–103.

37. 6; Plut. *Pomp.* 33). Moreover, Rome's careless treatment of Armenia hardly suggests that they considered it to be of prime strategic significance in protecting their eastern possessions or in preventing Parthian advance.[1] At no time did Rome go to war with Parthia simply because of Armenia; indeed, her control of the kingship of Armenia was so nominal as to be often ineffective.[2] Tacitus sums this up in the opinion he ascribes to Quadratus' council in AD 52 as they discuss whether to intervene in Armenia – 'emperors had often bestowed Armenia, under the guise of making a generous gift, but really to disrupt the native population' (*Ann.* 12. 48). On the other hand, after Lucullus and Pompey the Romans considered Armenia to be within their sphere of interest (*Ann.* 13. 34); and their prestige and ability to influence friendly kings demanded that they keep a high profile there.

In 31 BC Augustus had at least 200,000 Italians under arms, mastery of the resources of the Roman world, and opportunities for intervention provided by Tiridates, a claimant for the Parthian kingship; moreover, he was present personally in the East, and needed military glory against a foreign enemy. Yet he ignored the tradition of military action against Parthia followed by Crassus, Ventidius, and Antony, and also the plan of conquest formulated by Julius Caesar. This cannot have been due to lack of determination or capability, since he undertook large-scale campaigns of conquest elsewhere throughout his reign, willingly appointed effective commanders, and took advice from senior associates like Agrippa. But, although he needed the laurels of a great conqueror, he could not afford embarrassing setbacks, and in the light of recent history – the rapid conquest of Gaul but several reverses in Parthia – it must have seemed that the northern provinces would be a more fruitful field for a decisive victory. Augustus recognized that war with Parthia would be a perilous venture because of the

---

[1] For discussion of wider strategic and military issues, see Luttwak 1976, especially pp. 25–30, 45–8, 105–11; Mann 1979, 175–83; Isaac 1990, 372–426.

[2] Sherwin-White 1984, 337, suggested that the upper Euphrates and Araxes valleys provided an easy passage between Roman Anatolia and the Parthian provinces. However, this route took at least twelve weeks' march and there is no sign that the Parthians ever contemplated it.

tactical difficulties, and that the Parthians had a permanent presence in eastern affairs. From the start his policy was not merely to avoid war with Parthia, but to establish negotiating terms. He realized the value of diplomacy based on the threat of military intervention, to achieve an accommodation over Armenia and establish mutual spheres of interest, in effect, a balance of power that could still be presented as a great Roman triumph.[1]

Augustus' personal prestige and complete mastery of the Roman world enabled him to impose his will on foreign policy, and to employ his children and relations as especially high-ranking personal envoys to the Parthian king, Phraates. Indeed, the developing importance of diplomacy in Romano-Parthian relations is reflected in the status of the envoys and the increasing formality and protocol of meetings.[2] Moreover, the emperor exploited the pretender Tiridates, who had kidnapped Phraates' son and established himself strongly enough to issue coins in Seleuceia in May 26 and March 25 BC, and who was sufficiently persuaded of Roman good will to describe himself as 'Friend of the Romans' on his coinage (Dio, 51. 18, 53. 33; McDowell 1935, 222). In 20 BC Augustus himself travelled to the eastern provinces, but there was no summit with Phraates – diplomacy was not sufficiently advanced for that, and Augustus wished to avoid a public demonstration of equality. He must have realized that if Phraates had met him he would not have grovelled as a suppliant in the way that Augustus was to suggest in his propaganda. Augustus quietly set Tiridates aside and returned Phraates' son; in exchange Phraates handed over the standards captured at

---

[1]   Brunt (1963, 174–5 (= 1990, 104–6); 1990, 456–77) holds that Augustus' other preoccupations prevented any attack on Parthia from 31–20 and after 2 BC. This does not seem to me to fit the facts of Augustus' relations with Parthia (cf. also Sherwin-White 1984, 331–2), and in any event begs the question why Parthia was so low on his list of priorities. Brunt also believes that Augustus was aiming in general at undefined expansion of Roman power. I accept that the emperor was not constrained by a merely defensive policy, but do not find that incompatible with a willingness to use diplomacy where appropriate to achieve more limited objectives.
[2]   Augustus found some channels of diplomacy already in place – exchanges of letters and meetings of high-ranking envoys using interpreters of Greek, Latin, and Parthian (cf. Plut. *Crass.* 28–31). For Greek as the language of diplomacy in the East, see Millar 1988, 364–6.

Carrhae. This was important as a propaganda coup, but also and probably more significantly, the return of the standards deprived the Parthians of an important bargaining counter.[1]

But this was only the first step. There was still the problem of the long-term relationship between the two empires and the status of Armenia. Diplomatic contact reinforced by gifts[2] doubtless continued behind the scenes. We see this in the exchange of letters between the new king Phraataces and Augustus in AD 1. The Parthian had written to explain his activity in Armenia and to demand back his brothers who were in Rome. Augustus' reply omitted to call Phraataces 'king' and demanded that he lay aside the royal name and withdraw from Armenia. This was a tough public stance to support the personal mission to the East on which his adopted son Gaius had embarked. In a further letter, Phraataces styled himself 'king of kings' and referred to Augustus merely as Caesar. These well-modulated insults reveal a remarkable knowledge of the political set-up in the other country. But it is clear that both sides knew how to keep the insults within reasonable limits, as part of the diplomatic manoeuvring, and they did not undermine the attempt to find a negotiated settlement. In Armenia, Parthian intrigue had secured the return of Tigranes as king at the expense of Artavasdes who had had Roman support. But Tigranes wrote to Augustus carefully refraining from calling himself 'king' and providing gifts; these Augustus accepted, thus accepting the diplomatic initiative, and instructed him to go to meet Gaius with good expectations.[3]

The high-level personal meeting between Gaius and Phraataces was crucial for the development of diplomacy. The protocol was elaborate. They met on an island in the Euphrates with equal retinues, and subsequently Gaius joined the king for a formal

[1] According to Dio (54. 9), in a letter to the senate in 20 BC Augustus suggested that he might be satisfied with existing Roman territory; the emperor presumably was referring only to the East, and this passage cannot be taken as a reliable indication of his long-term policy (Brunt 1990, 461–2). However, it is significant that Augustus was prepared to recognize publicly a limitation to his ambitions for territorial aggrandizement in Armenia and Parthia.

[2] Note Augustus' gift of an Italian slave girl, Musa, to Phraates in 20 BC. She was eventually to become queen (Joseph. *AJ* 18. 39–43).

[3] Dio, 55. 10. Tigranes subsequently died in battle.

banquet on the Parthian side; then the king came to dine on the Roman side. This made a great impression on Velleius, then a young military tribune (Vell. Pat. 2. 101):

> Early in my military career, as a tribune of the soldiers I was lucky to witness this splendid and memorable moment when the distinguished leaders of two great empires and mankind met, with the Roman army on one side, the Parthian on the other.

From this meeting in AD 1 a formal treaty emerged, which was to be cited by the Parthians in AD 18, 49 and 61, when King Vologaeses hesitated about warlike moves in view of the 'unbroken treaty' with Rome.[1] According to Dio, Phraataces undertook to keep out of Armenia, while Augustus agreed to keep the king's brothers out of the East and thereby away from internal Parthian politics.[2] Moreover, Rome recognized the Euphrates as a demarcation line between the two empires. In 62 King Vologaeses wrote to Corbulo complaining about the establishment of Roman forts on the east bank of the Euphrates and demanding that the Euphrates should form the boundary as it had before (Tac. *Ann.* 15. 17). This suggests that the river was part of the original treaty, and that is confirmed by Velleius' description of the conference between Gaius and Phraataces with the symbolism of meetings in the middle of the river and then on both banks, pointless unless it was to indicate the boundary.[3] This

---

[1] Tac. *Ann.* 2. 58, 12. 10, 15. 1; Dio, 55. 10 a; Vell. Pat. 2. 101; Sherwin-White 1984, 326–8. Ziegler 1964, 47–8, and others have placed this treaty in 20 BC on the grounds that *foedus* is used by some sources to describe the agreement of 20; but it is impossible to ascribe a precise meaning to this word in a poet (Prop. 4. 6. 79) or a late writer (Oros. 6. 21); Velleius uses *societas*, which is also imprecise. It may be argued that 20 BC is the correct context for a treaty because the Parthians were then granted friendship (*RG* 29. 2). But that need not imply a treaty; cf. *RG* 32. 2 where Augustus also speaks of Phraates seeking friendship *c*.10 BC.

[2] Phraates had sent four of his sons to Rome *c*.10 BC. It was often expedient for a Parthian king to dispose of political rivals in this way (cf. Joseph. *AJ* 18. 41–2; Tac. *Ann.* 2. 1, 15. 1). Note that the Latin *obses* did not necessarily have the pejorative implication of the English 'hostage' (Braund 1984, 12–15).

[3] Note also that when in 35 L. Vitellius escorted Tiridates, the candidate backed by Rome for the Parthian throne, he turned back at the Euphrates (Tac. *Ann.* 6. 37). The subsequent meeting of Vitellius and the Parthian king Artabanus was held in the middle of a bridge across the Euphrates (Joseph. *AJ* 18. 101).

was indeed a concession by Augustus since the Romans did not usually recognize a formal delimitation of their power. The nature of this meeting also demonstrated the status of Parthia as a comparable power; but once again Augustus could distance himself by not meeting Phraataces in person.

The treaty of AD 1, although it did not amount to an alliance (*contra* Sherwin-White 1984, 327), defined spheres of influence more clearly. Both sides could now accept that Armenia should not be a cause of war between them; they could keep diplomatic face and represent the situation there as it suited them. So Augustus preserved notional Roman sovereignty by seeking to nominate a king of Armenia. He could then threaten the Parthians with greater Roman involvement, since he realized that the possibility of a permanent Roman military presence would be more damaging to them than a loose Parthian suzerainty would be to the Romans, as the Parthians considered the Armenians to be racially akin and thought of the country as their third kingdom after Parthia itself and Media Atropatene. The consequence, though, was that having committed himself to this level of intervention, he subsequently found it difficult to withdraw completely. But as long as Roman troops were not stationed permanently in Armenia, the Parthians were prepared to refrain from direct military support for their own interests, although they were not prevented from trying to exercise influence in Armenia, as the sequel shows. Consequently, when Paetus spoke of Rome's control of Armenian kings, the Parthians replied that the real power lay with Parthia.[1] On the Roman side the treaty was backed up by the presence of three or four legions in Syria and initially three in Egypt,[2] a high-prestige force of concentrated fire power, and by the threat of diplomatic intervention through support for rival candidates for the Parthian throne.

It is not clear how far public opinion in Rome approved of Augustus' policy and how far it had to be persuaded. The ordinary

---

[1] Tac. *Ann*. 15. 14. For the notion that armed intervention in Armenia by Rome could lead to hostilities with Parthia, see *Ann*. 2. 4 (AD 16).
[2] It is not clear whether three or four legions were permanently stationed in Syria. There may also have been a legionary garrison in Galatia in the early Empire (Keppie 1986, 412–13).

people will have been happy with the handouts and games provided by a leader who had himself triumphed three times in 29 BC. It is unlikely that they had strong opinions about war with Parthia. Similarly, the Italian soldiers who had survived the fighting of the long civil wars perhaps yearned for more settled conditions, especially since opportunities for booty would now be more restricted and Augustus was moving towards a regulated system of pay and discharge bonuses. The military dynast will not have been under pressure from his troops to fight in Parthia; doubtless there were veterans of Antony who remembered how difficult that could be. It is the upper classes in Rome who arguably might have most resented the preference for diplomacy rather than war, either because of imperialist aspirations and anger at previous blows to Rome's military honour, or because of the restriction of opportunities for senatorial military glory, prestige, and aggrandizement. But the campaigns of Crassus and Antony had provided a warning that this was not a lucrative area for military glory, despite romantic notions some may have had of emulating Alexander. Moreover, the civil wars had been disastrous for the upper classes; a period of peace and recuperation was desirable, and it would soon be discovered that real influence lay now in other areas, particularly in having the ear of the emperor. The governorship of Syria itself, it may be argued, was sought more for the prestige it brought through the whole range of its administrative responsibilities, than for any opportunities of military glory that might accrue (Campbell 1975, 25–6).

Nevertheless, there must have been people in Rome who still expected war with Parthia. Having been prepared for this by the campaigns of Crassus and Antony and the bellicose plans of Caesar, they doubtless expected the young leader to seek every opportunity for military glory. Augustus himself may have given an impression of greater military activity than was in reality intended, or perhaps the comments of his entourage were misunderstood. Many contemporary authors, writing probably before 20 BC, recount the disgraceful defeat of Crassus and the loss of the standards, and the military skill of the Parthian bowmen and heavy cavalry, but emphasize that they are destined to be crushed by Augustus and led in triumph; these victorious campaigns might even extend to the Chinese, Indians, and

British.[1] All this does not mean that there was necessarily a strong public opinion in favour of war, only that some elements of the upper classes expected it. Poets were not puppets of the regime, but would not go out of their way to express sentiments known to be contrary to Augustus' views or policies. It is notable that after 20 BC the tone changes. Roman power stretches everywhere and peace has been achieved, founded upon Parthian subservience, symbolized by the return of the standards. Phraates has accepted Augustus' jurisdiction and power (*ius* and *imperium*).[2] This is well illustrated by Propertius, who in his earlier work had imagined the Euphrates under Roman control and a campaign against India. After 20 he takes a different approach. The Parthians admit defeat but only through an agreement, and if there is any prospect of further Roman advance, it is to be deferred so that Gaius and Lucius Caesar, the emperor's grandsons, can win some glory. Perhaps this was one of the ways in which Augustus justified his reluctance to push the Parthians further in 20 BC.[3]

Augustus himself could introduce into public discussion the facts that suited him, namely the difficulty of coping with Parthian military techniques, and the return of the standards, since that was to be the one highly visible gain of his diplomatic approach. He set out to make diplomacy seem respectable, even glorious, so he concealed what he later was to recognize himself, namely the comparability of Rome and Parthia. Both the meeting of Gaius and Phraataces and the formal agreement which limited

---

[1] e.g. Hor. *Epod.* 7. 1–10; *Odes,* 1. 12. 53–6, 19. 11–12, 2. 13. 17–18, 3. 2. 3–4; Virg. *Ecl.* 10. 59–60; *Georg.* 1. 509; *Aen.* 6. 792–5, 851–3, 12. 855–9; Prop. 2. 10. 13–18, 14. 23, 27. 5, 3. 4. 4–10, 5. 47–8, 9. 25–6, 54, 12. 3–12, 4. 3. 35–6, 67–8.

[2] Hor. *Odes,* 4. 5. 25–7, 15. 5–12, 23; *Epist.* 1. 12. 27–8, 18. 56–7; Virg. *Georg.* 3. 30–3 (these lines were probably revised by Virgil shortly before his death in 19 BC); *Aen.* 7. 601–6, 8. 726–8; Ovid, *Fasti,* 5. 580–98; *Tr.* 2. 227–8. On contemporary literature see Brunt 1963 and 1990, 443–6; Mann 1979, 176–7; Wissemann 1982.

[3] Prop. 4. 6. 79–84. Ovid, *Ars Am.* 1. 177 ff., writing in 2 BC, does predict great conquests in the East, but he may have misunderstood the purpose of Gaius' intended mission, or was perhaps attempting to flatter the prince. There is no need to suppose that Augustus would always wish to make his intentions entirely clear.

Roman ambitions as much as it did Parthian were omitted from the *Res Gestae*. On the other hand, he exaggerated the return of the standards and Roman control of Armenia, and implied that this was a final solution, in order to convince the doubters that all this was for the good of Rome:

> Greater Armenia . . . I could have made a province, but following the example of our ancestors I preferred to grant the kingdom to Tigranes . . . When the same people (the Armenians) later rebelled and went to war, I quelled them through the agency of my son Gaius Caesar and handed them over to be ruled by king Ariobarzanes . . . I forced the Parthians to return to me the spoils and standards of three Roman armies and to seek as suppliants the friendship of the Roman people. Those standards I deposited in the innermost shrine of the temple of Mars the Avenger.
>
> (*RG* 27. 2; 29. 2)

Moreover, coins celebrate 'the recovery of the standards', with a representation of a kneeling, humbled Parthian, and 'the capture of Armenia' (Ehrenberg and Jones 1976, nos. 26, 28). In the *Res Gestae* Augustus sought to leave an overall impression of Roman advance and glorious conquest (26. 1); this was appropriate for the great *imperator* who had rescued the state from disintegration, in order to show that the army of the Roman people had been put to good use. Elsewhere in this work Augustus arranged the facts to suit his point of view, and no less so in his description of his dealings with Parthia. Yet he does make clear that his basic objective was friendship and diplomatic rapport with Parthia, not war:

> Phraates . . . sent all his sons and grandsons to me in Italy not because he had been overcome in war, but because he sought our friendship by pledging his children.
>
> (*RG* 32. 2)

It is likely that the diplomatic approach found a receptive audience in Rome and that a fairly typical viewpoint was that of the Italian municipal aristocracy as expressed by Velleius Paterculus, who clearly welcomed the Romano-Parthian rapport.[1]

---

[1]   Vell. Pat. 2. 101; cf. 2. 91. Note Tacitus' praise of Tiberius' astute use of diplomacy (*Ann.* 6. 32). See also Campbell 1984, 394–401.

Diplomacy after Augustus

The policy of achieving limited, but defined objectives by diplomatic contact was, in my view, consistently followed up to the early second century. Decisions were made by emperors and their upper-class advisers who were doubtless much influenced by precedent and tradition (Millar 1977, 259–72; 1982, 4–7). The channel of high-level meetings continued, using the formality and protocol that provided a framework inside which diplomacy could be worked out. This was able to cope with the upset in 35 when Artabanus took advantage of the death of Artaxias III[1] to install his son as king of Armenia. Artabanus' long reign had probably increased his confidence, and Roman inactivity in the East may have led him to think that they would not trouble to intervene. Matters were settled by Augustus' method – disruption in Parthia, a display of force, limited support for a Roman nominee in Armenia, and close diplomatic contact; so, at the end of Tiberius', or possibly at the start of Gaius' reign, King Artabanus met L. Vitellius the governor of Syria, who, in the absence of the emperor or a suitable prince, was the most senior official available. The meeting took place on a bridge of boats across the Euphrates, each side having an appropriate retinue, and was followed by a feast organized by Herod Antipas, the Jewish tetrarch and Roman ally. It is interesting that as part of the ceremonies Vitellius and Artabanus sacrificed to the legionary standards and images of Augustus and the reigning emperor, emphasizing the notional presence of the imperial family. The result of this diplomacy was to perpetuate the agreements made in AD 1.[2]

Vologaeses' attempt to install his brother Tiridates as king of Armenia in 52 subverted the diplomatic rapport. Nero and his advisers took vigorous measures and Domitius Corbulo was despatched as special commander. It is significant that soon after Corbulo's arrival in Armenia messages recommending peace were sent to Vologaeses. The Parthian king was initially unwilling to

---

[1] Artaxias had been installed in Armenia in 18 by Germanicus, who was approached by Artabanus with the offer of a personal meeting at the Euphrates. Germanicus replied politely, but apparently nothing came of it (Tac. *Ann.* 2. 56, 58).
[2] Suet. *Calig.* 14. 3, 19. 2; *Vit.* 2. 4; Dio, 59. 27; Joseph. *AJ* 18. 101.

allow his brother to hold Armenia as the gift of a foreign power
(Tac. *Ann.* 13. 34). This strongly implies that Vologaeses had been
offered this compromise, and that from the start Rome accepted
as a possible option the installation of a Parthian nominee with
Roman approval. This is confirmed by Corbulo's subsequent
message to Tiridates that he should petition Nero for a safe throne
without fighting (13. 37). He can hardly have offered this without
Nero's approval; elsewhere the commander was reluctant to act
without imperial instructions (15. 17). Only in 60 was a Roman
nominee, Tigranes, put forward for Armenia. Although this was
perhaps a preferred option, it is possible that the Romans
recognized that a Parthian-backed king might be more stable and
still not a threat to them. Tigranes indeed proved unsuitable
because he upset the Parthians by making unprovoked attacks on
Adiabene, forcing both Rome and Parthia to become involved.

Up to this point, despite a background of imposing military
preparations, Corbulo's activities had enhanced the importance of
negotiation according to the pattern established by Augustus. He
astutely used letters and meetings to keep in close contact with
Vologaeses, while also deploying substantial military force, which
was not only to intimidate the Parthians but also to preserve
Rome's face with her allies in the region.[1] Tacitus summarizes
the gist of Roman diplomatic approaches at this time: there was
no need for war; both sides had had their successes; peace and
order suited everyone; Parthia had internal problems while Rome
was at peace everywhere.[2]

After an agreement for joint withdrawal from Armenia,
Caesennius Paetus was sent out as special commander, with
instructions probably to demonstrate Roman military strength in
order to secure Armenia for Tigranes or another more amenable
candidate, or to persuade the Parthians to accept suitable terms

---

[1]   Dio, 62. 23 (secret diplomacy); see, in general, Warmington 1969, 85–
99; for the legions, Keppie 1986, 415–17. Isaac 1990, 29, asserts:
'Corbulo's eastern campaigns turned a diplomatic conflict regarding
Armenia into a military one'. But this does not fit the facts as presented
by our only major ancient sources, Tacitus and Dio.
[2]   Tac. *Ann.* 15. 27. Nero, however, refused to support the Hyrcanians,
who were in revolt from Parthia.

for the crowning of Tiridates.[1] Paetus' disastrous defeat and
capitulation at Rhandeia gave Parthia the upper hand in Armenia
and harmed Rome's standing. Corbulo, who was now solely
responsible for the execution of Nero's policy, had large forces at
his disposal, but it was sophisticated diplomacy that repaired the
damage. First, there was a preliminary meeting with the king's
high-ranking envoy Monaeses on the bridge which Corbulo had
built across the Euphrates, now with its central section removed,
perhaps symbolizing the absence of Roman aggression across the
river. Here he broached the key issue – that Vologaeses' brother
Tiridates could receive the crown of Armenia if he went to Nero in
person. Vologaeses' envoys to Rome were at first unsuccessful in
resolving the matter, although they apparently accepted the
principle of Roman sovereignty. But Corbulo had soon arranged
a meeting with Tiridates at Rhandeia where, amid a combination
of personal contact and formality, Tiridates agreed to relinquish
his crown and receive it back from Nero. A great feast completed
the ceremony.[2]

Vologaeses then wrote to Corbulo to ensure that the correct
protocol was applied to his brother's trip to Rome, which
amounted to a 'state visit'. This gives an excellent indication of the
degree of understanding and sophistication reached in Romano-
Parthian relations by the mid-first century. Tiridates was not to be
exposed to any suggestion of subjection, should not surrender his
sword, should be allowed to greet provincial governors and not be
kept waiting at their doors; in Rome he was to receive the honours
due to a consul (Tac. *Ann.* 15. 31). At the crowning ceremony
in Rome, Nero provided an interpreter for the crowd and
emphasized the importance of a face-to-face meeting with

---

[1] Tac. *Ann.* 15. 6 records Paetus' boast that he intended to install the
tribute and government of Rome in Armenia. It is possible that Paetus
exaggerated or misunderstood his instructions, since the sequel shows
that annexation of Armenia was not an option. Dio, 62. 20 suggests that
Paetus' instructions were confined to making sure that nothing new
happened in Armenia.

[2] Tac. *Ann.* 15. 29–30. When Corbulo and Tiridates met, the king
dismounted as soon as he saw the general, who followed suit, and then
both men clasped hands; the meeting was concluded with an embrace. As
both armies paraded in full array, Tiridates laid his crown before a statue
of Nero.

Tiridates. Both sides had made concessions; Tiridates prostrated himself before Nero in public, calling him master; but he refused to surrender his sword, which in a nice diplomatic solution was nailed to its scabbard (Dio, 63. 1–7; Suet. *Nero*, 13). The ceremony was followed by games and a sumptuous banquet. In response to Nero's frequent letters urging that he visit Rome, Vologaeses eventually proposed a meeting in Asia, since it was easier for Nero to cross the sea. Nothing came of it. Vologaeses probably did not wish to commit himself further, for, although Nero presented the settlement as a triumph for Rome, and Tacitus could suggest that Tiridates was little more than a captive and that Rome always valued real power rather than its meretricious trappings (*Ann.* 15. 29, 31), the Parthians reckoned that they had come off the better, as we see from the story of Terentius Maximus, the false Nero, who was able to raise some support among the Parthians in 79/80 by claiming that he was the emperor who had given Armenia back to them (Dio, 66. 19; John of Antioch, *FHG* iv, p. 578, fr. 104). But this was what Augustus had intended, that Armenia should be part of diplomatic bargaining and not a cause of war.

Thus by the end of the mid-first century AD there was a pattern of diplomatic contact, though by no means a rigid system.[1] Letters sometimes expressed the central points at issue but were more generally used to arrange meetings or the next step in the diplomatic process; they were carried on the Roman side by centurions and other junior officers (e.g. Tac. *Ann.* 15. 5). Emissaries were of high rank and in close contact with the top man; for envoys travelling through hostile territory escorts were provided.[2] It is possible that before envoys were despatched formal authorization was required; one condition of the truce negotiated by Paetus with the Parthian king was that the king

---

[1]   It may not be very helpful to assume with Millar 1988, 364, 368 that the apparatus of internal diplomatic exchanges, for example, with Greek cities, could be applied to external relations, since the range of matters to be discussed was so much greater and the emperor was dealing not with a subject community, but with a large power, where sometimes he might have to take the initiative; moreover, the mechanism of diplomatic contact was different.

[2]   When Parthian envoys appeared before Nero and gave an account of events in Armenia contradicting that of Paetus, the emperor was able to

should have the right of sending envoys to Nero (ibid. 15. 14). Time was presumably needed to make arrangements for their passage to Rome. The governor's role was often to facilitate the diplomatic process by arranging for the conveyance of envoys and letters. For example, we find Marius Maximus, governor of Syria Coele, writing to the tribunes, prefects, and *praepositi numerorum* in the province, enclosing a copy of his letter to the procurator concerning the subsistence and travel arrangements (along a carefully delineated route) for Goces, a Parthian envoy to Septimius Severus and Caracalla (Chaumont 1987, 422–47). Occasionally a governor might communicate directly with the \king, or even meet him. But usually governors were limited by their *mandata*, and in my view were not free to formulate policy, though of course their reports might influence the emperor and his advisers (Campbell 1984, 348–54). Envoys were held to be sacrosanct; when Ardashir sent Severus Alexander four hundred tall, handsome Persians in order to intimidate the Romans, Alexander refused to return them, but sent them to villages in Phrygia; he felt unable to execute them because of their status as envoys, non-combatants, and mere messengers for their master (Herodian, 6. 4).

We see another aspect of diplomatic contact in 75 in the relations between Vespasian and Vologaeses, who wrote offering the assistance of 40,000 Parthian bowmen in the civil wars. Vespasian politely declined, but thanked the king, inviting him to send envoys to the senate in the knowledge that the peace, and so presumably the treaty, was secure (Tac. *Hist.* 4. 51; Suet. *Vesp.* 6. 4). Subsequently, Vologaeses asked the emperor to help him against the Alani and requested either Titus or Domitian to accompany the force. Vespasian, however, refused to get involved in what he wisely thought was none of his business; the treaty and friendship had never extended to an alliance (Dio, 66. 15; Suet. *Dom.* 2. 2; above, p. 225). In view of all this it is difficult to accept the argument that the expansion of Cappadocia by the incorporation of the newly-annexed Commagene, the stationing of a legionary force in the province in 72, and the road-building

question personally a centurion who had accompanied the group from the East (Tac. *Ann.* 15. 25; cf. 27, 14. 25).

and other activities in Syria[1] were aimed directly at the Parthians, because, after Nero's settlement of 66, Armenia had been
ruled by Tiridates, brother of the Parthian king. The garrison in
Cappadocia could protect Roman interests against the Scythians,
Sarmatians, and Alani, as well as any Parthian threat, and also
keep order throughout Anatolia, where previously there had been
few Roman troops. After the Jewish revolt the previous concentration of troops in Syria may have seemed unsuitable both in size
and location. Road-building was part of the general Roman
policy to facilitate control and communications west of the
Euphrates.

The breakdown of diplomacy, AD 115–235

As the framework of diplomacy became more formal and regular,
so deviations from it had greater importance and, indeed, their
own diplomatic significance. The giving of gifts could complete a
deal or simply be a gesture of good will, as when Vologaeses sent a
gold crown to Titus to mark the defeat of the Jews; Titus accepted
the gift and gave a banquet for the king's envoys. But to refuse to
accept gifts and honour their bearers could be a mark of
diplomatic disapproval and warning, as could a refusal to reply to
messages or to send a suitable envoy. Trajan's presence in the East
should have allowed the development of diplomatic channels, but
his activities in fact did much to damage them. He was not
interested in compromise or negotiation, but set out to look for
opportunities of conquest. Diplomacy, where employed, was used
aggressively. When, during his journey to Syria in 113, the
emperor was met in Athens by envoys of King Osroes seeking
peace and bringing gifts, he refused to accept the gifts or to make
any reply. This was a warning that some of the usual diplomatic

---

[1] Bowersock 1973, 133–40; Isaac 1990, 36–42; Brunt 1990, 457. Commagene was included in Cappadocia because its king, Antiochus, was
alleged to be intriguing with the Parthians (Joseph. *BJ* 7. 219–29) and was
presumably deemed to be unreliable. For legionary dispositions, see
Keppie 1986, 420–4. An inscription of AD 75 indicates that Syria then had
four legions; Keppie suggests that Cappadocia may have had praetorian
status, with one legion.

channels were not open. Subsequently, Parthamasiris, nephew of Osroes and his nominee as king of Armenia, wrote to Trajan styling himself 'king'. He got no reply. When he wrote again he omitted 'king' and asked for the governor of Cappadocia to be sent to him as an envoy. This was a typical diplomatic approach. But again he got no answer to his letter and Trajan sent the governor's son instead, which looks like an insult (Dio, 68. 17, 19). The continuing importance of these ideas in the third century can be seen in the exchange between Odenath of Palmyra and Shapur I, the Persian king, who treated the former's letters with contempt. Ordering his gifts to be thrown into the river, he said 'Who is this and where does he come from that he dares write to his own master?' (Peter the Patrician, *FHG* iv, p. 187, fr. 10).

When Trajan finally met Parthamasiris at Elegeia, he conducted negotiations in his tent, but then insisted that the Parthian speak from the tribunal, thinking that the publicity would prevent any distortion of what was said. Clearly this meeting lacked the civility, cordiality, and trust of earlier conferences where the negotiating was done in secret and the results revealed in public displays. Indeed, according to Dio, Parthamasiris had the preconceptions of Romano-Parthian diplomacy typical of the first century: there had been no military defeat; he was there by agreement to negotiate; there was the precedent of Nero's diplomacy; he expected to be king of Armenia. He must have been astonished when Trajan declared that Armenia was to be a Roman province.[1]

Even worse was to follow. After leaving, Parthamasiris was killed in a scuffle with his Roman escort. Trajan tried to evade responsibility by saying that Parthamasiris had broken the agreement and had justly met his fate. Yet as Fronto shrewdly observed, the killing of a man who had come in good faith to a conference damaged Rome's credibility in diplomatic terms.

It would have been much better for the reputation of the Romans if the suppliant had left unharmed rather than been punished even justly; for in events like this, the reason for the deed is obscure, only the deed itself remains under public scrutiny; and it is much better to ignore an

---

[1] Dio, 68. 20. For detailed discussion of the aims and course of Trajan's wars in the East, see Lepper 1948; Angeli Bertinelli 1976, 3–22.

injury and keep international public opinion on your side, rather than
to avenge one and have it turn against you.

(Fronto, 2. 212–14 Haines)

This is a good statement of the pragmatism that had characterized
Roman diplomacy with Parthia from the time of Augustus. By his
invasion of Parthia, which clearly took the Parthians by surprise
since they were expecting the usual diplomatic exercises, Trajan
undermined the relative stability of the region.

In the period after Trajan, our meagre source material makes it
difficult to establish the importance of diplomacy. Nevertheless,
between AD 113 and 217 there were four major wars involving
Rome and Parthia, in three of which the Romans as aggressors
invaded Parthian territory and indeed created a new province in
northern Mesopotamia, whereas from 31 BC to the early second
century AD there were no wars.[1] It is surely a reasonable
conclusion therefore that war, even if not necessarily the preferred
option, was now more readily accepted as a solution than before,
although the framework of diplomacy was still in place and
contacts continued.[2] As Parthia degenerated into a dynastic
struggle between the brothers Artabanus V and Vologaeses V,
Caracalla's offer to marry Artabanus' daughter should probably
be seen as an attempt to encourage internal disarray, since he
boasted in a letter to the senate that the brothers' dispute would
damage Parthia.[3]

[1] Isaac 1990, 53, argues that periods of major warfare came at intervals
of fifty years or more. But the first interval he mentions (36 BC–AD 52) is
almost ninety years, and this is achieved only by counting as a major war
Corbulo's operations. Tacitus makes clear that Rome and Parthia were
intent on avoiding war in Nero's reign, and in no sense can these events be
compared to the wars of the second century.
[2] Hadrian, for example, returned the Parthian king's daughter captured
by Trajan, and promised to return his golden throne, though he failed to
do this (SHA *Hadr.* 13. 8; *Ant. Pi.* 9. 7). For a Parthian ambassador on
the way to Septimius Severus, see above, p. 233. There is no evidence for
the view of Ziegler 1964, 132, that the Parthian king concluded a peace
with Severus on the basis of the status quo.
[3] Dio, 77. 12, 78. 1; Herodian, 4. 10–11. Caracalla had a great admiration
for Alexander, who had married a Persian princess, and this emperor's
eccentric actions are not a safe guide to Roman policy at this time.

Conclusion

Millar has argued that the concept of war in the East was concretely embodied in the strategic priorities chosen by emperors, and that the most significant choice was the occupation of Mesopotamia and the readiness to fight repeated wars for it.[1] But it is surely remarkable that despite the pre-eminence of eastern wars in Graeco-Roman culture, and their own warlike traditions, Rome and Parthia preserved the peace in the East for almost 150 years. Early in Augustus' reign there were three or four legions stationed in Syria and three in Egypt. Even after Severus' annexation of Mesopotamia and the stationing there of two legions, Rome's eastern territories (including Egypt) were garrisoned by only eleven legions, two of which were in Judaea with a primary task of watching the Jews. The major concentration of legions (sixteen) remained on the Rhine and Danube. Mesopotamia was occupied late in relation to Rome's other territories and was defended because the balance of power had changed and Rome, under pressure from the Persians, found it diplomatically impossible to withdraw safely. Lucius Verus had invaded Mesopotamia because he needed to reassert Roman influence after the defeat of Severianus. Septimius Severus annexed it because after bloody civil war he needed to gain political prestige for his new dynasty by a war against a foreign people, and thought that he could fight Parthia without excessive risk of widespread reprisals.

Augustus' diplomatic framework survived because of the respect in which he was held and because it worked. Emperors, who from the late first century were expected to command in person, were in general conservative and, in my view, avoided large-scale campaigns of aggrandizement and annexation (Campbell 1984, 390–401). Moreover, for a time the self-interest of the two empires coincided in avoiding war, which left them free to consolidate their control and intervene more profitably elsewhere. But there was necessarily an unpredictable element in diplomacy, since it was conducted at the behest of autocratic rulers who could at any time exercise their inexplicable whim

[1] Millar 1982, 20, 22. Isaac 1990 also believes that the frontier policy of Rome in the East was intermittently but persistently aimed at expansion.

without restraint. Perhaps by the end of the second century there was a feeling in Rome that Parthia was weaker now and unlikely to respond effectively to aggression. If so, this was misguided. The decline in diplomatic contact may have made it more difficult to cope with the Sassanids of Persis who were predominant after the overthrow of Artabanus V by Ardashir probably in 224, and who had no reason to trust the idea of talking to Rome or appeasing her since they could point to the unprovoked invasion of Iranian territory by Trajan, Septimius Severus, and Caracalla, acts of aggression largely unavenged by the Arsacids. To a Roman embassy Ardashir replied that weapons, not words, would settle the matter. As pressure built up on other frontiers the resurgence of an aggressive power in the East was very damaging to Roman interests in that it absorbed much of her attention and resources, and brought a serious setback in the defeat and capture of the emperor Valerian at Edessa in 260 by Shapur I, who celebrated the new order: 'And Syria, Cilicia, and Cappadocia we burned with fire, and ruined, and pillaged'.[1]

Bibliography

Angeli Bertinelli, M. G. (1976), 'I Romani oltre l'Eufrate nel II secolo d.C.', *ANRW* ii. 9. 1. 3–45.
Bickerman, E. J. (1980), *Chronology of the Ancient World* (London).
Bowersock, G. W. (1973), 'Syria under Vespasian', *JRS* 63: 133–40.
Braund, D. C. (1984), *Rome and the Friendly King: The Character of the Client Kingship* (London).
Brunt, P. A. (1963), review of H. D. Meyer, *Die Aussenpolitik des Augustus und die augusteische Dichtung*, *JRS* 53: 170–6; = 'Augustan imperialism', in Brunt 1990, ch. 5 (pp. 96–109).
—— (1990), *Roman Imperial Themes* (Oxford).
Campbell, J. B. (1975), 'Who were the "viri militares"?', *JRS* 65: 11–31.
—— (1984), *The Emperor and the Roman Army 31 BC–AD 235* (Oxford).
—— (1987), 'Teach yourself how to be a general', *JRS* 77: 13–29.
Chaumont, M. L. (1987), 'Un document méconnu concernant l'envoi d'un

---

[1] From Shapur's trilingual inscription at Naqsh-E Rustam, translated in Frye 1984, 371–3. Versions of this chapter were delivered at Leicester University and at Mount Allison University, New Brunswick. I am grateful to those who contributed to the discussion, and especially to David Buck and John Rich, who read the text in detail and offered valuable comments and advice.

ambassadeur parthe vers Septime Sévère (P. Dura 60B.)', *Historia*, 36: 422–47.

Colledge, M. A. R. (1967), *The Parthians* (London).

Crawford, M. H. (1974), *Roman Republican Coinage* (Cambridge).

Debevoise, N. C. (1938), *A Political History of Parthia* (Chicago).

Ehrenberg, V., and Jones, A. H. M. (1976), *Documents Illustrating the Reigns of Augustus and Tiberius*, 2nd edn (Oxford).

Frye, R. N. (1962), *The Heritage of Persia* (London).

—— (1984), *The History of Ancient Iran* (Handbuch der Altertumswissenschaft, iii. 7; Munich).

Gruen, E. S. (1990), 'The imperial policy of Augustus', in K. A. Raaflaub and M. Toher (eds), *Between Republic and Empire: Interpretations of Augustus and his Principate* (Berkeley, Los Angeles, and Oxford), ch. 18 (pp. 395–416).

Isaac, B. (1990), *The Limits of Empire: The Roman Army in the East* (Oxford).

Keaveney, A. (1981), 'Roman treaties with Parthia *c*.95–*c*.64 BC', *AJP* 102: 195–212.

—— (1982), 'The king and the war-lords: Romano-Parthian relations *c*.64–53 BC', *AJP* 103: 412–28.

Kennedy, D., and Riley, D. (1990), *Rome's Desert Frontier from the Air* (London).

Keppie, L. F. J. (1986), 'Legions in the east from Augustus to Trajan', in P. Freeman and D. Kennedy (eds), *The Defence of the Roman and Byzantine East* (British Institute of Archaeology at Ankara Monographs, 8; BAR International Series, 297; Oxford), pp. 411–29.

Kissinger, H. A. (1979), *The White House Years* (London).

Lepper, F. A. (1948), *Trajan's Parthian War* (London).

Luttwak, E. N. (1976), *The Grand Strategy of the Roman Empire from the First Century AD to the Third* (Baltimore and London).

McDowell, R. H. (1935), *Coins from Seleucia on the Tigris* (Michigan).

Mann, J. C. (1979), 'Power, force and the frontiers of the empire', *JRS* 69: 175–83.

Millar, F. G. B. (1977), *The Emperor in the Roman World* (London).

—— (1982), 'Emperors, frontiers and foreign relations, 31 BC to AD 378', *Britannia*, 13: 1–23.

—— (1988), 'Government and diplomacy in the Roman empire during the first three centuries', *International History Review*, 10.3: 345–77.

Rey-Coquais, J.-P. (1978), 'Syrie romaine de Pompée à Dioclétien', *JRS* 68: 44–73.

Reynolds, J. M. (1982), *Aphrodisias and Rome* (London).

Sherwin-White, A. N. (1984), *Roman Foreign Policy in the East 168 BC to AD 1* (London).

Timpe, D. (1975), 'Zur augusteischen Partherpolitik zwischen 30 und 20 v. Chr.', *Würzburger Jahrbücher für die Altertumswissenschaft*, N.F. 1: 155–69.

Warmington, B. H. (1969), *Nero: Reality and Legend* (London).

Wheeler, M. (1954), *Rome beyond the Imperial Frontiers* (London).

Wissemann, M. (1982), *Die Parther in der augusteischen Dichtung* (Frankfurt).

Ziegler, K.-H. (1964), *Die Beziehungen zwischen Rom und dem Partherreich* (Wiesbaden).

∞ 10 ∞

Philosophers' attitudes to warfare under the principate

Harry Sidebottom

> Caesar seems to provide us with profound peace,
> there are no wars any longer, nor battles, no
> brigandage on a large scale, nor piracy, but at
> any hour we may travel by land, or sail from the
> rising sun to its setting.
>
> (Epictetus, 3. 13. 9)

The Roman empire under the principate had banished war to the social and geographic periphery. For the majority of the inhabitants of the empire, wars (as far as they were considered still to exist at all) were almost always the business of professional soldiers on distant frontiers.[1] The experience of Greek philosophers under the principate was unlike that of their predecessors. It is thus worthwhile to examine their attitudes to warfare, and to see in what ways their attitudes were shaped by their distinctive historical experience.

I have taken as case studies three philosophers: Musonius Rufus, Epictetus, and Dio of Prusa. All are mainstream philosophers in being to some extent Stoics (Musonius a rather heretical Stoic, Epictetus a 'cynicizing Stoic', and Dio an 'eclectic Stoic') at a time when Stoicism was the dominant philosophical system, which partly underpinned the morality of upper-class society.[2] All are 'Greek' in

[1] The classic expression of this ideology is the oration *To Rome* of Aelius Aristides.

[2] On the dominance of Stoicism see, briefly, MacMullen 1966, 46 ff. On the philosophical alignment of Musonius see Lutz 1947; van Geytenbeek 1963. On Epictetus see Brunt 1977. On Dio see von Arnim 1898; Moles 1983 and 1990.

that they taught philosophy in Greek, and all are professional in that they taught others, and did not continuously pursue any other career.

Philosophers' interest in warfare

In the Classical and Hellenistic ages warfare was seldom a very distant reality, and philosophy concerned itself with warfare. Plato and Aristotle discussed various aspects: who should participate in warfare,[1] their education,[2] the strategic site and defensive works of the ideal state,[3] its military command and organization,[4] as well as problems concerned with justice *within* warfare such as the ·ewards and punishments due to one's own combatants[5] and the treatment of the enemy.[6] Warfare could be considered an inevitability, normally held to be caused by man's acquisitive nature.[7] It may thus be thought unsurprising that neither Plato nor Aristotle produced a systematic discussion on the justice *of* war.[8]

[1]   Plato, *Rep.* 374 a–e, 425 a, 457 a–b, 466 d; *Laws*, 6. 785, 7. 804–6; Arist. *Pol.* 1264 b 34–40, 1267 a 16–1268 b 4, 1297 b 10–25, 1321 a 5–25, 1329 a 2–26.
[2]   Plato, *Rep.* 403 c–404 e, 466 e–467 e, 522 c–e, 537 d, 539 e; *Laws*, 7. 794–6, 813–4, 8. 829–34; Arist. *Pol.* 1271 b 1–9, 1334 a 16–b 4, 1338 b 8–1339 a 10.
[3]   Plato, *Rep.* 415 d; *Laws*, 6. 778–9, 8. 848; Arist. *Pol.* 1327 a 20–4, 1330 b 17–1331 a 19.
[4]   Plato, *Laws*, 5. 746, 6. 755, 760–1; *Critias*, 118–19; Arist. *Pol.* 1322 a 29–b 6, 1327 a 40–b 17.
[5]   Plato, *Rep.* 468 a–469 b; *Laws*, 11. 921–2, 12. 942–5.
[6]   Plato, *Rep.* 469 b–471 c; Arist. *Pol.* 1255 a 3–b 3, 1255 b 37–40, 1256 b 23–6, 1328 a 7–10.
[7]   Inevitability: Plato, *Laws*, 1. 625–6, cf. 628, 5. 737; Arist. *Pol.* 1265 a 20–6, 1267 a 17–35, 1291 a 6–9. Cause: Plato, *Rep.* 373 d–e; *Laws*, 3. 678–9; Arist. *Pol.* 1267 a 17–35; *Eth. Nic.* 1160 a 15–20.
[8]   Some relevant texts: Plato, *Laws*, 1. 628, 7. 803; Arist. *Pol.* 1255 a 3–b 3, 1255 b 37–40, 1256 b 23–6, 1324 b 10–40, 1328 a 7–10, 1333 b 37–1334 a 3, 1334 a 15. On Aristotle's views on war see Defourny 1977, but cf. Barnes 1986, especially p. 45: 'c'est en vain qu'on cherche dans la *République* de Platon ou dans la *Politique* d'Aristote une théorie de la guerre juste'. It is, however, unsafe to deduce from this, as Barnes appears to do, that Greek philosophers were uninterested in war. If war could be seen as an inevitability, the justice *of* war may well have appeared relatively unproblematic and thus was not discussed in contrast to justice *within* war which was discussed.

While the early Stoa may have been uninterested in war,[1] the middle Stoa, as mediated to us by Cicero, did discuss warfare. In the course of producing arguments to justify Rome's acquisition and possession of an empire, the middle Stoa, and above all Panaetius, may have widened philosophical debate on warfare to include the systematic discussion of the justice *of* war (Erskine 1990, 192–200; cf. Barnes 1986, 45 n. 21).

Under the principate, Greek philosophers continued to have a certain level of interest in war, although war was now usually seen as (at most) a very distant reality, and any direct experience of war was an exception.

In AD 69 war came to Musonius in the heart of the empire. The philosopher went as an envoy to the Flavian troops of Antonius Primus.

> Making his way among the companies, he began to warn those in arms, discoursing on the blessings of peace and the dangers of war. Many were moved to ridicule by his words, more were bored; and there were some ready to jostle him and to trample on him, if he had not listened to the warnings of the quieter soldiers and the threats of others and given up his untimely wisdom.
>
> (Tac. *Hist*. 3. 81)

Tacitus shows that Musonius felt competent to lecture on war. Although there is no extended discussion of war in what survives of Musonius' teaching (only a small part of the whole), he does on occasion draw images and illustrations from war (e.g. 14. 44. 32 ff., 7. 58. 17 ff., 9. 72. 6 ff., 19. 120. 18 ff.).

As far as we can tell, Epictetus never gave an extended discussion on war. For Epictetus war was an irrelevance. It was more important to overthrow the citadel of vice within each man than to overthrow the external citadels of tyrants (4. 1. 86 ff.). Epictetus discounts the importance of war as a topic for discussion, compared to the important issues with which he deals. Would his audience rather hear someone talk about incomes and revenues, peace and war, or the real issues of happiness and

---

[1] This, however, may be a misapprehension caused by Zeno in the *Politeia* failing to fix his ideal society in time or place, and thus freeing himself from any necessity to discuss its relations with other states (Erskine 1990, 23, 30, 32).

unhappiness, success and failure, or slavery and freedom (3. 22. 84)? Epictetus does, however, frequently draw images from war, and apply them both to himself and to the role of the philosopher.[1]

Dio of Prusa both frequently drew images from war, often applying them to the role of the philosopher,[2] and explicitly discussed war. *Oration* 22 carries the title *On Peace and War*. However, what we have of *Oration* 22 is only a fragment (Highet 1983, 81), and the main theme of the fragment is not peace and war, but the relative utility of the advice given by the philosopher and the orator. The philosopher considers the general aspect, should war be entered into, as well as more specific questions, such as when should war be entered into, with whom, and after what occurrence or non-occurrence (*Or*. 22. 3). The orator considers specifics: should the Athenians make war on the Peloponnesians, should Alexander cross to Asia, and the like. Yet in the orator's deliberations more general issues will arise: is it right to go to war with those who have not provoked war by a wrongful act, or if a wrong has been done how serious was it (*Or*. 22. 3–4)? From their respective starting points the philosopher and the orator come to cover much the same ground. The advantage the philosopher has is that he has deliberated in advance on the general issues, and so is not caught at a loss when a specific instance arises. The orator on the other hand has not considered the matter before, and knows no more than anyone else (*Or*. 22. 4; cf. 13. 22 ff.). A philosophical education is necessary to deliberate on important affairs of state, including peace and war (*Or*. 26. 7–8). A justification for this view can be found in the Euboean oration. The philosopher is not better in skill or craft than an individual craftsman, but, unlike the craftsman, he knows when it is advantageous to act and when it is not advantageous to act (*Or*. 7. 6 ff.).

---

[1]   e.g. 1. 6. 7–8, 16. 4, 3. 24. 31 ff.; applied to himself, 1. 9. 24 ff., 29. 29; role of philosopher, 1. 22. 38, 24. 6, 3. 22. 24; 3. 24, 85, 112.

[2]   e.g. *Or*. 1. 31, 4. 138, 6. 39, 16. 6, 20. 1, 74. 3–4; role of philosopher, 8. 20 ff., 13. 37, 35. 3, 77/8. 37–8, 40.

Negative attitudes to warfare

Philosophers appear usually to have had metaphysical and general objections to war. Dio, as was to be expected from an eclectic philosopher who normally drew more heavily on Stoicism than on any other brand of philosophy, had strong metaphysical and cosmological objections to war. The universe was a living being (*Or.* 36. 29 ff.). At 40. 35 ff. Dio tells how the universe runs on friendship and concord, peace and justice are present in it, and all things are governed by reason; there is thus peace in the heavens. At 1. 42–3 Dio speaks of the administration of the universe and the world; it is governed by divine reason, and because we are kin to it we live under the same commonwealth (*politeia*). Man's partnership in the universe, however, does not produce concord in mortal affairs (*Or.* 74. 26). For, as we are told at 38. 11, while concord (*homonoia*) unites the elements and there is no strife (*stasis*) in divine affairs, we fall short of the divine because some men are not sensitive to the *homonoia* (which reason has implanted) in them, but love its opposite *stasis*, and from that wars and battles follow. The disturbance caused by wars and *stasis* is not, like the disturbance caused by the cyclic destruction of the world, only an apparent disharmony which is in fact part of a greater plan for harmony (*Or.* 36. 47 ff.). *Stasis* and wars are to be interpreted as an actual disturbance of the universe, as far as man can disturb it, caused by man's wickedness or ignorance.[1]

Epictetus, as we have seen, regarded war as an irrelevance. He, however, also seems to have generally regarded it as bad, to the extent that its opposite was good. Control over moral purpose, the true business of a man, led to correct judgements, which produced love in a household, *homonoia* in a city, and peace among states (4. 5. 34–5). Logically, war was generally bad

---

[1] *Or.* 1. 43. Dio can call Zeus the dispenser of peace and war, e.g. *Or.* 12. 22, which seems to imply that war has a divine purpose. But it is not profitable to expect complete doctrinal consistency in Dio (Brunt 1977, 39). At 12. 78, Dio lists divine portents of war, while at 38. 18, he denies that any divine portent is a signal for war. Dio uses philosophy as a didactic tool to reach the desired conclusion within each oration (Moles 1978, 89–90; 1983, 253–4).

because it was caused by faulty judgements (4. 5. 28 ff.). The wise man remains at peace with all men no matter what they do (4. 5. 24).

As the teacher of Epictetus (Lutz 1947, 8–9), and as a fellow Stoic, Musonius can probably be assumed to have agreed with Epictetus that war was both an irrelevance to the inner man and at the same time generally bad. Tacitus' story of Musonius lecturing the troops implies that the philosopher was opposed to war in general, a position which may be supported by Musonius' denial that even self-defence justified the use of force (10. 78. 26 ff.):

> to scheme how to bite back the biter and to return evil for evil is the act not of a human being but a wild beast, which is incapable of reasoning that the majority of wrongs are done to men through ignorance and misunderstanding, from which man will cease as soon as he has been taught.

At more mundane and specific levels, war seems normally to have been regarded as bad. Dio spoke against 'false war'. To claim to be fond of war (to be *polemikos*) and then to avoid battle and seize prisoners at home and put them to death, was as bad as the degenerate form of Persian hunting. This statement comes at the end of an oration, *On Kingship*, to Trajan.[1] The reference is to Domitian's supposedly fake triumphs in the previous reign, which Pliny abused in the *Panegyric* (17), and is thus intended as a graceful compliment to Trajan. It is to be noted that Dio leaves open the implication that to be genuinely fond of war (*polemikos*) would be a good thing.

Wars without a motive were condemned.[2] In an oration on concord (*homonoia*), Dio held that war without a motive was madness and a desire for evil brought about by madness (*Or.* 38. 17). In the Trojan oration it is said to be no disgrace to retreat after making peace if one is campaigning against a country which is of no concern to one (*Or.* 11. 151). For Epictetus, all wars could be seen as motiveless. Why do you fight? If the enemy are wise men, why fight them, and, if they are fools, why do you care (3. 22. 37)?

---

[1]   *Or.* 3. 138; Moles 1983; *contra*, Desideri 1978, 297 ff.
[2]   A traditional view, cf. Arist. *Pol.* 1333 b 29–31; *Eth. Nic.* 1177 b 9–11; Polyb. 3. 4. 10–11; Cic. *Rep.* 3. 35.

Wars which had a discernible motive were often not treated more leniently. Wars inspired by glory or ambition could be seen as bad (hardly a novel position: cf. Cic. *Off.* 1. 38, 74, 3. 87). The educated man (the *pepaideumenos*) will not be led to desire foolish things because of glory, says Dio (*Or.* 38. 29), who wrote *Orations* 66 to 68 to combat the notion that glory might be good. Musonius held that the pursuit of glory was unworthy (7. 56. 19–20). The emperor Trajan was considered to be ambitious and motivated to war by a desire for glory.[1] It is thus surprising to find Dio composing *Oration* 4, *On Kingship*, under Trajan.[2] This work has been characterized by Moles as 'fundamentally a criticism of, or a warning against certain aspects of Trajan's character and policy' (Moles 1983, 252). 4. 116 ff., on the problems of the ambitious spirit, would have had obvious relevance to Trajan, as would 4. 43 ff., which contained in the words of Moles 'a swinging attack on mindless militarism' (ibid. 273). A philosopher can thus be seen attacking the pursuit of glory by military means under an emperor who was thought to be devoted to just that practice.

Wars motivated by material gain could also be looked on as bad (again an unremarkable stance for a moralist: cf. Plato, *Rep.* 373 d–e; Arist. *Eth. Nic.* 1160 a 15–20). In *Oration* 13, Dio told the Romans that they did not need the things they regarded as worth fighting for – silver, gold, ivory and so on (35). Quarrels, *stasis*, and foreign wars are all said to be motivated by greed (*Or.* 17. 10). Dio told the men of Tarsus that unlike them the Athenians and Spartans fought for real power, if one can call self-seeking that.[3] Epictetus castigates the confusion of self-interest with what is good (1. 22. 14):

> If it is in my interest to have a farm, it is my interest to take it away from my neighbour; if it is my interest to have a cloak, it is my interest to steal one from the baths. This is the source of wars, *stasis*, tyrannies and plots.

---

[1] Fronto, 2. 213 Haines; Dio Cass. 68. 17. 1. Pliny stressed in a letter to the emperor his own ambition to enhance the glory of Trajan (*Ep.* 10. 41).
[2] Moles 1983, 251 ff.; Jones 1978, 115 ff.; *contra*, Höistad 1948, 219–20; Lepper 1948, 194 ff., 204–5; cf. Desideri 1978, 287 ff.
[3] *Or.* 34. 51; see also *Or.* 11. 63–4, plunder a bad motive for war; and *Or.* 79. 6, Macedonians, etc., fools to overthrow empires to gain wealth.

It was ignorance of this distinction between the good and self-interest that led the Athenians and Spartans to fight each other, the Thebans to fight both of them, 'and in our own days' the Romans to fight the Getae (Epict. 2. 22. 22). The discourses are thought to have been delivered in about AD 108 (Millar 1965, 142). Again we find a philosopher criticizing the motives for which the present emperor had gone to war.

Fighting for liberty could also be disparaged. At *Or.* 38. 16–17, Dio lists the things men have fought wars for: kingly power, freedom, territory they did not have, and control of the sea. But other, and wiser, men have put war aside and concentrated on things of the highest value. The point is made more explicit at *Or.* 80. 3: to achieve freedom many wars have been waged by all peoples, but they were fools for they were in love with a counterfeit of freedom. Epictetus agrees: individuals and whole cities have been destroyed for political freedom, which is not true freedom (4. 1. 171–2).

The denial of the validity of fighting for political freedom logically denies the validity of wars of self-defence. Here the views of the philosophers of the principate are in contrast to those of their predecessors. Plato, Aristotle, and Cicero all accepted the validity of wars of self-defence.[1]

That various effects of war could be seen as bad can be discerned from the works of Dio. War encouraged irreligion. When Dio visited Olbia he found that not a single statue remained undamaged in the sanctuaries, and the same was true of the funeral monuments.[2] War encouraged irreligion in another way, by the breaking of oaths. In *Oration* 74, Dio argued that Philip of

---

[1]   Plato, *Rep.* 422 d–423 a; *Laws*, 5. 737; Arist. *Pol.* 1333 b 37–1334 a 3; Cic. *Rep.* 3. 34–5. 'Self-defence' also covered one's allies: Plato, *Laws*, 5. 737; Cic. *Rep.* 3. 35, *Off.* 2. 26; see also the *Rhetorica ad Alexandrum*, 1425 a 10–16.

[2]   *Or.* 36. 6; such damage took a long time to repair – Dio thought the last sack of Olbia had been about 150 years earlier, 36. 4. Sanctuaries commonly caused a tension between the ideology and reality of warfare. There was a widespread cultural veto on the despoiling of temples. Yet temples both contained treasure and were often tactically strong buildings. Ways round the problem were to claim that the enemy had already violated the sanctuary by turning it into a fortress, or that the god willingly gave up his treasures (Grant 1980, 181–8).

Macedon was equipped with all the weapons of war, including perjury. He was always seizing cities by breaking oaths or suborning traitors. He found the first method more congenial – it was far cheaper (*Or*. 74. 14; cf. Onasander, 34).

War was seen to curtail the normal functioning of society. In peacetime Dio tells us (*Or*. 38. 19):

> We bedeck ourselves with garlands, offer sacrifice, and hold high festival; but we do quite the opposite in time of war, just as in time of mourning – we shut ourselves within the gates, live in dread of everything, and abandon ourselves to despair. At such times women wail for their husbands and children for their fathers.

War was regarded as ruinously expensive. As we have seen, Dio said that quarrels, *stasis*, and foreign wars were due to the desire for more, but the result of them was to deprive both sides even of a sufficiency.[1] The Rhodians of Dio's day rededicated statues, whereas ancient Rhodians had not. Their ancestors had all the same expenses as them, while the heaviest outlays suffered in earlier times no longer existed. For the expenditures of war – and the ancient Rhodians were continuously at war – cannot be compared to the expenditures of peace (*Or*. 31. 101–2).

War could be seen to threaten urban life. The city of Olbia no longer corresponded in size to its ancient fame, occupying only a fraction of its former walls. The reason was its repeated seizure and continuous wars. Other cities on the shores of the Black Sea had fared even worse. The populations of some were no longer united to form cities (*Or*. 36. 4 ff.). Such a threat to urban life was a threat to the Hellenic way of life, for to live settled in villages was to live like barbarians (*Or*. 47. 10).

That Greek philosophers of the principate generally disapprove of warfare is unremarkable. More striking is the openness with

---

[1] *Or*. 17. 10, above; cf. *Or*. 11. 79, hunger and disease generally oppress the losers. The economic costs of war had long been recognized (Grant 1980, 179–80). In the *Republic*, Plato discussed the level of devastation suitable to be inflicted on an enemy territory (470 a–471 c). Again, a certain tension between ideology and reality can be detected. Hanson 1983, in brief at 1989, 3–8, has shown that in reality there were strong technico-military limits on the level of devastation a Greek army could inflict.

which, as we have seen, they sometimes criticize the wars of the reigning emperor. Their condemnations of warfare are generally comparable with those of their predecessors. Yet their flirtation with pacifism, the condemnation of wars of self-defence, is distinctive.[1] Here their historical experience appears to have shaped their attitudes. It is easy to disapprove of wars of self-defence when there is no plausible likelihood of having to fight one.

Ambiguous attitudes to the preparations for war and the practitioners of war

A range of attitudes to the preparations for war can be reconstructed from the orations of Dio of Prusa. In *Oration* 4, where he is criticizing Trajan's military aspirations, Dio makes Diogenes (the *persona* he is adopting in that speech) condemn preparations for war. The king is compared to the King-bee who 'has no sting, since he requires no weapon against anyone. For no other king will challenge his right to be king or battle him' (*Or.* 4. 60 ff., 4. 8). In this oration the preparations for war are consigned to the category of the useless, because no one will attack a true king.

In another work *On Kingship* (*Or.* 3), the preparations for war can be depicted in a less negative light. Fortifications, arms, siege engines, and troops are necessary for the king, as without them his authority cannot be maintained. But Dio does not see what gratification they can give, for they belong to the category of the useful but not pleasurable. They are anyway only useful in war; in peace – if such a thing is possible – they are a useless burden (*Or.* 3. 92 ff.; cf. 1. 63).

In *Oration* 1, *On Kingship*, Dio puts a more positive value on the preparations for war, if not without a certain ambivalence. The king should not neglect his soldiers, but nor should he pamper them or they will become useless. The king should be fond of war (*polemikos*) because making war rests on him, but he should be fond of peace (*eirenikos*) for there is nothing else worth

[1]   Epict. 4. 1. 171–2, 5. 24; Mus. 10. 78. 36 ff.; Dio, *Or.* 38. 16–17, 80. 3. Dio wrote a work, now lost, praising the pacifist sect of the Essenes (Syncellus, p. 317. 24–6).

fighting for. Yet he who is best prepared for war is most likely to live in peace (*Or.* 1. 27 ff.; cf. 32. 43, 62. 4). In this oration the preparations for war are to be considered in the category of the useful even in times of peace, because they guarantee the continuance of that condition.

Philosophers could look favourably on the participants in war, and regard the moral effects of war on the participants as good, if they were at a considerable distance – either in time or space. In an attempt to shame contemporary Rhodians into better behaviour, Dio told them that their ancestors had been both honourable in settling wars as well as brave in fighting them (*Or.* 31. 19).[1] The ancient Rhodians, and indeed anyone else who had won power and glory, had done so because they had men who were both lovers of honour and regarded posthumous fame more highly than death (*Or.* 31. 20). War, like a storm at sea, can rouse even the basest of souls, the Rhodians were assured (*Or.* 31. 165). The degenerate modern Alexandrians were told that the ancient Athenians, Megarians, and Corinthians became lovers of toil (*philoponoi*) because they had to fight to defend their homelands. The Spartans kept their good name because they were lovers of honour (*philotimoi*) as well (*Or.* 31. 17, 32. 92–3).

Warriors could also be seen as morally good, and the effects of war as morally bracing, if they were distant in geographic terms. In *Oration* 36, Dio told his native Prusans what he claimed to have found out about the people of Olbia on the north coast of the Black Sea during a visit there in the summer of AD 97. The Olbians, living on the fringe of the Greek world, are surrounded by warlike barbarians (*Or.* 36. 4). They no longer speak Greek distinctly (ibid. 9), and have adopted Scythian arms and costume (ibid. 7). Nevertheless, Dio portrays them as a mixture of 'Homeric hero' and 'philosopher-in-arms'.[2] They are always in a state of war, and because they are perforce warlike they love

---

[1] In my view orations 31 and 32 are to be dated to the time of Trajan, and are thus the work of Dio as a philosopher (Sidebottom 1992).

[2] Dio's interlocutor, the significantly named Callistratus, is highly regarded by his townsfolk for his beauty, his martial prowess, and his love of philosophy (*Or.* 36. 8).

Homer.[1] Although expecting a Scythian attack, almost all the inhabitants assemble under arms to hear Dio tell them his version of the ordering of the universe (ibid. 15 ff.). A philosopher would enjoy the sight of them for, all bar one, they have the long hair and beards that Homer praised.[2]

Warriors who are not specified as being far away in time or space are usually not viewed so positively by the philosophers. The practitioners of war can be conceded to have, or need, courage.[3] But even this is not always given them. Dio claims that, whereas athletics calls for courage (*andreia*), physical strength and temperance, all warfare needs is *eupsychia* – a lesser form of courage which lacks the moral element of *andreia*.[4]

The soldier's life, in the view of a philosopher, appears to have been marked by three main features: discipline, toil, and risk. The soldier is subject to a general's orders. He springs to his feet on command, he eats, takes up his weapons, falls in, advances and retires only at his general's command.[5] The good king should not relax the drill or hard work of his soldiers (Dio, *Or.* 1. 29; cf. 1. 21–2). The good king should make himself known to his soldiers, who face peril and hardship to defend his kingdom (Dio, *Or.* 1. 28; cf. Epict. 4. 1. 159–60). Epictetus speaks of all three features: if soldiers do not heed discipline none of them will dig a trench, construct a palisade, watch through the night, or risk his life in combat (2. 24. 31 ff.).

These were just the features that a philosopher would claim marked his own life. For example, Dio boasted of his courage, was always keen to stress his trials and tribulations in exile, and

---

[1] *Or.* 36. 9–10; some are fond of Plato too (ibid. 26), but all are uncorrupted by modern philosophy.

[2] *Or.* 36. 17; Homer in fact had nothing to say about beards. From possible fragments preserved in Jordanes' *Getica*, collected in *FGH* 707, and from a programmatic statement at *Or.* 12. 21, it appears that Dio's lost *Getica* presented the Getae as 'philosophers-in-arms'.

[3] e.g. Dio, *Or.* 1. 1 ff., 3. 5, cf. 79. 5; cf. Mus. 4. 40. 30 ff., with 4. 40. 32 ff.

[4] *Or.* 29. 9; as the work is a funeral oration for a young boxer, Dio has a special reason for privileging athletics over warfare. See also 29. 15–16: athletes fight the best, soldiers the worst; athletes fight opponents again and again, soldiers only once; soldiers' equipment often gives them victory.

[5] Dio, *Or.* 14. 6; cf. Epict. 1. 29. 29, 2. 6. 15, 3. 22. 97, 24. 34–5.

emphasized the philosopher's need for discipline.[1] But these features do not bring the soldier the benefit they bring the philosopher. For the occupation of the military life, which men actively seek, if practised successfully runs the risk of engendering *hubris*.[2] Military skill does not make one a better man (Dio, *Or.* 4. 46 ff.). For a military life is not a good thing in itself, it is only good if a man enters into it after philosophical deliberation.[3]

Philosophers' attitudes to soldiers appear to have usually been a mixture of alienation, contempt, and antipathy.[4] In the Olympian oration Dio tells of a visit to an army camp. He felt completely useless: he could not ride, was not an archer, could not cut timber, dig a trench and so on (*Or.* 12. 18). He also expressed his complete alienation. He was a peaceful observer of war – all around were swords, spears, horses, and armed men. The soldiers had no time to listen to speeches – indeed it was a wonder that they could stand the sight of Dio (*Or.* 12. 18–19; cf. 6. 60, 9. 1, 20. 8).

Philosophers' dislike of soldiers found expression in unflatter-ing comparisons. Soldiers were like sheepdogs, which were renowned for their viciousness.[5] They were compared to sailors, and the bad company kept on ships was proverbial.[6] They were likened to pedagogues, and they were generally thought of as being of such low status that they were like hired labour for the grape harvest.[7] Serving on a campaign was said to be like being a convict (Epict. 4. 1. 39; cf. 3. 24. 29). When Epictetus thought of

---

[1] Dio, *Or.* 45. 1, courage; Moles 1978, 97, hardship in exile; *Or.* 70. 8, discipline; cf. Epict. 3. 24. 31 ff.; Mus. 7. 58. 17 ff.

[2] Dio, *Or.* 80. 1, common occupation; *Or.* 3. 131, sought after; *Or.* 57. 6 and Epict. 3. 24. 85, *hubris*.

[3] Dio, *Or.* 24. 4; 69. 3–4; see below on the philosophically educated man whose duty impels him to fight.

[4] Certain sub-types of soldier were especially disliked. Bodyguards, with their associations with tyrants, always appear in a bad light: Epict. 4. 1. 88–9, 7. 1 ff.; Dio, *Or.* 6. 38, 10. 5. Mercenaries, who make up the majority of the bodyguards of tyrants in Greek history, are characterized as boastful, drunken, overdressed, and cowardly, Dio, *Or.* 77/8. 26.

[5] Dio, *Or.* 1. 28; see Firmicus Maternus, 6. 31. 15, on viciousness of sheepdogs.

[6] Dio, *Or.* 1. 29; Philostratus, *VA.* 5. 20, on bad company on ships.

[7] Dio, *Or.* 32. 51, 7. 114, for low status of pedagogues.

soldiers he did not see them as a guard or a protection, but as a threat (4. 27. 7):

> I have learned that what is born must also die . . . it makes no difference to me whether a fever shall bring that about, or a roof-tile, or a soldier; but if I must make a comparison, I know that the soldier will bring it about with less trouble and more speed.

Thus Greek philosophers under the principate appear only to have approved of the participants in warfare if they were at a considerable distance in space or time. Close contemporaries were normally regarded with feelings of alienation and hostility. This is in marked contrast to the attitude of earlier Greek philosophers. Neither Plato nor Aristotle exhibits comparably negative views of warriors. Plato, in the ideal state of the *Republic*, gives the second highest status in society to the warrior class (414 b, 415 a). It is the courage of the warriors which puts courage in the whole state (429 a–430 c). Aristotle held that it was in battle that man exhibited the noblest type of courage (*Eth. Nic.* 1115 a 29–35).

The armed forces of the Greek city-state were not a distinct group separated from the rest of society. By contrast, the armed forces of the principate were a standing professional army. Civilians tended to be wary, with good reason, of contact with soldiers.[1] The practice of warfare had been banished to the social periphery. The historical experience of Greek philosophers under the principate appears to have shaped their predominantly negative attitudes.

Positive attitudes to warfare

Philosophers could on occasion consider wars to be good, sometimes for the same reason that we have seen them usually being considered bad. The wars which won approval were usually a very distant drum indeed. Musonius approved of the wars of the Amazons, which proved their courage (4. 44. 32–3). Ancient wars for political freedom could also be viewed in a positive light.

---

[1]   e.g. Apuleius, *Metam.* 9. 39, with Millar 1981, 68. On the interaction of soldier and civilian under the later Empire, see MacMullen 1963.

Musonius approved of Dion of Syracuse raising a mercenary army and fighting to free Sicily (9. 72. 6 ff.). Dio of Prusa, possibly with his namesake in mind, applauded the countless exiles who had fought wars against the odds in opposition to the tyrannies or democracies which had driven them out. Such men considered it a great thing even to die on their native soil.[1] Ancient wars fought for the political freedom of others could also be applauded. The Thebans beat the Spartans at Leuctra and made the Spartans give back the Messenian territory and settle the helots, and 'not a man says that the Thebans acted unjustly, but all agree nobly and justly' (Dio, *Or.* 15. 28).

It was not always specified that fighting for political freedom had to be ancient history to be good. Musonius compared men to fighting cocks who stand firm to the death, even though they have no concept of virtue. As humans do, it is more fitting that we stand firm, when we are suffering for a good purpose – to help friends, benefit our city, or defend wives and children, or, best of all, to become good (7. 58. 17 ff.). For Musonius, the king must be fearless in defence of his subjects (8. 60. 9 ff.).

The justification for fighting for political freedom being a good thing, when, as we have seen, political freedom was not in the philosophers' eyes real freedom, was that the wise man must do his duty to his city and his neighbours. Man should, as Musonius put it, look to the common good, not his own (14. 92. 16 ff.). Dio claimed that if called on he would personally have taken up arms to help his friends in Olbia (*Or.* 36. 28). The only warlike action that Epictetus appears to have spoken in favour of was Socrates, when it was his turn to be a soldier, being the first to leave home, and then running the risks of battle ungrudgingly – because it was his duty (4. 1. 159–60).

Occasionally, contemporary wars, the perceived motives of which would usually have been considered bad, can be referred to in an unpejorative way. When Dio spoke at Olympia, he had just returned from the Danube frontier where preparations for one of

---

[1] *Or.* 13. 16. At 32. 48, Dio says that good men and tyrannicides are everywhere remembered because they died saving their native land. At 25. 6, Dio approves of Philip winning the Macedonians political independence, and, at 31. 104, he approves of the ancient Rhodians' wars for security.

the Dacian wars were under way. He says he went to the Danube
to see one side fighting for empire and power, and the other for
freedom and their native land. Dio passes no explicit judgement
on the motives of either side.[1]

Dio is the only one of the philosophers considered in this
chapter to have produced an extended philosophical justification
for war. *Oration* 2, *On Kingship*, leads up to the allegory of the
bull, where the message of the work lies (*Or.* 2. 65 ff.). In this
section the king is compared to the bull, who uses his strength for
the good of his herd and not himself. He leads the herd to pasture,
and when a wild beast appears he does not flee, but fights it in
front of the whole herd, thus bringing aid to the weak and saving
the multitude. Just, Dio says (*Or.* 2. 69), like a true king.
Sometimes another herd will appear and the bull will fight its
leader for victory, so that all will acknowledge his superiority and
the superiority of his herd (*Or.* 2. 70). In case anyone had missed
the allegory, Dio spells it out at 2. 71–2. The bull is a lesson in
kingship. The king must save his subjects, planning for them, if
need be fighting for them, protecting them from lawless tyrants,
'and as regards other kings, if any such there should be, he must
strive with them in a contest of virtue (*arete*), seeking if possible to
overcome them for the benefit of mankind at large' (*Or.* 2. 71).

This simple and elegant theory rests on the central theme of
Hellenistic and Roman political philosophy: that the king is a king
because of his virtue (*arete*), which he shows in the giving of
benefits – in the exercise of the virtue of benevolence
(*philanthropia*). The theory can justify any war, be it aggressive
and without provocation, for the king's *philanthropia* makes it a
duty for him to fight tyrants to free their subjects from them so
that the king can give them benefits. The king's *philanthropia* also
makes it a duty for him to fight other kings. The winner will be
shown to have greater *arete*, and thus will give greater benefits to
the defeated king's subjects. The king is thus justified in any war
because he fights for the benefit of mankind.[2]

The king is to be contrasted to the tyrant who fights, as he rules,

[1] *Or.* 12. 20; cf. above on Epictetus' views on the motivation of the
Dacian wars, 2. 22. 22 ff.
[2] Contrast *Or.* 2. 65 ff., to *Or.* 1. 84, where Herakles casts down tyrants,
but honours kings, and, by implication, still aids Trajan in this task.

purely to benefit himself. This is shown at *Oration* 6. 50. The tyrant fears war, but also fears peace. He fears war because he has to stir up his subjects by imposing taxes and making them take the field. 'So when there is war, tyrants want peace, and when peace has been made, they at once want war.' The motivation to (or from) war is for the tyrant only a calculation of his own interest.

The range of concepts which made up Dio's justification for war proved long-lived and adaptable.[1] Yet the theory appears to be seriously flawed. Dio's model of war involves hand-to-hand combat only between kings. Under the principate emperors never indulged in such monomachy (Campbell 1984, 65–9). Possibly this very dissonance between ideology and reality shows a philosopher's attitudes being shaped by his historical experience. The principate was an autocracy, and from the start was recognized as such by its subjects (Millar 1984). It could be argued that society's concentration on the personality and role of the autocrat led to the personality and role of others being downgraded or ignored. On this interpretation, Dio's attitude to war (war as *solely* the province of one individual) was shaped by his historical experience (living under an autocracy).

Conclusion

The selection of material to illustrate the attitudes to warfare of Musonius, Epictetus, and Dio, gives a partial and somewhat misleading impression of the overall content of their teaching, which was, in the main, directed to the conduct of ordinary life, and drew examples from many areas other than warfare (cf. Millar 1965, 148).

The philosophers appear to have had next to no first hand

---

[1] In the fourth century, Themistius, who drew heavily on Dio, Scharrold 1912; Valdenberg 1924, 558, 572 ff.; Dagron 1968, 85 ff., employed them to justify Valens' treaty with the Goths, e.g. Them. *Or.* 10, and Theodosius' settlement of the Goths within the empire (Them. *Or.* 16). For Themistius, so great was the *philanthropia* of the emperors that they wished to extend to the barbarians the benefit of peaceful conquest, e.g. Them. *Or.* 10. 131 c ff.

experience of warfare,[1] and to have almost exclusively drawn their knowledge of warfare from classical texts.[2] They accepted that the Roman empire had brought peace to its subjects.[3] The perception that warfare did not impinge directly on the ordinary lives of the majority of the inhabitants of the empire, coupled with tenets of Stoic philosophy, led to what can be seen as significant omissions in the philosophers' stated views on warfare. In an analysis of stated ranges of attitudes what is not discussed can be as significant as what is discussed.

It is interesting to compare the objections to warfare of philosophers of the first and second centuries AD with the 'peace movement' of the later tenth, eleventh, and twelfth centuries AD (well summarized by Contamine 1985, 270 ff.). The peace movement had as its theoretical underpinning metaphysical and cosmological objections to war comparable to those of the philosophers. The two main products were the concepts of the Truce of God, by which certain times were held to be unsuitable for war, and the Peace of God, by which certain categories of place, goods, and persons were to be exempt from war. These attempts to limit the horrors of war find few echoes in the works of the philosophers under the principate. For the philosophers only two categories of persons were to be protected in war: heralds and the dead. At *Oration* 75. 9 Dio states that law protects heralds in war, and that it is 'because of law that the slain are deemed no longer to

---

[1] Dio tells of two visits to war zones, *Or.* 12. 16 ff. and 36. 1 ff., but specifically states that on neither occasion did he witness any fighting. Musonius lectured the Flavian troops in AD 69 before the fighting, although he may have seen the ensuing battle, because Tacitus says that the battle was fought the same day with the inhabitants of Rome watching as if at a gladiatorial show (*Hist*. 3. 83).

[2] For example, when Dio wished to give examples of perjury in war he listed Pandarus, Tissaphernes, Philip, and Lysander: drawn respectively from Homer, Xenophon, probably Theopompus, and Xenophon again (*Or.* 74. 14–15; cf. 18. 8 ff.). Some knowledge may have been derived from conversations with high-placed friends. Epictetus has a charming story of reluctant dinner guests who do not want to be bored by the host's endless stories of his battles in Moesia (1. 25. 14 ff.).

[3] Epict. 3. 13. 9; cf. Dio, *Or.* 31. 104, 125, 32. 69. Dio, unlike Epictetus, dealt with piracy as if it were a contemporary problem (*Or.* 14. 11–12).

be foes, nor are hatred and insult wreaked upon their bodies' (cf. 76. 5).

This lack of any large-scale attempt to mitigate the effects of war on the part of men who were generally predisposed against war can be attributed to two factors. First, as we have seen, philosophers usually had no first hand experience of war – the empire was seen to be at peace, with war banished to the geographic periphery. Plato, for whom war was a less distant reality, did, it should be noted, produce rules for the limitation of the effects of war (*Republic* 466 d ff.). Second, the evils of war – death and slavery – were not evils at all for the philosophers. Epictetus in conversation:

> these are the falls that come to mankind, this is the siege of the city, this is the destruction of it – when men's correct judgements are torn down, when these are destroyed.

Epictetus' interlocutor asks:

> then when women are driven off into captivity and children are enslaved, and when men themselves are slaughtered, are not all these things evil?

Epictetus replies with a question:

> where do you get the justification for adding this opinion?
>
> (1. 28. 25 ff.)

As Epictetus put it (3. 3. 15), death lies outside the moral purpose. As Musonius put it (6. 54. 30 ff.), neither death nor anything which is free from wrong is an evil. The ex-slave Epictetus held that being taken a prisoner should not affect a man (3. 24. 65–6). Musonius claimed that Diogenes remained a free man while enslaved by pirates (9. 74. 8 ff.), and Dio wrote *Orations* 14 and 15 on the 'bars do not a prison make' theme.

The separation of Greek society from the armed forces which protected it led to another significant omission in the philosophers' stated views. For Plato and Aristotle, the different ways one should behave towards Greek and barbarian enemies were important (Plato, *Rep.* 469 b–471 c; Arist. *Pol.* 1255 a 3–b 3). While philosophers under the principate continued, at times, to employ the concept of dividing the world into Greeks and barbarians (e.g. Dio, *Or.* 3. 38), there was little point in applying it any longer to discussions of warfare.

Although war was a distant reality, and the commonly perceived evils of war (death and slavery) were not evils at all, mainstream Greek philosophers under the principate had a certain level of interest in war and claimed competence to lecture on it. Their attitudes to warfare were generally negative. War was seen as a disturbance of the cosmos caused by man's wickedness or (and it amounted to much the same) by his ignorance. Warfare could also be seen as an irrelevance to the inner man caused by faulty judgements (and the two views were not incompatible). Given their general hostility to war it is not surprising that at more mundane and specific levels philosophers usually regarded war in a negative light. The causes of war (glory, greed/gain, political freedom, or self-defence) were normally seen as bad (for all could be interpreted as faulty judgements). Similarly, the effects of war (irreligion, expense, the threat to the normal functioning of society, and the threat to urban life) were seen as deleterious.

The philosophers' criticism of war to some extent went against the general ideology of the Roman Empire. Rome under the Republic had been an extremely aggressive and militaristic state (Hopkins 1978, 25–37; Harris 1979; North 1981), and, although somewhat weakened under the principate (the wisdom of further imperial expansion could be doubted), the military ethos was still deeply embedded in Roman society.[1] It is indicative of the philosophers' range of attitudes to warfare that, although the inherent dangers of criticizing the emperor were known, both Epictetus and Dio of Prusa condemn the perceived motivation of the reigning emperor in going to war.[2]

Although generally negative, views on the preparations for war were touched by a certain ambiguity. The preparations for war could

---

[1] Mann 1979; Brunt 1990; Isaac 1990. Although their freedom of action was now more circumscribed, the Roman élite still subscribed to the concept of military glory (Campbell 1984, 317–62).

[2] Such criticism was probably facilitated by Trajan playing the role of the *civilis princeps*. Trajan was against treason charges on principle (Pliny, *Ep.* 10. 82). Similar criticism would have been much riskier under Domitian, whose reign Epictetus is probably thinking of when he talks of the dangers of criticizing Caesar (4. 13. 5–6; cf. Millar 1965, 142–3).

never belong to the category of the pleasurable, but could at times (yet not at all times) belong to the category of the useful. The practitioners of war could be regarded as good, and the effects of war on them as morally good, if they were at a distance in time or space. More normally, philosophers' attitudes to soldiers (who were in themselves part of the preparations for war – never pleasurable and only sometimes useful) were marked by antipathy, contempt, and alienation. Military skill did not make one a better man. For the military life was not a good thing in itself, but only became a good thing if entered into after philosophical deliberation.

Like the participants in war, wars themselves could sometimes be viewed in a positive light, usually if they were at a considerable distance, and conducted for political freedom. Wars fought for political freedom (and strictly political freedom was not freedom at all) could be seen as good if undertaken by a philosophically educated man whose virtue impels him to do his duty and fight.

It is indicative of the flexibility within the range of attitudes to warfare which could be expressed by mainstream Greek philosophers that Dio of Prusa, who in *Oration* 4, *On Kingship*, produced a swinging attack on militarism, could also in *Oration* 2, *On Kingship*, produce a cover-all philosophical justification for war.[1] Applying the central nexus of concepts of Hellenistic and Roman political philosophy (the king's virtue, *philanthropia*, and the giving of benefits) to war, Dio constructed a theory which justified any act of war. The king's virtue and its corollary, his possession of the virtue of benevolence (*philanthropia*), make it the king's duty to fight other rulers in order to exercise his *philanthropia* towards their subjects and give them benefits. This simple and elegant theory was to prove long-lived and adaptable when, after the third-century crisis, war became a less distant reality for late antique philosophers.

The distinctive historical experience of Greek philosophers under the Roman principate appears to have shaped their views on warfare in three ways. First, the rule of an autocracy seems to have removed discussion of warfare from the context of society as

---

[1] It is unfortunate that we know nothing of the circumstances which influenced the composition of these two works. See now Moles 1990 on their contexts, a subject to which I intend to return elsewhere.

a whole to that of the individual. Second, the relegation of participation in warfare to the social periphery (the removal of the armed forces from the context of the Greek society they protected) can be seen to have induced a generally negative attitude to the participants in warfare, and to have made the conceptual division of the world into Greeks and barbarians redundant in the context of discussions of warfare. Third, the relegation of warfare to the geographic periphery may have facilitated a flirtation with pacifism (the denial of self-defence as a legitimation of war), and an avoidance of the construction of any theories to ameliorate the horrors of war.

The distancing of warfare from the leading practitioners of ideology can be interpreted either as bringing an agreeable openness and flexibility to their theorizing, or, more plausibly, as causing a loss of ideological cohesion and an absence of moral force. In Philostratus' fiction, Dio of Prusa can quell a mutinous army with a quotation from Homer (*Lives of the Sophists*, 488). When Musonius Rufus tried the same trick in reality, he was lucky to escape without a good beating.

Bibliography

Barnes, J. (1986), 'Cicéron et la guerre juste', *Bulletin de la Société Française de Philosophie*, 80: 41–80.

Brunt, P. A. (1973), 'Aspects of the social thought of Dio Chrysostom and of the Stoics', *Proceedings of the Cambridge Philological Society*, 19: 9–34.

—— (1977), 'From Epictetus to Arrian', *Athenaeum*, 55: 19–48.

—— (1990), 'Roman imperial illusions', in *Roman Imperial Themes* (Oxford), ch. 18 (pp. 433–80).

Campbell, J. B. (1984), *The Emperor and the Roman Army 31 BC–AD 235* (Oxford).

Contamine, P. (1985), *War in the Middle Ages* (Oxford).

Dagron, G. (1968), 'L'empire romain d'orient au IVᵉ siècle et les traditions politiques de l'hellénisme: le témoignage de Thémistios', *Travaux et mémoires: Centre de Recherche d'Histoire et Civilisation Byzantines*, 3: 1–242.

Defourny, M. (1977), 'The aim of the state: peace', in J. Barnes, M. Schofield, and R. Sorabji (eds), *Articles on Aristotle*, i: *Ethics and Politics*, pp. 195–201 (London).

Desideri, P. (1978), *Dione di Prusa: un intellettuale greco nell' impero romano* (Messina and Florence).

Erskine, A. (1990), *The Hellenistic Stoa: Political Thought and Action* (London).

Grant, R. M. (1980), 'War – just, holy, unjust – in Hellenistic and early Christian thought', *Augustinianum*, 20: 173–89.

Hanson, V. D. (1983), *Warfare and Agriculture in Classical Greece* (Pisa).

—— (1989), *The Western Way of War: Infantry Battle in Classical Greece* (New York).

Harris, W. V. (1979), *War and Imperialism in Republican Rome 327–70 BC* (Oxford).

Highet, G. (1983), 'Mutilations in the text of Dio Chrysostom', in R. J. Ball (ed.), *The Classical Papers of Gilbert Highet* (New York), pp. 74–99.

Höistad, R. (1948), *Cynic Hero and Cynic King: Studies in the Cynic Conception of Man* (Uppsala).

Hopkins, M. K. (1978), *Conquerors and Slaves* (Cambridge).

Isaac, B. (1990), *The Limits of Empire: The Roman Army in the East* (Oxford).

Jones, C. P. (1978), *The Roman World of Dio Chrysostom* (Cambridge, Mass., and London).

Lepper, F. A. (1948), *Trajan's Parthian War* (Oxford).

Lutz, C. E. (1947), 'Musonius Rufus: "the Roman Socrates" ', *Yale Classical Studies*, 10: 3–147.

MacMullen, R. (1963), *Soldier and Civilian in the Later Roman Empire* (Cambridge, Mass.).

—— (1966), *Enemies of the Roman Order: Treason, Unrest, and Alienation in the Empire* (Cambridge, Mass.).

Mann, J. C. (1979), 'Power, force and the frontiers of the empire', *JRS* 69: 175–83.

Millar, F. (1965), 'Epictetus and the imperial court', *JRS* 55: 141–8.

—— (1981), 'The world of the *Golden Ass*', *JRS* 71: 63–75.

—— (1984), 'State and subject: the impact of monarchy', in F. Millar and E. Segal (eds), *Caesar Augustus: Seven Aspects* (Oxford), ch. 1 (pp. 37–60).

Moles, J. L. (1978), 'The career and conversion of Dio Chrysostom', *JHS* 98: 79–100.

—— (1983), 'The date and purpose of the fourth kingship oration of Dio Chrysostom', *Classical Antiquity*, 2: 251–78.

—— (1990), 'The kingship orations of Dio Chrysostom', in F. Cairns (ed.), *Papers of the Leeds International Latin Seminar*, 6 (Leeds), pp. 297–375.

North, J. A. (1981), 'The development of Roman imperialism', *JRS* 71: 1–9.

Scharrold, J. (1912), *Dio Chrysostomus und Themistius* (Burghausen).

Sidebottom, H. (1992), 'The date of Dio of Prusa's Rhodian and Alexandrian Orations', *Historia*, 41: 407–19.

Valdenberg, V. (1924), 'Discours politiques de Thémistius dans leur rapport avec l'antiquité', *Byzantion*, 1: 557–80.

van Geytenbeek, A. C. (1963), *Musonius Rufus and the Greek Diatribe* (Assen).

von Arnim, H. (1898), *Leben und Werke des Dio von Prusa* (Berlin).

The end of the Roman army in the western empire

Wolfgang Liebeschuetz

The title is more of a slogan than a confident conclusion. The Roman army did come to an end and not a trace of it is left today – but it is impossible to prove a negative and it will never be possible to state that on such and such a date the last Roman regiment was disbanded. So this chapter sets out to prove rather less, namely that the fifth-century army in important ways behaved differently from the army of the fourth century, and that *regular* units were ceasing to be what decided battles.

We begin with a definition of what is meant by the regular Roman army. I mean the regular professional force with its unique record of victory going back to Augustus and Marius and beyond. This was possibly the most successful military organization of all history and it continued to perform up to expectations at least up to 378 when Valens was defeated at Adrianople. That was the end of invincibility, but not the end of the army. Around 400 somebody compiled the *Notitia Dignitatum*, a list of all the units in the armies of both halves of the empire. It was a formidable force which Jones (1964, 418–60) estimated at 645,000. Jones's estimate is certainly much too high. He did not take into account the high likelihood that unit strength in the late Roman army was very much smaller than in the early Empire. This is quite apart from the probability recognized by Jones that the *Notitia* represents paper establishments likely to have been much larger than the forces actually available (Liebeschuetz 1990a, 41; Duncan-Jones 1990, 105–17).

There is no doubt that the regular units listed in the *Notitia* included a considerable proportion of men of Germanic or other non-citizen origin (Hoffmann 1969, 81–3, 141–5, 299; Liebeschuetz 1990a, 11–25). The proportion of regulars of barbarian origin is debatable. Recently, Elton (1990) has argued that the proportion was much smaller than has been generally thought, perhaps around twenty-five per cent. But that their numbers were significant at all levels is not in doubt. One reason may be that the imperial authorities found it difficult to recruit citizens over large areas of the empire. For example, when Alaric invaded Italy late in 401 and Stilicho needed to assemble an army strong enough to drive him out, he withdrew troops from Raetia, the Rhine and Britain (Claudian, *BGet.* 412–22). He enrolled large numbers of recently defeated barbarians (ibid. 106, 462–7). But he did not hold conscription in Italy and publicized the fact (ibid. 463).

While regular units might include a considerable proportion of men who were of barbarian origin or even recruited beyond the frontier, Roman armies of this period also included large numbers of units ᵼade up entirely, or almost entirely from barbarians of various kinds. These were the so-called federates (Olympiodorus, fr. 7. 4 Blockley). These are not included in the *Notitia* because they were enrolled only for a particular emergency, even though they might eventually become part of the regular army (e.g. the Honoriaci of Orosius, 7. 41). The distinction between regulars and federates is usually made clear in the sources. The former are regularly described as 'soldiers', the latter as barbarians, or federates, or by a tribal name (e.g. Goths or Huns).[1]

Federates were basically of two kinds. First, there were tribal groups, either settled, or merely garrisoned in particular regions of the empire and receiving *annona* in return for military assistance. The most notable or notorious of these groups were the Visigoths

---

[1] Barbarians and soldiers are clearly distinguished in Zosimus' account of the Gainas crisis (5. 13. 2, 17. 2, 18. 10, 20. 2, 26. 4–5) and of the fall of Stilicho (5. 31. 5, 33). Constantine, who was Augustus from 407 to 411, was proclaimed and joined by regular soldiers (Olympiodorus, fr. 13 Blockley), but later needed barbarian reinforcements (ibid. fr. 17). In 398 Gildo commanded 'soldiers' as well as barbarians (Orosius, 7. 36), as did the usurper Gerontius in 411 (Zosimus, 6. 5). Jovinus in 411 relied on Alans and Franks (Gregory of Tours, *Hist. Franc.* 2. 9).

in Aquitaine (Wolfram 1987, 174–6; Goffart 1980, 103–26) and the Burgundians in what is still called Burgundy.[1] Second, there were the units recruited for the duration of campaigns from barbarian groups within or without the empire, e.g. from Goths, Franks, Huns, Alans or from a combination of different tribes, sometimes under their own chiefs, sometimes under officers appointed by the empire (Liebeschuetz 1986). In view of the circumstances of raising of such units it is difficult to see how their fighting skills and indeed their equipment can have been other than native and tribal. They were, as it were, 'off the peg' soldiers. That federates played an indispensable role in armies of even the early fifth century is shown most strikingly in the case of Stilicho's Italian army, the last Roman army to check Alaric's Goths in direct military confrontation. This army became completely ineffective when after the death of Stilicho its federates, said to have been 30,000 strong, deserted to Alaric (Zosimus, 5. 35. 6). Castinus, who led a Roman force against the Vandals in Spain in 422, was similarly crippled when his Gothic federates deserted him (Hydatius, 77).[2]

The thesis of this chapter is that in the course of the first half of the fifth century, the regular army, that is the class of units listed in the *Notitia*, became unimportant as compared with the federates. The thesis is not that within fifty years every unit mentioned in the *Notitia* had disappeared. Some, perhaps a considerable number, may well have survived as garrison troops into the Gothic and Merovingian periods. But what I hope can be shown is that regulars ceased to be the decisive element in field armies. The men who increasingly came to decide battles were barbarian federates.

It has been brought out very clearly by Matthews (1975) and Elton (1992) that the military efforts of the western empire were far from unsuccessful in the first half of the fifth century. Admittedly, 410 saw Alaric capturing Rome, but subsequently at

---

[1] Goffart 1980, 127–61. Against Goffart I would still maintain that both Visigoths and Burgundians were allotted land, not the tax revenue of land. But Goffart's views deserve a fuller discussion than they have so far had.

[2] I cite Hydatius' chronicle from Mommsen's edition (*MGH, AA* xi. 1–36).

least the outline of Roman control was re-established in Italy, Gaul and perhaps Spain, and maintained up to at least 450 (Matthews 1975, 329–51; Demougeot 1979, 465–507). This was largely due to the efforts of two able generals Constantius (*PLRE* ii, s.v. Fl. Constantius 17) and Aetius (*PLRE* ii, s.v. Fl. Aetius). The rest of this chapter will be largely devoted to demonstrating the decisive role of federates in the success won by these two men.

In the case of Constantius there is no doubt that he did command a regular army. The summary of the western lists shows indications of a recent reorganization of the field armies (Jones 1964, 1425–6, with tables 6–7 on pp. 1434–6). A striking feature of this new organization is the transfer of no fewer than 21 former *limitanei* from frontier defence into the field army of Gaul (Jones's table 7). It is likely that this reorganization was undertaken by Constantius when he restored imperial control of Gaul after the breaking of the Rhine frontier in 406/7 and the collapse of the power of the usurper Constantine (cf. Demougeot 1975; Mann 1991, 218). But it is evident that Constantius did not normally use the reconstituted army in the traditional Roman way to bring the enemy to battle and to destroy him. He did this once to destroy the usurper Constantine in 411 (Sozomen, 9. 13–15; Orosius, 7. 42), but more often he used a Fabian strategy to put pressure on the Gothic enemy by preventing them from getting supplies (Orosius, 7. 43. 1; Hydatius, 60; *Chron. Gall. 452*, 72).[1] He won two of his most striking successes by employing the wandering warrior band of Alaric's Goths, now led by Athaulf, to defeat first the usurper Jovinus (Olympiodorus, fr. 18 Blockley), and later one of the two Vandal nations in Spain (Jordanes, *Get.* 163–6; Hydatius, 70). It was, of course, nothing new that the Romans should assign to *auxilia* of one kind or another the most exposed position in battle, and thus preserve the lives of legionaries (Tac. *Agr.* 35). But that the regaining of control of a major province should have been left entirely to an 'allied' band operating independently without any overall control by a Roman commander would have been unthinkable before 378, and reflects a defensive strategy totally different from that of the early Empire

---

[1]   The Gallic Chronicles of 452 and 511 are edited in *MGH, AA* ix. 646 ff. On the chronicle of 452 see Muhlberger 1990.

and even of the late Empire until the disaster of Adrianople, and not indeed adopted before the fall of Stilicho.

While some of his most important victories were won by independently operating federates – or by control of corn supply – Constantius undoubtedly did command a regular army. But this was not entirely an army of the old type, for it included a core of personal followers of barbarian origin, later known as *bucellarii*. We hear of these men only because they were inherited by Constantius' widow Galla Placida (Olympiodorus, fr. 38 Blockley). Personal followings of barbarians of this kind seem to have been a regular feature of armies at this time. They are also witnessed in the case of Stilicho (Zosimus, 5. 34), and of Constantius' younger contemporary Boniface (Augustine, *Epist.* 220. 6). Boniface's force in Africa consisted largely of Gothic federates (Possidius, *Life of Augustine*, 28, cf. 17). The combination of federates and *bucellarii* may well explain the close ties between Boniface and his troops, and his ability to hold on to his command in the face of three successive armies sent by the imperial government to depose him. Boniface's son-in-law and successor Sebastian is also recorded as having had a considerable military following (Priscus, fr. 4 Blockley; cf. Clover 1979). It may be that Sebastian in fact took over his father in law's *bucellarii*, and that it was the importance of *bucellarii* in Boniface's force that enabled Sebastian to 'inherit' Boniface's army (Hydatius, 99). As we will see, the career of Aetius, the second of the great commanders of this period, was made possible by his having a personal following of Huns.

It may therefore be that the very close ties between armies and their commanders, which is a feature of the military history of the period and recalls the last century of the Republic, was a consequence of the army's including a strong core of *bucellarii* and other soldiers who had been recruited by the commander personally.[1] A number of important armies turned into private armies. One example is the African army of Heraclian, the killer of Stilicho, which in 413 backed its commander's attempt to invade Italy and become emperor (Orosius, 7. 12–14). In 422 Boniface quarrelled with his fellow commander Castinus during

[1] On recruitment by the commander and its possible relationship with the enrolment of *bucellarii*, see Liebeschuetz 1986; 1990a, 36–8.

operations against the Vandals in Spain. He promptly abandoned the campaign and, presumably with his troops, 'invaded' Africa (Prosper, *Chron.* 1278;[1] Hydatius, 78; *Chron. Gall. 511*, 571). Subsequently he became the imperial commander in Africa, but, when first in 424 and again in 427 attempts were made to give him a successor, he refused to go and fought successful wars against generals sent from Italy to depose him (Prosper, *Chron.* 1286, 1294). Eventually he is said to have called in the Vandals to help him against yet another army of the government (Procop. *Vand.* 1. 22–6; Prosper, *Chron.* 1295). This tendency of the imperial government to lose control of its armies was a serious weakness which undermined its ability to cope with major dangers, above all the Goths and Vandals.

The career of Aetius, the last great commander of the western empire, illustrates the importance of private forces in war and politics in the second quarter of the fifth century. In fact it is likely that Aetius' achievements would have been impossible without his following of Huns. Aetius had an extremely active and on the whole successful military career. What can we say about the character of the army that he used to fight his campaign? We have no comprehensive narrative of his campaigns. Deductions about his military resources must be made from isolated fragments of evidence which might not give typical information. While that qualification should be remembered, it nevertheless looks as if not only the success of Aetius' army, but even his position of commander-in-chief of the western empire, depended on the fact that he had at his personal disposal a strong force of Hun federates.

Aetius established personal relations with the Huns during a period as a hostage at a Hunnish court (Gregory of Tours, *Hist. Franc.* 2. 8). In 423–5 he held the court office of *cura palatii* under the usurper John, on whose behalf he went on an embassy to the Huns. He returned in 425 with powerful reinforcements. When Aetius arrived in Italy John had already been defeated. In spite of his having been on the usurper's side Aetius was made *magister militum* by the government of Valentinian III and Galla Placida (Prosper, *Chron.* 1288; *Chron. Gall. 452*, 100). There followed

---

[1]   On the chronicle of Prosper of Aquitaine, edited in *MGH, AA* ix. 341–485, see Muhlberger 1990.

seven years of successful campaigning, mainly in Gaul. In 432 he fought and lost a battle at Rimini in Italy against Boniface, now a rival general of Valentinian III (Prosper, *Chron.* 1310; *Chron. Gall. 452*, 109, 111). He lost his command and, when his life was threatened, fled for help to the Huns. Soon after he returned to Italy, and, with Hun support – presumably in the form of *bucellarii* – had himself reinstated (Prosper, *Chron.* 1310; *Chron. Gall. 452*, 112). There followed five or so years of successful campaigning in Gaul and on the Rhine. In 440 he settled a group of Alans at Valence in the Rhone valley, in 441 other Alans under Goar in Armorica. In 443 he settled the remains of the Burgundians in Savoy and around Geneva. He had now established some kind of peace and order in Gaul. Then in 451 Attila invaded Gaul with a huge force of Huns and other subject barbarians. Aetius mobilized the Germanic federates settled in Gaul and led the alliance to victory over Attila in the battle of Chalons. Soon after, in 454, Valentinian III himself assassinated Aetius. The integration of his large forces into the palatine army created a problem which Valentinian hoped that Majorian, who had served with Aetius, would solve (Sid. Ap. *Carm.* 5. 306–8). But Valentinian was soon after killed by Optila and Thraustila, two of the former followers of Aetius (Jordanes, *Rom.* 334).

Aetius' career began with his leading a large number of Huns to the aid of the usurper John in 425. We are told that he persuaded these men to go home after the defeat of John (Prosper, *Chron.* 1288; Jordanes, *Rom.* 328). But it is remarkable that this officer who had been on the losing side in a civil war was immediately promoted to high military command by the victors. It looks as if even after the departure of the Huns from Ravenna he was still a powerful figure, which he would have been if he kept back a powerful force of Huns as his personal following (*bucellarii*). In that case, his first group of successful campaigns was fought with an army which had at least a federate core. We lack the evidence to say more.

The evidence is slightly better for the second series of campaigns from 436. In 432 Aetius was defeated in a civil war and forced into exile at the court of the king of the Huns. With his help he made peace with the emperor and had his successor exiled and himself reinstated (Prosper, *Chron.* 1310; *Chron. Gall. 452*, 112). It is likely that the help consisted of Hun *bucellarii* and that he kept the force for subsequent campaigns. Certainly we are told that it was with a force of Huns that he all but destroyed the defeated Burgundians in 436 (Prosper, *Chron.* 1322; *Chron. Gall. 452*, 118). In the same period Litorius, Aetius' second-in-command, led a force of Huns. With these he defeated the Armoricans in 435–7 (Sid. Ap. *Carm.* 7. 246–7), and marched through Auvergne to relieve Narbonne in 437 (ibid. 7. 248). In 439 he attacked the Goths outside Toulouse, where he was captured by the Goths and his army lost (Prosper, *Chron.* 1335). Subsequently we are told that Roman Gaul was defenceless, and Aetius helpless. It looks as if Litorius' mainly Hunnish force had made up a large part of Aetius' army (Sid. Ap. *Carm.* 299 ff.).[1]

Of course, Huns did not make up the whole of Aetius' army in Gaul in the 430s. But this does not mean that the bulk of it consisted of Romans. When Avitus took part in Aetius' campaign of 436 against the Burgundians, his military conduct is said to have surpassed that of Heruli, Huns, Franks, Sarmatians, Salians and Gelonians (Sid. Ap. *Carm.* 7. 235). Presumably all those barbarians were federates fighting in recognizable tribal units.

We have miserably little information about the composition of the armies of Aetius' ceaseless campaigning. Evidence is fullest for the campaign of 451 and the famous battle of Chalons. Now for the first time we have a reasonably full description of battle and combatants. The king of the Goths commanded one wing, Aetius commanded the Romans on the other, and in between were Alan federates. But, according to Jordanes at least (*Get.* 190–1), the Roman force too seems to have consisted entirely of federates: Franks, Sarmatians, Armoricans, Liticians, Burgundians, Saxons, Riparians, Olibriones (once Roman soldiers, now federates). There is no reference to Roman soldiers. This is to some extent confirmed by a line of Sidonius' panegyric in honour of Avitus. According to this, Aetius crossed the Alps to meet Attila with only a small force, not including regulars (Sid. Ap. *Carm.* 7. 329: *rarum*

---

[1]   But Aetius did have sufficient forces to conduct a siege and attack a fortified town (Merobaudes, *Panegyric* 2, p. 271–2), before negotiating peace (ibid. 272, lines 185–90, with the commentary of Clover 1971, 58–9).

sine milite ducens robur in auxiliis). So Attila seems to have been checked by what was virtually a federate army.

If Aetius came to Gaul in 451 without a strong regular force, it was not because he had left a powerful regular field army to guard Italy. For, when Attila in 452 invaded Italy across the Julian Alps, there was evidently no army to challenge him or even to attack his rear during the three months' siege of Aquileia. Attila captured Aquileia and Milan. What checked him appears to have been hunger and disease (Hydatius, 154). Military opposition is mentioned as coming from units sent by the eastern emperor Marcian to attack the Hun homelands in Pannonia (ibid.).

That there was only one major army, and that there was no effective field army in Italy while Aetius was campaigning in Gaul was nothing new. When in 440 a Vandal naval attack on the coast of Italy was feared, Valentian III ordered soldiers and federates to defend the coast and cities, but the situation was bad enough for him to call on citizens to arm themselves for self-defence. He encouraged them by the prospect that Aetius would soon arrive with a strong army (*Nov. Val.* 9). After Aetius' assassination Italy was even weaker. When Geiseric's Vandals camped outside Rome in 455 they seem to have met with no resistance at all. They then proceeded to plunder the city for a fortnight without any intervention by a Roman army (Procop. *Vand.* 1. 5. 1). In the following decades the conflicts of successive contenders for the western empire seem to have been fought largely by federates.[1]

Thus it looks as if by 450 the bulk of the field army (or armies) in the West consisted of federates. This does not mean that no regular units survived. The contrary is likely to have been the case,[2] but it may be that they were mostly tied down in garrison duties. But when a large expeditionary force was needed it seems

---

[1] e.g. in 456 Avitus depended on Goths and federates (Priscus, fr. 32 Blockley; Prosper, *Chron.* 1375). In 461 Majorian dismissed his federates and, when left with only his followers, was seized and killed by those of Ricimer (Priscus, fr. 36. 2 Blockley). In 472 Ricimer, supported by barbarians, overthrew Anthemius (Priscus, fr. 64 Blockley).
[2] Bachrach 1971, 33–4, suggests that the *'milites* who garrisoned fortifications and the *laeti* who protected fortresses and served as *antrustiones* in *centenae . . .* as well as other remnants of the late Roman military establishment were militarily significant' in sixth century Merovingian Gaul.

that it was raised for the duration of the campaign, largely from barbarians.[1] This is confirmed by the laws related to the recruiting tax in the Theodosian Code. These give the impression that the government preferred the levy of recruits to be converted into money, which could then be used to hire barbarians.[2] It was indeed for this very purpose that the Goths had originally been admitted into the empire in 376 (Amm. Marc. 31. 4. 4).

What was the reason for this reliance on foreigners in general and federates in particular? It is unlikely to have been actual shortage of Roman manpower. Jones's view (1964, 1040–5) that there was a general decline of population all over the empire is certainly not right (Liebeschuetz 1990a, 16, 19). But even if there was a marked decline in the western provinces, particularly those badly affected by invasions, there are still likely to have been plenty of individuals who could have been called up, but who, for whatever reason, were not enrolled. A process of demilitarization affecting all classes can certainly be observed over the whole imperial period of Roman history. In our period there is evidence for resistance by landowners to the call-up of peasants even in periods of military crisis. Landowners were able to sabotage recruiting by comparatively simple tactics of evasion.[3] It must be remembered that in most of the fifth century, and particularly in Gaul, patriotic 'Roman' behaviour, and support of the imperial army, were not the only defensive options available. The alternative was cooperation with the barbarians (Harries 1992; Teitler 1992).

At the same time settled federates were willing and even eager to provide troops, and individual barbarians, both within the empire and without, were ready to serve.[4] For them, military service in

---

[1]   e.g. Majorian's expedition against the Vandals (Sid. Ap. *Carm.* 5. 470 ff.).

[2]   e.g. *CTh* 11. 18. 1 (AD 409): *tirones, quoniam pretia exhausti aerarii necessitas flagitavit . . .*; cf. *Nov. Val.* 6. 3 (AD 444). This does not mean that the levy of recruits had been totally abandoned, cf. *Nov. Val.* 6. 1 (AD 440) and 6. 2 (AD 443).

[3]   *Nov. Maj.* 2. 4: 'powerful persons whose overseers . . . contumaciously keep themselves on their landed estates in order that no command of a judge or summons may come to them'.

[4]   On Alaric's Goths in search of employment see Liebeschuetz 1990a, 55–85. Alaric's successor Athaulf left Italy to fight for the usurper Jovinus, but then fought for Honorius against him (Olympiodorus, fr. 18. 20).

the pay of the empire meant a chance of profit. Moreover, the Germans were professional fighters. They would not need much training, particularly if they served in tribal units, using their native tactics. It was agreed that barbarians had very great military qualities. It was the highest praise for a Roman soldier for his warlike capacities to be compared favourably with those of a barbarian (Sid. Ap. *Carm.* 5. 238–54, 518–32, 7. 235–40). So it is not, perhaps, surprising that when a Roman general needed to raise a large army quickly he called for barbarian federates.

In the East as well as the West the empire was meeting many of its long-term frontier defence needs by alternatives to paid career soldiers. Frontier defence soldiers, the *limitanei*, were in the fifth century settled on land (Jones 1964, 653–4 n. 108). Certain categories of land (*agri limitotrophi*) were burdened with the duty of providing supplies and recruits of spearmen for the frontier (*CTh* 5. 12. 2 (AD 415); *Nov. Th.* 5. 2 (AD 439), 3 (AD 441)). Prisoners of war were settled with the obligation to provide troops as *laeti* (Jones 1964, 620 n. 26). Defence of frontier regions was devolved to frontier tribes. This happened on long stretches of desert frontier in North Africa (Jones 1964, 652–3 nn. 103–4) and in Syria/Palestine (Shahid 1984). It was in a sense comparable to the settlement of federates in the western province. The institution of *bucellarii* represented a limited 'privatization' of part of the state's role of providing a standing defence force (Gascou 1976). In these circumstances it is not perhaps surprising that permanent field armies of paid career soldiers were allowed to run down.

Bibliography

Bachrach, B. S. (1972), *Merovingian Military Organization 481–751* (Minneapolis).

Blockley, R. C. (1981–3), *The Fragmentary Classicizing Historians of the Later Roman Empire* (Liverpool).

Cesa, M. (1984), 'Romani e barbari sul Danubio', *Studi Urbinati*, 57: 63–99.

—— and Sivan, H. (1990), 'Alarico in Italia: Pollenza e Verona', *Historia*, 39: 361–74.

Clover, F. M. (1971), *Flavius Merobaudes: A Translation and Historical Commentary* (Transactions of the American Philosophical Society, 61 (1); Philadelphia).

—— (1979), 'Count Gainas and Count Sebastian', *American Journal of Ancient History*, 4: 65–76.

Demougeot, E. (1975), 'La *Notitia Dignitatum* et l'histoire de l'empire d'occident au début du Vᵉ siècle', *Latomus*, 34: 1079–134.

—— (1979), *La Formation de l'Europe et les invasions barbares*, ii: *De l'avènement de Dioclétien (284) à l'occupation germanique de l'empire romain d'occident (début du Vᵉ siècle)* (Paris).

Drinkwater, J. F., and Elton, H. (eds, 1992), *Fifth-century Gaul: A Crisis of Identity?* (Cambridge).

Duncan-Jones, R. (1990), *Structure and Scale in the Roman Economy* (Cambridge).

Elton, H. (1990), *Aspects of Defence in Roman Europe* AD *350–500* (unpublished D.Phil. thesis; Oxford).

—— (1992), 'Defence in fifth-century Gaul', in J. F. Drinkwater and H. Elton (eds), pp. 167–76.

Gascou, J. (1976), 'L'institution des bucellaires', *Bulletin de l'Institut Français de l'Archéologie Orientale*, 72: 143–56.

Goffart, W. (1980), *Barbarians and Romans: The Techniques of Accommodation* (Princeton).

Harries, J. (1992), 'Sidonius Apollinaris, Rome and the barbarians: a climate of treason', in J. F. Drinkwater and H. Elton (eds), pp. 298–308.

Heather, P. (1991), *Goths and Romans 332–489* (Oxford).

Hoffmann, D. (1969), *Das spätrömische Bewegungsheer und die Notitia Dignitatum* (Epigraphische Studien, 7.1; Düsseldorf).

Jones, A. H. M. (1964), *The Later Roman Empire 284–602* (Oxford).

Liebeschuetz, J. H. W. G. (1986), 'Generals, federates and bucellarii in Roman armies around AD 400', in P. Freeman and D. Kennedy (eds), *The Defence of the Roman and Byzantine East* (BAR International Series, 297; Oxford), pp. 463–74; = Liebeschuetz 1990b, ch. 19.

—— (1990a), *Barbarians and Bishops: Army, Church and State in the Age of Arcadius and Chrysostom* (Oxford).

—— (1990b), *From Diocletian to the Arab Conquest* (Great Yarmouth).

Mann, J. C. (1991), 'The *Notitia Dignitatum* – dating and survival', *Britannia*, 22: 215–19.

Matthews, J. (1975), *Western Aristocracies and Imperial Court* AD *364–425* (Oxford).

Muhlberger, S. (1990), *Prosper, Hydatius and the Gallic Chronicler of 452* (ARCA 27; Leeds).

Shahid, I. (1984), *Rome and the Arabs: A Prolegomenon to the Study of Byzantium and the Arabs* (Washington).

Teitler, H. C. (1992), 'Un-Roman activities in late antique Gaul: the cases of Arvandus and Seronatus', in J. F. Drinkwater and H. Elton (eds), pp. 309–17.

Wolfram, H. (1987), *A History of the Goths*, trans. T. J. Dunlop (Berkeley).

∞ 12 ∞

Landlords and warlords
in the later Roman Empire

Dick Whittaker

Introduction: the barbarian invasions

In AD 503, when the Byzantine emperor Anastasius mustered the largest ever army (or so Procopius says) against the Persians, Joshua the Stylite, who was witness to the war, wryly remarked, 'To the Arabs of both sides this war was a source of much profit and they wrought their will on both kingdoms.'[1] This example demonstrates how the people who emerged under the ominous, but vague name of Saracens were to some extent the creation of the great powers who used them. But it also throws light on the nature of the so-called barbarian invasions of the later Roman Empire, since the Saracens were not a new, unknown hoard of invaders, but a people who had long been known to the Romans and had even been a part of the Roman empire.

Ammianus describes the Persians in his day as making war 'by theft and banditry rather than . . . in pitched battles' (Amm. Marc. 16. 9. 1: *per furta et latrocinia potius quam . . . per concursatorias pugnas*). This phrase corresponds closely with his analysis of the principal mode of warfare by the Saracens, a people 'like rapacious kites' (14. 4. 1), who were 'well suited for guerilla raiding' (23. 3. 8: *ad furta bellorum appositi*). I am not here concerned whether Ammianus did justice to the Saracens or

[1] The example is drawn from Isaac 1990, from which I have greatly profited. See my review, *TLS*, 22 Mar. 1991.

fully understood the difference between the relatively stable federations, such as the Lakhmids and Tanukhids, and nomadic bands of pastoralists (Shahid 1984, ch. 7). The fact is that Ammianus was an eastern, military man who perceived the pressures on the eastern frontier as created principally by guerilla raids.

Ammianus' perception was shared by other contemporaries with direct experience, such as Jerome or the author of the *Ammonii Monachi Relatio*, who told of kidnapping and raids on monasteries by small bands of Saracen marauders. Even the emperor Julian described the Saracens as no more than 'bandits' (*Or*. 1. 21 b). An important, recent analysis of the eastern frontier concludes, therefore, that the whole idea of an organized frontier 'system', with some sort of continuous, impenetrable barrier from the Caucasus to the Gulf of Aqabah, is a modern myth, and that it is impossible to prove that the Persians had any general aggressive intention to occupy Roman territory.[1] It seems in general that the real threat on the eastern frontier came not from head-on clashes between great armies, but from the steady infiltration, increase in population and organization of the Arabs, which the very stability of the Roman empire encouraged.

All this, as I have argued elsewhere (Whittaker 1989, ch. 3), finds interesting parallels on the western frontiers, although naturally no one would want to suggest that the threats were precisely similar. I am thinking of the example of the Rhine frontier in about 350 where the German bandit, Charietto, thrived near Trier with a band of robbers. Since he also made profits by successfully killing other Germans who crossed the Rhine, he was employed by Julian as part of his military force (*PLRE* i, s.v. Charietto). Or there is the story given by Zosimus (4. 48), of how Theodosius tried to deal with the barbarian raiders near Salonica who were hiding in the marshes. His remedy was to take a small band of horsemen and ride continuously around the countryside hunting them out. They were, says Zosimus, 'like ghosts instead of men'. As Ammianus the soldier knew, the Romans themselves were often better advised to deal with barbarian invasions 'in

---

[1]   Isaac 1990, ch. 1, especially p. 52. However, in my opinion Isaac unduly minimizes the threat from the Saracens (pp. 72–4).

small divisions and by stealthy and guerilla warfare' (31. 7. 2: *particulatim perque furta magis et latrocinia*).

The disruption such raiders caused was selective but continuous. And yet the rural community coexisted with them and, in our stories, could not always identify them by dress or language. They were absorbed into the countryside 'like ghosts'. Even after the Goths had won their shattering victory at Adrianople in 378, they disappeared, says Themistius, 'like a shadow' (*Or.* 16. 206 c). Many of them had been living in the Thracian countryside round about for several years (Amm. Marc. 31. 6. 5–6). Charietto apparently had no difficulty living with his bandits, even in the territory of the imperial capital of Trier. The Saracen captors of Malchus, the monk, operated in the region between Beroea and Edessa, far within the Roman provinces of Euphratensis and Osrhoene (Jerome, *Life of Malchus*, 4 = *PL* xxiii. 58); but when the Saracen queen, Mavia, had a disagreement with the Arian emperor Valens, she simply withdrew beyond the frontier (Rufinus, *Hist. Eccl.* 2. 6).[1] The frontiers of the barbarians, whatever the Romans may have imagined, were in fact extending deeper into the Roman empire.

Many have asked the question, on how many occasions the 'barbarian invasions' really were what we would regard as invasions. This is not, of course, to disregard the seriousness of the great set-piece field battles like Strasbourg or Adrianople, nor the devastating effect of the irruptions into Gaul and Italy in the early fifth century for those inhabitants who lay in the path of the invaders. The real problem is to assess the importance of these dramatic but isolated events in comparison to the more banal but continual pressure of the small bands of infiltrators.

I have not seen anyone challenge the arguments put forward by Delbrück in his famous *Geschichte der Kriegskunst* in 1920 concerning the strength of Roman and barbarian armies. After careful analysis of the figures given by our sources for the battles of the fourth century and the *Völkerwanderung* of the fifth

---

[1] Discussed in detail by Shahid 1984, 142–52; cf. Bowersock 1980, 141. Compare also the Namara inscription to a Lakhmid king buried inside the Roman province between Bostra and Damascus, who, to judge from the exploits on his inscription, seems to have been a federate leader who, like Charietto, came over to the Romans; see below p. 290.

century, Delbrück – who was a pupil of Clausewitz and no fool on
military matters – came to the conclusion that most of the tribal
movements never consisted of more than 5,000 to 15,000 fighting
men, and in some cases, like that of the Burgundians in the mid-
fifth century, the numbers were even as low as 3,000 men
(Delbrück 1980, 285–99). Ammianus' figure of 243 Roman dead
at Strasbourg, Delbrück thought, was a more accurate guide to
the size of the forces engaged in battle than the thousands upon
thousands of Alamanni reported by Libanius and Ammianus. We
must, therefore, be on our guard against the rhetorical fervour of
partisans like Ammianus, who speaks of the barbarians flowing
like lava from Etna (31. 4. 9). Aetius' glorious victory over the
Salian Franks at *vicus Helena*, enthusiastically hailed by Sidonius
(*Carm.* 5. 219–29), turns out to be no more than a 'minor skirmish'
when the Romans broke up a wedding party (James 1988, 57).

Of course, there were from time to time larger but also more
ephemeral federations which, typically in our reports, lacked
cohesion and organization. The great Gothic migration in 376
was, in Ammianus' simplistic account, divided under the leadership of at least seven or eight chieftains with their followers. There
were reports of a 'mob' (*multitudo*) of unknown *nationes* 'wandering around the Danube', says Ammianus, 'scattered with their
families' (31. 4. 2). Similarly with the Alamans, it was their hydra-
headed, multi-tribal organization – or lack of it – which made
them so tricky to contain in Ammianus' narrative (e.g. 27. 10. 5).
Gregory of Tours was baffled by the constant references to *reguli*
and *duces* in Sulpicius Alexander's history of the fourth-century
Frankish invasions (*Hist. Franc.* 2. 9). Attila's Huns included the
Akatziri, described by Priscus as having 'many rulers by clans
(*phyle*) and families (*gene*)' (fr. 11, 259 Blockley). It is the 'multiple
structure' of the Arab federates that makes it impossible to
identify the many phylarchs who lived on the eastern borders of
Roman rule (Shahid 1984, 544).

The real difficulty is to imagine what was really happening,
when we talk in broad terms about the collapse of the frontiers
and the changes inherent in that process during the later Roman
Empire. This chapter is an attempt to concentrate on two of those
changes – those in the countryside and those in the army. For they
were, I believe, closely linked, and it was the developments which
took place in these areas especially which eased the transition

from the Roman empire to the barbarian kingdoms. One of the features which has struck some modern commentators about the Frankish conquest in the West, for instance, is the relatively peaceful character of the process.[1] I believe that is correct, not because the Franks were gentle invaders, but because out of the violence of the countryside there emerged a *modus vivendi* and a military structure which permitted Roman and invader to accommodate to each other.

Soldiers as landlords and rural patrons

The later Roman Empire was a period when notoriously the poor became increasingly dependent on the arbitrary will of the landed rich. It is usual, since Fustel de Coulanges, to cite the disappearance of the tenancy contracts of *locatio-conductio* in evidence. In fact, some non-technical references to land contracts do continue to appear in Vulgar Law in Augustine's Africa and Byzantine Egypt, and also in Euric's Code in Gaul and perhaps even in seventh-century Merovingian formularies.[2] Although there obviously was a diminution in the practice, I suspect that many contracts were increasingly verbal and that the absence of legally referable, written contracts was less important than the breakdown of traditional, unspoken social contracts of patronage in return for services between landowners and the poor, whether or not tenancy was involved. This breakdown was accelerated by

[1] Wallace-Hadrill 1962, 3; James 1988. Some of the papers in Drinkwater and Elton 1992 (kindly shown to me in advance of publication by Dr Drinkwater) place greater stress on the dislocation of the period than I have done here. However, the collapse of the central Roman authority did not lead to chaos and military anarchy everywhere, largely because of the local protection agencies discussed in this paper.

[2] See Levy 1951, 62, 90–3. The African example, which refers to an *inquilinus*, reads: *locata est enim tibi domus . . . non donata* (Augustine, *Enn. in Ps. 148*, 11 = *PL* 37. 1945). For Byzantine Egypt see e.g. *PLondon* 1695 (AD 531), a five year contract, and *PRG* iii. 39 (AD 584), a protest at the termination of a contract. Note Levy's comment about Euric's code (*lex* 12) – 'a contract about equivalent to . . . *locatio-conductio rei*', and his citation of a reference even in Merovingian *formulae*.

the growth of the twin process of soldiers becoming landlords and landlords becoming soldiers.

The first part of this process, that is, of soldiers turning into landlords, is the central, though coded, message of Libanius' celebrated 47th oration, which we tend to regard as a general discourse on *patrocinium*. It is really an attack on military officers, particularly those of the *laterculum minus* on the frontiers, who were purchasing property from *curiales* and encouraging peasants, both tenants and free villagers, to become their *oiketai* – their 'domestics' (sections 21, 24), turning farmers into 'brigands' (section 6) and undermining the very structure of the empire (Carrié 1976). It was, says Libanius, like appealing to the barbarians outside the empire.

This was loaded language, whose technical significance only becomes apparent in the next century. *Oiketai, oikia*, and *familia*, for instance, at that period regularly signal the presence of semi-private armies, when, for instance, Procopius describes the retinue of Belisarius (*Secret History*, 4. 13). A fragment of Malalas (cited by Mommsen 1910, 243) tells us that 'villagers' formed part of the special bands enrolled under Leo. Brigandage was always the standard charge made by the administration when legislating against such accretions, as when we find the Theodosian Code attacking *patrocinium* for encouraging bandits (*CTh* 1. 29. 8, AD 392). Themistius' attack on rich aristocrats for driving peasants to seek out barbarians (*Or.* 8. 115 c) was, I suspect, partly a reference to the fact, on which I shall have more to say below, that barbarians were becoming the new, military landlords on the Roman *limites*.

Harmand's commentary on Libanius' speech searches, without much success, for examples of soldiers who purchased property in Syria, often called 'forts' or, in Libanius' language, *pyrgoi*. He cites the case of Silvanus, who possessed a property in south-eastern Syria Prima, a *dux*, according to the inscription, who had taken the interesting, perhaps prudent, course for a frontier officer, of marrying the daughter of Saracen phylarchs.[1] Another estate has been identified on the Damascus–Palmyra road belonging to a Rufinus, a *dux limitis* (*CIL* iii. 6660). There is

[1] Harmand 1955, 155. I assume the plural means a long line; for references, see *PLRE* ii, s.v. Silvanus, 8.

no proof in either case that the officers used their position to purchase land, an important reminder to us of the limitations of epigraphic evidence. After all, Libanius' example of his own uncle, a *strategos*, who ended up with a modest estate of ten *oiketai*, proves that these things happened. Nor is there anything intrinsically surprising in soldiers using their money to purchase land in the area where they served. In so far as some of these soldiers were men of barbarian origin who perhaps married into local families, this process helped to integrate them into the imperial system.

The same development is illustrated by the Abinnaeus Archive in fourth-century Egypt. There Abinnaeus himself was becoming one of the land bosses – the *geouchoi*. In one of the papyri, *PAbin.* 61, one can even detect a formal written contract of tied labour which thus backed *patrocinium* with civil law.[1] It reads:

> To Flavius Abinnaeus, *praepositus* of the camp at Dionysias etc. . . . I, Julius, agree to act as surety for Ammonius, son of Souk of the village of Taurinon: whenever he is wanted, I myself, Julius, will produce him, as set down, and I give my consent to this under examination.

If this is indeed, as it appears to be, a reference to a contract upon the person and his personal service, it is at the very least a fourth-century example of the contract of *paramone*, service as a retainer of the household, an *oiketes* or *katadoulos pais*, known in the next centuries (e.g. *POxy.* 1112; *PStrass.* 40). But it is also getting close to Marc Bloch's 'homme de corps' – the henchman bound by personal ties to a master, which he regarded as the defining characteristic of medieval serfdom, as opposed to the conventional view of the 'serf de la glèbe', tied to the land. Certainly there is no mistaking the tone of the personal relationship between Abinnaeus and another peasant attested in *PAbin.* 36:

> To the master of my life, to the owner of my strength, to the *praepositus* Abinnaeus: from Pallas . . . I earnestly beseech you that you . . . give my wife some sheep . . . You know, my lord, that I have none. I am your servant forever.

It is impossible to tell from the context whether Pallas was a

---

[1] Rémondon 1965, 142. The text of the Abinnaeus Archive is published by Bell *et al.* 1962.

colonus or free peasant, but the whole archive is nevertheless a graphic portrait of rural patronage on a desert frontier of the Fayum in the mid-fourth century.

That stimulates me to wonder about other desert frontiers in the Roman empire, especially the Tripolitanian frontier, where we have no papyri or Libanius, but certainly many inscriptions and many fortified farmhouses, the 'gsur', which must have been very like the Syrian *pyrgoi*. Some of these were official *centenaria* of the local frontier army, the forts of local tribunes and *principes* of units of *gentiles*, but most we know to have been the private estates of these same military officers (Elmayer 1985). This is not a precise analogy with the Syrian or Egyptian examples, since most of the officers in Tripolitania, apart from the *praepositi limitis*, appear to have been local aristocrats, who were very prosperous and had large settlements attached to their farmhouses. Therefore the Tripolitanian estate owners, men like Julius Masthalul, Julius Nasif and Flavius Isiguari (*IRT* 886, from Bir ed-Dreder), illustrate both halves of the twin process, soldiers as landlords and landlords as soldiers. The evidence of the Nessana papyri in Palestine suggest that the Theodosian camel corps posted there in the sixth century was also recruited from local landowners (Kraemer 1958, no. 24, etc.).

When we turn to the western provinces, it is strange that we have no obvious reference at all to the Syro-Egyptian phenomenon of military landlords. Can we really believe that it did not exist (as Carrié 1976, 175, supposes)? More probably, in my view, the explanation lies simply in the different kinds of sources available to us. After all, even in the earlier Empire it is generally believed that soldiers in Gaul bought farms in the vicinity of their camps (Drinkwater 1983, 67). There are, however, a few clues – I put it no higher than that – that the practice was becoming increasingly common in the West during the later Empire. Perhaps, for instance, *patrocinium* and property lies behind the edict (*CTh* 7. 1. 10) addressed by Valentinian to Jovinus, the Gallic *magister militum* on the western front in 367, forbidding soldiers from taking away with them freeborn men 'by pretending that they are kinsmen (*propinquitas*) or attendants (*lixae*)'. Interesting in itself is the assumption of the legislation that such household retinues were large enough to create serious worries about evasion of military service, whether they involved *coloni* or not. I also believe that the legislation in 384 (*CTh* 7. 1. 12) complaining of soldiers 'wandering through private property', when they should have been with their units, could refer to their own property. Later, under Valentinian III, soldiers of Numidia and Mauretania who 'wandered away' from frontier posts were obviously landowners, since they were formally conceded a month's leave to visit their 'household and land' (*familia et possessiones*: *Nov. Val.* 13. 13, AD 445).

At all events, there must be a strong *a priori* presumption that on the Rhine–Danube front there was some growth of military landlordism. Ammianus' attack on Constantius' courtiers who were 'raised at one bound from base poverty to vast riches' goes on to attack those soldiers who sought 'even houses of marble' (22. 4. 3, 6). But no doubt, as in Tripolitania, the situation was often confused by the presence of native *gentiles*. Where did all those Frankish and Alaman grandees who served in the Roman army have their families and land? Some, we know from Ammianus, had property beyond the frontiers (e.g. 20. 4. 4). But some must surely have held estates in 'Toxandria' and the Rhinelands under Roman control, in exactly the same way as the Saracen Tanukhids almost certainly held land in North Syria (Shahid 1984, 545). Charietto with his band of retainers lived around Trier. The German Petulantes apparently had some property in the provinces, since they complained bitterly, when about to be posted by Julian, that their families who had been freed from the Alaman would again be exposed to invasion (Amm. Marc. 20. 4. 10). The family of Arbogast certainly had large estates on the Moselle by the time that his heir was count of Trier, and Merobaudes posssessed estates in Baetica and near Troyes in Gaul (*PLRE* ii, s.v. Arbogast, Merobaudes).

These are, of course, only scraps of evidence, although, as we shall see, there is some circumstantial corroboration from archaeological evidence that the phenomenon of military patronage was not unknown in northern Gaul and Germany. There is also a very general argument in support of the proposition. The fourth century, it is generally believed, witnessed the emergence of new landowning gentry in Gaul, consisting mainly of men who had sought and found their fortunes at the imperial court. Camille Jullian compared such men to the bourgeois parvenus at the court of Henri IV and Louis XIII (Jullian 1926, 128; Stroheker 1948,

12–14). It seems very likely that some would have begun as military officers. Jovinus (mentioned above) seems to have had property at Rheims, where he built a church and recorded his military service (*CIL* xiii. 3256). But, unlike in Syria, during most of the fourth century, emperors took up residence on the Gallic frontier and therefore military patronage vied and overlapped with court patronage, making it impossible – perhaps even pointless – to judge in which capacity the new noblesse acquired their property and powers of patronage.

In short, it seems reasonable to conclude that soldiers, particularly officers, on active service, became increasingly powerful locally through their attachment to the land in the regions in which they served. The phenomenon was not an invention of the later Empire but the culmination of a long process, since legislation against soldiers forming local attachments had been relaxed in the second century. The change in the later Empire was one of degree: properties became greater and state controls over the exercise of private patronage became weaker. And, above all, there was the additional factor that the soldiers were now often men who had entered Roman service as federate leaders.

Landlords as soldiers

We have more evidence for the other half of the twin process: landlords turning to militarism. With the growth of huge estates and concentration of property ownership in the later Empire came control of large numbers of dependants who could be mustered for military action. Again, this was not an invention of the later Empire. The rebellion in Africa in 238 by the estate owners at Thysdrus against the emperor Maximinus, when rural workers, interestingly called *oiketai* by a contemporary Greek historian (Herodian, 7. 4. 5), joined forces with the aristocratic *iuvenes*, is an early example of how landlords could use their bands of *amici* and *clientes* forcefully in a period of crisis. Zosimus tells of an estate owner at Selge in Pamphylia who resisted Tribigild and his Goths in 399 by calling upon his *oiketai* and farmers 'who, he says, were trained in many battles with neighbouring bandits' (Zos. 5. 15. 5). Armed battles between retainers seem to have been quite common, like the example of two brothers who were estate owners in Cappadocia, each with his own 'army of workers' (*stratos . . . hypocheirion*: Gregory of Nyssa, *Life of Gregory Thaumaturgus* = *PG* 46. 9269).

The legislation of the fourth century provides clear evidence for the central administration's concern about the growing independence and inaccessibility of rich estate owners, who were recruiting soldiers from the army, offering sanctuary to deserters and, of course, in the stereotyped language of the time, aiding and abetting robbers. Hence their attraction to peasants unwilling or unable to pay their taxes. Egypt illustrates what this meant in personal terms. The citizens of Theadelphia in 332 protested against Eulogios, the owner of an estate in the Oxyrhinchite nome, for giving protection to five tax payers with their families; yet 'Eulogios, their landlord', they complain, 'together with Arion the winegrower and Serapion the farmer, has prevented us with violence from approaching even the entrance of his estate . . .' (*PThead.* 17). This does not, of course, mean that peasants and *coloni* were turning into full-time private soldiers, but that landlords were using their increasing powers of patronage to bind peasants to their personal allegiance, including the use of violence, if needed.

The legislation is set in more global terms. In 396 we have the well-known ban on soldiers entering private service (*privatum obsequium*), which the law says had been going on for some time (*CTh* 7. 1. 15). In the Theodosian Code, the first of a group of seventeen laws which are listed under the title 'concerning deserters and those who shelter them' (*CTh* 7. 18) is dated 365. The laws rise to a climax in the 380s, but without apparently much effect, since they continue almost unabated into the fifth century. Obviously it was going to be difficult to maintain a tight control, if the authorities took such a relaxed view of military duties as is reflected in the Abinnaeus Archive, where soldiers seem grossly underemployed and regularly off on expeditions hunting gazelle, or farming.

It is equally hard to be impressed by the severity of the legislation against soldiers taking absence without leave when we read the edict of 413: 'If anyone should spend a year without leave of absence . . . in slothful ease, he shall be demoted below his next ten inferiors'. But if a year seems a long time for a soldier to be absent without leave, what follows is even more remarkable: the law prescribes that only if a soldier is absent for four years, 'shall he be removed from the official register and granted no pardon' (*CTh* 7. 18. 16). What were the soldiers doing for four years in slothful ease?

The language of *latrones* and deserters, native *duces* and their *servitia*, *rustici* and *coloni* is also very much at the core of the scattered rural movements from the third to fifth centuries in Gaul and Spain, which we call the Bagaudae (Van Dam 1985, 30) and of the circumcellions in Africa. Rightly, in my view, regarded as more than simple jacqueries, these upheavals were perhaps no more than extreme forms of local armies of dependants, taking aim at the traditional *domini-curiales* of the *civitates*. Just as Libanius compared desertion from the patronage of local *curiales* to going over to the barbarians, so too the image of passing beyond the frontiers and going over to the barbarians was used of Gallic dissidents (ibid. 40–2). If it is correct that the Seine and Marne were the primary regions of such disaffection,[1] we must also ask to what extent this was a reflection of the proto-settlements of Frankish war bands.

It is not my concern here to enter the controversy about how much aid the circumcellions gave to the rebellions of Firmus and Gildo in fourth-century Africa (recently played down by Gabbia 1988). But it is of great significance that, in addition to the support of local Máuri tribes and some regular Roman army units, Ammianus' account of Firmus' revolt includes references to his

---

[1] Drinkwater 1984. It is only proper to point out that Drinkwater strongly disagrees with Van Dam's (and my) interpretation of the Bagaudae (most recently, Drinkwater 1989). His main arguments are that it is impossible to identify any known prominent landowner associated with the Bagaudae movement, and that there was no continuity of Gallic élites from early to late Roman periods. To which I respond: (1) we know so little of later Gallic élites that I have no confidence in the argument from silence; in Africa, by way of comparison, we know nothing about the origins of the house of Nubel before the fourth century, although they were obviously extensive landowners; (2) a change of élites during the disturbances of the third century does not preclude continuity of conditions of extreme rural dependence associated with early Gallic nobles. Drinkwater 1992 develops the interesting idea that the fifth-century movement was caused by refugees from the barbarian invasions putting unacceptable pressure upon land in southern Gaul.

satellites, hired *plebs*, and *servi* accompanying him (29. 5. 36, 39), and that the Theodosian Code mentions the massive estates of Gildo and his *satellites* (*CTh* 7. 8. 7, AD 400, 9. 42. 19, AD 405). The language can be compared to legislation passed a few years later after the disgrace of Stilicho, when punishment was ordained for those who gave their resources 'in law or in body' (*iure vel corpore*) to Stilicho, his son and other *satellites* (*CTh* 9. 42. 22, AD 408). This, as we shall see later, is the vocabulary used of *bucellarii*, those semi-private household retinues that became the major mobile strike forces of the fifth century. We might here just note Diesner's reminder that Gildo's rebellious retinue was defeated just one year after the edict I referred to earlier, forbidding soldiers to enter into *privatum obsequium* (Diesner 1972, 324).

These men were not barbarians from the mountain or desert fringes of the empire. The House of Nubel in the Kabylie, from which Firmus and Gildo stemmed, was a world of large fortified estates, *castella* and *centenaria*, in which banditry was endemic. But the builders of these *castella* – which make one think of Tripolitania again – played a dual role as Mauri chiefs and Roman officials; thoroughly absorbed into the imperial court and army, yet leaders of 'tribal' bands of the local *gentes*. From the fourth to the sixth century a series of such figures pass across the scene from the *rex gentium Maurorum et Romanorum* at the old Roman fort of Altava to Koceïla, king of Awreba near Tlemcen, whose real name was perhaps Caecilius. It was these men who kept alive the Roman and the Christian name in Africa.[1]

What is important to note here, however, is how close these Roman landlords were to the world of the federate warlords. It is quite difficult to distinguish between a Saracen *malek* or phylarch in the service of Rome, who, like the Mauri chiefs, was settled with land on Roman territory and absorbed into the Roman

[1] Camps 1985. It may not be too fanciful to note here a further parallel with the Bagaudae, whose leaders Amandus and Aelianus were also called native usurpers but who were regarded as local heroes of Christianity in the fifth century. Later medieval tradition associated Saint-Maurdes-Fossés with a place called *castrum Bagaudarum* and viewed the rebel *latrones* as *custodes* of the Christian faith; see Jullian 1926, 14; Giardina 1983, 383–5; Van Dam 1985, 54.

administration, and the Saracen warrior leader, serving Rome with his federate band but equally prepared to serve Persia. I am thinking of the chieftain commemorated in 328 on the inscription at Namara near the Druz Mountains in Syria, called 'king of all the Arabs', who forced many tribal chiefs to become 'phylarchs of the Romans' (Bowersock 1983, 138–47; Shahid 1984, 31–53; Bellamy 1985), or of Mavia in the reign of Valens, the Tanukhid queen, whose daughter married Victor the *magister equitum*, and who fought for the right to have a Christian catholic bishop against the Arian emperor (*PLRE* ii, s.v. Mavia; Shahid 1984, 142–52). How different were they from the phylarch Podosaces, whom Ammianus calls a *latro* because he served the Persians (Amm. Marc. 24. 2. 4)?

These African and Arabian examples can be likened to the various Gallic and Frankish *reguli* who kept alive the Roman name. Men like Syagrius of Soissons, who was called *rex Romanorum* by Gregory of Tours, but was a king without a kingdom (James 1988, 70–1), or Arbogast of Trier, who spoke 'the true Latin of the Tiber . . . even though the Roman writ has perished at our border' (Sid. Apoll. *Epist*. 4. 17), or Childeric of Tournai. We are accustomed to think of Childeric as a Frankish invader, but he was buried with his Roman *fibula* of office and Bishop Remigius of Rheims seems to imply in a letter to Clovis that Childeric had been administrator of Belgica Secunda, as was his more famous son (James 1988, 78). In this last example, the Roman landlord has merged into the federate warlord as part of the process of change.

The problem about conceptualizing this change, as James (ibid. 79) has recently reminded us, is that Gregory of Tours in the sixth century, followed by many historians since, could only conceive of the Franks' entry into Gaul as a violent barbarian invasion, culminating at Soissons where Syagrius fell fighting symbolically as the last defender of Romania. In fact, the fifth century in Gaul was the culmination of a less dramatic process of integration of Germanic chiefs with their 'Gefolgsleute' into the burgeoning *demi-monde* of estate owners surrounded by their fighting retinues. The organization of armed retinues was not simply the creation of the invaders, since we can see parallel developments in Africa and the East. Nor was it German federate leaders but Romano-Spanish court grandees, Veranius, Didymus,

Theodosiolus and Lagodius, cousins of Honorius, who raised troops from the slaves and *coloni* of their Spanish domains in 408-9 in order to stop the usurpation of Constantine III (*PLRE* ii, s.v. Veranius).

Likewise, a bishop of the Church, such as Hilary of Arles, was acting as a typical Roman landlord when he raised his armed band as an irregular force (stigmatized as an *abominabilis tumultus* at *Nov. Val.* 17.1, AD 445). Synesius' natural pride at having organized the defence of Cyrene when he 'enrolled companies of officers with the resources I had at my disposal' (*Epist.* 125) is matched by the occasion when he raised a similar band of irregulars to protect his private estates at Ausamas (MacMullen 1963, 138, cf. p. 140 for parallels). Gregory of Tours records a long line of bishops with militant bands; like Hilary of Arles or Cantinus of Auvergne (Clermont), they played havoc with the property of their neighbouring brethren. Sidonius Apollinaris as bishop of Clermont famously led the defence of his city in the 470s. One plausible reason for the conversion of Clovis, when threatened by the Alamans at Tolbiac, was that this might enable him to tap the considerable resources of the Church (Bachrach 1972, 7-8).

It might be argued that these examples of fifth-century Roman estate owners and bishops active in resistance are isolated and come late in a century which was otherwise marked by general helplessness in the face of the barbarian onslaught. But that is to forget the sparseness of the sources for this period. In fact the law codes of the later fourth century give an indication of the problem which only became fully evident when the central state armies disintegrated – a process which is itself most unclear (Jones 1964, 612; Liebeschuetz above, ch. 11).

The archaeology of change

The archaeology of Gaul provides some corroborative evidence of the rise and similarity of warlords and landlords. Much of the recent boom in graveyard analysis appears to confirm the generally peaceful course of integration and the 'invisibility' of the barbarian invaders, just because it has been so difficult to identify them. Here I shall pick only three characteristics, since I have discussed the subject elsewhere (Whittaker 1989, ch. 3, with detailed references).

(1) Undoubtedly one of the major features of the changing face of the countryside was considerably more nucleation of rural sites, particularly in the northern provinces of Germany and Belgica. Small farms disappeared, many *vici* were abandoned or removed to old Iron Age hilltop sites, while larger villas, like St Ulrich, Echternach etc. survived, expanded and were often fortified. The château of Claudius Postumus Dardanus near Sisteron acquired new ramparts 'for the protection of everyone' in the early fifth century, and for good measure was called Theopolis (*CIL* xii. 1524; Jullian 1926, 141). This looks like clear evidence of concentration of property holdings, the increased isolation and inaccessibility of estates and the compulsion on peasants to seek the refuge of the rich. It seems that in some cases the villages on the estates grew larger (Wightman 1981; 1985, 246–50). The process is vividly evoked in the words of Salvian (*de gub. Dei*, 4. 14): 'Those who, when driven by the terror of the enemy, flee to the *castella* . . . and give themselves over to the yoke of being *inquilini*'.

(2) At many forts the Gallo-Roman burials are replaced by Germanic styles of interment. The most celebrated is the cemetery at Krefeld-Gellep on the Rhine at the Roman fort of Gelduba, whose 5,000 or more graves have long been known. They look like *gentiles* or federate troops. But closer to my theme is the more recently studied site of Vireux-Molhain in the Ardennes, a small Roman fort opposite a *vicus*, reinforced in the mid-fourth to mid-fifth century by Germanic groups, estimated at about twenty-five men and women per generation (Lemant 1985; James 1988, 48). We can only conjecture what the social relations between the soldiers in such forts and the neighbouring villagers were like, but these sites provide the perfect setting for military, rural patronage in the style described by Libanius.

(3) Most important of all is the integration of Germanic and Gallo-Roman burials. This is so complete that it is virtually impossible to tell whether a 'Germanic' burial with weapons is in reality that of a German or not, since much of the military style of the artefacts – belts, buckles, etc. – is common to both Germans and late Roman officers. My favourite example comes from Landifay (Aisne), where a 'German' buckle is inscribed with a

portrait of a Roman cavalry officer and his wife who is not dressed with the tell-tale *fibulae* normal for German women (Erison 1978). Pretty clearly, however, many of the burials are German, especially those containing distinctive Frankish weapons like the throwing-axe.

Many of these burials are not associated with military camps at all, but based on Roman villas. Frequently the German burials are grouped in clusters of about twenty to thirty around a richer central grave, presumably that of a minor leader surrounded by his *Gefolgsmänner*. But these clusters are often to be found in cemeteries otherwise composed of typically Gallo-Roman graves, looking, as one commentator remarks, like 'the indigenous, rural Gallo-Roman population who remain where they were' (A. Dasnoy, in Fleury and Périn 1978, 68–79). From the evidence at Abbeville-Homblières near St Quentin it has been argued that there was a German-owned villa worked by Gallo-Roman labour. In the case of the cemetery adjacent to the Roman villa at Frénouville near Caen, it is impossible to detect a break in continuity of population from the late third to the late seventh century, only in the mode of burial over a long period and in the orientation of the graves in the mid-fifth century (Böhme, cited by James 1988, 49; Pilet 1980, 171).

In other words, just as the villas of rich Gallo-Roman landlords concentrated the resources of rural land and labour on their estates, so the same process was taking place on the rural sites of the German warlords. Childeric's grave-goods are linked to a series of chieftains' graves of the Flonheim-Gültingen group scattered from the Ardennes to south of the Somme. It is only historical prejudice which says that they must date from after the battle of Soissons in 486. More probably they reflect the conditions of northern Gaul in the early fifth century (James 1988, 76–7).

Changes in the army

It is time to return to the army itself. I began by saying that frontier defence was less a problem of large pitched battles than of infiltration by small groups of guerilla raiders. It appears that, just as the federate settlements and civilian villas were consolidating into more isolated, nucleated units, military developments were moving in the same direction. Constantine's *comitatenses*, and still more the regional *comitatenses* which had grown up under his successors, appear to have become by the end of the fourth century more and more like a static militia, based upon the cities for the purpose of supplies – a feature already evident to Ammianus (16. 4. 1, cf. 31. 16. 8). This tendency was perhaps encouraged by the forced cantonment of units of *laeti* and *gentiles* upon public lands attached to cities or forts. It is well known that many towns in modern France take their names from such units, for example, Salmaise (ancient Sarmatia) near Langres, where a prefect of Sarmatian *gentiles* was stationed.[1]

That kind of degeneration of the field army was also a feature of the Byzantine army. But the corresponding evolution was a *force de frappe* in the fifth century. The force was made up overwhelmingly of 'federates' – a term which by the time of Honorius had lost all sense of being applied exclusively to barbarians, if we are to believe Olympiodorus (fr. 7. 4, p. 158 Blockley) – who were probably often *ad hoc* irregulars; federates, but also *bucellarii*. The *bucellarii* were, again according to Olympiodorus, both Roman and foreign, defined by the scholiast on Basil (60. 18. 29) as 'those who eat the bread of someone, on the condition of becoming his trusty'. The word in Greek is *parameinontes*, meaning literally 'those who stay alongside', which comes to mean 'those who are faithful'. It is used regularly in the fifth and sixth century and corresponds pretty closely to 'gentlemen-in-waiting' – the same sense as the Latin word *satellites*. Procopius, for instance, calls them, 'those who stand behind when the commander is dining' (*Vand.* 4. 28).

There is no need for me to repeat all that has been said about the *bucellarii* from Mommsen to Liebeschuetz (Liebeschuetz 1986, with references to earlier treatments). But the institution is usually discussed in terms of the army of the eastern empire, as though it post-dated the collapse of the West. Whereas, in fact, as the examples collected by Diesner (1972) show, it had firmly established itself in the western empire by the later fourth century. Indeed, I would argue that it is precisely through this institution

[1]   *Not. Dig. Oc.* 42. 61. In Langres itself a suburb was called Laticensis (modern Lassois), surely from a laetic unit (Bachrach 1972, 34).

that one can see most clearly the transition from the later Empire to the medieval German kingdoms in the West. Titus, the leader of a unit of *bucellarii* who, according to the *Life of Daniel Stylites* (60–4), was invited to serve under Leo in the East, came from Gaul.

A good deal of the debate about *bucellarii* in the past has ranged around the question of whether they herald the advent of feudalism by virtue of the personal oath of allegiance they gave to their leader (e.g. Bachrach 1967; Gascou 1976). But, apart from the fact that medievalists now use the term 'feudalism' less freely than some classical historians, most of the argument about private – as opposed to public – armies is misplaced. Procopius is clear that the private contract (perhaps for what was later called *paramone*) was supplemented by the *sacramentum* to the emperor (*Vand.* 4. 18). But obviously the public oath was of limited relevance if the patron rebelled, or if imperial rule was not recognized; the loyalty of the soldiers then became private *obsequium*.

This ambiguity is well captured by Sidonius when describing the siege of Clermont in 474, at a time when the ties with an unknown western emperor were of the most tenuous and there was no imperial army in sight. In a letter to Ecdicius, Sidonius lauds the exploits of this great landlord, who with a *comitatus* of barely eighteen *sodales* – 'fewer than your table normally has guests' – managed to cut his way through and put to flight 'several thousand' Goths without loss (Sid. Apoll. *Epist.* 3. 3. 3–4). Gregory of Tours improves upon these incredible figures by giving Ecdicius only ten companions (*Hist. Franc.* 2. 24). But I think we are here victims of terminology rather than of rhetoric. Those who rate a mention are only Ecdicius' free *satellites*, his *amici* (whence the reference to his table), who are sometimes called *clientes*. No publicity was given to the far more numerous lesser *clientes*, *servi* and *coloni* in attendance on each companion – in Procopius' language, we have the *doryphoroi* without the *hypaspists* (cf. Procop. *Secret History* 4. 13).

This is not unlike like the example of Sarus, the Goth whom we know to have had two to three hundred personal followers. When he died fighting against Athaulf's army of 10,000, he is said to have had only eighteen or twenty men, according to the strict account of Olympiodorus (fr. 18, p. 183 Blockley), one of whom we know was called Belleridus, termed a 'domestic' (*PLRE* ii, s.v. Sarus). In Ammianus' account of the followers of Firmus, he distinguishes between *satellites*, the *plebs* whom Firmus 'had hired for much pay' and the '*servi* who accompanied him' (29. 5. 34–6). In the case of Ecdicius and his companions, Sidonius goes on to say that he collected 'a kind of army', but it is impossible for us to be certain what kind of army this was. Was it a band of rural workers from the fields, which any patron-landlord could arm, like those noted earlier in Pamphylia, 'trained in many battles against bandits'? Or were they bands of private *bucellarii*, whom Delbrück compared to the *Kriegsknechte* of the Cinquecento? Was there any difference by now?

One thing that makes me think that there was not much difference is that at exactly the same time as Ecdicius was carrying out his heroic exploits at Clermont, not far south at Narbonne King Euric was passing legislation concerning the rights of *bucellarii* in relation to their private masters. But in the *antiqua* commentary (5. 3. 1) on Euric's Code, the word *bucellarius* is replaced by the phrase 'placed in patronage' (*in patrocinio constitutus*; cf. Delbrück 1980, 390). That shows how close the concept of patronage is to the terms of service of *bucellarii*. But again I insist that it is not incipient feudalism that we find in this relationship, but something not too far from the quite separate phenomenon of serfdom. The description of the *satellites* of Stilicho, which I cited earlier, was of those who had given themselves *iure vel corpore* to their patrons; that is, they had pledged their bodies. When Marc Bloch defined the early serf as an 'homme de corps', he also believed the relationship had its origin in *patrocinium* (Bloch 1963).

There is little doubt in my mind, either, that the parallels between the Byzantine *parameinontes* and the Frankish *trustiones*, defined in Salic Law as *in truste dominica* ('in their lord's trust'), are closer than is normally recognized. While the remnants of the Roman army continued to operate in the towns, just as in the eastern army, the countryside was controlled by these semi-private bands. The practice of wearing exotic clothes, a characteristic of the eastern *bucellarii* (Gascou 1976, 151), is certainly matched by the description of the magnificent *comitantes* of Sigismer, one of the Rhine Franks, going to a wedding in *c*.469; uniform of hairskin shoes, bare lower legs and arms, a tight fitting multi-coloured garment from knee to shoulder; each wearing a green mantle with crimson border, a sword hanging from the shoulder by a studded baldric, a shield of silver with a golden boss – 'the gleam from which showed their rank and their devotion (*censum et studium*)' (Sid. Apoll. *Epist.* 4. 20).

The central characteristic of the *bucellarii*, as we know them in the East, was their attachment to the 'distinguished houses', as a kind of *annona* levy upon the estates of the rich. It was not unlike the *functio navicularia* for transport, which was well known in the fourth century as a burden on the title of some estates. Maintaining the *bucellarii* was 'a fiscalisation of the *servitium militare*,' a levy upon the *oikos* to provide *hospitalitas*.[1] The reform, as we see it illustrated in the Egyptian papyri, turned the estates of rich landlords, which had *de facto* become centres of military organization, into a part of the public administration.

In the West in the fifth and sixth centuries we have, as far as I know, no formal information about how the army was maintained. But it is evident from Procopius that in Gaul some units of the regular army and *laeti* continued to man the towns and forts, simply transferring their allegiance from Romans to Franks (James 1988, 83). In the sixth century there were still units of *laeti* in the Auvergne (Bachrach 1972, 14–15). That was the case also in Noricum in the fifth century, where the Life of St Severinus gives us a vivid picture of feeble units of soldiers virtually cooped up in the garrison towns which were eventually forced to pay tribute to the Rugi (best studied by Thompson 1982, ch. 10). In Noricum, as in Frankish Gaul, it is clear that the control of the countryside was in the hands of what are called robbers. But these robbers were evidently in some cases bands under a war leader like Ferderuchus, who eventually came to control the town of Favianis (Vienna?) (*Life of Severinus*, 42. 1).

The situation recounted in the *Life of St Geneviève* sounds very similar. Childeric, the Frank, appears to be in control of the countryside for the whole period of ten years, while Geneviève is with the 'Romans' holding out in Paris. In Gaul it is significant that many of the fourth- to fifth-century Frankish cemeteries of

[1] Gascou 1976, 151; *POxy.* 156, for instance, directs others in the Oxyrhinchite nome to enrol two men as *bucellarii* and provide them with *annona*.

Picardy and elsewhere were rural but within a short range of the major towns of Beauvais, Vermand, Amiens, Soissons, etc., indicating fairly clearly the strategic points from which the various Frankish warlords came to control the *civitates* by the end of the fifth century (James 1988, 222).

Warlords in history

I have used the term 'warlord' to describe some of the actors, such as federate chiefs, in the later Empire, who controlled personal armies and I have tried to separate them from landlords, although, as I have argued, the distinction became increasingly blurred as the state army declined. The word itself inevitably invites comparisons with that period of Chinese history in the late nineteenth and early twentieth century which is particularly associated with warlordism, the breakdown of the Ch'ing Manchu empire and the ill-fated attempt to establish a republic after 1911. But even Chinese experts now feel the need for closer definition and analysis of the phenomenon. Historians, complains one of them, often regard their task as merely to reproduce the chaos of their sources and not to clarify them (Lary 1980, 460). The same might be said of the later Roman Empire and its historians.

Chinese warlordism was not simply born from the extremes of regionalism and provincialism provoked by the breakdown of central administration. It was the product of two separate forces. One was a long period of organized violence throughout the nineteenth century, particularly on the fringes of the empire, where chronic banditry, rural poverty and weak infrastructures inevitably created the natural conditions for a fragmentation of politics (Fairbank and Feuewerker 1986, 12). For the poor, ties of kinship with the rich gentry and the protection they offered were stronger than the conflicts of class, and whole villages were often turned into protective dependencies of landlords. The system worked after a fashion as long as the 'moral economy' of reciprocal benefits between rich and poor were respected. But during the nineteenth century the rich increased the pressures on the poor and reduced the conditions of tenancies to oral contracts of shorter leases, often of only one year.

The pressures developed into a series of movements of rural

unrest, frequently millenary in character – like the White Wolf robber band or (later) the Spirit Boxers – culminating in the late nineteenth-century Taiping Rebellion. The upshot was the raising of local militias. The gentry selected, or themselves became, local generals, who in turn appointed lesser gentry. They with their followers created extreme factions and fictive kinship groups (Lary 1980, 460). But for all this, they were not warlords. The gentry remained loyal to and bolstered up the central Manchu government, despatching their taxes to Beijing and often themselves entering the civilian bureaux (Sutton 1980, 3–4).

The other force was the result of a new military class, the Ch'ing dynasty's last attempt to control from the centre by modernizing the Chinese army, a central organization loyal to the Manchus – after a fashion. But, when the Republic after 1911 failed to unite the country, they took to direct rule in the provincial governor-ships. Now indeed there was not merely a loss of bureaucratic control, but what has been described as a 'disintegration of political authority' (Lary 1980, 448), leading to 'a patchwork of local satrapies' (Sutton 1980, 6) and personal armies. Warlordism, in short, was really the phenomenon of the military specialist officer corps and included men like Sun Yat-sen and Chiang Kai-shek, who emerged as generalissimos.

Essential, however, although not fully understood, was the relationship between the two forces of landlords and warlords. In some cases it is difficult to distinguish one from the other. But in all cases it is clear that the gentry and their networks, including local bureaucrats, were necessary to the warlord for the extraction of surpluses and control of the land, including the supply of soldiers. Both parties had an interest in the union and warlords, therefore, had no radical political goals. This much was clear to Mao Tse-tung, when he wrote (Mao Tse-tung 1913, i. 176):

> If the peasants do not arise and fight in the villages to overthrow the privileges of the feudal-patriarchal landlord class, the power of the warlords and of imperialism can never be hurled down root and branch.

Even the rural unrest resulted in 'rebellions, not revolutions', to use a cliché of Chinese historians. That is, the movements of religious zealots and peasant dissidents found no bridge between social banditry and political actions, and therefore they usually degenerated into yet further local militia at the disposal of warlords and gentry – as happened to the Boxers.

This very brief and, to the expert, probably simplistic summary presents a number of striking similarities with the conditions of the later Roman Empire, whatever the differences: (1) the general conditions of violence, endemic banditry and peasant oppression; (2) the contrast between the 'moral economy' of the patronage offered by the curial gentry, as presented by Libanius, and its decay, due to forces of factionalism, against which he and later Salvian protest; (3) the appearance of rural movements, frequently millenarian in aim (like the circumcellions) but without trace of real political objectives beyond those attached to the gentry; (4) the appearance of a new, military élite in the intrusive *gentiles* and federates, centred on the court and intended to reinforce the imperial bureaucracy, but disintegrating into something like local satrapies as political authority collapsed. Court offices were held by Childeric and Clovis (probably), by Alaric and even by Attila the Hun.

Obviously the 'fit' is not perfect and it is possible to see many differences, not least the amount of aid from foreign powers given to the Chinese warlords, which had no equivalent in the later Empire. But the similarities are enough at least to make the point that warlordism in the Roman Empire was not the simple product of rural gentry and protectionism, but of those factors in combination with the Germanic warleaders and their armies. The warlord and the landlord must be kept as separate phenomena. It is the relationship between the two which created the continuity of Roman administration and law into the so-called barbarian kingdoms.[1]

Bibliography

Bachrach, B. S. (1967), 'Was there feudalism in Byzantine Egypt?', *Journal of the American Research Center in Egypt*, 6: 163–6.
—— (1972), *Merovingian Military Organization, 481–751* (Minneapolis).

[1] I must express my thanks to Wolf Liebeschuetz and John Drinkwater for the comments they offered on the first draft of this chapter. I hope I have repaid their care by explaining or correcting the points they raised.

Bell, H. I., Martin, V., Turner, E. G., and Van Berchem, D. (1962), *The Abinnaeus Archive: Papers of a Roman Officer in the Reign of Constantius II* (Oxford).

Bellamy, A. (1985), 'A new reading of the Namarah inscription', *Journal of the American Oriental Society*, 105: 31–48.

Bloch, M. (1963), *Mélanges historiques* (Paris).

Blockley, R. C. (1981–3), *The Fragmentary Classicizing Historians of the Later Roman Empire* (Liverpool).

Bowersock, G. W. (1980), 'Mavia, queen of the Saracens', in *Studien zur antiken Sozialgeschichte: Festschrift F. Vittinghoff* (Cologne), pp. 477–95.

—— (1983), *Roman Arabia* (Harvard).

Camps, G. (1985), 'De Masuna à Koceila: les destinées de la Maurétanie aux VIᵉ et VIIᵉ siècles', in *Histoire et archéologie de l'Afrique du nord (IIᵉ Colloque International, Grenoble 1983)* (Bulletin archéologique du Comité des Travaux Historiques, 19B; Paris), pp. 307–25.

Carrié, J.-M. (1976), 'Patronage et propriété militaires au IVᵉ siècle', *Bulletin de correspondance hellénique*, 100: 159–76.

Delbrück, H. (1980), *History of the Art of War*, ii: *The Barbarian Invasions*, trans. W. J. Renfroe (Lincoln and London).

Diesner, H.-J. (1972), 'Das Bucellarietum von Stilicho und Sarus bis auf Aetius (454–455)', *Klio*, 54: 321–50.

Drinkwater, J. F. (1983), *Roman Gaul* (London and Canberra).

—— (1984), 'Peasants and Bagaudae in Roman Gaul', *Classical Views/Echos du monde classique*, 3: 349–71.

—— (1987), *The Gallic Empire: Separatism and Continuity in the North-western Provinces of the Roman Empire, AD 260–274* (Historia Einzelschriften, 52; Stuttgart).'

—— (1989), 'Patronage in Roman Gaul and the problem of the Bagaudae', in A. Wallace-Hadrill (ed.), *Patronage in Ancient Society* (London).

—— (1992), 'The Bacaudae of fifth-century Gaul', in J. F. Drinkwater and H. Elton (eds), pp. 208–17.

—— and Elton, H. (eds, 1992), *Fifth-century Gaul: A Crisis of Identity?* (Cambridge).

Elmayer, A. F. (1985), 'The centenaria of Roman Tripolitania', *Libyan Studies*, 16: 77–84.

Erison, V. (1978), 'La tombe de guerrier de Landifay (Aisne)', in Fleury and Périn (eds), pp. 39–48.

Fairbank, J. K., and Feuerwerker, A. (eds, 1986), *The Cambridge History of China*, xiii: *Republican China 1912–49*, part 2 (Cambridge).

Fleury, M., and Périn, P. (eds 1978), *Problèmes de chronologie relative et absolue concernant les cimetières mérovingiens d'entre Loire et Rhin* (Paris).

Gabbia, C. (1988), 'Ancora sulle "rivolte" di Firmo e Gildone', *L'Africa Romana*, 5: 117–29.

Gascou, J. (1976), 'L'institution des bucellaires', *Bulletin de l'Institut*

Français de l'Archéologie Orientale, 76: 143–56.

Giardina, A. (1983), 'Banditi e santi: un aspetto del folklore gallico tra tarda antichità e medioevo', *Athenaeum*, 61: 374–89.

Harmand, L. (1955), *Libanius: discours sur les patronages* (Paris).

Isaac, B. (1990), *The Limits of Empire: The Roman Army in the East* (Oxford).

James, E. (1988), *The Franks* (Oxford).

Jones, A. H. M. (1964), *The Later Roman Empire 284–602* (Oxford).

Jullian, C. (1926), *Histoire de la Gaule*, viii: *Les Empereurs de Trèves, ii: La terre et les hommes* (Paris).

Kraemer, C. (1958), *Excavations at Nessana*, iii: *Non-literary Papyri* (Princeton).

Lary, D. (1980), 'Warlord studies', *Modern China*, 6: 439–70.

Lemant, J.-P. (1985), *Le Cimetière et la fortification du bas-empire de Vireux-Molhain (Ardennes)* (Mainz).

Levy, E. (1951), *West Roman Vulgar Law* (Philadelphia).

Liebeschuetz, J. H. W. G. (1986), 'Generals, federates and bucellarii in Roman armies around AD 400', in P. Freeman and D. Kennedy (eds), *The Defence of the Roman and Byzantine East* (BAR International Series, 297; Oxford), pp. 463–74.

MacMullen, R. (1963), *Soldier and Civilian in the Later Roman Empire* (Cambridge, Mass.).

Mao Tse-tung (1913), *Chi-ch'u chan-shu (Basic Tactics)* (Hankow).

Mommsen, T. (1910), 'Das römische Militarwesen seit Diokletian', *Gesammelte Schriften* (Berlin, 1910), vi. 206–83.

Pilet, C. (1980), *La Necropole de Frénouville* (BAR International Series, 83; Oxford).

Rémondon, R. (1965), 'Militaires et civils dans une campagne égyptienne au temps de Constance II', *Journal de savants*: 132–43.

Shahid, I. (1984), *Rome and the Arabs: A Prolegomenon to the Study of Byzantium and the Arabs* (Washington).

Stroheker, K. (1948), *Der senatorische Adel in spätantiken Gallien* (Tübingen).

Sutton, D. S. (1980), *Provincial Militarism and the Chinese Republic: The Yunnan Army, 1905–25* (Ann Arbor).

Thompson, E. A. (1982), *Romans and Barbarians: The Decline of the Western Empire* (Madison).

Van Dam, R. (1985), *Leadership and Community in Late Antique Gaul* (California).

Wallace-Hadrill, J. M. (1962), *The Long-haired Kings* (London).

Whittaker, C. R. (1989), *Les Frontières de l'empire romain* (Annales littéraires de l'Université de Besançon, 390).

Wightman, E. M. (1981), 'The fate of the Gallo-Roman villages in the third century', in A. King and M. Henig (eds), *The Roman West in the Third Century AD* (BAR International Series, 109; Oxford).

—— (1985), *Gallia Belgica* (London).

Index